THE COMPLETE GUIDE TO GOVERNMENT REAL ESTATE LEASING

VOLUME I

THE COMPLETE GUIDE TO GOVERNMENT REAL ESTATE LEASING

VOLUME I

By Jamie A. Scruggs

Real Estate Media Group

Cover Image: Wisconsin State Capitol Building

The Complete Guide to Government Real Estate Leasing, Volume 1

Printed in the United States of America

Real Estate Media Group, LLC
1658 North Milwaukee Avenue, Suite 315
Chicago, IL 60647

ISBN: 978-0-9983075-0-3

CONTENTS

PREFACE

Government real estate leasing is an optimistic business. Federal, state, and local government agencies work with property owners to reach lease terms that are often substantially different than standard private-sector real estate leases. This relationship works well because the approximately 90,000 units of government in the United States need to maximize the utility of their real estate requirements, while property owners recognize that the approximately 150,000 government tenant leases in the US have stable, long-term institutional ratings that have a higher investment value than most private-sector tenants they lease property to.

The Complete Guide to Government Real Estate Leasing, Volume I, is an in-depth review of the business relationship between government tenants and the property owners leasing space to them. As with all great relationships, it is the journey that matters, with the long-term goal of having a mutually beneficial business relationship. With this goal in mind, the volumes of *The Complete Guide to Government Real Estate Leasing* provide the reader with:

1. the ability to understand how property owners and investors can profitably service government real estate leases and
2. an understanding of how government agencies use contemporary real estate leasing practices to implement policies and processes at the federal, state, and local levels of government.

Both property owners and government agencies will benefit from reading the volumes of *The Complete Guide to Government Real Estate Leasing* because it is a comprehensive guide to how government agencies and property owners complete their respective roles in government real estate leasing.

Volume I Contents

Chapter One begins with a review of leasing policy at the federal, state, and local levels along with a review of notable government real estate leases and lease portfolios. Chapter Two reviews how government agencies post new lease requirements and how property owners can find new government real estate lease requirements. Chapter Three is a review of government real estate lease models, with lease examples provided from various government agencies. *Chapter Four* provides a review of the government real estate lease proposal process with an in-depth analysis of the US General Services Administration (GSA) request for lease proposal form, the RLP R100 (dated March 2016).

How to Read Volume I

The reader should consider the following two items when reading each chapter:

First, the chapters are written so the reader can obtain a working understanding of the various policies, processes, and practices that make up the foundation of government real estate leasing. The reader should approach each chapter with the understanding that the items in the chapter provide an overview of a select portion of each level of government real estate leasing.

Second, *The Complete Guide to Government Real Estate Leasing, Volume I,* is the start of the discussion on the complexity of government real estate leasing. This complexity is ultimately about how a government agency and a property owner can work together to optimize their individual organizational policies, processes, and practices in order to meet their respective real estate leasing needs.

After almost three years of writing *Volume I* and the forthcoming *Volume II,* I have found that the complexity of these two items, while incredibly immense, is understandable, measurable, and in a position to be both optimized and standardized.

Volume II

The forthcoming book, *Volume II*, will continue the journey through government real estate leasing with a review of negotiating government real estate leases, financial analysis of lease proposals, lease administration, and an in-depth review of the US GSA lease form, L100 (dated March 2016). Look for additional volumes to be published with a variety of topics concerning government real estate leasing.

The Fine Print

A government real estate lease is a contract that needs to be reviewed by an attorney. I am not an attorney and I cannot offer legal advice. You should not take any action concerning topics presented in the volumes of *The Complete Guide to Government Real Estate Leasing* without first seeking the advice of an attorney.

Acknowledgments

Volume I would not have been completed without the tremendous support and contributions of Dr. Dennis Eisen, Diana Parks Curran, J.D., and Brian Adelstein. All three individuals are unquestionably major figures in the world of government real estate leasing today. Their individual biographies are at the end of the book with contact information. I highly recommend their professional services to anyone who needs them. Also, Anthony Galto, an exceptional artist, was of considerable assistance in the design and image selections for *Volume I.*

Finally, I would like to give a big thank you to both you the reader for supporting the publication of *The Complete Guide to Government Real Estate Leasing* and to those organizations and individuals in the government real estate leasing industry that have provided me with a career and a profession.

Fraternally,
J.S.
Washington, DC
Chicago, IL
2016

FOREWORD

By Diana Parks Curran

The world of government real estate leasing can be perplexing for both the initiated and uninitiated. The author, Jamie Scruggs, has a unique perspective of experiencing and working with government real estate leasing from the orientation of both the government tenant agency and private-sector property owner. This unique perspective allows the introspection and experience necessary to write this guide to government real estate leasing. I share this perspective, and I welcome *The Complete Guide to Government Real Estate Leasing* as a resource that can benefit all involved in government leasing, regardless of whether holding a perspective oriented toward the government or private-sector side of the real estate lease.

The experience and pointers available through this publication are valuable and place importance on understanding and mastering the perspectives and motivations both parties bring to the table when working to achieve a signed government real estate lease. I have provided legal representation in this field for over two decades, with almost equivalent time spent in each camp, as either, formerly, an assistant regional counsel for the US General Services Administration or, currently, as an attorney providing legal services to private-sector property owners. With this industry experience, I find the book's engaging insights useful for better understanding the needs and objectives of property owners and government tenants.

The author suggested that I provide as part of writing the foreword a brief review of what a real estate lease is in terms of obligations arising out of a legally enforceable contract. In law school, students are instructed to view rights in real property as a bundle of sticks that an owner can dole out in a complete bundle, such as a fee simple conveyance of real property, or as a few of the sticks from the bundle, such as a conveyance of a leasehold interest when a property owner enters into a real estate lease agreement to allow another party the right to occupy or use all or a portion of the real property for a defined period of time for a defined amount of consideration, or rent.

In government real estate leasing, we find there is an added element of risk allocation created by the government tenant in its real estate lease contracts. This risk allocation is generally accomplished through a shifting of risk away from the government tenant (lessee) and toward the property owner (lessor). In the context of government real estate leasing, it becomes apparent to the careful reader of this work that risk is largely shifted away from the government tenant and toward the property owner, making for a unique set of concerns that merit special consideration and knowledge when seeking or competing for award of a government real estate lease, whether by an experienced property owner, seasoned government employee, real estate contractor, or the property owner new to government real estate leases.

In government real estate leasing, the management and allocation of risk has a monetary value. This risk has to be considered and managed by both parties in order to make a bargain that is fair and adequately compensated for via the payment of lease rent for not only the use of the property but the government's general aversion to risk associated with that leasehold interest in real property. *The Complete Guide to Government Real Estate Leasing* stresses that for both parties to the real estate lease to be successful, this contractual agreement must create a mutually beneficial business relationship that can be achieved if:

1. a fair and sustainable profit or return is generated for the property owner and the government tenant is able to maximize its use of the leasehold interest and
2. both parties can meet the reasonable goals of the other party, as stated in the lease contract.

The author advocates for an open and integrative exchange of information, especially between the government's real estate leasing contact person and the property owner. This approach encourages a fair and open leasing environment. This exchange of information should produce an equitable outcome for all concerned, which is a lease that works and meets the intentioned needs of both parties for the duration of the lease term.

I trust this publication will offer the government real estate leasing industry the author and I both serve insights that will advance the goals of forming a real estate lease contract that unambiguously, clearly, and fully addresses the needs of both government tenants and property owners.

Best regards,
Diana Parks Curran
Atlanta, GA
2016

INTRODUCTION

By Dennis Eisen, PhD

Government real estate leasing has changed significantly since I started in the business in 1973. Over the years I have seen countless changes in the way government agencies and the private sector conducts their real estate leasing activities. The one constant that remains is that government agencies are still tasked with making sure their leasing activities protect both the mission of the government tenant agencies and the taxpayers who are paying the rent.

Government real estate will forever be an important component of our nation's economy at federal, state, and local levels of government, for the simple reason that space must be provided for the millions of government employees who work not just in office buildings but in laboratories and courthouses, in storage centers and archives, in border stations and customs enforcement, in clinics and hospitals, in defense and intelligence agencies, in social service and public health centers, in control towers and weather stations, in prisons and police stations, in libraries and post offices, and in numerous other places conducting governmental functions required for efficient operation of the country.

In preparing to write this introduction, I decided to relate some of my experiences in government real estate leasing as a way to discuss both the complexity and ever-changing nature of the government real estate leasing business.

I arrived in Washington, DC, in 1966 as a newly minted PhD. with a double major in mathematics and computer science and spent the first few years helping to write war-gaming programs for the Pentagon. But by 1973 my attention had turned to developing computer programs for the analysis of real estate deals for friends and acquaintances, which led to an offer from the US General Services Administration (GSA) to bring some order to the federal lease acquisition process.

In those bygone days the federal government did not have software programs for determining whether real estate space needs were best satisfied through new construction, repair, and alteration of existing space, leasing, or lease-construction. Nor were there computer software programs for rapid and efficient comparison of multiple lease offerings received in response to solicitations for offers, especially those containing options to purchase the leased property. Nor were there any software programs for allocating the technical resources in advance of needed services for handling lease renewals or architectural services across US GSA's various regional offices. Nor were there any software programs for conducting long-range planning of the nation's future space needs and corresponding funding impact on the Federal Buildings Fund, this being the revolving fund into which rental income and other receipts are deposited, and out of which are drawn the US GSA's operating expenses for salaries, lease payments, and construction funding.

It soon became my responsibility to develop computer software modeling tools for the US GSA's real estate lease-versus-buy decisions. The following are brief descriptions of these software models with the approximate date which I started working on them:

1. The Automated Prospectus System (TAPS) is a detailed computer model that produces the year-by-year financial history of a lease, typically used in support of larger US GSA lease prospectuses that must be approved by the Office of Management and Budget (OMB) and authorized by Congress before the US GSA can issue a Request for Lease Proposal (RLP). The TAPS model consisted of 500 lines of code when it was first developed in the early 1980s, and 20 years later had grown to 50,000 lines of code as its overall capability and level of detail had expanded to include such features as alternative financing, lease construction, repair and alteration, third-party out-leasing, and measurements expressed in metric units (1980).
2. The LEASE model is used for the evaluation of lease proposals submitted in response to RLPs, which could accommodate a wide range of purchase options for the leased building, both during the lease term or upon expiration of the lease (1982).
3. The MANPOWER model is used by the US GSA to ensure that the right number and mix of personnel are in place as old leases expire and must be recompeted, old buildings repaired or replaced, and new facilities constructed. With the exception of fire, flood, and similar disasters, these aforementioned events are predictable and are completely amenable to having the right people in place at the right time (1984).
4. The PLANS model takes the predicted rate of population growth and combines this with the associated growth rates of the civilian and mission-oriented agencies to arrive at a five- and ten-year forecast of the amount of space needed to accommodate the federal workforce and how much it will cost the federal government to do so for the incremental space that will have to be leased or built in order to do so (1986).

Needless to say, a number of federal, state, and local government agencies adopted these software modeling tools. I worked extensively with the US Department of Veterans Affairs (VA) to adopt the aforementioned TAPS and LEASE models for evaluating lease-versus-build alternatives for US VA clinics and hospitals. Use of these software models, for example, permitted rapid evaluation and determination of the winning offer for replacement of a US VA hospital that was condemned as a result of the Loma Prieta earthquake in northern California in 1989. The RLP was announced on a Monday, bids received and opened on Friday, evaluations conducted on Saturday, the Source Selection Committee's report completed on Sunday, and the winner announced by the US VA administrator the very next day. The entire process took just seven days from RLP to award.

Over a 20-year period starting in the mid-1980s, I worked extensively with the Federal Aviation Administration (FAA) to adopt the TAPS model to examine build-versus-lease construction alternatives for the replacement of the nation's aging control towers at the nation's airports, each new one substantially taller and wider than its predecessor because of the lengthening of airport runways and incorporation of more and more technology. FAA's version of the TAPS model was converted to an automated processing system that could evaluate the entire FAA lease inventory of 10,000 operating leases to determine which, if any, should have been classified as capital versus operating leases. This is an important distinction from a budgetary standpoint because whereas the continuing lease payments of an operating lease can be paid for out of the agency's ongoing annual budget, in the case of capital leases a great portion of the entire cost of the lease must be budgeted for in the year the lease commenced; this is a budgetary hurdle few if any agencies can readily meet.

It must be emphasized that my computer model efforts for the federal government were not static affairs and have undergone numerous modifications over the years due to changes in tax law, accounting standards, and public real estate policy. When I first started with the US GSA, for example, lease payments over the term of the lease were expressed in difficult-to-understand *constant* dollars, a system that was changed to the present-day discounted cash flow methodology in 1986. Further, a lease was a lease until the Budget Enforcement Act of 1990 split federal government leases into three variants labeled capital, operating, and lease purchases, in accordance with the controversial OMB lease scoring rules that required completely different rules from an accounting standpoint as described above for the FAA.

Notable changes to government real estate lease models over the years have included:

1. elimination of bargain-price purchase options, meaning that purchase option prices cannot be set below the fair market value of the property at the time of option exercise;
2. distinctions between special versus general purpose property, wherein general-purpose property can be amortized over the term of the lease but special-purpose property must be accounted and budgeted for in its entirety up front;
3. leases on private versus government-owned land, for which different budgetary and scoring rules apply;
4. enhanced-use leases, in which developers can lease underutilized property on federal land, introducing moneymaking improvements to the property while paying rent (or providing in-kind services) to the federal government;
5. amortization methods for tenant improvements, by which the up-front cash outlays by property owners can be recaptured over the firm term of the lease in a variety of different ways;
6. minimum lease payments, which include both net lease payments and real estate taxes when accounting for the cost budgeting of capital leases;
7. build-to-suit properties, meaning those real estate projects built to the unique specifications of the federal government;
8. cancellation versus noncancellation operating leases, by which rental payments under an operating lease can be budgeted for on a year-by-year basis only if the lease has a bone fide cancelation clause or, if not, must be budgeted for in a lump-sum manner in the first year of the lease;
9. liquidated damages, in which a payment to be made by the federal government upon cancelation of a lease (whenever exercised) must be accounted for in the federal agency's budget up front in the year the lease commenced;
10. imputed interest, which is the complex formula by which the difference between the total lease payments and their up-front write-off of a capital lease are distributed over the remaining term of the lease.

By 1995, enough changes had taken place in federal government real estate leasing that I published *Decision Making in Federal Real Estate: How the Government Decides Whether and with Whom to Lease, Build or Buy*. But changes in federal government leasing continued to occur, so in 2005, I started the highly regarded industry quarterly newsletter that is now called the *Journal of Government Real Estate* in order to keep practitioners in the field of federal government real estate abreast of new developments as they happen. And in 2009, I helped form the National Federal Development Association, a nonprofit trade association devoted to bringing members of the private-sector and federal government real estate community together for communication purposes and exchange of information and ideas.

So here we are in 2016, 20 or so years since I published *Decision Making in Federal Real Estate*, and I'm very happy to see that another individual with extensive experience in government real estate leasing, Jamie Scruggs, has undertaken the tremendous effort to pull together the vast array of information needed to pursue government real estate leases. The following are a few reasons why *The Complete Guide to Government Real Estate Leasing* is an essential companion for those interested in government real estate leasing:

Government-Leased Properties Are a Great Investment

Investing in buildings and other facilities leased to federal, state, and local government agencies can be a very rewarding experience, in good measure due to the high credit ratings of the tenant agencies, the high likelihood of lease renewal, and the long-term tenure of the government agency that occupies the leased property. A large majority of government agencies that lease space have A credit ratings or better, meaning that rent payments are backed by a government agency that will rarely if ever default on a lease or fall behind in its lease rent payments. When it comes to renewability and tenure, government agencies are almost immutable. A great many of them deliver vital services to the community in which they are located, which requires they stay in a community for many generations.

The long-term presence of the government tenant in the community, its high credit rating, and the stability that the government tenant brings to the property makes government-leased properties one of the most sought after real estate investments in the real estate market today.

Understanding the Government Lease

There are so many considerations that are part and parcel of a government lease that the only way to avoid misunderstandings, control costs, minimize delays, and establish effective communication between the property owner (lessor) and government tenant agency (lessee) is by coming to an understanding of each and every clause that can have a financial impact on the property owner's bottom line and by selecting and working with an experienced set of contractors and consultants who will help in pricing labor, materials, and other building components properly to begin with, and who can be called upon in negotiation meetings between the property owner and the government. Real estate investors who have failed to do their homework have been burned, and cases are legion wherein lessors and developers of government-leased facilities have been forced to declare bankruptcy because of inadequate preparation and insufficient understanding of the government's real estate lease acquisition process and protocols.

Government Employees and Contractors

Most government agencies have employees hired specifically to work on their real estate leases or hire private-sector real estate firms they contract for completing their government agency real estate lease assignments. This book will help government employees and contractors understand the various policies, processes, and practices that government agencies utilize at different levels of government. Equally important, this book will help the government employee and contractor understand how property owners and real estate firms approach their real estate leasing policies, processes, and practices at various stages of the government real estate leasing cycle.

Professors and Students

Another group that this book should appeal to are teachers and students at our country's universities and colleges. Government real estate is big business and employs many, many thousands of people in the federal, state, and local agencies that have oversight responsibility for providing safe, secure, and efficient workplaces for government workers. As each generation of realty specialists, real estate analysts, and real estate contracting officers retire or otherwise leave the workforce, they must be replaced by the next generation of similar workers.

The difficulty is that at virtually all colleges and universities with real estate or urban planning departments, the course work uniformly concentrates on real estate construction and real estate development. It is my hope that *The Complete Guide to Government Real Estate Leasing* might slowly but steadily be adopted by the academic world and eventually form the basis of a formal college curriculum in government leasing. Just think of the savings to government agencies that must spend big dollars on contract instructors to prepare every new hire on the basics of government leasing that should have been part of their academic training as real estate majors. The lease inventory of the federal government alone consists of more than 46,000 leases, and there must be many times this number held by state and local governments, which is why this book must be given serious consideration at every level of government as well as every academic department of real estate throughout the country.

In summary, I would say that my training in government real estate was self-taught and slow, but by absorbing what's inside these covers, whether you're a practitioner or neophyte, you'll avoid many of the pitfalls along the path toward mastering the field of government real estate. Read, study, and enjoy the opportunity!

With warmest regards,
Dr. Dennis Eisen
Washington, DC
2016

Los Angeles City Hall Reflected

CHAPTER ONE:

GOVERNMENT REAL ESTATE LEASING

IN THIS CHAPTER

1. **Government Real Estate Leasing Overview**
2. **Government Real Estate Leasing Policies**
3. **Notable Portfolios and Leases**

Government real estate leasing in the United States involves almost every government agency at the federal, state, and local levels of government. Government real estate leasing can be described as any real estate leasing activity undertaken by a government entity. These leasing activities can be internal leasing transactions within a governmental body whereby one agency leases property to another or it can be those leasing activities that involve a government agency looking to lease property from a private-sector property owner. This chapter will cover (1) an overview of government real estate leasing; (2) the real estate leasing policies of a number of government real estate agencies at the federal, state, and local levels of government; and (3) a review of notable government real estate leases and portfolios of private-sector property owners with government real estate leases.

GOVERNMENT REAL ESTATE LEASING OVERVIEW

To grasp the enormity of the total universe of government leases in the US it is best to look to the numbers. According to the US Census Bureau, in 2012, there were 89,004 local governments in the United States; local governments include 3,031 counties, 19,522 municipalities, 16,364 townships, 37,203 special districts, and 12,884 independent school districts, which, when combined with the federal and state governments, comes to 89,055 units of government.[1] Many of these government entities will have multiple subgovernment entities or subagencies within them that will create a multiplier of agencies beyond the 89,055 units of government listed above. Most of these units of government will have some level of real estate leasing activity with the private sector, whether it is for a million-square-foot office lease or a 500-square-foot warehouse storage lease.

To estimate the current number of real estate leases government agencies have with the private sector could be conservatively estimated at 150,000 office and warehouse leases with an average size of 5,000 square feet per lease, for a government-leased footprint of 500 million square feet.[2] Adding into this calculation the number of government agencies with private-sector ground leases, land leases, structures, ports, etc., could add another 50,000. By comparison, in 2015 Starbucks, Walmart, and McDonald's combined had 32,053 stores in the United States.[3]

Most large government agencies have both internal and external leasing activities, while smaller government agencies will typically own the real estate they are occupying, with a smaller number of private-sector leases in their lease inventory. Government leasing activities that occur internally will often be silent to the public, while external leasing activities will usually be published for public review and consideration. A significant difference among government agencies that do external leasing is whether they are required to compete their real estate leases or if they can sign a lease with a building owner without conducting a competitive bid process. Government agencies required to compete their real estate leasing activities for external leasing activities will follow some type of regulated and public process, which can range from simple lease acquisition requirements to overly complex rules and regulations, depending on the size of the lease requirement and which agency is procuring the leased space.

Regardless of whether a government agency is required to compete its real estate leases, it will most likely follow some type of internal authorization process to start the lease transaction process for a government tenant going into a private-sector leased space. These internal authorizations will take the form of an approval process that requires the government agency to formally authorize the government tenant or government real estate agency handling the government lease to determine the following items before getting started on the new real estate lease action:

1. The estimated budget for the lease term, including lease rents and leasehold improvements;
2. How the budget will be funded;
3. Lease term;
4. Geographical area the leased space is to be located in;
5. Any additional special requirements that may be required such as secured parking, building setbacks, and LEED certifications.

At this point in the process, after the initial tenant agency approvals are completed, the decision-making process can split off in multiple directions. Smaller government agencies may be able to immediately select their desired property location along with signing the property owner's lease, while larger government agencies may need to take a more detailed and lengthy approach to their leasing activities. Government entities like the US federal government will undertake a detailed and comprehensive approach to their real estate leasing activities for even the smallest leases. The standard approach for large government agencies at the state and federal levels after the approval process is:

1. Assign the leasing action to a government leasing contact (GLC) to start the new lease transaction.
2. The GLC will determine the lease forms and process specific to the lease size and standards specific to the government tenant.
3. Advertise the lease requirement if required.
4. Visit properties or have property owners submit property information that can be used to select the winning property.
5. Conduct a competitive procurement or approval process that determines which property owner will be awarded the lease.
6. The GLC will make the award of the lease to the property owner, which will either be on the government tenant's lease form or the property owner's own lease document.
7. The leasehold improvements, which are the shell and tenant improvements to the leased space based on the tenant's design intent drawing, will then be completed, along with acceptance and occupancy of the leased space.

Most property owners will naturally expect the difficult part of government real estate leasing process ends with the award of the government lease, but challenges do remain for the property owner during the management of the lease, which can include issues specific to government tenants such as:

1. Correctly tracking and billing operating costs with lease language that is not standard to private-sector leases.
2. Billing for real estate tax expenses.
3. Dealing with government tenant complaints that can be unique for property owners who may only do net leases where the private-sector tenant is responsible for the day-to-day maintenance of the leased space.
4. The approval process for even minor repairs or renovations can often require multiple levels of GLC approvals and bids when required.
5. Government tenants may have very specialized requirements in the leased space that may be difficult to manage for even the most experienced property manager.

The management of government-leased properties is slightly easier for those companies that specialize in working on government real estate lease transactions and managing the properties once the government lease is in place. Most large real estate companies now have departments or staff dedicated specifically to government real estate leasing and property management. In the last 15 years, the trend for the largest real estate firms has been to pursue contracts with government real estate agencies to represent them on their real estate lease transactions as their real estate broker. These large real estate companies with government real estate representation agreements in turn will often hire smaller real estate firms to assist in the real estate lease transaction. This is because these small firms can either satisfy the government's real estate brokerage contract requirements for small business set-asides or can assist in the government real estate lease transaction due to their specialized knowledge on a given government tenant or specific geographic region.

GOVERNMENT REAL ESTATE LEASING POLICIES

The long-term health of a government's real estate portfolio—the taxpayers' portfolio—is driven by its real estate policies. These policies are typically initiated by the executive or administrative branches of a government agency. At the federal level, the president's administration sets its agenda for the real estate portfolio using input from the US General Services Administration (GSA). The US GSA, which provides real estate services to most agencies of the federal government, is often tasked with implementing and codifying the executive branch's agenda through real estate policy directives that federal agencies then follow. At the state and local levels real estate leasing policy is driven more by the long-term goals of the individual agency's real estate needs along with being responsive to the shifts in both the economies and population demographics of these states and local governments.

Federal Real Estate Leasing Policies

Not all federal agencies use the GSA for their real estate leasing services. While the GSA owns and leases over 427 million square feet of office and warehouse space in 8,705 buildings domestically, there are, according to the GSA's *FY 2013 Federal Real Property Profile (FRPP) Summary Data Set (Data Set)*, 18 federal agencies reporting owned and leased holdings in FY 2013 that do not include the GSA in their real estate representation figures. These 18 federal agencies occupied almost three billion square feet of owned and leased space in 344,579 buildings around the world.[4] In 2015, the GSA published its *FY 2014 FRPP* data with domestic and US territory numbers only, which is a departure from previous years, which had included most global figures for the portfolio. The *FY 2014 FRPP* compared to the *FY 2013 FRPP* shows a smaller pool of properties when compared to the entire global US federal government-owned and -leased inventory.

Not included in the GSA's FY 2014 *Data Set* are real estate inventory numbers for the US Postal Service (USPS). In 2015, the USPS reported a real estate inventory of 194,220,092 square feet of owned space in 8,524 owned buildings along with an inventory of 78,144,453 square feet of leased space in 23,314 leased properties.[5] Also not included in the FY 2014 *Data Set* are the federally owned and managed public-domain lands. In 2012 the Department of the Interior reported that federally owned and managed lands, including public-domain lands, equal almost 629 million acres; this amounts to almost 28 percent of the 2.27 billion acres of land in the United States.[6] This is a massive portfolio of property for the federal government to own, lease, and manage. By some accounts, the federal government ranks fourth globally in the amount of owned land and property, behind the holdings of the Queen of England, China, and Russia.

US General Services Administration

When looking for a starting point for examining the federal government's real estate policies, it is best to start with the GSA's Public Building Service (PBS). PBS is the arm of the GSA that leases space for numerous federal agencies, including the Federal Bureau of Investigation and the Social Security Administration. PBS is also the caretaker of federal properties the GSA owns, occupies, and leases to other federal agencies across the country. PBS's real estate policies are numerous and address almost all the federal government's real estate leasing activities since the formation of the GSA in 1949.

Narrowing the focus to policies currently in place finds that PBS sets the policy baseline for the federal government's real estate policy. This policy baseline is best described by PBS as its "basic policy" to lease quality space that is the best value to the federal government, is located in a central business district (with some exceptions), is accessible by persons with disabilities, and is sustainable and provides a safe work environment.[7]

The bulk of PBS's real estate policies are found in the *PBS Leasing Desk Guide* (*Desk Guide*). The *Desk Guide* sets forth the guiding principles and policies for GSA employees engaged in government real estate contract activities. The policies in the *Desk Guide* also apply to federal agencies leasing space under delegated authority from the GSA. In 1996 the GSA administrator granted GSA leasing authority to all federal agencies. Known as "delegated authority," this change permits federal agencies to lease their own space without using the GSA as their real estate representative. If a federal agency uses the GSA for its real estate needs, that agency becomes either a tenant in federally owned GSA-managed space or a subtenant to the GSA, with the GSA holding the primary lease with the private-sector property owner. The GSA has a separate occupancy agreement with the federal agency to which it is subleasing the space. The costs for managing that space are usually added to the lease payments made to the GSA by the subtenant leasing the space from the GSA. The GSA typically has special clauses in its occupancy agreements that allows the federal agency to vacate the leased space before GSA's lease term expires with the private-sector landlord; the GSA is typically left paying the remainder of the lease term rents regardless of the whether the space is still occupied by the federal agency subtenant. As recently as 2014, the GSA made changes to its leasing delegation authorization process. Some of these modifications centralize the GSA delegation authorization process and require additional oversight of federal agencies, which now are required to show they can manage and administer their own leases.[8] To better understand the GSA's leasing authority and the GSA's authority to delegate this authority to other federal agencies, it is best to look at the United States Code (USC) Title 40, formally known as the Public Buildings Act of 1959.[9] USC Title 40 is the most frequently mentioned code in the two main bodies of work that deal with the GSA's delegated authority (and a multitude of other GSA policies): the *Desk Guide* and the GSA's *General Reference Guide for Real Property Policy* (*Reference Guide*). The *Reference Guide* details almost every major policy for the steps in a federal agency's real estate transaction cycle, ranging from delegated authority to leasing, ownership, property management, and disposal.

GSA-Delegated Authority

GSA describes its self-delegation authority in the *Delegation of Authority Manual* (*Delegation Manual*). The *Delegation Manual* explains in exhaustive detail the GSA administrator's activities granting delegated authority to the GSA administrator along with various GSA departments, including the Public Building Service, the Civilian Board of Contract Appeals, and each of the GSA regional administrators, with attention paid to the officials who work in each GSA Region.[10]

While the *Delegation Manual* does an excellent job of detailing GSA's delegated authority, it is best to return to the *Desk Guide* for the big picture of authority delegated to the GSA and to other federal agencies. For authority delegated to the GSA itself, the *Desk Guide* states:

> The Administrator of General Services is authorized by [Title] 40 U.S.C. §585 to enter into lease agreements to accommodate Federal agencies in buildings (or improvements) that are in existence or will be erected by the Lessor. The agreement may not bind the Government for more than 20 years. The Administrator has delegated leasing authority to Regional Commissioners, who, as Heads of Contracting Activities, further delegate the authority by issuing leasing warrants to LCOs.
>
> Option periods: Renewal option periods, exercisable at the sole discretion of the Government, in the original contract can be used to extend this time beyond 20 years. However, in no case can the exercised firm term of the lease exceed 20 years.[11]

The GSA's policies for itself differ from those established for other federal agencies, as stated in the *Desk Guide*:

> Delegations of lease acquisition authority to Federal agencies are made to the head of the agency or designee. The authority delegated may be for an individual lease action or a class of similar leases, such as Department of Defense recruiting activities. Agency heads are required to exercise the delegated authority per this Desk Guide, where it implements applicable laws, executive orders (EOs), regulations, Office of Management and Budget circulars, and other GSA policies that implement laws, EOs, and regulations.
>
> FMR Bulletin 2008-B1, dated November 19, 2007, limits lease acquisition delegations to 19,999 rentable square feet or less of general-purpose space. Specific agencies have been granted categorical and special-purpose lease acquisition delegations in the FMR. Agencies must request specific authorization to exercise the special-purpose delegated authority if the requirement is for 2,500 rentable square feet or more. If the requirement is 2,499 rentable square feet or less, then the agency may proceed without specific written authorization from GSA.[12]

The above *Federal Management Regulation (FMR) 2008-B1* reference was updated with the 2014 publication of *FMR Bulletin C-2*, which "clarifies the conditions, restrictions and reporting requirements specified in the GSA delegation of authority."[13] One policy item to note from the 2014 *FMR Bulletin C-2*, which seems to have always been on the books in one form or another, states that "Federal agencies will not be granted a delegation of leasing authority if suitable Government-controlled owned or vacant leased space is available."[14] The 2014 *FMR Bulletin C-2* goes on to list, with added emphasis, the forty-seven major laws, regulations, executive orders, and OMB circulars that make up the GSA and the executive branch's real estate lease policy.

DoD's Use of GSA-Delegated Authority

Federal agencies that have GSA-delegated authority typically incorporate, as they are required to do, the policies dictated in the *Desk Guide* with additional agency-specific policies added to those required by the GSA. The Department of Defense (DoD) real estate activities mentioned in the *Desk Guide* paragraph above reflect that while the DoD does not typically use the GSA for its real estate activities, it is still bound to the policies of the executive branch, the GSA, and its own internal real estate directives. It is also subject to additional DoD directives added to incorporate policies specific to its agency-specific mission needs.

Among the most important DoD regulations today are the DoD offsets required by the Base Realignment and Closure Act (BRAC) of 1990, which, as of early 2016, had not yet been approved for future base closings.[15] In the GSA's *Customer Guide to Real Property* (*Customer Guide*), GSA-delegated authority is described for each of the major federal agencies looking to lease space with private-sector property owners. The *Customer Guide* explains in detail what an agency with GSA-delegated authority can do to pursue different types of lease uses and lease terms. It sets forth the ways DoD uses real estate space, ranging from typical office space to armories and mess halls. DoD's lease authority for lease terms range from single-year (fiscal year) leases up to 20-year leases that include option periods.[16]

The *Desk Guide* references additional sources for federal government real estate policies. These sources include the *Federal Management Regulation* (*FMR*) guide, which contains procedures for operating under the *FMR*, and the *GSA Acquisition Manual* (*GSAM*), which contains agency items that govern the leasing process. The *Desk Guide* has an excellent appendix section that includes information on the OMB Circular A-11 (titled "Capital Lease Scoring"). This information describes how to determine whether a federal agency's real estate lease is a capital lease or an operating lease. Not included in the *Desk Guide*, but still important to the federal government's real estate policy, are all of GSA's Realty Service Letters and Lease Acquisition Circulars. Lease Acquisition Circulars are described by the GSA on the GSA's website as the "final authoritative source of leasing policy and guidance."

Policy Memorandums

The June 2010 Presidential Memorandum *Disposing of Unneeded Federal Real Estate* (*Disposing Memo*) describes the ongoing challenges with the federal government's real estate portfolio and the executive branch's efforts at the time to address or at least acknowledge these challenges:

> For decades, the Federal Government, the largest property owner and energy user in the United States, has managed more real estate than necessary to effectively support its programs and missions. Both taxpayer dollars and energy resources are being wasted to maintain these excess assets. In addition, many of the properties necessary for the Government's work are not operated efficiently, resulting in wasted funds and excessive greenhouse gas pollution.
>
> Past attempts at reducing the Federal Government's civilian real property assets produced small savings and had a minor impact on the condition and performance of mission-critical properties. These efforts were not sufficiently comprehensive in disposing of excess real estate and did not emphasize making more efficient use of existing assets. To eliminate wasteful spending of taxpayer dollars, save energy and water, and further reduce greenhouse gas pollution, I hereby direct executive departments and agencies (agencies) to accelerate efforts to identify and eliminate excess properties.

In 2012, the Office of Management and Budget (OMB) issued a follow-up to the 2010 *Disposing Memo*. Titled Memorandum M-12-12, *Promoting Efficient Spending to Support Agency Operation* (*Promoting Efficiency*), this memo echoes the *Disposing Memo* policy with the following statement:

> The President has been clear that wasteful spending is unacceptable, and that the Federal Government must strive to be more efficient and effective. That is why the President and the Vice President launched the Campaign to Cut Waste and charged agencies with going line-by-line through their budgets to identify areas of unnecessary spending or opportunities for greater efficiency or cost savings.
>
> The President directed each agency to reduce its combined costs in a variety of administrative categories by not less than 20 percent in Fiscal Year (FY) 2013 from FY 2010 levels. Agencies have since developed plans for achieving these cuts, and the President's FY 2013 Budget identifies $8 billion in reduced costs as a result of Executive Order 13589.

It is clear from both the 2010 *Disposing Memo* and the 2012 *Promoting Efficiency* memo that the executive branch is looking to establish a more efficient and effective real estate policy for the federal government.

Freezing the Footprint

It is important to remember, however, that while the 2010 *Disposing Memo* was written to address disposal of unneeded federal real estate, the 2012 *Promoting Efficiency* memo further addresses what was considered at the time to be the administration's most prominent real estate policy position, which states:

> Agencies must also move aggressively to dispose of excess properties held by the Federal Government and make more efficient use of the Government's real estate assets. Agencies are already streamlining operations and using existing properties to meet the directive in the June 10, 2010 Presidential Memorandum (Disposing of Unneeded Federal Real Estate-Increasing Sales Proceeds, Cutting Operating Costs, and Improving Energy Efficiency) to produce no less than $3 billion in civilian real property cost savings by the end of FY 2012.
>
> As of the date of this memorandum, agencies shall not increase the size of their civilian real estate inventory, subject to exceptions as described below. Acquisition of new Federal building space (where approval of such acquisition occurs following the date of this memorandum) that increases an agency's total square footage of civilian property must be offset through consolidation, co-location, or disposal of space from the inventory of that agency.
>
> In identifying consolidations, co-locations, or disposals of property to offset acquisition of new Federal building space, an agency may include civilian buildings from its own inventory that were, in accordance with the June 10, 2010 Presidential Memorandum, reported as excess to the GSA or otherwise disposed of.
>
> Additional guidance will be provided for carrying out this section, including defining those properties to which this section applies and when a property may be identified as an offset, as well as establishing a process to identify exceptions to this section's requirements where appropriate, such as to comply with legal requirements, to reduce costs, to protect national security, or to allow for the effective accomplishment of agency missions.

Implementing Policy

A year later, in 2013, OMB published a memo titled *Implementation of OMB Memorandum M-12-12 Section 3: Freeze the Footprint* (*Implementation Memo*) that explains in detail the meaning of the 2012 *Promoting Efficiency* memorandum statements above (and perhaps indicates the origin of the "freeze the footprint" phrase). The 2013 *Implementation Memo* states:

> Consistent with Section 3 of the Office of Management and Budget Memorandum (OMB) M-12-12, Promoting Efficient Spending to Support Agency Operations, all Chief Financial Officers (CFO) Act Executive branch departments and agencies (agencies) shall not increase the total square footage of their domestic office and warehouse inventory compared to the FY 2012 baseline. This Memorandum clarifies the "Freeze the Footprint" policy.
>
> a. Baseline for Measurement. Any agency's total square footage for office and warehouse space shall remain at its FY 2012 baseline level. Agency baselines will be calculated based on the FY 2012 Federal Real Property Profile (FRPP) data . . .[17]

This baseline for measurement can be found by analyzing the previously discussed FY 2014 *Federal Real Property Profile Summary Data Set* (*Data Set*). The *Data Set* is an Excel spreadsheet found in the *FRPP* section of the GSA's website. The FY 2014 *Data Set*, published in 2015, includes FY 2012 through FY 2014 inventory data for comparison.

The inclusion of the additional FY data is a departure from previous *FRPP* reports prior to FY 2013, which provided only the published year's inventory data. The inclusion of the previous years' data is no doubt an attempt to measure adherence to the 2012 *Promoting Efficiency* memo.

Establishing the Baseline

Analyzing the FY 2014 *Data Set* for office and warehouse space baseline numbers referenced in the 2012 *Promoting Efficiency* memo (not including the full

USPS reported inventory)[18], we start with the "Key Statistics" numbers in the FY 2014 *Data Set.* The "Key Statistics" data set is found in the first of 21 tabs in the *Data Set* spreadsheet. The "Key Statistics" numbers provide inventory data on the federal government's owned and leased buildings, structures, and land for FY 2012 through FY 2014.

To compare the FY 2012 baseline numbers to the FY 2014 numbers, it is best to first focus on the owned and leased building square footages listed among the "Key Statistics." FY 2012 shows 2,565,023,590 square feet of owned space in 272,063 buildings and 302,072,246 square feet of leased space in 23,146 buildings. This total of 2,867,095,836 square feet of owned and leased space in 295,209 buildings can be used as one method to establish the "Freeze the Footprint" FY 2012 baseline for measurement. It is important to remember that in 2015 the GSA did not include all internationally owned and leased properties in the FY 2014 *Data Set*—the GSA only included domestic and US territory data.

The FY 2014 numbers show a reduction in owned space, totaling 2,505,805,423 square feet in 254,083 buildings. There is a decrease in the amount of leased space, to 294,163,456 square feet. Meanwhile, the number of leased buildings decreased to 21,112. The total owned and leased square footage for FY 2014 is 2,799,968,879 square feet; this is a year-over-year *decrease* of 47,968,393 square feet. The number of owned and leased buildings also decreased in FY 2014 by 10,897 buildings. This decrease is mainly due to the drop in federally owned buildings reported in FY 2014.

Office and Warehouse Trends

In further analysis of these baseline numbers in the FY 2013 *Data Set,* we find very useful data in the "Office Trend by Agency" ("Office Trend") and "Warehouse Trend by Agency" ("Warehouse Trend") tabs, which report the office and warehouse data for all the reporting federal agencies. The "Office Trend" data show that the office space numbers for FY 2013 *increased* from FY 2012 by 0.43 percent, a 3,462,158 square feet total increase. The largest users of office space, the GSA and the Department of the Army (Army), added 1.44 percent and 1.40 percent to their office space inventory, respectively. This works out to 7,444,735 square feet of growth for these two agencies that lease a combined 529,325,568 square feet of space, compared with the total 801,379,275 square feet of office space owned and leased in the FY 2013 *Data Set.*

Looking at the FY 2014 *Data Set* numbers is challenging given that the total international numbers have been removed. Analyzing the FY 2014 *Data Set* finds that there are square footage decreases for most of the agencies, with notable decreases going to the GSA and the Army getting closer to their FY 2012 reported numbers. The overall percentage change for the office data shows a percentage decrease of 1.42 percent from FY 2013 to FY 2014.

The "Warehouse Trend" tab data shows that the reported FY 2013 warehouse numbers shed 8,027,507 square feet, or 4.43 percent, of owned and leased warehouse space from FY 2012 to FY 2013. The largest users of warehouse space, the Army and the GSA, showed the largest decreases in use from FY 2012 to FY 2013, with 10.41 percent and 4.01 percent respective decreases on 7,840,940 square feet of warehouse space. In FY 2013, the Army and the GSA had a combined inventory of 87,937,806 square feet of warehouse space. The data show a total FY 2013 warehouse inventory of 177,129,540 square feet for all reporting federal agencies.

The FY 2014 *Data Set* numbers show that there was an overall decrease of warehouse space of 3.92 percent from FY 2013. Most agencies reported decreases, with only a handful of agencies reporting increases. The Army showed the largest decrease in its square footage use of warehouse space, shedding 6.44 percent of its warehouse inventory while the GSA showed a small increase in its use of 0.28 percent.

Comparison of the reported inventory numbers for the FY 2012 baseline, and the subsequent years' data to FY 2014 shows that the "Freeze the Footprint" policies may have been met for that period.

Reduce the Footprint

In 2015, the federal government updated the 2013 Freeze the Footprint memo to move from the Freeze the Footprint policy to a Reduce the Footprint policy in FY 2016. The updated memo, dated March 25, 2015, states in the summary:

> Consistent with Section 3 of the Office of Management (OMB) and Budget Memorandum M-12 12, Promoting Efficient Spending to Support Agency Operations (May 11, 2012), all Chief Financial Officers (CFO) Act Executive Branch departments and agencies shall move aggressively to dispose of surplus properties held by the Federal Government, make more efficient use of the Government's real property assets, and reduce the total square footage of their domestic office and warehouse inventory relative to an established baseline. This Memorandum supersedes OMB Management Procedures Memorandum 2013-02 (March 14, 2013) and clarifies existing policy to dispose of excess properties and promote more efficient use of real property assets. OMB and the General Services Administration (GSA) will annually monitor the continuing implementation of this policy. As part of this process, each agency will develop and submit a Real Property Efficiency Plan in lieu of a Revised Real Property Cost Savings and Innovation Plan. GSA will support policy implementation through data management and analytics to identify real property efficiency opportunities.[19]

The above summary changes some of the reporting requirements for federal agencies from the Freezing Memo to the new Reducing Memo but the biggest change, as the name implies, is that agencies are required in FY 2016 to not only continue to freeze but also to reduce their real property footprint over the next several years.

Current Actions and Looking Ahead

As part of the FY 2016 budget request for the federal government a document titled *Government-Wide Real Property Management* was published, which covers the federal government's real estate policies, strategy, and a plan for the future. Highlights related to this document are as follows.

National Strategy

1. Issue the policy of Reducing The Footprint policy to move from a policy of "freezing" to "reduction."
2. Create decision tools using the Federal Real Property Profile (FRPP) and performance benchmarking data.
3. Improve the FRPP data.
4. Utilize the GSA Federal Building Fund consolidation program to support implementation of these policies.

Key Budget Items

1. GSA Federal Buildings fund consolidation program: Provides $200 million of Federal Building Fund money to support consolidation of leases into government owned buildings to decrease lease costs and increase efficiency. Additional consolidation alternatives include consolidation of high cost leases into a single lower cost lease along with consolidation of multiple owned locations into a more densely populated owned location.
2. Reproposal of the Civilian Realignment Property Act (CRPA): The CRPA has been mentioned numerous times over the years with some support at the federal level and in the private-sector. Here are the objectives of the CRPA as discussed in the budget request document:

Objectives of the CRPA:

1. Support timely disposal of assets and realignment of the inventory.
2. Streamline the legal framework to accelerate disposal and realignment.
3. Eliminate O&M costs associated with unneeded properties.
4. Enhance portfolio efficiency and allow agencies to benefit from sale proceeds.

Moving forward, as the budget request document states, the federal government is looking to:

1. Implement both the National Strategy and the Reduce the Footprint policy.
2. Monitor and refine the policies to meet the reduction goals.
3. Focus on improving FRPP data.
4. Engage Congress on real property legislation.

United States Postal Service Real Estate Leasing Policy

The United States Postal Service (USPS) has the largest and longest-running inventory of single-agency leased spaced in the US. In 2012, the USPS posted it had about 27,000 post offices nationwide. With 3,537,438 square miles of land in the United States to cover, that is one distribution point for every 131 square miles in the US. Whether owned or leased, the USPS currently has a post office in every major market and in most rural markets in the US. Looking at the historical numbers of post offices[20] in the US finds that from 1901 to the present day the history of the USPS post office inventory is one of contraction:

1901: 77,000 post offices nationwide.

1950: 41,000 post offices nationwide.

1969: 32,000 post offices nationwide.

1971: US Postal Department becomes the US Postal Service.

1975: 30,000 post offices left nationwide, the Government Accounting Office (GAO) wants to close 12,000 buildings.

1976: Congress places moratorium on closures.

1977: The moratorium on closures is lifted.

2012: 27,000 post offices nationwide.

While not all post offices may be leased, there are non–post office USPS locations that are leased across the country. The USPS in its FY 2015 annual report states that the USPS executed over 6,000 leases in FY 2015, with lease rates for leases over $50,000 negotiated at 8.4 percent below market value.[21] The USPS in 2011 hired the private-sector real estate company CB Richard Ellis (CBRE) to act as its sole real estate broker on a number of USPS lease negotiations. The number of leases CBRE has negotiated on behalf of the USPS varies depending on the published statistics, but according to one report, *Postal Service Management of CBRE Real Estate Transactions,* CBRE negotiated 1,698 leases during FY 2012 and FY 2013 along with negotiating 5,660 leases from January 2013 to March 2015.[22] Of the 5,660 leases, 90 percent where negotiated at or below market rental rates.

The report mentioned above states that the real estate objectives of the USPS are "to acquire, lease, build, and expand facilities to support operations. Challenges in the economy, shifts in technology, and other factors have led to a change in the Postal Service's real estate goals and objectives. Currently, the Postal Service's Facilities organization is focused on consolidating and disposing of excess space and vacant properties in an effort to optimize operations, generate revenue, and reduce real estate expenses." One of the main tools of this effort to reduce and consolidate post offices utilizes a USPS program called POStPlan, started in 2012, that allows the USPS to reduce service hours at post office locations across the US. In 2016 a substantial number of post offices nationally closed their locations, consolidated, or have worked under reduced hours.

STATE AND LOCAL GOVERNMENT REAL ESTATE LEASING POLICIES

The real estate leasing policies of state and local governments are not uniform nationally in their approach to managing their real estate lease portfolios. Local government policies are even more varied from the states, with little to no input or oversight from the voting public. Larger states and local governments that have more resources and larger populations tend to have a more sophisticated approach to their real estate activities, while smaller government entities tend to have smaller portfolios with policies that are more inconsistent or outdated when compared to their larger government counterparts.

State Government Real Estate Leasing Policies

There are several challenges when reviewing the real estate policies of state governments that need to be discussed to achieve a perspective on what it is that most states are doing related to their real estate leasing inventory. This perspective is not to place any negative light on a state's leasing efforts but rather to point to the complexity of what each of their efforts entail. To start with the major challenge first, since there are no national standards for government real estate leasing, it can be difficult to translate the way one state agency performs its real estate leasing transactions compared to another. This is often carried over to the various governmental bodies or agencies within a state, which may be using its own separate individual lease forms or deviating from a state-approved form by signing a property owner's lease without following the state's own mandated lease guidelines. Second, states do not follow a standardized national format in how they report their real estate leasing activities, as some state governments do not report any leasing activities to the public while other states report data that is either inconsistent or irregular in its publication from year to year. Third, unlike the federal government, which is fairly transparent relative to its state counterparts, most state agencies do not readily divulge basic real estate leasing data to the general public. Fourth, the internal decision-making process for state governments can be difficult due to the term of leases they can sign because some states sign long-term leases, while others are limited to signing leases subject to annual budget appropriations that can force an agency to terminate a lease early in the lease term if agency funding is cut. Finally, while most states tend to cluster their owned government properties at the seat of their state government, which is usually the state capital, states run into the issue of whether to lease or own in locations that are not geographically convenient for owning but leasing for the long term can create issues both financially and politically.

The above challenges aside, there are many state governments that do spend a considerable amount of time and energy determining what the best policies are for their individual real estate lease inventories. For example, the state of Florida currently releases a yearly lease inventory report, and the state of Texas publishes a biannual master facility plan. Both the Florida and Texas reports are excellent in that they cover the methodologies and policy objectives for their lease inventory decision-making practices.

The Texas biannual 2014 report *The Master Facilities Plan Report*[23] (*Report*) is worth reviewing in that it discusses its statutory reporting requirements, budget constraints, population impacts, and consolidation efforts. The *Report*'s executive summary states:

> The Master Facilities Plan Report is a comprehensive report that satisfies statutory reporting requirements found in Texas Government Code, Title 10, Chapters 2165 and 2166. The Master Facilities Plan Report addresses the status and costs associated with TFC-owned and leased inventories, current utilization statistics, future state agency requirements, relevant real estate market information, and provides strategies to ensure efficient utilization and operation of state assets. Understanding the fiscal challenges facing the State of Texas, the Commission is proactively pursuing strategic initiatives that will leverage existing resources to improve utilization, operational efficiencies, and provide cost savings. It is important to note that these initiatives are multi-year plans and projects that require

> substantial groundwork and investment to yield maximum financial and operational benefits to the State.

The *Report* goes into great detail regarding the needs for the owned and leased property portfolio for the state. This is relevant for the state in understanding what the long-term goals are as it relates to its future private-sector real estate leasing objectives. Some states will signal what their long-term intentions are for their leased inventory based on what their plans are for their owned portfolio.

The *Report* discusses what is becoming more common at the state level, which is for states to have some type of lease consolidation plan to reduce the footprint of their lease inventory portfolios:

> A similar effort, the Commission's Statewide Lease Consolidation Program is a tactical plan aimed at reducing state lease expenditures and the State's dependence on commercial lease facilities in the metropolitan areas outside of Austin where the State has maintained a historical presence. With an eye toward long-term savings by consolidating leases into new regional service centers, the Commission is currently aligning its lease portfolio expirations.
>
> This will enable the state to take advantage of opportunities to buy or lease existing facilities large enough to provide for cost-effective consolidation of facilities.

The consolidation plan goes on to state that consolidating administrative office space has proven to reduce the volume of space required by 10 to 20 percent in recently completed state-owned renovations. Further, the *Report* states that:

> Government Code, Section 2166.1061 requires that the Commission determines the cost-benefit of consolidating leases into centralized sites and develops plans to implement viable lease consolidations. The field of candidates is to be derived from counties where the State leases office space and the population exceeds 75,000 people. In Fiscal Year 2013, approximately 3 million square feet of administrative sites located in 34 counties and 43 cities made up the initial evaluation field within requisite counties. Candidate cities for lease consolidation are determined according to the following criteria: two or more leases exist in the requisite city; all of the state leases in the city will expire by 2017; savings can be achieved through improved efficiencies; and adequate facilities are or may become available. According to the selection criteria outlined above, eight cities were determined to be candidates for lease consolidations by the year 2017. For the last 3 years, TFC's leasing services program has been positioning candidate lease expirations of 131 leases to allow an orderly transition into 17 consolidated leased sites.

Consolidating 131 leases into 17 may not be a huge number when compared to Texas's 2016 lease inventory of 1,424 leases, but what is not discussed in detail is what the size of the leases are or where they are located.

Another item that is relevant to review for state decision makers when making lease inventory decisions is determining whether a state should build or lease. For Texas, the build-versus-lease (BBL) review is part of its statutory requirements as discussed in the *Report*:

> TFC performed buy and renovate versus build versus lease ("BBL") analyses for 33 candidate cities. TFC is required by statute to ensure that when building or buying office space, total occupancy costs will not exceed the cost of leasing when calculated over the term of the bond debt, typically 20 years. The BBL evaluation includes cost-benefit analyses which incorporate planning, land acquisition, design, demolition, construction, management, fixed equipment, telecommunication, building start-up and occupancy life-cycle costs. TFC performs these analyses every biennium as required by statute. The analyses included the current and projected market conditions, the industry estimating parameters, the current state lease costs, the current real estate market asking rates, the Texas Public Finance Authority's quoted interest rates, and the individual studies in the real estate markets of the 33 cities. The Commission's BBL methodology and procedures were audited by the State Auditor's Office ("SAO") in early 2000. Upon their review, which included input from CB Richard Ellis real estate professionals and the City of Austin's planning department, the TFC BBL

> methodology was approved by the SAO. Real estate fundamentals and financial market conditions have significantly changed since then.
>
> The results of the BBL analyses revealed several key factors that pose challenges for the feasibility of buying and renovating or building new facilities in the 33 cities: a) the state's lease rates are extremely favorable at this time; b) the desire to maintain cost neutrality when relocating tenant agencies from older and less expensive space into newer space reflective of current market asking rates; c) the current one to one parking space allocation practice, which unnecessarily increases project cost; and, most significantly, d) the 20-year cost-benefit time frame utilized in the analyses. Collectively, these challenges are magnified when attempting to construct buildings of monumental stature with useful life cycles in excess of 50 years. The typical original term of a state lease is 5 to 10 years with as many renewal options as desired, effectively resulting in tenancy of 15 to 30 years at a single location. In most cases, these leases are only replaced due to the limitations of further expansion of the facility to meet requirements for the expansion and growth of agencies. The Commission's historical lease data indicates this is the case in the majority of the 33 cities previously cited. It is reasonable to assume the State will maintain its long term presence, perhaps 50 to 100 years or more, in these communities.

These statements regarding the BBL analysis go to the heart of what states are considering when they make lease inventory decisions. One could argue that this analysis is based on the principles of marginal utility. Marginal utility would apply here to states that are looking to understand their consumption levels for owning and leasing, with diminished utility given to owned locations that are going to be in a geographic location for only a short period of time.

The following is an overview of state government leasing policies and activities that are relevant due to their size and publicly available information.

California

California is one of the largest states in the country, with a large portfolio of real estate leases and owned property for the state's government activities. The California Department of General Services Real Estate Division's Real Estate Leasing and Planning Section (RELPS) handles a majority, but not all, of the state's leasing activities. The inventory for the number of state leases tracked by the Real Estate Division in 2016 shows there are 2,299 leases with the private sector for a total of 16,373,309 square feet of leased space with another 5,293,024 square feet of storage and other space leased. The total annual rent in 2016 for all leased space is $491,051,267.[24] As with the federal government's *FRPP* data, the RELPS inventory is limited to collecting leases from a certain number of agencies within the state and does not collect data, or at least release the figures publicly, for all leases the state has with the private sector.

Florida

The Florida Department of Management Services (DMS) is tasked with oversight of the state's lease procurement process. While DMS manages less than 1 percent of the total number of state-owned facilities, it manages the second-largest portfolio in terms of square footage. DMS reported in 2015 it has 794 leases with the private sector, with 6,466,501 square feet of leased space and combined total annual rents of $125,176,825.89.[25] Like most states, the state of Florida follows a decentralized model for its real estate portfolio, with several agencies managing their own real estate activities. This decentralized model would indicate by most standards a portfolio that is hard to keep track of but the state does a good job of tracking and analyzing its portfolio from year to year. According to one report, the challenges of this decentralized model is that it is "managed differently across agencies, creating little consistency relating to the staffing, management or operations of their real estate programs. This decentralization limits the state's ability to realize strategic goals and cost-savings initiatives."[26]

Texas

The state of Texas real estate leases are managed and overseen by the Texas Facilities Commission (TFC) State Leasing Services department. TFC reported in 2016 an inventory of 1,424 leases, with several of these leases being shown to be at the same location with the same agency, for a total combined square footage of 10,271,311 square feet.[27] The TFC states, "Lease expenditures totaled $153.6 million during Fiscal Year 2013. Office space accounts for 86%, or 8.9 million square feet, of the TFC-leased inventory and $138 million of total lease costs. Warehouse, laboratory, print shop, parking and other support facilities make up the balance of the leased inventory totaling 1.4 million square feet at a cost of $15.6 million per year. TFC also manages single office leases in the District of Columbia, New York, California, Illinois, and Oklahoma. Of the 34 tenant agencies in the Commission's leased inventory, more than 90% of commercially-leased office space is occupied and paid by 10 agencies or departments."[28]

Illinois

The state of Illinois real estate leases are managed and overseen by the Department of Central Management Services Bureau of Property Management (BOPM). BOPM reported in 2015 that its lease inventory consisted of 358 leases with the private sector, with 6,702,065 square feet of leased space for a combined total annual rental rate of $86,547,372.00.[29] A majority of these leases are clustered in Springfield and Chicago.

The State of Illinois has a lease consolidation program and in a 2010 press release gave the following as examples of its real estate lease cost reduction efforts:[30]

1. IDOT Springfield, Division of Traffic Safety moved to state owned space: Total cost reduction $1.7 million.
2. DHS Chicago (59th and Ashland) moved to other existing leased space: Total cost reduction $1.3 million.
3. DCEO Springfield: the old lease of $2.3 million per year was reduced by 51 percent to $1.1 million: Total savings $1.2 million.
4. DCFS Springfield: the prior lease was $1.0 million; the office was split in two for a total lease cost of $432,140.00, reduced by 57 percent for a total reduction of $575,874.00.

Local Government Real Estate Leasing Policies

Understanding the real estate policy for local governments at the county and municipal levels is a complex undertaking. Unlike federal and state governments, most local governments carry out their real estate leasing activities with little or no public reporting required. Even the largest local government agencies perform their leasing activities without advertising or publishing their real estate leasing activities. The reasons for this are mostly a lack of interest by the public in their local government's real estate leasing activities or limited resources available for local government agencies to actively report and publish these activities. Adding to this is the fact that most private-sector real estate leases with local government agencies, aside from the largest of local governments, are infrequent and small enough to not be reviewed by the public and competing property owners.

One city that is very transparent in its real estate leasing activities, whether required by statute or code, is the City of New York. New York City, when compared to other local governments' published data, has the largest number of private-sector leases in its real estate lease inventory. New York City publishes its lease inventory online along with some references in its annual budget as to what its leasing costs are. Chicago is another local government entity that posts information, although sporadically and limited in scope, regarding its private-sector leasing activities. The City of Chicago may be the best representation of a local government with leasing activities that rises to the level of warranting some level of reporting but that is perhaps not so large as to require a centralized database like New York City.

Like their federal and state counterparts, the cities of New York and Chicago are focused on the current trend of consolidating and downsizing their lease inventory whenever possible. The City of Chicago in its *2015 Annual Financial Analysis*[31] states:

> Property rental and building services in 2005 were $30.0 million and grew thereafter with increasing rental and building services costs, to $38.9 million, or 12.4 percent of contractual services expenses, in 2008. Since 2008, rental and related expenses have steadily decreased to $28.3 million as the City reduces the number of properties that it leases. The City is maximizing the utilization of City-owned space, such as City Hall, and reducing long-term rental expenses while grouping similar departmental functions together in order to increase efficiencies and facilitate beneficial coordination. Space consolidations in the past year include City operations moving from two previously leased locations to City-owned facilities, as well as a facility where the City does not pay rent. Space consolidations are on-going and the City estimates that, once complete, the cost of these relocations and related renovations will be fully recouped with lease savings within three years.

What is most intriguing about the various moves and consolidations is that while these decisions are not the easiest to make, they are usually made with only a single property owner. Most local governments (including Chicago and New York City) are not required to competitively bid their private-sector leases. As stated in the New York City *2015 Annual Summary Contracts Report*,

> **Leases/Lessee Negotiation Agreements**
>
> Leases are agreements entered into between the City and a landlord for use of real property by the City. In certain situations, the agreement for the use of real property by the City can take the form of a "license." The acquisition and use of the real property through a Lease is not subject to the competitive bidding requirements of the PPB Rules or GML § 103. As required by the Charter, most Leases for real property are negotiated and entered into by DCAS, generally on behalf of other City agencies, community boards and borough president's offices.

One item that needs to be considered when reviewing the lease inventory data for local governments is that other units of government within a local government's body, such as the school system, transportation authorities, and libraries, may not be included in the local government's lease inventory data but counted separately as its own data set.

The following is a review of the lease inventory information for the cities of New York and Chicago.

City of New York

The Department of Citywide Administrative Services (DCAS) Asset Management Office is the department that oversees the city's owned buildings and commercial rental properties. The Asset Management Office also negotiates and administers the leases the city has with the private sector.

In 2016, a majority of the publicly available lease inventory data for the city can be found in three places:

1. The city's Integrated Property Information System (IPIS)[32] lease database in the New York City OpenData website.
2. The city's Planning Department website, which has its city-owned leased property (COLP)[33] data available for download.
3. The city posts its yearly lease contract activity in its annual fiscal year budget reports.[34]

The top two lease inventories referenced above offer a large amount of data to sort through. The IPIS data provide the most extensive report available, with 689 leases listed along with an assortment of other data for its owned properties. The COLP data have a 2014 post date and are less extensive than the IPIS data, listing 748 leases. Neither data set reports annual lease rent payment amounts or with whom leases are signed. One may assume that the data from the COLP and IPIS inventory are different due to the lease inventory contracting from 2014 to 2016. The lease transaction data in the FY 2015 annual report data show there were 96 leases entered into that FY for a lease contract value of $1,271,086,165; this value is for the total lease payments owed for the full term of the lease. Almost half of the total lease contract value in FY 2015 was for the New York City lease at the Four World Trade Center building, with total lease payments of $577,876,144 owed for the full term of the lease.

City of Chicago

The city of Chicago's real estate leasing activities are handled primarily by the city's Bureau of Asset Management, with, in 2015, a reported leased inventory of 55 leases and 454 owned properties. Unlike the City of New York, the City of Chicago does not post its city lease inventory activities in a centralized location for public review. The city does post its individual lease actions in a central database when the leases are up for city council approval. These leases are generally published in the general mix of other budget line-item approval requests. Alternatively, the City of Chicago's public school system, which is not included in the posted lease and owned properties listed above, posts a majority of its leases in an online database along with the actual leases it has executed as either the lessor or lessee.

Looking at a 2011 lease inventory for the city shows that the city had a total of 59 leases, which includes 42 office leases, 7 warehouse leases, and 10 land leases, for total annual rents of $19,816,894. The office inventory has a leased square footage of 1,154,277 square feet, with the warehouse inventory being 392,895 square feet. In a 2015 budget hearing statement, it appears that a few of these leases have been closed or consolidated into other owned and leased locations.[35]

NOTABLE PORTFOLIOS AND LEASES

A review of government real estate leasing would not be complete without a discussion of the notable government real estate leases and the portfolios of leases held by the various national real estate property firms. A good place to look when reviewing the notable portfolios of properties that house government tenants is the public companies that are required to report their holdings. It's worth noting that while some public companies may have several million square feet of government-leased space in their property portfolios, these holdings represent but a fraction of the overall government-leased properties in the US. In 2015, The top ten property owners of government tenant leases leased approximately 33 million square feet of the estimated 500 million square feet of government-leased space in the US. Most of these property owners are real estate investment trusts (REITs) or investment funds.

Notable Portfolios

The largest holder of government real estate leased properties in 2015 is Government Properties Income Trust (NYSE: GOV), a REIT, that states that it "is an Office REIT that focuses on properties that are leased to U.S. and state government agencies." GOV has 71 properties with 10,700,964 square feet of space with almost 94 percent of the square footage leased to various government agencies and a market capitalization of $1.01 billion in 2016.[36, 37] By way of comparison, in 2016, the largest REIT in the US, Simon Property Group, has a market capitalization of $57.46 billion.[38]

Another REIT that has a significant number of government tenants in its portfolio of properties is Corporate Office Properties Trust (COPT) (NYSE: OFC). COPT had, in 2015, 65 leases with the federal government for a total of over 3.8 million square feet with annual rents of over $140 million in 2015.[39] The federal government, in 2015, represents over 22 percent of COPT's top 20 office tenants, with its next largest tenant being the Boeing Company.

A REIT that has a significant presence in the Washington, DC, market is Vornado Realty Trust (NYSE: VNO), which reported in its 2015 annual report that it leases over 3.5 million square feet to the federal government, with revenues in 2014 on these leases of over $133 million.

Notable Leases

Discussing the leases in government real estate that are notable is not an easy task. Most but not all of the information regarding the larger government leases is publicly available at the federal level, sporadic at the state level, and almost nonexistent at the local level without working with local government officials in a Freedom of Information Act request capacity.

While large leases get most of the attention, it is important to consider that there are smaller leases that may be unremarkable in themselves but when they are part of an agency's national or state effort to lease space in a short period of time, the logistics can be mind-boggling. Also, there are some agencies like the Federal Emergency Management Agency (FEMA), which is required to go into a market based on some event that necessitates FEMA to sign sometimes very large leases with a property owner in a compressed time period (sometimes in less than 24 hours). While all government real estate leases are notable and unique, the following are leases are notable for either their size or the leasing action undertaken by the government agency to complete its agency leasing goals.

US Census Bureau–Census 2010 Leases

The US Census Bureau's Census 2010 leasing action, like the leasing actions for previous decennial US Censuses, are incredibly complex, with a large number of leases across the US. The Census 2010 leases, 507 of them, were for a short term and required the necessary build-out for a traditional office space. The following review of the Census 2010 leasing action is taken from a follow-up report by the Census Bureau in 2012:[40]

> The United States Constitution requires a census of population and housing to be conducted every ten years of people living in the United States. Prior to the actual census enumeration activities, a widespread network of temporary Regional Census Centers and Local Census Offices are opened to manage the collection of decennial data. As has been done in past censuses, a space acquisition program is established to lease the temporary office space. For the 2010 Census, 12 Regional Census Centers, one Puerto Rico Area Office, and 494 Local Census Offices were opened. These offices were located in all 50 states, the District of Columbia, and Puerto Rico. All major field operations were conducted from these temporary offices.
>
> The 2010 Census Space Acquisition Program was considered a success, although throughout the program a number of challenges were encountered. Six of the twelve Regional Census Centers opened later than originally planned, as did a number of Early Local Census Offices, due to lease acquisition challenges. The Early Local Census Offices were further impacted by the Non Response Follow-Up Re-plan, which occurred during their design and build-out phase. None of the delayed openings affected operational activities. Between the Early Local Center Offices and Local Census Offices acquisition phase the Census Bureau and other program stakeholders took into consideration lessons learned from the Early Local Census Offices experience and made adjustments for the Local Census Offices phase, adjusting activities and process steps beginning with the acquisition process through Office Computing Equipment deployment. These changes resulted in an improved and more efficient process for the remaining 344 Local Census Offices, which opened on schedule. The Census Bureau was able to start closing offices early and closed the last of the 494 Local Census Offices a few weeks before the scheduled finish date.
>
> The total cost of the Space Acquisition Program was $330,778,430. Total costs include General Services Administration rent, Tenant Improvements, Operating Expenses, Department of Homeland Security Federal Protective Service fees, Reimbursable Work Authorizations, Security Work Authorizations, General Services Administration Fees, and miscellaneous expenses related to the 2010 Census.

The US Census 2010 leasing action described above is both massive and complex in its scale and the effort required to complete it. It is interesting to note that the US Census 2010 offices were required to be located in each Congressional District, with some districts having either no or very limited traditional commercial office space available for lease at the time the leasing action occurred. The limited amount of available leased space and the demands on the lease occupancy schedule required that the Census 2010 leasing teams be very creative in the approach and use of the space they needed to find to make the leases work for the Census 2010 offices.

Alexandria, VA

Looking at single-lease transactions, the US GSA has one of the largest leases in the US for leased space as a tenant. The US Patent Office has almost 2.4 million square feet of leased space, with rent payments in 2015 of over $72 million.[41] The building's lessor, LCOR, completed the building in 2005 with a lease end date of 2024.

Kansas City, MO

Another large lease is the Department of the Treasury leased space in Kansas City, Missouri. This lease is number five in square footage and number four in lease rental payments in the US GSA's December 2015 lease inventory data set. The US GSA released a superseding lease request in 2013 for this lease that states:[42]

> The General Services Administration (GSA) proposes a superseding lease of up to 1,140,000 rentable square feet (RSF) and 4,900 parking spaces for the Department of Treasury. The Kansas City Service Center is the primary location for continued processing of individual taxpayer paper returns and is expected to retain this function even as the transition to electronic filing is being adopted by taxpayers to an increasing degree. This proposed request serves to enhance the Government's leasehold interest in the current facility, based on the Department of Treasury determination of ongoing need and the current lessor's offer to extend and improve the terms of the lease.

City of New York

The City of New York's lease at the Four World Trade Center building is one of the largest municipal leases in recent history. The lease is for the city's Human Resources Administration office. The city has a 15-year lease that started in January 2015 for 581,642 square feet for total lease payments of $577,876,144.[43]

State of Illinois

The State of Illinois administrative headquarters lease in the City of Chicago is for a five-year term starting in January 2014 for 242,831 square feet, with lease payments in 2015 of $6,091,341.[44]

State of Texas

The State of Texas lease in Austin for the Department of Assistive and Rehabilitative Services is for 10 years starting in December 2015 for a total of 184,000 square feet.

CHAPTER SUMMARY

This chapter reviewed the following topics related to government real estate leasing:

- An overview of government real estate leasing.
- The real estate leasing policies of a number of government real estate agencies at the federal, state, and local levels of government.
- A review of various notable government real estate lease transactions and portfolios of private-sector property owners with government real estate leases.

NOTES

[1] https://www.census.gov/newsroom/releases/archives/governments/cb12-161.html.

[2] The numbers used to estimate the total number of government leases with the associated average rents and square footage in the US is an estimate only, as the official numbers are currently not available or don't exist. For comparison of the estimated figures, the 2012 Commercial Buildings Energy Consumption Survey states that there are 5.6 million commercial properties in the US comprising 87.4 billion square feet of floor space. http://www.eia.gov/consumption/commercial/reports/2012/preliminary/.

[3] http://money.cnn.com/2012/12/05/news/companies/starbucks-new-stores/; http://www.statista.com/statistics/256040/mcdonalds-restaurants-in-north-america/; http://www.statista.com/statistics/269425/total-number-of-walmart-stores-in-the-united-states-by-type/.

[4] *FY 2013 FRPP Summary Data Set* (MS Excel spreadsheet), tab 7: Buildings (Washington, DC: US GSA).

[5] https://about.usps.com/who-we-are/financials/annual-reports/fy2015.pdf.

[6] Ross W. Gorte, Carol Hardy Vincent, Laura A. Hanson, and Marc R. Rosenblum, *Federal Land and Ownership: Overview and Data* (Washington, DC: Congressional Research Service, February 8, 2012), Table 1, pp. 4 and 2.

[7] *PBS Leasing Desk Guide, 2010* (Washington, DC: US GSA), 5.

[8] "Lease Delegations," US GSA, accessed September 6, 2014, http://gsa.gov/portal/category/106099.

[9] *General Reference Guide for Real Property Policy* (Washington, DC: US GSA, 2010), 2.

[10] *GSA Delegations of Authority Manual* (Washington, DC: US GSA, revised 2011).

[11] *PBS Leasing Desk Guide, 2010*, 3.

[12] *PBS Leasing Desk Guide, 2010*, 4.

[13] *Federal Management Regulation (FMR) Bulletin C-2* (2014).

[14] *FMR C-2*, 5.

[15] *http://www.thefiscaltimes.com/2015/12/18/Congress-Pentagon-Don-t-Even-Think-About-Closing-Military-Bases.*

[16] *Customer Guide to Real Property* (Washington, DC: US GSA), 76.

[17] Danny Werfel, "Implementation of OMB Memorandum M-12-12 Section 3: Freeze the Footprint," Management Procedures Memorandum No. 2013-02 (Washington, DC: Office of Management and Budget, 2013).

[18] Some USPS numbers included in the FY 2013 *Data Set* are not part of the USPS primary inventory.

[19] https://www.whitehouse.gov/sites/default/files/omb/financial/memos/implementation-reduce-the-footprint.pdf.

[20] Figures are taken from a write up of a speech given by Mark Strong, "Are Postal Closures Inevitable, Based on USPS History?," at the 2014 AUSPL Conference: http://auspl.com/wp-content/uploads/2014/05/Mark-Strong-story.pdf.

[21] https://about.usps.com/who-we-are/financials/annual-reports/fy2015.pdf, p.51.

[22] https://www.uspsoig.gov/sites/default/files/document- library-files/2015/sm-ar-15-003.pdf

[23] http://www.tfc.state.tx.us/divisions/facilities/prog/planning/FINAL%20-%202014%20TFC%20Master%20Facilities%20Plan%20Report%20(WEB).pdf.

[24] http://www.dgs.ca.gov/resd/Home/SPIhomepage/SPISummary.aspx.

[25] http://www.dms.myflorida.com/content/download/118552/650855/2015_Master_Leasing_reportpdf.pdf, p. 3.

[26] http://www.dms.myflorida.com/content/download/118552/650855/2015_Master_Leasing_reportpdf.pdf, p. 39.

[27] http://www.tfc.state.tx.us/divisions/facilities/prog/leasing/inventory for 01/16.

[28] http://www.tfc.state.tx.us/divisions/facilities/prog/leasing/.

[29] https://www.illinois.gov/cms/agency/property/leasing/Documents/November-2015-CMS-Lease-Inventory.pdf.

[30] http://www3.illinois.gov/pressreleases/ShowPressRelease.cfm?SubjectID=2&RecNum=8577.

[31] http://www.cityofchicago.org/content/dam/city/depts/obm/supp_info/2016Budget/AFA%20-%202015%20(with%20Press%20Release).pdf.

[32] https://nycopendata.socrata.com/Housing-Development/IPIS-Integrated-Property-Information-System-/n5mv-nfpy.

[33] http://www1.nyc.gov/site/planning/data-maps/open-data.page.

[34] http://comptroller.nyc.gov/wp-content/uploads/documents/FY15_Annual_Contracts_Report.pdf.

[35] Statement by David J. Reynolds, Commissioner, Department of Fleet & Facility Management, 2015 Budget Hearing.

[36] http://finance.yahoo.com/q?s=GOV, company data from 2/2/2016 and 2/5/2016

[37] http://s2.q4cdn.com/091245771/files/doc_financials/quarterly/2015/q3/GOV_3Q15-Supplemental_102915.pdf.

[38] http://finance.yahoo.com/q?uhb=uhb2&fr=uh3_finance_vert_gs&type=2button&s=spg, company data from 2/5/2016.

[39] http://investors.copt.com/Cache/1500077257.PDF?Y=&O=PDF&D=&FID=1500077257&T=&IID=103010.

[40] https://www.census.gov/2010census/pdf/2010_Census_Space_Acquisition_Assessment.pdf.

[41] http://finance.yahoo.com/q?uhb=uhb2&fr=uh3_finance_vert_gs&type=2button&s=spg.

[42] http://www.gsa.gov/graphics/pbs/fy13_leaseprogram_Internal_Revenue_Service_Lease.pdf.

[43] http://comptroller.nyc.gov/wp-content/uploads/documents/FY15_Annual_Contracts_Report.pdf.

[44] http://www.illinois.gov/cms/agency/property/leasing/Documents/January-2015-CMS-Lease-Inventory.pdf.

Marin County Civic Center Interior

CHAPTER TWO:

NEW GOVERNMENT REAL ESTATE LEASES

IN THIS CHAPTER

1. **New Lease Requirement Postings**
2. **Government Lease Inventory Reports**
3. **Government Agency Reports**
4. **Additional Search Options**

For most property owners and real estate agents, finding new government real estate leases can be a challenge, as most simply don't know where to start. There are multiple ways to find new government real estate leases, from basic searches to advanced techniques that experienced government real estate professionals use. Basic searches are usually limited to large government agencies, such as those of the federal government and those state agencies that have a large volume of new lease requirements and the resources to advertise and regularly update their listing databases (smaller government agencies with less new real estate lease volume may require more advanced techniques to find new leases). This chapter will review how to find new government real estate leases through (1) new lease requirement postings, (2) government lease inventory reports, (3) government agency reports, and (4) additional search options.

NEW LEASE REQUIREMENT POSTINGS

The best place to start when searching for new government real estate leases is with the basic search functions of a large government agency's new lease requirements website. Large government agencies like the federal government and larger states have dedicated websites to make searching for new lease requirements relatively easy, while smaller states and local governments may lack the new lease transaction volume and resources to support a website with updated postings of their new lease requirements as they become available. This section will focus on government agencies that maintain an active database of new lease requirement postings, with other sections of this chapter reviewing methods to search for new lease requirements with smaller agencies that do not maintain a new lease requirements website database.

When starting the new government lease requirement search for any given area, it is best to start with the new lease requirements for the federal government and narrow the search to state and local government agencies. It's important to remember when reviewing the sample search items in this chapter that although a government tenant agency may request information in its requirements posting, it is often limited in nature, with the government lease contact (GLC) often asking for additional information to be submitted after the property has been submitted for review and a market survey has been completed.

Federal New Lease Requirement Postings

The federal government is typically required to advertise a majority of its real estate lease transaction activities whether it is for a lease renewal, extension, or a traditional new lease in the market. These new lease announcements are typically found online through the federal government's FBO.gov website. While a majority of new lease requirements are found on the FBO.gov website, there is a current trend for some new lease requirements for the US GSA to be placed into the Advanced Automated Acquisition Program (AAAP) system, which is discussed later in this chapter.

Federal Business Opportunities (FBO.gov)

FBO.gov is the federal government's main website where buyers (the federal government) and sellers (the private sector) can access the federal government's new business opportunities announcements and notifications for awarded business opportunities. A majority of federal agencies use the FBO.gov website for their real estate transactions, including the US GSA, USDA, Department of Veterans Affairs, and the Bureau of Land Management.

Most of the federal government's real estate lease requirements are currently posted on the FBO.gov website. The largest poster of new real estate lease requirements on FBO.gov is the US GSA. The US GSA posts new government real estate leases, lease renewals, and most new lease actions for the public to submit lease proposals on. As discussed in Chapter 1, the US GSA is the federal agency that procures a large amount of leased space for its federal customer agencies, such as, for example, the US Social Security Administration (SSA).

Getting Started on FBO.gov

If you are new to the FBO.gov website, it is best to review the website's "Getting Started" section for an overview of how the website works. To gain access to most of the website's functions it is best to register as a vendor, which allows one to search for new lease opportunities and to receive email notifications when a new lease requirement is posted that meets your online search criteria.

Using the FBO.gov Website

The following is the basic approach to using the FBO.gov website to find new lease requirements.

Step 1: Login

Log in to the FBO.gov website with your username and password.

Step 2: Advanced Search

You will see that there are many options and tabs to choose from on the website. Go to the "Advanced Search" tab, which will allow selection of a geographic area for the new lease requirements, along with a multitude of other options that may not necessarily be applicable to your search criteria.

Once you've selected your geographical area to search, the advanced search function should be blank as to what you need to select. Go to the "Classification Code" selection box and scroll down to "X-Lease or rental of facilities" and select and click on the "Search" button.

Step 3: Reading the Results

The advanced search results will give you an array of search results that are ordered on the website by the Opportunity, Agency/Office/Location, Type/Set-aside, and (date) Posted On columns. Let's look at the following example to assist in reading the search results.

Figure 2.0: Sample FBO Search Results Example

Opportunity	Agency/ Office/ Location	Type/Set-aside	Posted On
US Government Seeks to Lease 19,199 ABOA SF of Office Space in Chicago, IL X -- Lease or rental of facilities	Chicago	Presolicitation (Modified)	February 10, 2018

Clicking on the Opportunity Links in the advertisement gives us the following requirement example with Sections added for further analysis at the end of the advertisement sample.

Figure 2.1: Sample Federal Lease Requirement Advertisement

FBO Advertisement Sample

(SECTION A)

Synopsis:

State: Illinois

City: Chicago

Delineated Area:

North: Ogden Street

East: Michigan Ave

South: Cermak Avenue

West: Austin Street

Minimum Sq. Ft. (ABOA): 19,199 ABOA SF
Maximum Sq. Ft. (ABOA): 19,659 ABOA SF
Space Type: Office

Parking Spaces (Total): Per City Code

Parking Spaces (Surface): Per City Code
Parking Spaces (Structured): None Parking
Spaces (Reserved): Two

Full Term: 15 Years

Firm Term: 10 Years

(SECTION B)

Additional Requirements:

Proximity to Public Transportation

Contiguous Space

Offered space must meet Government requirements for fire safety, accessibility, seismic and sustainability standards per the terms of the lease. A fully serviced lease is required. Offered space shall not be in the 100-year flood plain.

Interested Respondents should include Building Owners, or if a Broker, please include the Exclusivity Agreement, Representation Letter, or Listing Contract granting the exclusive right to represent the building by the Building Owner, in your expression of interest.

Expressions of interest must include:

- Building name and address and location of the available space within the building.
- Rentable square feet available, and expected rental rate per rentable square foot, fully serviced.
- ANSI/BOMA office area (ABOA) square feet to be offered and expected rental rate per ABOA square foot, fully serviced. Indicate whether the quoted rental rate includes an amount for tenant improvements and state the amount, if any.
- Date of space availability.
- Building ownership information.
- Amount of parking available on-site and its cost. Include whether expected rental rate includes the cost of the required Government parking, if any.
- Energy efficiency and renewable energy features existing within the building.
- List of building services provided.

The above sample US GSA requirement is an excellent lease requirement for a property owner in the Chicago real estate market. Let's review the requirement in closer detail on what the property owner should be looking for in Sections A and B.

Review of Figure 2.1 Advertisement

Section A

Delineated Area:

This is the geographic area the government tenant is seeking to lease space in. The boundaries that make up the delineated area are often not flexible. If you have a property outside this area, you should call the GLC to inquire if you can offer your property for lease. The GLC may be able to tell you about other lease requirements that your building may qualify to offer on or place your property on a list of properties that are available for future leases.

Square Footage:

Federal government agencies often quote their lease square footage requirements as a usable or rentable square foot number. The sample requirement quotes the requirement in ABOA square footage, which means the area "where a tenant normally houses personnel, and/or furniture, for which a measurement is to be computed" as stated by the American National Standard Institute/Building Owners and Managers Association (ANSI/BOMA).[1]

The usable square footage number in the sample advertisement is quoted with a range that specifies a minimum required usable square footage amount. It is rare for a government agency to pay for more usable square footage than what is listed in the advertised requirements. It is important to determine what square footage measurement method the GLC is using for the lease requirement to ensure that the space available will meet the advertised lease requirements.

Space Type:

This is an important criteria to consider when pursuing government leases. In the sample requirement the space type is listed as office. If your building is considered retail or light industrial, it would be prudent to call the GLC before submitting your property. Government agencies that have high customer traffic counts, like the US SSA, may do well in a retail setting because retail properties are often situated near public transportation, and these property types usually have higher parking counts than their office or industrial counterparts. Alternatively, government agencies with a law enforcement function or those seeking a lower tenant visibility profile will sometimes seek light industrial properties to keep out of areas that have high pedestrian foot traffic, heavy vehicle traffic, and residential neighborhoods.

Parking:

Parking is an important requirement for government agencies with a high volume of visitors to the leased location or for government agencies that require secured, fenced parking to securely move guests and goods and services into a leased space. Parking per "code" is not always the best measurement for what the government agency requires, as code-required parking can differ from property type to different parts of the delineated area.

If your property has a low parking count or a tight parking configuration, it is recommended that you call the GLC to discuss the parking requirements. Discussing irregular property characteristics with the GLC up front will avoid spending time on a lease that may not work for the government tenant agency.

Lease Term:

The lease term for most federal government lease contracts are going to be quoted in full and firm terms, with the firm term being less than or equal to the full term. Most government agencies will include in their lease requirements a cancellation option after the firm term has expired. Some government agencies are restricted as to how long the lease terms can be. For instance, some agencies are only able to commit to a 1-year firm term with multiple option periods, while others are able to sign leases with 20-year firm terms or more. If you find a lease requirement with a low firm term number, you may want to ask the GLC if the agency will consider a longer firm term to make the lease rental income viable for your property to propose on.

Section B

Additional Requirements:

This area is important, as these requirements will typically be incorporated into the lease and often need to be discussed with the GLC to confirm whether the offered property can meet these additional requirements. Some items that are important to review here are:

- Is there a bus stop requirement?
- Is first floor space or contiguous space on one floor required?
- Seismic certification?
- Are LEED and/or Energy Star required?

Remember to ask the GLC if there are exemptions or waivers available if your property is unable to meet any of the advertised lease requirements. Make sure that if there are any requirements your property cannot satisfy that you have these requirement deficiencies waived or exempted in writing from the GLC and made part of the lease documents as applicable. Simple items such as not confirming that the leased property can meet the bus stop requirement might void the government real estate lease if the requirement is found not to have been met after the lease is signed.

Expression of Interest Due:

If you have read the requirements thoroughly and need more time to submit the property, you should call the GLC to request more time to submit the property. This is an opportune time to discuss with the GLC how well the market is responding to the new lease requirement and if the GLC has any questions or comments about the property you are submitting. It is common for some GLCs to extend the property submittal date to property owners who have legitimate reasons for being delayed in submitting property information as part of their formal expression of interest.

Items to include with property submittal:

The items requested to be submitted in the sample advertisement are rather extensive and require the property owner to do some work to complete the property submittal items. It is best to call the GLC to confirm if they really need all the items requested as part of the property submittal. Request that the GLC send you an email stating what items can be sent after the government has accepted your property for a property submittal as part of the request for lease proposal (RLP) process.

Other FBO.gov items to consider:

The new lease requirements posted on the FBO.gov website will sometimes mention that the government agency is currently located in an existing leased location and that the GLC will be using the advertisement to determine what properties are available in the marketplace before proceeding with an RLP. The advertisement may mention that the GLC will add the costs to move the government tenant to a new location as part of the RLP financial analysis, which should alert you that you might need to be very competitive on your RLP lease rental rates if you want to move the government tenant from its current leased location.

The FBO.gov site has a function to track the changes to the lease requirement advertisement that will often allow you to track lease requirement changes as they are made. Reviewing the track changes function can tell you how long the lease requirement has been in the market, with some track changes showing lease requirements in a given market for several years before being canceled or awarded.

The FBO.gov lease requirement advertisements have a "watch this opportunity" button that will allow you to receive an email if there are any changes to the requirement. It is best to follow up with the GLC to inquire on the status of the advertised lease requirement you are interested in.

STATE NEW LEASE REQUIREMENT POSTINGS

The new lease requirement postings for states are not consistent in their approach and process from state to state. The states with the largest state leasing activity are currently California, Texas and Florida. This section reviews how California and Texas, each with large lease inventories, approach their new lease requirements.

State of California New Lease Requirement Postings

The State of California posts new real estate lease requirements through a private vendor portal that is best accessed through the California Department of General Services website.

The State of California real estate lease requirements search platform follows the federal FBO.gov website format, with some differences. The following is a sample lease requirement advertisement for the State of California with an overview of each section.

Figure 2.2: Sample State of California Lease Requirement Advertisement

Wanted to Lease

By the State of California - San Luis Obispo

(SECTION A)

The State Water Resources Control Board is looking for approx. 27,000 nusf of office space in the City of San Luis Obispo, 85 plus parking spaces. Buildings submitted must: 1) Be Asbestos Hazard-free upon occupancy, 2) Accommodate State plans, specs., seismic safety, Americans with Disabilities Act (ADA) and applicable codes (California Building Code & Title 24), 3) Be close to public trans., and 4) Comply with Disab. Vet. Bus. Enterprise requirements. The State of California will, where cost effective, give preference to those buildings, which demonstrate LEED or Energy Star compliance. Please refer to http://energystar.gov for further details.

(SECTION B)

Person authorized to represent such properties must respond to contact person by response date with address, map & project by email or in writing.

Project # - 5555

City - San Luis Obispo

County - San Luis Obispo

Agency - State Water Resources Control Board

Type of Space - Office

Parking Spaces - 85

Boundaries:

North – Palm Street

East – Santa Rosa Street

South – Pismo Street

West – Carmel Street

The above sample lease advertisement requirement is an excellent lease requirement for a property owner with vacancy in the San Luis Obispo real estate market. Let's review the advertised requirement in closer detail to determine what the property owner should be looking for in sections A and B.

Review of Figure 2.2 Advertisement

Section A

Space Type and Square Footage:

The State of California's new lease requirement advertisement example starts out the advertisement for leased space with the square footage requirement requested as an approximation versus a range as seen in the FBO.gov new lease requirement example in Figure 2.1.

The square footage requested in sample 2.2 is quoted in net usable square footage, which means the area "where a tenant normally houses personnel, and/or furniture, for which a measurement is to be computed" as stated by the ANSI/BOMA.[2] For most state leases it is best to contact the GLC to confirm what their expectations are for how to measure the space. You don't want to submit a property for a requirement where the property owner and the government tenant aren't in agreement on how much space will be leased due to differences regarding how to measure the space.

Building Submittal Requirements:

For the submittal requirements we see that the State of California is focused on the following requirements in section A of the sample advertisement for their leased space:

1. Asbestos Hazard-free space upon occupancy, which according to the California GSA states:

   Buildings constructed before 1979 must be certified in writing to be free from hazards from Asbestos Containing Material (ACM). The certification must be provided by an industrial hygienist certified by the American Board of Industrial Hygiene (ABIH) or an Environmental Protection Agency (EPA) Asbestos Hazard Emergency Response Act (AHERA) Certified Inspector.

   If the building was constructed subsequent to 1979, a photocopy of the Occupancy Certificate issued by the city or county building department is all that is required prior to the execution of the lease.[3]

2. Accommodate State plans, specs., seismic safety, Americans with Disabilities Act (ADA) and applic. codes (California Building Code &

Title 24) – the California GSA states that for seismic safety:

> All facilities the State occupies must be evaluated for the ability to meet a seismic performance objective of substantial life safety. The State's Space Planner will complete an initial screening of the property. If required, the State may request a structural evaluation performed by an independent licensed structural engineer and the certification must be completed and signed.

3. Be close to public transportation. This item should be followed up with the GLC to confirm the type of public transportation and within what distance from the property it is required.
4. Comply with Disabled Veteran Business Enterprise (DVBE) requirements. That is, as the State of California GSA website states, "A Lessor who is utilizing a certified DVBE firm to fulfill the full DVBE participation goal must commit to performing at least 3% of the lease contract amount with Lessor's firm or in combination with other DVBE firms."[4]
5. The requirements posting states that "The State of California will, where cost effective, give preference to those buildings which demonstrate LEED or Energy Star compliance." This preference, although not a requirement for this advertisement, should be carefully considered, as both items can be difficult for a property owner to obtain after the lease is signed if the costs and the design have not been closely considered. Property owners should fully understand the costs and the process involved in obtaining the LEED certifications and energy compliance certifications before signing a lease. The property owner should consult with both an architect and a general contractor to arrive at an estimate for the costs for this item.

Section B

Project Contact:

A property owner should always, if possible, contact the GLC to discuss the property considered for lease to the government agency. Contacting the GLC will allow the property owner and the GLC to prescreen both the property and the prospective government tenant for the property.

Project Description:

The project description posted here for the advertisement is straightforward. Most state lease requirements are not flexible in the delineated area boundary requirements, but there is generally more flexibility with state government lease requirements than their federal government counterparts. If your property does not meet the exact requirements as posted in the advertisement, you should contact the GLC to discuss whether there's any flexibility in the requirements so that your building can be considered. Also, there may be other government leasing requirements in the market that your property is qualified to offer on.

Looking further into the State of California's new lease requirements advertisement website you will find that the state details the steps necessary for property owners interested in leasing space to the state on its "Guide to Leasing Space to the State"[5] web page.

Figure 2.3: State of California's "Guide to Leasing Space to the State"

"Guide to Leasing Space to the State"

As Administered by the Department of General Services (DGS)

Step 1: View the State's Lease Advertisements

The best way to find out if the State is in need of leasing space in your area is to view all current advertisements on the Bid Sync website. You can view all of the state's current advertisements listed for space needs in Bid Sync by clicking the following link in this paragraph. When that site opens, type the word "lease" (without the quotes) in the search box and click the search button.

Step 2: Determine If Your Property Fits the State's Guidelines

Determine if your property meets the state's needs by answering the following questions:

- Is it located in the site boundaries?
- Is there adequate space available in your building? (Note that the state leases on a net usable square foot basis instead of rentable square feet.)
- Is the building LEED certified or Energy Star Compliant?

The State of California will, where cost effective, give preference to those buildings that demonstrate LEED or Energy Star compliance. See http://www.energystar.gov for further details.

- Does the space meet all state lease requirements?

Step 3: Review the State's Leasing Process

Listed below are some important lease issues:

- DGS leases space on a net usable square foot (not rentable square foot) basis.
- DGS desires full-service rates, which include utilities, janitorial, and maintenance services.
- DGS requires that the lessor include in the lease rate a Tenant Improvement ("TI") allowance.
- The state pays monthly rent in arrears.
- DGS does not enter into binding letters of intent.
- DGS requires that the standard state lease form be used.
- The state has lease requirements pertaining to ADA, structural evaluation, Disabled Veteran Business Enterprise (DVBE), and California Environmental Quality Act (CEQA) requirements. Depending on the age of the building, asbestos and lead criteria might also be a factor.

Step 4: Respond to the Advertisement

Now that you have determined that your property fits the state's needs, respond to the contact information on the advertisement before the specified deadline date. DGS will analyze all responses submitted before the deadline date and contact all prospective listings.

Step 5: Viewing the Property

DGS will review all prospective listings and narrow the listings in anticipation of site visits.

Step 6: DGS Will Request Lease Proposals

DGS will review all toured properties and request formal lease proposals from the selected sites.

State of Texas New Lease Requirements Postings

The State of Texas new lease requirement advertisements can be found on the State of Texas website in the Texas Facilities Commission section.

The following is a sample State of Texas advertisement for a new lease requirement:

Figure 2.4: Sample State of Texas Lease Requirement Advertisement

Sample Lease Advertisement

Lease of 7,886 sq. ft. of office space in Richmond or Rosenberg for office for the Health and Human Services Commission (HHSC)

(SECTION A)

Agency Requisition Number: 123

The Texas Facilities Commission (TFC) has identified a need for lease office space to meet the requirements of the Health and Human Services Commission (HHSC). Pursuant to Texas Government Code, Section 2167.054, TFC is soliciting offers for 20,000 sq. ft. of usable office space in the City of Richmond or Rosenberg, Fort Bend County, Texas, under the guidelines provided in Texas Government Code, Chapter 2167. All proposals must meet the requirements outlined in this request for proposals (RFP) to be considered for evaluation by TFC.

Agency: Texas Facilities Commission

Agency Requisition Number: 111-222

Previous Price Paid: N/A

Solicitation type: 21 Days or more for solicitation notice

(SECTION B)

Note: You will need to download all of the following files for specifications and other required document, including a HUB subcontracting plan (if required).

Help: Right Click to and choose "save file as" or "save target as."

The above State of Texas advertisement for lease space is different from what we've seen for the FBO.gov and the State of California. One of the main differences in the State of Texas lease advertisement example is that it includes the lease documents as part of the advertisement. The following is a review of the sample lease advertisement sections.

Review of Figure 2.4 Advertisement

Section A

Open Date:

The first item posted here is the lease proposal open date. This date is typically the date a government agency will open the lease proposals they have received from property owners. The lease proposal open date may be an open or closed event to the public. For opening events open to the public the government agency may allow interested parties to see which properties submitted lease proposals along with the submitted lease proposal information.

Project Description:

The project description listed here states who the government tenant agency will be along with the size of the space with the associated space measurement method. The description also mentions when the space is to be delivered for occupancy along with the contact information.

Section B

Section B is where the advertisement posts the required packages that property owners are to complete to be considered for the state lease. In this advertisement we see that there are two links that the GLC has for property owners to download and complete as part of the property submittal process.

The first link, "Package 1" posted in the sample advertisement, is for the State of Texas RLP document that is provided for property owners to complete as part of their lease proposals. This sample RLP document has five sections along with an exhibit that the property owner must complete and submit per the submittal schedule in the RLP documents.

The second link, "Package 2," is for an addendum document that amends the items in the RLP and is made part of the RLP. The specific document included here in the sample makes some changes to the initial RLP document.

It is a best practice to contact the GLC to discuss any addendum items to confirm these items are correctly incorporated into the property owner's lease proposal.

LOCAL GOVERNMENT NEW LEASE REQUIREMENT POSTINGS

While most local city and county governments own the real estate they occupy, there is also a continuing need for leased space with private-sector property owners to supplement their real estate needs. Per the US Census Bureau, in 2012, 89,004 local governments existed in the United States; local governments include 3,031 counties, 19,522 municipalities, 16,364 townships, 37,203 special districts, and 12,884 independent school districts.[6] Each of these local governments, with some exceptions, will have leasing activity with the private sector, whether it be for a small amount of warehouse storage space or large-scale leases for commercial and industrial properties.

Undertaking the search for new local government lease requirements can be a challenge for some property owners, as there is rarely an easily identifiable source for new lease requirement postings for local governments. Compounding this challenge is that most local governments typically do not have formal notification requirements for these new leases that would reach a large audience beyond county and city business connections.

The easiest way to start the search for local government leases is to contact the government agency or department you seek to lease space to and inquire as to who the point of contact is for new lease requirements. There are some local government agencies that do maintain an online database, with Los Angeles County being one that is easy to navigate. The following is a review of a sample Los Angeles County new lease requirement posting.

Los Angeles County New Lease Requirement Postings

Los Angeles (LA) County's new lease requirement postings can be found at the LA County Real Estate Division website.

The LA County Real Estate Division website typically has several "space needs" posted on its website with the title of the space need given, which when clicked brings you to a PDF of the new lease requirement. Here's a sample of an LA County new lease requirement advertisement.

Figure 2.5: Sample LA County Lease Requirement Advertisement

County of Los Angeles Request for Office Space Replacement

The County of Los Angeles, Chief Executive Office, Real Estate Division is issuing this Request For Office Space Replacement for the County of Los Angeles Departments of Community and Senior Services and Parks and Recreation, Headquarters Administrative Programs.

Purchase or Lease:

Community and Senior Services have a requirement of approximately 60,000 sf. contiguous and Parks and Recreation requires 67,000 sf. contiguous.

The space use could be combined for a total need of 130,000 sf. The departments have a parking requirement of 4 parking spaces per 1,000 (square footage) and area boundaries within a 20 mile radius of 2000 N Fuller Avenue, Los Angeles, California 90046.

Potential Selection Criteria:

Proximity to Public Transportation, availability of affordable housing for County employees, use of historic buildings, economic development potential, and compatibility with local land use plans. County will need property detail information to assess estimated construction and ongoing operational costs. Properties submitted will only be accepted if submitted by the owner, principal and/or the listing broker.

The County reviews all sites listed on CoStar. For any questions regarding this notice please contact as listed in the advertised requirement.

The LA County advertisement for new leased space contains several differences from the previous advertisements reviewed in this section that point to the LA County GLC perhaps looking for expressions of interests to include the requested information in the sample advertisement with additional property submittal data requested by the GLC after the initial property data have been submitted by the property owner. It would be best to call the GLC to review this type of advertisement, as there may be additional items that are not included in the advertisement that would assist the property owner in proposing space to the GLC as part of the new lease proposal.

GOVERNMENT LEASE INVENTORY REPORTS

Government agencies with large real estate lease inventories typically have some type of lease inventory report that is generated on an annual, quarterly, or monthly basis. Government lease inventory reports are a great place to identify government real estate leases that may be expiring in your geographical area of interest.

Some of the largest users of private-sector leased space in the federal government are the US GSA and the USPS, both of which post their lease inventories online. The US GSA posts its lease inventory monthly as an expiring lease report, while the USPS updates its national inventory on a less frequent basis. Most states publish their lease inventory in some fashion, with larger states like California and Texas publishing their lease inventory in a manner that allows research on the properties in the portfolio similar to the manner in which the US GSA and the USPS post lease inventories publicly and online.

Federal Lease Inventory Reports

The US GSA currently posts its expiring lease report on a monthly basis at its website under the "Lease Inventory" section. The US GSA posts its inventory of leased properties in an Excel format that is easy to analyze with almost every data point needed for a thorough understanding of the leases expiring in a specific market. Most often the lease inventory report will correlate with the active US GSA real estate lease projects in the market.

If there is a US GSA real estate project listed on the FBO.gov website, you should check the Expiring Lease Report to confirm if there is a similar lease in the report. If there is any confusion regarding whether the new US GSA lease requirement is a new lease being competed against an existing lease location, it is best to contact the GLC to inquire if the new US GSA lease requirement is a new lease for the market or if there is already an existing leased location in the market.

In some cases, the US GSA Expiring Lease Report will not show a property listed that is an existing leased location by the federal government because the federal agency did not use the US GSA for the original lease, or it may be left out of the inventory for national security reasons. There are instances in which the expiring lease is not going to be active after the lease expires due to colocations, consolidations, or a change in agency requirements that takes that agency out of the market. There are times when the expiring lease will trigger a purchase option in the lease that a government agency will exercise to purchase the leased building from the lessor.

When reviewing a government lease inventory report it is best to see what leases are coming up within the next two years in your area of interest, as this is the typical lead time for most government leases to start their leasing process with a new lease requirement. Advertisements for a new lease action will generally be posted 18 months to 2 years before a new lease is signed with a property owner. Also, when reviewing the lease inventory, examine the rents in the inventory for the lease you are interested in to determine if your property can be competitive with the current lease rental rates. If you find an expiring lease that you think would be a good fit for your property, you should contact the GLC and discuss when the expiring lease will be competed in the market as well as introducing your property to the GLC for consideration on other leases that may be expiring.

The USPS posts its expiring lease report on its website. The USPS lease inventory is separated by state and provides a lot of information to determine what the best approach is for a specific lease at any given location.

State Lease Inventory Reports

Several states post expiring lease reports online, with the State of Florida being a good example to review.

The State of Florida has several ways to view the state lease expirations.

One way is to view the entire owned and leased inventory through the SOLARIS Facility Inventory Tracking System (FITS), which shows both the owned and leased inventory along with the lease start and end dates, along with the addresses and rents paid for the leased space.[7]

The State of Texas posts its expiring lease report online with all the data points one could need for the various leases, including information about whom to contact at the state for further information on the expiring lease.[8]

GOVERNMENT AGENCY REPORTS

Most government agencies at the federal and state levels will publish annual reports that seek approvals for their budget needs and requirements for their real estate lease inventory. Some agencies report more frequently than others or publish special reports detailing specific requirements or budget requests depending on new laws or political decisions that require agencies to expand, consolidate, or spend money on improvements to existing leased space. Government agency reports are often an excellent source of information on what specific federal and state agencies are planning each year. The federal government is less consolidated in its reporting, as some federal agencies publish their own reports whereas states will often have one or two main reporting bodies that cover a majority of the leases for that state.

Federal Government Agency Reports

The federal government represents the largest single user of leased real estate in the US. Looking at the federal agencies individually, we see that the USPS and the US GSA post upcoming leased inventory requirements on an annual basis, with special reports published occasionally. The US GSA publishes a report annually listing prospectus level leases, which are leases that (for FY 2014) are greater than $2,850,000 per year in costs.

Other agency reports that are useful to research for new lease requirements are DoD and BLM reports, which have a greater impact on specific regions of the country that have a large military and BLM presence. The Department of Veterans Affairs has published many reports detailing their ongoing need for medical space in different parts of the country.

Prospectus Leases

The US GSA has several postings for their leases that include leases that are very large, typically called "Prospectus Leases," which are, as of FY 2014, greater than $2,850,000 per year in costs.[9] These lease projects are usually listed by the US GSA on its website for each year they are being considered.

The following table shows two sample leases of the approximately 13 US GSA prospectus leases for FY 2015.[10]

Exhibit 2.10: Sample of US GSA Prospectus Leases for FY 2015

Name	City	State
Federal Aviation Administration	Hawthorne	CA
Department of Education	Washington	DC

Reviewing prospective-level lease projects can be educational to see how the largest leases are budgeted for, advertised, negotiated, and ultimately awarded to a property owner. The following is a sample prospectus lease request for review purposes.

Exhibit 2.11: Sample US GSA Prospectus Lease

Prospectus - Lease

Executive Summary

The US General Services Administration (GSA) proposes a replacement lease of up to 229,000 rentable square feet (RSF) for leased space currently located in the Southeast. The replacement lease will provide continued housing for the tenant and will improve the tenant's office and overall utilization rates from 153 to 102 usable square feet (USF) per person and 226 to 188 USF per person, respectively. As a result of the improved utilization, the replacement lease will reduce the rentable square footage of the requirement by 12 percent, a 30,432 RSF reduction from the tenant's current occupancy.

Description

Occupant: Federal tenant

Lease Type: Replacement

Current Rentable Square Feet (RSF): 259,432 (Current RSF/USF = 1.08)

Proposed Maximum RSF: 229,000 (Proposed RSF/USF = 1.15)

Expansion/Reduction RSF: 30,432 RSF Reduction

Current Usable Square Feet/Person: 226

Proposed Usable Square Feet/Person: 188

Proposed Maximum Lease Term: 20

Expiration Dates of Current Leases: 2/8/2017

Number of Official Parking Spaces: 40

Scoring: Operating Lease

Maximum Proposed Rental Rate: $28.00 per RSF

Proposed Total Annual Cost: $6,412,100

Current Total Annual Cost: $4,819,272 (lease effective 3/09/1997)

This estimate is for fiscal year 2015 and may be escalated by 2.0 percent annually to the effective date of the lease to account for inflation. The proposed rental rate is fully serviced including all operating expenses whether paid by the lessor or directly by the Government. GSA will conduct the procurement using prevailing market rental rates as a benchmark for the evaluation of competitive offers and as a basis for negotiating with offerors to ensure that lease award is made in the best interest of the Government.

Lease award shall not exceed the maximum rental rate as specified in this prospectus.

New leases may contain an escalation clause to provide for annual changes in real estate taxes and operating costs.

The current lease includes 13,215 rentable square feet of space that was vacated by the tenant in 2010. The current total annual cost includes the rent associated with the vacancy. The entire lease is 272,647 rentable square feet.

Acquisition Strategy

In order to maximize the flexibility in acquiring space to house the tenant, GSA may issue a single, multiple award solicitation that will allow offerors to provide blocks of space able to meet the requirements in whole or in part. All offers must provide space consistent with the delineated area defined by this prospectus.

Justification

The tenant has developed a program of requirements for replacement space to house its Region Headquarters. The proposed requirements utilize new space standards developed to improve space efficiency and employee productivity and will reduce the tenant's footprint by 30,432 RSF. In the absence of this reduction, the status quo cost of continued occupancy at the proposed market rental rate would be $7,264,096 per year.

Summary of Energy Compliance

GSA will incorporate energy efficiency requirements into the Request for Lease Proposals and other documents related to the procurement of space based on the approved prospectus. GSA encourages offerors to exceed minimum requirements set forth in the procurement and to achieve an Energy Star performance rating of 75 or higher.

Resolutions of Approval

Resolutions adopted by the House Committee on Transportation and Infrastructure and the Senate Committee on Environment and Public Works approving this prospectus will constitute approval to make appropriations to lease space in a facility that will yield the required rentable area.

Interim Leasing

GSA will execute such interim leasing actions as are necessary to ensure continued housing of the tenant agency prior to the effective date of the new lease. It is in the best interest of the Government to avert the financial risk of holdover tenancy.

Certification of Need

The proposed project is the best solution to meet a validated Government need.

While the above prospectus lease sample may be outside the scope of what most property owners will have available to lease to a government agency, it is still a worthwhile exercise to read, as these reports provide clues as to which government agencies are moving, expanding, and consolidating. These large leases impact the space needs of these agencies on both local and national levels.

Federal Agency Records Search

There are several places to look for federal records dealing with current and upcoming real estate leases with the federal government. A simple key word search in Google will often yield more data on leases than can be absorbed in one sitting. It helps to know what agency best fits your property and/or government leasing requirements. It can be beneficial to perform a federal records search for federal agencies that are active in its real estate leasing efforts. A good example of a government agency currently procuring a large numbers of leases in 2016 is the Department of Veterans Affairs (VA). In a Congressional Report titled "Department of Veterans Affairs Major Medical Lease Authorization Act of 2013" the VA had requested funds and approvals for 27 leases across the country.[11] The report details the geographical area of consideration, the square footage, and type of space needed for each location. The following is a partial list of sections of this bill for review.

Exhibit 2.12: US Department of Veterans Affairs Report

House Report 113-284 - Department of Veterans Affairs Major Medical Facility Lease Authorization Act of 2013

Section-by-section analysis of the legislation

Section 1. Short title

Section 1 of the bill would provide the short title of the legislation as the Department of Veterans Affairs Major Medical Facility Lease Authorization Act of 2013.

Section 2. Authorization of Major Medical Facility Leases

Section 2(5) of the bill would authorize a lease for the Leeward Outpatient Healthcare Access Center in Honolulu, HI, for an amount not to exceed $15,887,370.

Section 2(9) of the bill would authorize a lease for an outpatient clinic consolidation in New Port Richey, FL, for an amount not to exceed $11,927,000.

Section 2(10) of the bill would authorize a lease for an outpatient clinic in Ponce, Puerto Rico, for an amount not to exceed $11,535,000.

Section 2(11) of the bill would authorize a lease for a lease consolidation in San Antonio, TX, for an amount not to exceed $19,426,000.

Section 2(12) of the bill would authorize a lease for a community-based outpatient clinic in San Diego, CA, for an amount not to exceed $11,946,100.

Section 2(20) of the bill would authorize a new research lease in Hines, IL, for an amount not to exceed $22,032,000.

Section 2(25) of the bill would authorize a community-based outpatient clinic in Phoenix, AZ, for an amount not to exceed $20,757,000.

Section 2(26) of the bill would authorize a lease for the expansion of a community-based outpatient clinic in Redding, CA, for an amount not to exceed $8,154,000.

Section 2(27) of the bill would authorize a lease for the expansion of a community-based outpatient clinic in Tulsa, OK, for an amount not to exceed $13,269,200.

The above bill is a good example of what a federal records search can yield for potential leases. It is important to follow the progress of these bills through to the final approval phases by the associated government agency. It is recommended that you follow-up with the GLC to inquire if and when these requirements would be posted as official lease requirements for a property owner to propose on.

ADDITIONAL SEARCH OPTIONS

Recent years have seen an increase in the options for searching for new government real estate leases. Several government agencies have embraced the use of technology to provide timely real estate lease requirement information to the private sector along with allowing property owners to submit properties to the government for future considerations, as is the case of the US GSA's Advanced Automated Acquisition Program (AAAP).

There are several private-sector firms that will do automated searches for their client property owners that provide specific results on a daily or weekly basis. It is a good practice for property owners who are interested in leasing space to government tenants to utilize the technology available to provide ongoing notifications for lease requirements as they become available in a given real estate market.

US Federal Government Automated Systems

The US federal government has been the leader in the automated acquisition programs for real estate leasing to government tenants. The US GSA's AAAP's system is becoming more and more widespread nationally. As the technology becomes mainstream, it is only a matter of time before state and local governments use these systems for their own real estate leasing activities.

Advanced Automated Acquisition Program (AAAP)

The AAAP system was expanded to all the US GSA regions nationally in 2015. For more information regarding the AAAP system we can look to the US GSA's AAAP website FAQ section:

> The AAAP is a multiple award platform that handles space requirements ranging from 500 square feet up to $2.85M net annual rent. The platform uses a pre-competed inventory of properties to meet the space requirements for various government agencies. It was created for the purpose of consolidating and streamlining the leasing process for a large volume of small leases, as well as for procuring space faster. The program offers the general public and businesses the opportunity to electronically offer building space for lease to the Federal Government. Using the AAAP procurement approach, the offer submission process is completely web-enabled, allowing all registered participants to submit and update offers to lease space to the Federal Government every month, in response to a Request for Lease Proposal (RLP).[12]

Real Estate Leases–Bid Vendors

There are several private-sector firms that, for a fee, will provide property owner members with notifications of government real estate leases that come on the market. Most of these private-sector firms do not cover the whole market but will typically capture leases that may go unnoticed by most property owners for government agencies that do not have a heavy presence in the local real estate market.

Contacting the Government Real Estate Leasing Representatives

It is recommended that you contact the GLC for the government tenant agencies in your real estate market. The majority of first- or second-tier real estate markets will have most levels of government as tenants in leased space in properties in that market. When contacting a government agency to inquire about its real estate leasing needs, it is best to directly contact the leasing office for that specific government agency. Most government agencies do not encourage property owners and real estate brokers to contact the local government tenant occupying the current leased space in question; most government agencies do, however, encourage people to contact the leasing contact representative for that government agency.

The Government Tenant Contacts You

Occasionally the GLC will contact the property owner regarding a lease that the building may be suitable for. Direct contact from an interested prospective tenant is the preferred method for completing most any real estate lease transaction. When the GLC contacts the property owner, it is best to be prepared with a host of questions to prequalify the government tenant before proceeding with submitting information for a market survey with the government tenant. The following is a list of prospective questions a property owner can ask the GLC when contacted by the GLC to discuss a particular property for lease.

1. Is this a new lease for the tenant agency, or is this tenant agency currently housed in a location that will also be considered for the new lease requirement?
2. Is the tenant agency looking to pay a market rental rate, or is there a restriction on the rents that can be paid?
3. Is this lease subject to an annual appropriations bill or budget approvals that would limit the amount of actual firm term on the lease?
4. What is the lease process? Is there a lease format that is specific to the government agency similar the US GSA's RLP process, or will the government agency use the property owner's lease form?

CHAPTER SUMMARY

This chapter reviewed the following items related to new government real estate leases:

- New lease requirement postings.
- Government lease inventory reports.
- Government agency reports.
- Additional search options.

NOTES

[1] http://www.acquisition.gov/gsam/current/html/part570.html, 570.102 Definitions.

[2] http://www.acquisition.gov/gsam/current/html/part570.html, 570.102 Definitions.

[3] http://www.dgs.ca.gov/resd/Programs/LeasingandPlanning/NewLease/LeaseRequirements.aspx.

[4] http://www.documents.dgs.ca.gov/resd/RELPS/leaserequirements/DVBEGuidelines.pdf.

[5] http://www.dgs.ca.gov/resd/Programs/LeasingandPlanning/NewLease.aspx.

[6] https://www.census.gov/newsroom/releases/archives/governments/cb12-161.html.

[7] http://www.dep.state.fl.us/lands/fl_solaris_public_files.htm.

[8] http://www.tfc.state.tx.us/divisions/facilities/prog/leasing/.

[9] http://www.gsa.gov/portal/content/101522.

[10] http://www.gsa.gov/portal/category/100435.

[11] House Report 113-284.

[12] https://aaap.secure.force.com/AAAP/PBS_AAAP_About_AAAP.

State of Texas Capitol Building Interior

CHAPTER THREE:

GOVERNMENT REAL ESTATE LEASES

IN THIS CHAPTER

1. **US Federal Government Leases**
2. **State Government Leases**
3. **Local Government Leases**

Government real estate leases are unique to the agencies that use them. Federal government leases typically follow the US General Services Administration (GSA) lease format, with the United States Postal Service (USPS) lease being a separate document entirely. Most states like California, Texas, and Florida use their own standard lease format when it comes to their real estate leasing actions. County and local city governments also have their own lease formats or rely on the property owner's individual lease when it comes to their real estate leasing activities.

When looking at private-sector real estate leases for commercial properties, most property owners make a distinction regarding whether a lease is a gross lease, a modified gross lease, or a net lease. Most government real estate leases with federal and state tenants will seek to have most if not all of the operating costs included in the lease rent payments, which would make the lease look more like a gross lease. The distinction between government real estate leases and private-sector leases has more to do with whether the government lease has firm terms, appropriation clauses, termination options, holdover language, etc.

Understanding the different lease types, formats, and models for each level of government will allow property owners the ability to determine if these leases are appropriate for their properties. Some government leases are for new space requirements in new property locations, while others are used for existing leased locations only. It is important to remember that government lease language and formats can change without notice, so it is a best practice for a property owner to work with an attorney when reviewing any lease documents for a new government tenant.

This chapter will review (1) US federal government leases, (2) state government leases, and (3) local government leases. Most of the leases reviewed in this chapter are not intended to cover every lease type available for each level of government but to provide a general overview of the leases that are common for that level of government.

US FEDERAL GOVERNMENT LEASES

The federal government relies, for the most part, on the US GSA lease format and lease guidelines for a majority of leasing activities that the federal government is involved in. There are exceptions to this, with some agencies currently using their own lease formats, such as the Department of Defense and the USPS. This section covers the various lease models and lease types for the federal government, with a focus on the US GSA and the USPS leases. It is important to remember when reviewing US GSA lease models and types that they will be used, generally, by other federal agencies for their own leasing activities when not using the US GSA for their leasing activities.

US General Services Administration Leases

There are several types of leasing activities that federal government agencies work on with property owners. It's important to note there is some distinction between a lease type and a lease model when discussing government leases, but for purposes of the review in this section it is assumed that the type of lease being used is to describe the event for a specific lease action, such as the type of lease being used for a lease renewal. The lease model term is often used to identify the lease method to complete the specific type of lease action. These two terms, the lease type and lease model, are sometimes used interchangeably, with the term "lease type" used most often to describe both the activity and the leasing method that the GLC will be using for the lease transaction.

The US GSA has three main types of leasing categories, which are: new or replacement leases, succeeding leases, and superseding leases. It is important for property owners (as part of their negotiations with the US GSA) to understand what type of lease action the GSA is intending to pursue with the property owner. There are several distinctions between what lease action is being used by the GSA that will signal to the property owner the GSA's intention to renew the lease, compete the lease in the open market, or to simply do a short-term extension to see what the tenant agency's options are. The US GSA may use one of the lease types or a combination of all three in the course of a lease transaction with a property owner.

US GSA Lease Types

New or Replacement Leases

The US GSA describes these leases in the GSA *Leasing Desk Guide* as "leases with new terms and conditions and new lease contract numbers, applicable for either a new requirement or to replace an existing expiring lease."

A majority of US GSA lease transactions taking place in the market for most property owners will be for a new or replacing lease.

Succeeding Leases

The US GSA describes these leases in the US GSA *Leasing Desk Guide* as "non-competitive (sole-source) lease acquisitions secured to cover continued occupancy of the current premises at the end of a lease term without a break in continuous tenancy. They establish new terms and conditions and have a new lease contract number. Such a lease would generally be used where acceptable new locations are not identified, or where acceptable locations are identified but a cost-benefit analysis indicates that award to an offeror other than the current Lessor will result in substantial relocation costs or duplication of costs to the Government, and the Government cannot expect to recover such costs through competition."

These leases can sometimes be competed in the market by the US GSA as a new lease, but if a new location is not identified as being a best value to the GLC, it can be converted to a sole-source procurement. A property owner that holds the current lease may not be told by the GLC that the sole-source procurement they are involved in is a sole-source procurement without competition. These US GSA leases typically do not have many tenant improvement requirements with the lease being signed by the tenant in near "as-is" condition with minor tenant agency work needed that can often include paint and carpet.

Superseding Leases

The US GSA defines these leases in the US GSA *Leasing Desk Guide* as "new leases that replace an existing lease before expiration. It is procured following non-competitive sole-source procedures. They establish new terms and conditions and have a new lease contract number. The Government considers executing a superseding lease to replace an existing lease when the Government needs numerous or detailed modifications to a space that would cause complications or substantially change the existing lease, or where better terms are available in a market."

As with a succeeding lease, the US GSA can consider superseding leases as being a new lease competed in the market place.

US GSA Lease Models

Starting in FY 2016 the US GSA began using a global lease model template, the GSA Form L100 that is currently being utilized to select the lease model for the lease action type from a single lease template. The previous lease models used by the US GSA utilized multiple templates to cover each specific lease type and specific model instead of the current use of a single lease model template to be used for almost all lease action types.

There are some exceptions to the use of the US GSA Form L100 under the current system in place when it applies to simplified leases, on-airport leases, and warehouse lease models. The following is an overview of the various lease models, most of which currently are being negotiated using the US GSA L100 template, currently used by US GSA, except for the exceptions noted above.

Simplified Lease Model

The US GSA describes the Simplified Lease as follows:

> A lease acquired under this acquisition method was previously referred to as a simplified lease acquisition threshold (SLAT) lease or "short form" lease. Those names have now been replaced with the term "simplified lease." The term "SLAT" is used only in conjunction with the monetary limit of this lease model, not for the lease model itself. This model is specifically for acquisitions with a net annual rent at or below the current threshold of $150,000, or the threshold as amended by the General Services Administration Acquisition Manual (GSAM). This acquisition method applies to a large percentage of all lease transactions by number while encompassing a small percentage of the overall net annual rent and transacted square footage.[1]

As stated above, most US GSA leases will be completed using the simplified lease model method.

Streamlined Lease Model

The US GSA describes the streamlined lease as follows:

> The streamlined lease model works best for lease procurements that exceed the simplified acquisition threshold (see Federal Acquisition Regulation (FAR) 2.101) up to a maximum of $500,000 net annual rent. The net annual rent must be calculated as the average annual rental amount for the lease term, plus option periods, and excluding the cost of services and utilities furnished by the lessor.
>
> This annual rent threshold is a general guide; Leasing Specialists are strongly encouraged to remain within the threshold amount. Do not use the streamlined lease for procurements requiring build-to-suit, major lease construction, complete rehabilitation or reconstruction of existing buildings, or when using a best value trade-off procurement methodology.[2]

The Standard Lease Model

The US GSA describes the standard lease as follows:

> The Standard lease model replaces the previous GSA tenant improvement SFO and should be used for new construction and lease acquisitions requiring extensive alterations, regardless of the dollar value of the acquisition and security level requirements. This lease model is designed for a best value trade-off or lowest price technically acceptable procurement. It may also be used for a sole source procurement if the succeeding/superseding lease model is not appropriate due to extensive alteration requirements.[3]

Succeeding and Superseding Lease Models

The US GSA describes succeeding and superseding leases as follows:

> The Succeeding/Superseding lease model should be used when space requirements have not changed and a stay in place solution is appropriate. This lease model is designed for space with minimal or no tenant improvements (that is, carpet and paint refreshing). Improvements such as carpet and paint refresh must be included in the rental rate and amortized over the firm term of the lease. This lease model is designed for a sole source procurement. If a tenant improvement allowance is needed or the acquisition is likely to be a sole source procurement, the RPLO should use the Standard lease model.[4]

The following figure shows the current lease models used by the US GSA for its various lease actions.

Figure 3.0: US GSA Lease Models

	STANDARD	STREAMLINED	SIMPLIFIED	SUCCEEDING/ SUPERSEDING
Net Annual Rent Dollar Threshold	N/A	\$150,000 to \$500,000	Under \$150,000	N/A
Unit-Specific Requirements	TI allowance allows refinement during design	DID schematic and/or detailed requirements– typical office space	DID schematic and/or detailed requirements– typical office space	"As is" or paint and carpet
ISC Security Requirements	All	Levels I, II, III	Levels I, II	All
TI Strategy	TI allowance	3 TI options	Upfront pricing of TIs (firm fixed price at lease award)	No TI
Procurement Method	Best Value Trade-Off or Lowest Price Technically Acceptable	Lowest Price Technically Acceptable	Lowest Price Technically Acceptable	Lowest Price Technically Acceptable
Additional Criteria	N/A	DID workshop No change to lease after final offer is submitted	Optional paragraphs for operating cost escalations and tax adjustments. Intent is to avoid use of these clauses if possible. Initial offer can be accepted as the final offer. No CD review	

The US GSA global lease model, the GLA L100 template, will be discussed in further detail in Volume II; the global RLP document and the GLA R100 are discussed in further detail in Chapter 4.

US Postal Service Lease

In contrast to the US GSA, the USPS uses a single standard form lease model for most of its leases with property owners regardless of the square footage or the length of the lease. The USPS lease format is fairly straightforward, with lease language that may be considered relatively easy to understand. The USPS lease is highly customizable to include various attachments and riders to the lease as needed. The USPS standard lease reviewed in this section is dated 2004 with General Conditions dated 2006 and riders and attachments from various dates.[5]

The typical USPS lease follows a standard lease model format that includes the following items with notes for further review.

USPS Standard Lease (2004)

1. General area—measured in net total USPS leased square footage and can include exterior platforms, parking, and driveways.
2. Lease term
3. Rental amount
4. Renewal options
5. Termination
6. Legal description
7. Signature page

General Conditions to USPS Lease (2006)

1. Choice of Law—typically states that federal law governs the USPS lease.
2. Recording requirements
3. Mortgagee's agreement information
4. Assignments
5. Applicable codes and ordinances
6. Sublease—does not typically state that USPS must give notice to property owner for permission to sublease the space.
7. Restoration and alterations
8. Claims and disputes—the USPS lease is subject to the federal Contract Disputes Act of 1978.
9. Hazardous and hazardous conditions clause
10. Facilities nondiscrimination
11. Clauses required to implement policies, statutes, or executive orders—there are several general clauses that may not apply to all property owners but these clauses should be read in detail to ensure the property owner is in compliance with the USPS lease contract.

Common Riders to the USPS Lease

Maintenance riders: There are different types of maintenance riders, which include maintenance responsibility by the property owner or the USPS. The type of maintenance rider used can have a significant impact on the property owner's costs to lease space to the USPS.

Real estate tax rider: There are different types of real estate tax riders that discuss either the property owner reimbursements for the real estate taxes by the USPS or no reimbursements of the real estate taxes by the USPS. The real estate tax language and reimbursement of real estate taxes by the USPS to the property owner are unique to USPS leases and should be understood completely by the property owner before proceeding with a signed lease with the USPS.

Utilities, services, and equipment rider: This rider to the lease is where most of the language for which services and utilities the property owner is responsible for providing to the USPS and how they will be paid for, by either the USPS or the property owner.

Mortgagee's agreement: The language and information requested may be new for most property owners, as this form needs to be completed by the property owner's lender if there is a mortgage on the property.

Additional Common Attachments

- Renewal Option Based on Market Value Rider
- Underground Storage Tank Rider
- Common Area Maintenance Rider
- Construction Rider
- Purchase Option Riders

Exhibits

- Legal Description
- Floor Plans
- Building Rules

Lease Amendments

- Lease Extensions
- Lease Renewals
- Landlord Designs and Improvements
- Modifications to Riders

Both the US GSA leases and the USPS leases are well suited to handle a variety of leasing tasks on a national basis. While federal lease actions are specifically geared toward having both the federal tenant agency and property owner agree to the specifics of the lease agreement, it becomes apparent as a property owner moves from a federal tenant agency lease to a state or local government lease that state and local government tenants are focused on their individual laws and regulations specific to their government agency and not those of other government agencies at levels above or below them.

STATE LEASES

Moving from federal leases to state leases can be a new experience for some government real estate practitioners due to the fact that most states use a standard lease model that is specific to that state and is not consistent nationally.

This section reviews the State of California standard lease, which has a number of interesting items that may be in contrast to other state leases. The contrast between the State of California and other states is remarkable when compared to states that are much smaller than California in that these smaller states use much shorter leases and do not incorporate many of the same rules and regulations that a larger state like California uses in its leases. There are multiple reasons for this lack of complexity for smaller state leases, but generally it is due to the amount of resources each state leasing department has and the amount of complexity required to get a deal done.

One of the largest areas of concern for property owners dealing with a new state tenant lease is that the state tenant may have a clause in the lease, commonly known as the "budget appropriations" lease clause, which allows the tenant to cancel the lease if the state tenant does not have budget approval for the lease payments for any given year which would allow the government tenant to cancel the lease. This budget appropriations language in effect creates a government lease that is a year–to–year lease versus a multiyear fixed-term lease. This type of year-to-year lease makes it difficult for some property owners to lease to state tenants because commercial lenders are not in favor of a tenant being able to cancel a lease early in the term of the lease contract.

State of California Lease

The State of California's Department of General Services Real Estate Services Division uses a standard form lease for all its leasing activities, which include several exhibits, forms, and lease checklists.[6] The state has several clauses that relate specifically to California state law that should be read closely by the property owner's attorney to ensure that the property owner will be in compliance with these laws.

The following is selected whole or partial lease paragraphs of note for further review from a sample State of California lease dated 2014 (italics have been added to individual lease sections for emphasis).

State of California Standard Form Lease

RESD Standard Lease (revised May 2014)

3. Early Termination.

The State may terminate this lease at any time effective on or after _____, by giving written notice to the Lessor at least thirty (30) days prior to the date when such termination shall become effective. *If the State fails to complete its move out within the notice period and remains in the premises, additional rent shall be paid and prorated on a thirty (30) day month, based on the actual number of days the State occupies the premises following the effective date of termination.*

4. Rent.

Rental payments shall be paid by the State, from legally available funds and subject to the California Constitution, in arrears on the last day of each month during said term as follows:

Rental payable hereunder for any period of time less than one month shall be determined by prorating the monthly rental herein specified based on the actual number of days in the month.

Rental shall be paid to Lessor at the address specified in Paragraph 5 or to such other address as the Lessor may designate by a notice in writing. *If the premises are not complete pursuant to Paragraph 6 by the date shown in Paragraph 2, it is understood and agreed by and between the parties that, at the State's sole option, the dates shown in Paragraphs 2 and 3 and the dates and dollar amounts shown in Paragraph 4 may be adjusted to the first of the month following the State's acceptance of the completed premises, such acceptance shall not unreasonably be withheld. If the State exercises this option, it is agreed the State will complete unilaterally an amendment to the lease to revise the herein above stated dates.* Any accrued rents for the period of time prior to the unilaterally adjusted commencement date will be paid in accordance with Paragraph 8. Additionally, it is understood and agreed between the parties that, at the State's option, the dates shown in the "CPI Escalator Operating Expenses" paragraph, if incorporated herein, shall be adjusted to reflect the time delay between lease commencement and the first of the month following the actual acceptance date. In the event this lease agreement contains a provision granting the State an Option to Purchase the premises, it is further agreed herein by the parties that, notwithstanding the provision of the Option to Purchase paragraph herein, the effective dates and corresponding purchase option prices of said Option to Purchase shall be adjusted consistent with any adjustment to the lease commencement date. Said "adjusted" purchase option dates shall be established consistent herewith and incorporated into said lease with a unilateral amendment by the State.

7. Notice of Completion and Access to Premises during Construction.

Lessor shall notify the State in writing by certified mail of the date the leased premises will be completed and ready for occupancy at least thirty (30) days prior thereto. Such notice shall be a condition precedent to the accrual of rental hereunder, except however, that if the State occupies the premises prior to the receipt of such notice or prior to the expiration of the notice period of such notice, rental shall commence to accrue as of the date of occupancy.

Following execution of this lease, and not more than sixty days (60) prior to completion of construction and occupancy under this lease, State or its contractors or other representatives shall have the right to enter the premises for the purpose of installing certain equipment such as, but not limited to, modular system furniture, and electrical and telecommunications cabling and equipment.

State agrees to indemnify and hold Lessor harmless from and against any claims, damages, or other injury suffered by Lessor as a result of the work to be performed pursuant to this right to enter the premises prior to State's acceptance and occupancy of the premises. Lessor agrees to indemnify and hold State and its agents, contractors or other representatives harmless from and against any claims, damages, injury or other harm suffered by reason of the negligence or other wrongful act of Lessor or any of Lessor's agents, contractors, or other representatives. In no event shall the exercise of this right of entry be construed so as to cause an acceleration of the occupancy date of this lease or the obligation of the State to pay rent.

Lessor and State shall each make all reasonable efforts to ensure that the respective construction and installation work is scheduled in such a manner so as to not interfere with or delay the other.

In the event that one or the other party causes a delay in the other party's work, such injured party shall be compensated in the following manner:

Delays caused by the Lessor: *Credit the State a compensating day of delay in the occupancy date and corresponding day of delay in payment of rent.*

Delays caused by the State: *Credit the Lessor a compensating day of payment of rent from the actual date of occupancy.*

Compensation will be in one-day increments.

The parties agree that this shall be the sole remedy for delay, in that the calculation of damages in any other manner is too uncertain and not susceptible of accurate determination.

9. Time Limit and Proper Tenancy.

No rental shall accrue under this lease, nor shall the State have any obligation to perform the covenants or observe the conditions herein contained until the leased premises have been made ready for occupancy in accordance with the provisions hereof. *It is specifically agreed that in the event the leased premises are not completed and ready for occupancy by the State on or before __, then and in that event the State may, at its option and in addition to any other remedies it may have, terminate this lease and be relieved of any further obligations hereunder, providing that a fair and reasonable allowance for the following delays shall be added to said time for completion:*

A. Acts of the State, its agents or employees, or those claiming under agreement with or grant from the State, or by

B. The acts of God which Lessor could not reasonably have foreseen or guarded against, or by Notice of Completion and Access to Premises during Construction Early Occupancy Time limit and Prior Tenancy

C. Any strikes, boycotts or like obstructive actions by employees or labor organizations and which are beyond control of Lessor, and which cannot be reasonably overcome, or by

D. Restrictive regulations by the Federal Government, which are enforced in connection with a National Emergency.

In the event that the State elects to occupy premises before the work on the premises specified in Exhibit A, B, and C is fully completed, the State will provide the Lessor with a punch list of work remaining to be completed (referenced as the State's "Punch List"). Lessor agrees that Lessor shall complete the remaining work no later than 14 calendar days from the date of receipt of said Punch List. *If said Punch List is not completed within the specified 14-day period, Lessor agrees that, beginning on the first day after said 14-day period following occupancy of premises by the State, rent may at the State's sole option be reduced to $ which is seventy percent (70%) of the base rent specified in paragraph 4 herein (excluding any amortization payments) until such time that the Punch List work is completed in full and that such completion of work is inspected and accepted by the State. The portion of the rent specified for amortization of tenant improvements, if any shall continue to be paid in full without interruption.*

It is understood and agreed that the rent reduction specified above does not relieve Lessor of its obligation to complete said work and the State shall maintain all other remedies specified in the Lease.

It is understood by all parties hereto that it shall be the Lessor's responsibility to remove any prior tenant.

17. Assignment and Subletting.

The *State shall not assign this lease without prior written consent of the Lessor,* which shall not be unreasonably withheld, but shall in any event have the right to sublet the leased premises.

22. Prevailing Wage Provision.

For those projects defined as "public works" pursuant to Labor Code §1720.2, the following shall apply:

A. Lessor/contractor shall comply with prevailing wage requirements and be subject to restrictions and penalties in accordance with §1770 et seq. of the Labor Code which requires prevailing wages be paid to appropriate work classifications in all bid specifications and subcontracts.

B. The Lessor/contractor shall furnish all subcontractors/employees a copy of the Department of Industrial Relations prevailing wage rates, which Lessor will post at the job site. All prevailing wage rates shall be obtained by the Lessor/contractor from: Department of Industrial Relations Division of Labor Statistics and Research 455 Golden Gate Avenue, 8th Floor San Francisco, California 94102 Phone: (415) 703-4774 Fax: (415) 703-4771 For further information on prevailing wage: http://www.dir.ca.gov/dlsr/statistics_research.html Inspection Destruction Subrogation Waived Prevailing Wage Provision.

C. Lessor/contractor shall comply with the payroll record keeping and availability requirement of §1776 of the Labor Code.

D. Lessor/contractor shall make travel and subsistence payments to workers needed for performance of work in accordance with the Labor Code.

E. Prior to commencement of work, Lessor/contractor shall contact the Division of Apprenticeship Standards and comply with §1777.5, §1777.6, and §1777.7 of the Labor Code and Applicable Regulations.

27. Holding Over.

In the event the State remains in possession of the premises after the expiration of the lease term, or any extension or renewal thereof, this lease shall be automatically extended on a month to month basis, subject to thirty (30) days termination by either party, and otherwise on the terms and conditions herein specified, so far as applicable. If the last rental amount shown in Paragraph 4 included the amortization of a capital sum expended by Lessor for certain alterations and improvements, as described in a separate paragraph herein, and the capital sum has been fully amortized, the holdover rent shall be reduced by the amount of the monthly amortization. *If the State fails to vacate the premises within the notice period and remains for an extended period, additional rent shall be paid and prorated on a thirty (30) day month, based on the actual number of days the State occupies the premises following the effective date of termination.*

Lease Exhibits and Additional Lease Information

Most of the information in this section on lease exhibits for the State of California leases is taken from the state's Department of General Services website.[7]

Lease Exhibit A

Lease Exhibit A is a CAD drawing of the floor plan, along with project notes of work to be completed.

Lessor must provide accurate electronic (CAD) drawings depicting the "as-built" condition of the space considered for lease, including common areas and paths of travel necessary for State tenancy. Lessor will be responsible for any rework, design changes, or change orders caused by inaccuracies in plans or discrepancies between plans and physical premises.

The State may request provision of architectural and design services by Lessor. If agreed, lessor shall secure the services of a licensed architect or Certified Interior Designer who shall prepare, after consultation with the State's space planner, a scope of work statement subject to review and approval by the State. A list of general requirements for the services will be provided subsequent to the request.

Lease Exhibit B

Lease Exhibit B is a document that outlines performance specifications for new construction, alterations, and existing construction.

Note: Unlike most private-sector tenants who lease space on a rentable area basis that includes a load factor for common areas, leased space as defined in Exhibit B, Division 1.00 (E), is based on a modified version of the BOMA definition of usable area that excludes all code required restrooms, utility rooms, and common areas.

Lease Exhibit C

Lease Exhibit C is a list of requirements for compliance with the State Fire Marshal, California Building Code (CBC), Americans with Disabilities Act (ADA), and Sustainable Measure Procedures.

Accessibility Checklist for State Leased Buildings and Facilities and Form G

Accessibility Survey Checklist

Lessors are required to provide an accessibility survey as described in Exhibit C, Division 3. The Accessibility Survey Checklist must be completed prior to executing a lease. Any Certified Access Specialist (CASp), ICC Accessibility Inspector or Plans Examiner, or a California-licensed architect can perform the checklist.

Form G

Form G verifies the space is 100 percent ADA compliant. It must be signed by the architect on the project and submitted to DGS prior to occupancy and beginning the rent.

Asbestos, Lead, and Seismic Information [8]

Asbestos

Buildings constructed before 1979 must be certified in writing to be free from hazards from asbestos-containing material (ACM). The certification must be provided by an industrial hygienist certified by the American Board of Industrial Hygiene (ABIH) or an Environmental Protection Agency (EPA) Asbestos Hazard Emergency Response Act (AHERA) certified inspector.

If the building was constructed subsequent to 1979, a photocopy of the occupancy certificate issued by the city or county building department is all that is required prior to the execution of the lease.

Lead

Buildings constructed before 1980 must be certified as free of hazard from lead-containing materials (LCMs). Paint chip samples and samples of other suspected LCMs shall be collected by a DHS lead-certified project designer for laboratory analysis to determine lead content.

If the building was constructed subsequent to 1980, a photocopy of the occupancy certificate issued by the city or county building department is all that is required prior to the execution of the lease.

Seismic

All facilities the state occupies must be evaluated for the ability to meet a seismic performance objective of substantial life safety. The state's Space Planner will complete an initial screening of the property. If required, the state may request a structural evaluation performed by an independent licensed structural engineer, and the certification must be completed and signed.

Sustainable Measures, Submetering, and Construction Waste Recycling

Sustainable Measures

All state-leased facilities are now subject to review and reporting procedures under Sustainable Measures/Authority sections of Exhibit C, Division 1, and Division 4.

Submeters

The state requests lessors to submeter the state-leased space for both utilities and water, where economically feasible, in order to report energy use data into the US EPA Energy Star Portfolio Manager and water use to a database as designated by the Department of Water Resources. The state also encourages lessors to participate in utility-sponsored energy conservation measures, using alternative financing.

Construction Waste Management Job Site Recycling

If a project requires tenant improvements or other construction, a plan must be submitted for the recycling of waste materials.

Disabled Veterans Business Enterprise (DVBE)

In recognition of the contribution disabled veterans have made to our country, this package provides program information and lessor guidelines for the Disabled Veterans Business Enterprise (DVBE) Program. Lessors are encouraged to comply with the DVBE program whenever possible.

LOCAL GOVERNMENT LEASES

Local government leases, leases that deal mainly with county and local municipalities, make up a bulk of the leasing activity on a national basis. However, due to the low leasing volume for most local governments, it is common for local government agencies to use a nonstandardized lease format for their leases. Conversely, large local government agencies like the County of Los Angeles and the City of Chicago use a standardized lease for their real estate leasing activities.

The County of Los Angeles standardized lease is written so that the county is covered for most things it should need to protect itself from. The City of Chicago also uses a standardized lease format that is thorough in its attempts to cover itself through language that covers most if not all of the legal items needed for a comprehensive lease agreement with the property owner. One of the main items both leases have in common is that these leases contain language that makes sure the property owner is aware of the laws, codes, statues, and requirements specific to doing a real estate lease with that level of government.

This section will cover leases for both the County of Los Angeles and the City of Chicago with sample paragraphs in the leases that could be of further interest to property owners.

County of Los Angeles Lease

The County of Los Angeles standard form lease is indexed for the property owner to easily identify areas that may need to be reviewed in more detail. The exhibits to the lease include a variety of items that are important to the tenant agency, which includes a detailed cleaning schedule that the property owner should review closely to confirm that it is correctly priced into the operating costs of the lease. A work letter will usually be attached to the lease if there are any tenant agency improvements needed to the leased space; the work letter will detail the costs for the tenant agency improvements with a discussion of how the tenant improvements will be paid.

The following are selected whole or partial lease paragraphs of note for further review from a County of Los Angeles lease (italics have been added to individual lease sections for emphasis).

COUNTY OF LOS ANGELES CHIEF EXECUTIVE OFFICE LEASE AGREEMENT

2. Premises.

(b) Tenant shall have the right within 90 days of approval of this Lease by the Board of Supervisors of the County of Los Angeles ("Board of Supervisors") *to field-measure and verify the exact footage of the Premises and/or the Building. All measurements shall be taken in accordance with the methods of measuring rentable/usable area as described in the Standard Method for Measuring Floor Area in Office Buildings, ANSI Z65.1-1996, as promulgated by the Building Owners and Management Association ("BOMA") International except that no penthouse mechanical room space shall be included in the measurement. Should this measurement be less than the square footage stated above, Tenant shall have the right to adjust such square footage and reduce the Base Rent in Section 1* accomplished by the mutual execution of a memorandum of understanding between the Landlord and the Tenant. Landlord acknowledges the space has been marketed at the above-indicated rental amount and in the event of subsequent physical measurements, *Landlord agrees there will be no adjustment made to either the square footage or the Base Rent in the event the measured square footage exceeds the amount represented by Landlord.* Should Landlord and Tenant not agree with respect to the results of the measurement conducted pursuant to this subsection (b) Landlord shall appoint an independent firm or person who is experienced in making such measurements whose determination with respect to which measurement is correct shall be final and binding upon the parties. Landlord and Tenant shall share equally in the fees of such firm.

4. Commencement and Expiration Dates.

(a) Term. The term of this Lease shall commence upon the Commencement Date and terminate on the Termination Date. Within 30 days of determining the Commencement Date, Landlord and Tenant shall acknowledge in writing the Commencement Date by executing the Commencement Date Memorandum and Confirmation of Lease Terms attached as Exhibit C. The Commencement Date shall begin 30 days after Tenant's Acceptance of the Premises. The term "Tenant's Acceptance of the Premises" as used in this Lease shall mean the date upon which the Premises are Substantially Complete, Tenant has inspected the Premises and Tenant has accepted the Premises. The term "Substantially Complete" or "Substantial Completion" as used in this Lease shall mean compliance with all of the following: (1) the shell and core of the Building are complete and in compliance with all applicable laws and codes, and all of the building systems are operational to the extent necessary to service the Premises, (2) *Landlord has sufficiently completed all the work required to be performed by Landlord in accordance with this Lease, including the installation of modular furniture systems, if so required (except minor punch list items which Landlord shall thereafter promptly complete), such that Tenant can conduct normal business operations from the Premises,* (3) *Landlord has obtained a certificate of occupancy for the Building, or a temporary certificate of occupancy for that portion of the Building that includes all of the Premises, or its equivalent,* (4) Tenant has been provided with the number of parking privileges and spaces to which it is entitled under this Lease, and (5) if Landlord is responsible for the installation of telecommunication systems, then such systems shall be completely operational.

(b) Termination Right. If the Commencement Date has not occurred within 60 days from the Projected Commencement Date, subject to Tenant Delays or Force Majeure Delays as provided in Landlord's Work Letter, which has been executed concurrently herewith, *Tenant may thereafter, at any time before the Commencement Date occurs, terminate this Lease effective* upon the giving of written notice to Landlord and the parties shall have no further obligations to one another hereunder.

7. Holdover.

If Tenant remains in possession of the Premises or any part thereof after the expiration of the Term of this Lease, such occupancy shall be a tenancy which is terminable only upon 90 days written notice from Landlord or 30 days written notice from the Chief Executive Officer of Tenant at the last monthly Base Rent payable under this Lease (as such Base Rent may be adjusted from time to time in accordance with this Lease) plus all other charges payable under this Lease, and subject to all of the terms, covenants and conditions of this Lease.

9. Damage or Destruction.

(d) Default By Landlord. If Landlord is required to repair and restore the Premises as provided for in this Section and Landlord should fail to thereafter pursue said repair and restoration work with reasonable diligence to completion, *Tenant may (a) declare a default hereunder, or (b) perform or cause to be performed the restoration work and deduct the cost thereof plus interest thereon at ten percent (10%) per annum,* from the Base Rent next due as a charge against the Landlord.

10. Repairs and Maintenance.

(d) Tenant's Right to Repair. If Tenant provides written notice (or oral notice in the event of an emergency such as damage or destruction to or of any portion of the Building structure and/or the Building systems and/or anything that could cause material disruption to Tenant's business) to Landlord of an event or circumstance which requires the action of Landlord with respect to repair and/or maintenance, and Landlord fails to provide such action within a reasonable period of time, given the circumstances, after the giving of such notice, but in any event not later than five days after the giving of such notice, then Tenant may proceed to take the required action (provided, however, that no such notice shall be required in the event of an emergency which threatens life or where there is imminent danger to property or a possibility that a failure to take immediate action could cause a material disruption in Tenant's normal and customary business activities). Tenant shall have access to the Building to the extent necessary to perform the work contemplated by this provision. *If such action was required under the terms of this Lease to have been taken by Landlord and was not taken by Landlord within such period (unless such notice was not required as provided above), and Tenant took such required action, then Tenant shall be entitled to prompt reimbursement by Landlord of Tenant's reasonable costs and expenses in having taken such action plus interest thereon at ten percent (10%) per annum. If not reimbursed by Landlord within ten days, Tenant shall be entitled to deduct from Base Rent payable by Tenant under this Lease the amount set forth in its invoice for such work.* The remedies provided in this Section are in addition to the remedies provided in Section 14.

15. Assignment and Subletting.

Tenant may assign, mortgage, encumber or otherwise transfer this Lease or sublet the whole or any part of the Premises *without first obtaining Landlord's prior consent:* provided, however, that no such assignment, subletting or other transfer shall relieve Tenant of any liability under this Lease unless Landlord has given its written consent thereto, which Landlord shall not unreasonably withhold if the assignee has a financial condition which is reasonably sufficient for it to be responsible for all future obligations under this Lease.

32. Irrevocable Offer.

In consideration for the time and expense that Tenant will invest, including, but not limited to, preliminary space planning, legal review, and preparation and noticing for presentation to the Tenant Real Estate Management Commission of Los Angeles County in reliance on Landlord's agreement to lease the Premises to Tenant under the terms of this Lease, Landlord irrevocably offers to enter into this Lease and not to revoke this offer until the Irrevocable Offer Expiration Date, as defined in Section 1.

Exhibits to the Lease

The following is a list of common exhibits and attachments to a County of Los Angeles lease:

- Exhibit A: Floor Plan
- Exhibit B: Commencement Date Memorandum
- Exhibit C: Cleaning Schedule
- Exhibit D: Tenant Estoppel Certificate
- Exhibit E: Subordination, Nondisturbance, and Attornment Agreement
- Exhibit F: Nondisturbance Agreement
- Exhibit G: Request for Notice
- Exhibit H: Community Business Enterprises Form

Landlord's Work Letter

- Landlord's Work Letter
- Addendum A: Base Building Improvements
- Addendum B: Tenant Improvements
- Addendum C: Memorandum of Tenant Improvements Costs

City of Chicago Lease

Reviewing local-level leases can be interesting when viewed from the federal and state level, given that most city leases, more commonly known as municipal leases, are focused on making sure that the property owner is adhering to the local ordinances and codes specific to the municipality that the property owner is leasing to. The City of Chicago lease is a good example of a municipal lease in that it is a well-written legal document geared toward equitably protecting the city, the city subtenant agency if applicable, and the property owner. It is important to note that some large municipalities may have other city government agencies, such as a public school system, that may have their own unique leases separate from the main municipal governing body along with leasing authority outside the control of the main city leasing department.

The following consists of selected whole or partial lease paragraphs of note for further review from a sample City of Chicago lease that was in use in FY 2015 (italics have been added to individual lease sections for emphasis).

ORDINANCE

BE IT ORDAINED BY THE CITY COUNCIL OF THE CITY OF CHICAGO:

SECTION 1: On behalf of the City of Chicago as Tenant, the Commissioner of the Department of Fleet and Facility Management is authorized to execute a Lease with _____, as Landlord, for use of approximately _____ square feet of commercial space located at _____ by the Departments of Finance, Buildings, and Administrative Hearings, as Tenant, such Lease to be approved by the City Comptroller, the Commissioners of the Buildings and Fleet and Facility Management, and approved as to form and legality by the Corporation Counsel in substantially the following form:

LEASE

2. Term.

The term of this Lease (the "Term") shall begin on the later of (i) the completion of the Build out by Landlord as defined in Section 11 below, *or (ii) the approval of the Lease by City Council and the execution of the Lease by the parties.* The Term shall end on _____, unless sooner terminated as set forth in this Lease.

5. Assignment, Sublease and Liens.

5.1 Tenant *shall not assign this Lease in whole or in part, or sublet the Premises or any part thereof without the written consent of Landlord in each instance.* Landlord shall not unreasonably withhold such consent.

6. Insurance and Indemnification.

<u>6.1 Insurance.</u> Landlord shall procure and maintain at all times, at Landlord's own expense, during the Term, the insurance coverages and requirements specified below, insuring all operations related to the Lease.

The kinds and amounts of insurance required are as follows:

(a) <u>Worker's Compensation and Employer's Liability Insurance.</u> Workers Compensation as prescribed by applicable law, covering all employees who are to provide a service under this Lease, and Employer's Liability Insurance with limits of not less than _____ each accident, illness or disease.

(b) <u>Commercial General Liability Insurance.</u> (Primary and Umbrella). General Liability Insurance or equivalent, with limits of not less than ____ per occurrence, for bodily injury, personal injury, and property damage liability. Coverage shall include the following: All premises and operations, products/completed operations, defense, separation of insured's, and contractual liability (not to include Endorsement CG 21 39 or equivalent). The City of Chicago shall be named as an additional insured under the policy. Such additional insured coverage shall be provided on CG 20 10 or on a similar additional insured form acceptable to the City. The additional insured coverage shall not have any limiting endorsements or language under the policy such as but not limited to, Landlord's sole negligence or the Additional Insured's vicarious liability. Landlord's liability insurance shall be primary without right of contribution by any other insurance or self-insurance maintained by or available to the City.

(c) Automobile Liability Insurance. (Primary and Umbrella). When any motor vehicles (owned, non-owned and hired) are used in connection with the Lease, the Landlord shall provide and maintain Automobile Liability Insurance with limits of not less than _____ per occurrence, for bodily injury and property damage. The City of Chicago shall be named as an additional insured on a primary, non-contributory basis.

(d) All Risk Property Insurance. All risk property insurance coverage shall be maintained by the Landlord for full replacement value to protect against loss of, damage to or destruction of property.

The Landlord shall be responsible for all loss or damage to personal property (including but not limited to materials, equipment, tools and supplies), owned, rented, or used by the Landlord.

6.2 Other Terms of Insurance. Landlord will furnish the City of Chicago, _____, original Certificates of Insurance evidencing the required coverage to be in force on the date of this Lease, and Renewal Certificates of Insurance, or such similar evidence, if the coverages have an expiration or renewal date occurring during the Term. Landlord shall submit evidence of insurance prior to execution of the Lease. The receipt of any certificate does not constitute agreement by the City that the insurance requirements in the Lease have been fully met or that the insurance policies indicated on the certificate are in compliance with all Lease requirements. The failure of the City to obtain certificates or other insurance evidence from Landlord shall not be deemed to be a waiver by the City. The Landlord shall advise all insurers of the Lease provisions regarding insurance. Non-conforming insurance shall not relieve Landlord of its obligation to provide insurance as specified herein. Nonfulfillment of the insurance conditions may constitute a violation of the Lease, and the City retains the right to terminate or suspend the Lease until proper evidence of insurance is provided.

The Landlord shall provide for 60 days prior written notice to be given to the City in the event coverage is substantially changed, canceled, or non-renewed.

Any and all deductibles or self-insured retentions on referenced insurance coverages shall be borne by Landlord.

Landlord hereby grants to the City a waiver of any right of subrogation, which any insurer of said Landlord may acquire against the City by virtue of the payment of any loss under the insurance. Landlord agrees to obtain any endorsement that may be necessary to affect this waiver of subrogation, but this provision applies regardless of whether or not the City has received a waiver of subrogation endorsement from the insurer(s).

Landlord expressly understands and agrees that any coverages and limits furnished by Landlord shall in no way limit the Landlord's liabilities and responsibilities specified in this Lease or by law.

Landlord expressly understands and agrees that its insurance is primary and any insurance or self-insurance programs maintained by the City shall not contribute with insurance provided by Landlord.

The required insurance to be carried is not limited by any limitations expressed in the indemnification language in this Lease or any limitation placed on the indemnity in this Lease given as a matter of law.

If Landlord is a joint venture or limited liability company, the insurance policies shall name the joint venture or limited liability company as a named insured.

If Landlord maintains higher limits than the minimums shown above, the City requires and shall be entitled to coverage for the higher limits maintained by Landlord. Any available insurance proceeds in excess of the specified minimum limits of insurance and coverage shall be available to the City.

Notwithstanding any provision to the contrary, the City of Chicago, _____ maintains the rights to modify, delete, alter or change these requirements at any time during the Term of Lease.

6.3 Mutual Indemnification. Landlord and Tenant shall indemnify and hold each other harmless against all liabilities, judgment costs, damages, and expenses which may accrue against, be charged to, or be recovered from either party by reason of any negligent performance of or failure to perform any of their obligations under this Lease.

8. Conflict of Interest and Governmental Ethics.

8.1 Conflict of Interest. No official or employee of the City of Chicago, nor any member of any board, commission or agency of the City of Chicago, shall have any financial interest (as directed in Chapter 2-156 of the Municipal Code of Chicago), either direct or indirect, in the Premises. *No such official, employee, or member shall participate in making or in any way attempt to use his or her position to influence any City governmental decision or action with respect to this Lease.*

8.2 Duly to Comply with Governmental Ethics Ordinance. Landlord and Tenant shall comply with Chapter 2-156 of the Municipal Code of Chicago, "Governmental Ethics," including, but not limited to, section 2-156-120, which *states that no payment, gratuity, or offer of employment shall be made in connection with any City of Chicago contract as an inducement for the award of that contract or order.* Any contract negotiated, entered into, or performed in violation of any of the provisions of Chapter 2-156 shall be voidable in the sole discretion of the Tenant.

9. Holding Over.

9.1 Any holding over by Tenant shall be construed to be a tenancy from month to month beginning on _____ and the rent shall be at the same rate as set forth in Section 3.1(j) of this Lease. During any holding over all other provisions of this Lease shall remain in full force and effect.

10. Miscellaneous.

10.10 Termination of Lease. Tenant shall have the *right to terminate this Lease for convenience without penalty by providing Landlord with ninety (90) days prior written notice at any time on or after the first day of the _____ lease year.*

10.13 No Brokers. The Department of Fleet Facility Management, Office of Real Estate Management, does not use brokers, tenant representatives, or other finders. Landlord does not use brokers, landlord representatives, or other finders. Tenant warrants to Landlord that no broker, landlord or tenant representative, or other finder *(a) introduced Tenant to Landlord, (b) assisted Tenant in the negotiation of this Lease, or (c) dealt with Tenant on Tenant's behalf in connection with the Premises or this Lease. Landlord warrants to Tenant that no broker, landlord or tenant representative, or other finder (a) introduced Landlord to Tenant, (b) assisted Landlord in the negotiation of this Lease, or (c) dealt with Landlord on Landlord's behalf in connection with the*

Premises or this Lease. Under no circumstances shall Tenant make any payments due hereunder to any broker(s). Under no circumstances shall Landlord make any payments due hereunder to any broker(s).

10.15 No Construction against Preparer. This Lease shall not be interpreted in favor of either Landlord or Tenant. Landlord and Tenant each acknowledge that both parties participated fully in the mutual drafting of this Lease.

11. Build out of Premises.

11.5 Build out Completion. *Landlord and Tenant warrant that final completion of the Build out, which is satisfactory to Tenant, is a condition precedent to Tenant's occupancy of the Premises. If Landlord is not able to complete the Build out by _____ ("the Build out Deadline"), Landlord may request an extension of the Build out Deadline by providing Tenant with written notice of the Build out delay and a written request for extension no later than _____. Upon receipt of such written notice and request, Tenant may grant an extension of the Build out Deadline for up to ninety (90) days. If Landlord does not complete the Build out within the ninety (90) day extension, Tenant shall have the right to terminate this lease.*

11.6 Cost of Build out. Landlord shall pay for the cost of the Build out, *without contribution or repayment from Tenant.*

12. Additional Responsibilities of Landlord.

12.18 Economic Disclosure Statement Affidavit Updates. Landlord shall provide Tenant with any material updates to the information submitted in Landlord's Economic Disclosure Statement and Affidavit. Tenant may also request such updates from time to time. *Tenant reserves the right to withhold rental payments under this Lease in the event Landlord fails to provide such updates.*

13. Additional Responsibilities of Tenant.

13.10 Repairs for Tenant Negligence. Vandalism, or Misuse. Tenant shall not destroy, deface, damage, impair, nor remove any part of the Premises or facilities, equipment or appurtenances, unless approved as part of an alteration, addition, or improvement under Section 4.5 of this lease. Subject to approval as set forth herein. *Tenant shall assume all responsibility for any repairs to the Premises necessitated by the negligence, vandalism, or misuse of the Premises or equipment therein by Tenant's employees, clients, invitees, agents, or contractors.*

In such case, Landlord shall notify Tenant in writing of such damage. At Tenant's option Tenant may perform such repairs with service providers suitable to Tenant and at Tenant's sole cost without further set off or deduction. In the alternative, Tenant may direct Landlord in writing to perform said repairs subject to full reimbursement to Landlord by Tenant of all costs associated with such repairs excluding any overhead and/or profit. Any repairs to the Premises effectuated by Landlord under this section shall only be performed by Landlord upon written approval and concurrent Notice to Proceed from the Commissioner of the Department of Fleet and Facility Management. Repair approval from any other department(s) shall be deemed invalid and of no force or effect. Repairs made without said written approval and concurrent Notice to Proceed from the Commissioner of the Department of Fleet and Facility Management shall not be reimbursable to Landlord.

14. Landlord Disclosures and Affirmations.

14.1 Business Relationships. Landlord acknowledges (A) receipt of a copy of Section 2-156-030 (b) of the Municipal Code of Chicago, (B) that it has read such provision and understands that pursuant to such Section 2-156-030 (b) it is illegal for any elected official of the City, or any person acting at the direction of such official, to contact, either orally or in writing, any other City official or employee with respect to any matter involving any person with whom the elected City official or employee has a "Business Relationship" (as defined in Section 2-156-080 of the Municipal Code of Chicago), or to participate in any discussion in any City Council committee hearing or in any City Council meeting or to vote on any matter involving the person with whom an elected official has a Business Relationship, and (C) notwithstanding anything to the contrary contained in this Agreement, that a violation of Section 2-156-030 (b) by an elected official, or any person acting at the direction of such official, with respect to any transaction contemplated by this Agreement shall be grounds for termination of this Agreement and the transactions contemplated hereby. Landlord hereby represents and warrants that no violation by Landlord of Section 2-156-030 (b) has occurred with respect to this Lease Agreement or the transactions contemplated hereby.

14.3 Prohibition on Certain Contributions - Mayoral Executive Order No. 2011-4. Landlord agrees that Landlord, any person or entity that directly or indirectly has an ownership or beneficial interest in Landlord of more than 7.5 percent ("Owners"), spouses and domestic partners of such Owners, Landlord's contractors (i.e., any person or entity in direct contractual privity with Landlord regarding the subject matter of this Agreement) ("Contractors"), any person or entity who directly or indirectly has an ownership or beneficial interest in any Contractor of more than 7.5 percent ("Sub-owners") and spouses and domestic partners of such Sub-owners (Landlord and all the other preceding classes of persons and entities are together, the "Identified Parties"), shall not make a contribution of any amount to the Mayor of the City of Chicago (the "Mayor") or to his political fundraising committee (i) after execution of this Agreement by Landlord, (ii) while this Agreement or any Other Contract is executory, (iii) during the term of this Agreement or any Other Contract (as hereinafter defined) between Landlord and the City, or (iv) during any period while an extension of this Agreement or any Other Contract is being sought or negotiated. This provision shall not apply to contributions made prior to May 16, 2011, the effective date of Executive Order 2011-4.

Landlord represents and warrants that from the later of (a) May 16, 2011, or (b) the date the City approached the Landlord or the date Landlord approached the City, as applicable, regarding the formulation of this Agreement, no Identified Parties have made a contribution of any amount to the Mayor or to his political fundraising committee.

Landlord agrees that it shall not: (a) coerce, compel or intimidate its employees to make a contribution of any amount to the Mayor or to the Mayor's political fundraising committee, (b) reimburse its employees for a contribution of any amount made to the Mayor or to the Mayor's political fundraising committee, or (c) bundle or solicit others to bundle contributions to the Mayor or to his political fundraising committee.

Landlord agrees that the Identified Parties must not engage in any conduct whatsoever designed to intentionally violate this provision or Mayoral Executive Order No. 05-1 or to entice, direct or solicit others to intentionally violate this provision or Mayoral Executive Order No. 2011-4.

Notwithstanding anything to the contrary contained herein, Landlord agrees that a violation of, non-compliance with, misrepresentation with respect to, or breach of any covenant or warranty under this Agreement or violation of Mayoral Executive Order No. 2011-4 constitutes a breach and default under this Agreement, and under any Other Contract for which no opportunity to cure will be granted, unless the City, in its sole discretion, elects to grant such an opportunity to cure. Such breach and default entitles the City to all remedies (including, without limitation, termination for default) under this Agreement, and under any Other Contract, at law and in equity. This provision amends any Other Contract and supersedes any inconsistent provision contained therein.

If Landlord intentionally violates this provision or Mayoral Executive Order No. 2011-4 prior to the closing of this Agreement, the City may elect to decline to close the transaction contemplated by this Agreement.

14.5 Failure to Maintain Eligibility to do Business with City. Failure by Landlord or any controlling person (as defined in Section 1-23-010 of the Municipal Code of Chicago) thereof to maintain eligibility to do business with the City as required by Section 1-23-030 of the Municipal Code of Chicago shall be grounds for termination of this Agreement and the transactions contemplated thereby. Landlord shall at all times comply with Section 2-154-020 of the Municipal Code of Chicago.

14.6 Cooperation with Inspector General and Legislative Inspector General. It is the duty of every officer, employee, department, agency, contractor, subcontractor, user of real property and licensee of the City, and every applicant for certification of eligibility for a City contract or program, to cooperate with the City's Legislative. Inspector General and with the City's Inspector General in any investigation or hearing undertaken pursuant to Chapters 2-55 and 2-56, respectively, of the Municipal Code of Chicago. Landlord understands and will abide by all provisions of Chapters 2-55 and 2-56 of the Municipal Code of Chicago.

14.7 2014 Hiring Plan Prohibitions.

1. The Tenant is subject to the June 16, 2014 "City of Chicago Hiring Plan", as amended (the "2014 City Hiring Plan") entered in Shakman v. Democratic Organization of Cook County, Case No 69 C 2145 (United States District Court for the Northern District of Illinois). Among other things, the 2014 City Hiring Plan prohibits the Tenant from hiring persons as governmental employees in non-exempt positions on the basis of political reasons or factors.

2. Landlord is aware that Tenant policy prohibits Tenant employees from directing any individual to apply for a position with Landlord, either as an employee or as a subcontractor, and from directing Landlord to hire any individual as an employee or as a subcontractor. Accordingly, Landlord must follow its own hiring and contracting procedures without being influenced by Tenant or Tenant employees. Any and all personnel provided by Landlord under this Lease are employees or subcontractors of Landlord, not employees of the City of Chicago. This Lease is not intended to and does not constitute, create, give rise to or otherwise recognize an employer-employee relationship of any kind between the Tenant and any personnel provided by Landlord.

3. Landlord will not condition, base, or knowingly prejudice or affect any term or aspect to the employment of any personnel provided under this Lease, or offer employment to any individual to provide services under this Lease, based upon or because of any political reason or factor, including, without limitation, any individual's political affiliation, membership in a political organization or party, political support or activity, political financial contributions, promises of such political support,

activity or financial contributions, or such individual's political sponsorship or recommendation. For purposes of this Lease, a political organization or party is an identifiable group or entity that has as its primary purpose the support of or opposition to candidates for elected public office. Individual political activities are the activities of individual persons in support of or in opposition to political organizations or parties or candidates for elected public office.

4. In the event of any communication to Landlord by a Tenant employee or Tenant official in violation of paragraph 2 above, or advocating a violation of paragraph 3 above, Landlord will, as soon as is reasonably practicable, report such communication to the Hiring Oversight Section of the Tenant's Office of the Inspector General ("OIG Hiring Oversight"), and also to the head of the relevant Tenant department utilizing services provided under this Lease. Landlord will also cooperate with any inquiries by OIG Hiring Oversight.

Exhibits to Lease

The following is list of common attachments to a City of Chicago lease:

Exhibit 1: Depiction of Premises

Exhibit 2: Floor Plan of Build-Out

Exhibit 3: Land Trust Parcel

Exhibit 4: Payment Schedules

Exhibit 5: Facility Improvements by Landlord

Exhibit 6: Economic Disclosure Statement and Affidavit Appendix A to Economic Disclosure Statement: Familial Relationships to elected City Officials and Department Heads. Appendix B to Economic Disclosure Statement: Building Scofflaw/Problem Landlord Certification.

CHAPTER SUMMARY

This chapter reviewed the following items related to government real estate leases:

- US federal government leases.
- State government leases.
- Local government leases.

NOTES

[1] *PBS Leasing Desk Guide,* 3-1, http://www.gsa.gov/graphics/pbs/LDG_Ch_3-Simplified_Lease_Acquisition_5-31-11_508.pdf.

[2] *PBS Leasing Desk Guide*, 4-1,"Streamlined Lease," http://www.gsa.gov/portal/mediaId/180555/fileName/LAC-2013-02.

[3] FSH 6409.12, *Leasing Officers' Handbook*, p. 3, section 31.11.

[4] FSH 6409.12, *Leasing Officers' Handbook*, p. 3, section 31.14.

[5] The USPS is currently looking at updating its standardized lease, which may begin use sometime 2017.

[6] http://www.dgs.ca.gov/resd/Programs/LeasingandPlanning/NewLease/LeaseRequirements.aspx.

[7] http://www.dgs.ca.gov/resd/Programs/LeasingandPlanning/NewLease/LeaseRequirements.aspx.

[8] Most of the exhibit information is taken from the CA DGS website, http://www.dgs.ca.gov/resd/Programs/LeasingandPlanning/NewLease/LeaseRequirements.aspx.

Flamingo, Chicago Federal Plaza

CHAPTER FOUR:

THE FEDERAL REQUEST FOR LEASE PROPOSAL REVIEW

IN THIS CHAPTER

1. **RLP Process Review**
2. **Review of GSA RLP Document**

The request for lease proposal (RLP) is one of the most important documents in government real estate leasing. The RLP document, also known as the request for proposals (RFP), is the culmination of the tenant agency's lease requirements, legal requirements, budget constraints, timelines, and terms. The RLP documents should ultimately answer the who, what, why, and when of the tenant agency's lease requirements.

Unlike private-sector real estate leasing, government real estate leasing is tasked with ensuring the tenant agency's specific lease rules, regulations, and requirements are integrated into the RLP documents that are then provided to the property owners for them to make offers on. The RLP document is typically sent to a property owner after the GLC completes the market tour and the offered property is deemed acceptable for a property owner to propose a lease to the tenant agency. Some government agencies skip the market tour altogether and have property owners submit the completed RLP documents without the government agency first visiting the offered property. Almost all federal agencies and most states will have property owners complete some type of RLP document before proceeding with negotiations and ultimately a lease is award by the GLC. This chapter will review (1) the common elements of an RLP proposal with (2) a review of the US GSA's real estate RLP document, the R100, which is currently used for most of the US GSA's real estate lease transactions with the private sector.

It is important to remember that not all government agencies share their RLP requirements with property owners and that not all RLP documents are the same for every agency at a specific level of government. In instances where the government agency doesn't share its RLP requirements with the property owner, it is important for the property owner to have a thorough understanding of what the tenant agency requirements are before signing a lease.

The RLP document itself can take many forms, from a single-page document that has a simple description of what the tenant agency requires to a complex document package that includes documents that must be signed and initialed by a property owner before negotiations with the GLC can begin. A majority of government lease RLP documents will have property owners complete documentation that will work to prescreen property owners to ensure that property owners can provide both the information required for the lease requirements and to give the government tenant, if they receive multiple RLP responses, an idea of what the market interest is for the RLP requirements.

Government agencies that do not use a formal public RLP process with a property owner will most likely have a truncated internal RLP process by which the GLC is tasked to actively select properties that fit the tenant agency's lease criteria without the property owner undergoing an extensive RLP process. The key to success in these situations is for the GLC and the property owner to have a clear understanding of what the tenant agency's specific rules, regulations, and requirements are before signing the lease. A simple attachment to the lease with these items can help bridge the gap between having no RLP documents versus having a lengthy RLP document process that both the GLC and the property owner may be seeking to avoid.

When a property owner reviews an RLP document for the first time there are several things to look for:

1. Look to see that the RLP document is properly addressed to whom it's supposed to go to along with the correct address of the offered property, along with the date for when the RLP submittal is due from the property owner to the GLC.
2. Check to see that the documents referenced in the RLP package are actually included in the RLP document. It's becoming more common for government agencies to include documents by reference only or with a reference to a document that is online.
3. Prioritize in order of importance those items that need to be completed for the RLP to be 100% complete by the RLP submittal due date. If there is a concern that the work required to complete the RLP submittal items by the RLP submittal due date will not been done in time, it is best to not delay in requesting that the GLC extend the RLP submittal due date, if possible.
4. After reviewing the first three items listed above, property owners should reflect on what it is the RLP documents are requiring the property owner to complete. Are the RLP documents written in what seems to be an overly complex fashion with a short RLP submittal timeframe? Or, ideally, are the RLP documents written in a way that is easy to understand with an RLP submittal time frame that seems realistic and doable? The answer to either of these questions will often set the tempo and mood for the rest of the RLP transaction process. There are times when an RLP package that is sent by the GLC to a property owner will appear to be poorly written and awkwardly formatted, with outdated forms that make RLP documents package appear incomplete. In instances where this is the case it is often due to formatting by the GLC and not an attempt to discourage property owners from submitting their properties for the RLP submittal.
5. Most RLPs will make circular references within the RLP and to the presumptive lease document, whether or not it is included in the RLP documents package. These references may be clearly stated or indirect in that an RLP section discusses specific items in the RLP document, with the lease document having a similar section that may be more or less defined on that same topic. Conversely, there may be statements or sections in the RLP that are not included in the lease, but still need to be negotiated or discussed with the GLC. Always double-check big-ticket items that are referenced in the RLP against similar items in the lease. An RLP is usually not the document that the property owner will be bound to; it's the lease

and the language within its four corners that matters. However, it's a good practice to keep a copy of the final RLP documents handy in case they are needed for reference purposes at some later date.

6. When reviewing the RLP for the first time, it can help to contact the GLC to ask for direction on how to best proceed. The GLC is often the same person who has compiled the RLP documents, so he or she will be a good source to discuss how the RLP documents should be completed, priorities of importance to the tenant agency, timelines, etc.

Using these six items as a primer to get started on the RLP review process will help considerably. The end result, or rather the successful conclusion to any RLP process for a property owner is to have completed the RLP so that the property owner wins the lease award with—*and this is more important than winning the lease award—the property owner having correctly priced the tenant agency lease requirements into their RLP offer.*

US GSA REQUEST FOR LEASE PROPOSALS (RLP) FORMAT

The government agency that offers the best example of the RLP document process is the US GSA. This chapter will review the US GSA RLP R100 document in detail. The US GSA RLP document is well written and this chapter review can be used as a guide when reviewing other government real estate lease RLP documents, whether for other federal agencies or state or local government tenants.

Keep in mind when reviewing any RLP document that most often the RLP document and the lease document are considered separate documents. Occasionally a government real estate RLP may include a lease in the RLP documents for reference purposes only or to be signed by the property owner and fully executed by the GLC at the completion of negotiations. In addition to the sample lease included in the RLP documents, there will typically be other documents that the GLC will want the property owner to complete as part of the RLP submittal process that will not become part of the final lease documents.

The following is a list of the various documents that are typically included in the US GSA RLP document package with reference to whether these documents will be included in the final lease document.

Exhibit 4.0

US GSA RLP Document Overview for the R100 RLP Document Package

DOCUMENT NAME	DOCUMENT TYPE	COMMENTS
Lease No. GS-XP-LX (Form L100)	Lease	This lease will generally be used at lease award.
Agency Requirements	Lease	Contains information for the tenant agency's specific build-out requirements.
Security Requirements for Level X	Lease	Contains additional information for any tenant agency TI and shell build-out security requirements.
GSA Form 3516, Solicitation Provisions	RLP	Outlines the provisions that control the RLP process.
GSA Form 3517B, General Clauses	Lease	Outlines the clauses that control the lease.
Proposal to Lease Space (GSA Form 1364)	RLP	Form for the offered lease rental rates and additional information as needed.
GSA Form 1217, Lessor's Annual Cost Statement	RLP	Form for the property owner's operating costs for both the property and the tenant agency's leased space.
GSA Form 3518	Lease	Contains the information for the property owner to certify themselves as an RLP offeror.
GSA Form 12000 for Prelease Fire Protection and Life Safety Evaluation for an Office Building	Lease	Property information form for the property's fire life safety information.
Security Unit Price List	Lease	Form used for security related items to be paid for by the tenant agency, the property owner or both.
Seismic Offer Forms	Lease	Forms to certify that the building meets the seismic requirements or exemptions as stated in the lease.

The main document of the RLP documents package is the GSA Form R100. The R100 document is generally divided into the following five sections:

- Section 1: Statement of Requirements
- Section 2: Eligibility and Preferences for Award
- Section 3: How to Offer
- Section 4: Method of Award
- Section 5: Additional Terms and Conditions

Understanding how these sections are incorporated into the R100 RLP document is significant to understanding how each section will not only impact whether a property owner will be successful in winning the proposal to lease space with the tenant agency but also will ensure the lease transaction doesn't fail to be successful after it's fully executed. The following is a list of the sections of the RLP R100 document in greater detail:

Section 1: Statement of Requirements

- Amount and type of space.
- Lease term and occupancy date.
- Area of consideration.
- List of RLP documents.
- Security requirements.
- Broker commission information.

Section 2: Eligibility and Preference for Award

- Layout efficiency.
- Flood plains.
- Seismic information.
- Historic preference.
- Accessibility and fire life safety.
- Energy Star.

Section 3: How to Offer

- Receipt of lease proposals.
- Pricing terms.
- Operating leases.
- Prospectus leases.
- Additional submittals.
- Tenant improvement information.
- Security costs.
- LEED.
- Operating costs.
- Separating utilities.

Section 4: Method of Award

- Negotiations.
- HUBZone.
- Award based on price.
- Other award factors.
- Present value price evaluation.
- Award.

Section 5: Additional Terms and Conditions

- Additional tenant agency requirements.
- Additional award and eligibility requirements.

The rest of this chapter will be a review the US GSA RLP document, the R100, in detail. The US GSA's lease document, the L100, which is sometimes included in the RLP document for reference and review by the property owner, will be reviewed in detail in Volume II. The following review includes a synopsis for most sections and paragraphs of the R100 document with section references to the L100 in Volume II as applicable. There are a handful of R100 sections that have been deleted from this chapter due only to their applicability to the review in this chapter.

As always, a property owner should, before proceeding with any response or submission to a government RLP document and lease, review these documents with a knowledgeable attorney and the designated GLC for the lease transaction.

US GSA FORM R100 (03/16) REVIEW

US GSA FORM R100 TABLE OF CONTENTS

GLOBAL RLP

Index Synopsis: The RLP index should be reviewed along with the US GSA Form L100 index if it is included in the RLP documents package. This review should be used as an overview to see what items are in the documents and to confirm if there are any inconsistencies or items deleted in one document but remaining in the other; for example LEED may be required in the R100 document but deleted from the L100 document.

SECTION 1 STATEMENT OF REQUIREMENTS

1.01 GENERAL INFORMATION (SEP 2015)

A. This Request for Lease Proposals (RLP) sets forth instructions and requirements for proposals for a Lease described in the RLP documents. The Government will evaluate proposals conforming to the RLP requirements in accordance with the Method of Award set forth below to select an Offeror for award. The Government will award the Lease to the selected Offeror, subject to the conditions below.

A. This Request for Lease Proposals (RLP) sets forth instructions and requirements for proposals for a Succeeding or Superseding Lease where the Government is currently in occupancy and possession of the leased Premises. Unless otherwise noted, the Government will accept the leased Premises in their current condition, with the exceptions outlined in the RLP documents. The Government will evaluate the proposal conforming to the RLP requirements in accordance with the Method of Award set forth below. The Government will award the Lease subject to the conditions below.

B. Included in the RLP documents is a lease form (GSA Form L100) setting forth the lease term and other terms and conditions of the Lease contemplated by this RLP and a GSA Proposal to Lease

Space (GSA Form 1364) on which Offeror shall submit its offered rent and other price data, together with required information and submissions. The Lease paragraph titled "Definitions and General Terms" shall apply to the terms of this RLP.

C. Do not attempt to complete the lease form (GSA Form L100). Upon selection for award, GSA will transcribe the successful Offeror's final offered rent and other price data included on the GSA Form 1364 into the lease form, and transmit the completed Lease, including any appropriate attachments, to the successful Offeror for execution. Neither the RLP nor any other part of an Offeror's proposal shall be part of the Lease except to the extent expressly incorporated therein. The Offeror should review the completed Lease for accuracy and consistency with his or her proposal, sign and date the first page, initial each subsequent page of the Lease, and return it to the Lease Contracting Officer (LCO).

D. The Offeror's executed Lease shall constitute a firm offer. No Lease shall be formed until the LCO executes the Lease and delivers a signed copy to the Offeror.

Section 1.01 Synopsis: While there are several important items in this section to consider, specific attention should be paid to paragraph D of this section. Paragraph A should alert the property owner to the intentions of the GLC while B & C are used to direct the property owner on how to complete the different forms included in the RLP documents package. Property owners should review the L100 if it is included with the RLP document. An attorney should review the RLP document and all documents related to the offer, as well as any lease awarded to the property owner before signing a lease with the GLC.

1.02 AMOUNT AND TYPE OF SPACE, LEASE TERM, AND OCCUPANCY DATE (SEP 2015)

A. The Government is seeking a minimum of _____ to a maximum of _____ of American National Standards Institute/Building Owners and Managers Association (ANSI/BOMA) Office Area (ABOA) square feet (SF) of contiguous space within the Area of Consideration set forth below. See Section 2 of the Lease for applicable ANSI/BOMA standards.

A. The Government is seeking ____ of American National Standards Institute/Building Owners and Managers Association (ANSI/BOMA) for Office Area (ABOA) square feet (SF) of Space within the existing location. See Section 2 of the Lease for applicable ANSI/BOMA standards.

Section 1.02.A. Synopsis: These two paragraphs detail the square footage required for the tenant agency. If the property submitted for offer can't meet the square footage required for this lease requirement then the GLC should be contacted to discuss any next steps. As noted, this specific RLP is following the ANSI/BOMA measurement method for measuring the leased space. It is common for different government agencies to use different space measurement methods and different language describing the measurement of the leased space.

B. The Space shall be located in a modern quality Building of sound and substantial construction with a facade of stone, marble, brick, stainless steel, aluminum or other permanent materials in good condition and acceptable to the LCO. If not a new Building, the Space offered shall be in a Building that has undergone, or will complete by occupancy, modernization or adaptive reuse for the Space with modern conveniences.

C. The Government requires _____ structured/inside parking spaces and _____ surface/outside parking spaces, reserved for the exclusive use of the Government. These spaces must be secured and lit in accordance with the Security Requirements set forth in the Lease. Offeror shall include the cost of this parking as part of the rental consideration.

D. As part of the rental consideration, the Government may require use of part of the Building roof for the installation of antenna(s). If antenna space is required, specifications regarding the type of antenna(s) and mounting requirements are included in the agency requirements information provided with this RLP.

E. Approximately _____ ABOA SF will be used for the operation of a vending facility under the provisions of the Randolph-Sheppard Act (20 USC 107 et seq.). The Government will control the number, kind, and locations of vending facilities and will control and receive income from all automatic vending machines. Offeror shall provide necessary utilities and make related alterations. The cost of the improvements is part of Tenant Improvement (TI) costs. The Government will not compete with other facilities having exclusive rights in the Building. The Offeror shall advise the Government if such rights exist.

E. The Government may provide vending machines within the Government's leased area under the provisions of the Randolph-Sheppard Act (20 USC 107 et. seq.). If the Government chooses to provide vending facilities, the Government will control the number, kind, and locations of vending facilities and will control and receive income from all automatic vending machines. Offeror shall provide necessary utilities and make related alterations. The cost of the improvements is part of Tenant Improvement (TI) costs. The Government will not compete with other facilities having exclusive rights in the Building. The Offeror shall advise the Government if such rights exist.

F. The lease term shall be _____ Years, _____ Years Firm, with Government termination rights, in whole or in part, effective at any time after the Firm Term of the Lease by providing not less than days' prior written notice.

G. The Lease Term Commencement Date will be on or about______, or upon acceptance of the Space, whichever is later.

Section 1.02.F.-G. Synopsis: These paragraphs cover the lease term, termination rights and rent commencement dates. It is important to understand the firm and non-firm term periods thoroughly. The termination right in this paragraph allows the GLC, with proper notice, to terminate the lease at any time after the firm term, which is different than an option to renew the lease after the firm term. The importance of these paragraphs can be overlooked by property owners failing to recognize there is a potential for 9-month to 2-year project design and tenant improvement build-out schedule from the time the lease is signed to when the space build-out is completed and accepted by the GLC. A good place to start the review of the project schedule is to review the "Schedule for Completion of Space" which can be found in the L100 lease document. The property owner needs to work with the GLC to determine a realistic schedule for the period starting from the initial offer, up to the final offer, award, design intent, construction start up to acceptance of the space and payment of rents by the GLC.

1.03 AREA OF CONSIDERATION (JUN 2012)

The Government requests Space in an area bounded as follows:

North _____

South _____

East _____

West _____

Buildings that have frontage on the boundary streets are deemed to be within the delineated Area of Consideration.

Section 1.03 Synopsis: The property owner should double-check that the offered property is within the area of consideration described in this section. If the property is not within the area of consideration, contact the GLC to discuss any next steps.

1.04 NEIGHBORHOOD, PARKING, LOCATION AMENITIES, AND PUBLIC TRANSPORTATION (DEC 2015)

A. Neighborhood and Parking: Inside City Center:

Space shall be located in a prime commercial office district with attractive, prestigious, and professional surroundings with a prevalence of modern design and/or tasteful rehabilitation in modern use. Streets and public sidewalks shall be well maintained. The parking-to-square-foot ratio available on-site shall at least meet current local code requirements, or in the absence of a local code requirement, on-site parking shall be available at a ratio of one (1) space for every _____ RSF of Space.

B. Neighborhood and Parking: Outside City Center:

Space shall be located 1) in an office, research, technology, or business park that is modern in design with a campus-like atmosphere, or, 2) on an attractively landscaped site containing one or more modern office Buildings that are professional and prestigious in appearance with the surrounding development well maintained and in consonance with a professional image. The parking-to-square-foot ratio available on-site shall at least meet current local code requirements, or, in the absence of a local code requirement, on-site parking shall be available at a ratio of one (1) space for every _____ RSF of Space.

C. Walkability and Amenities:

1. Employee and visitor entrances of the Building must be connected to public sidewalks by continuous, accessible sidewalks.

2. A variety of employee services, such as restaurants, retail shops, cleaners, and banks, shall be located within the immediate vicinity of the Building. The primary functional entrance of the Building shall be within safely accessible, walkable _____ foot distance of at least _____ instances of amenities, two of which must be inexpensive or moderately priced fast-food or eat-in restaurants. The remaining _____ instances must fall within at least _____ Categories shown below:

Diverse Use Category	Uses
Food Retail	Supermarket, Other food store with produce
Community-Serving Retail	Clothing store or department store selling clothes, Convenience store, Farmer's market, Hardware store, Pharmacy, Other retail
Services	Bank, Gym, Health club, Exercise studio, Hair care, Laundry, Dry cleaner, Restaurant, Café, Diner (excluding establishments with only drive-throughs)
Civic and Community Facilities	Adult or senior care (licensed), Child care (licensed), Community or recreation center, Cultural arts facility (museum, performing arts), Educational facility (including K–12 school, university, adult education center, vocational school, community college), Family entertainment venue (theater, sports), Government office that serves public on-site, Place of worship, Medical clinic or office that treats patients, Police or fire station, Post office, Public library, Public park, Social services center.

To be considered, amenities must be accessible from the Building by continuous sidewalks, walkways, or pedestrian crosswalks. Amenities must be existing or the Offeror must demonstrate to the Government's reasonable satisfaction that such amenities will exist by the Government's required occupancy date.

D. Transit Accessibility:

A subway, light rail, or bus rapid transit stop shall be located within the immediate vicinity of the Building, but generally not exceeding a safely accessible, walkable 2,640 feet from the principal functional entrance of the building, as determined by the LCO.

D. Transit Accessibility:

Stops for _____ or more public bus or streetcar lines usable by tenant occupants and their customers shall be located within the immediate vicinity of the Building, but generally not exceeding a safely accessible, walkable _____ from the principal functional entrance of the Building, as feet determined by the LCO. Stops for commuter bus service do not meet this requirement. Combined, the bus or streetcar stops must provide at least _____ trips per weekday or trip headways (time between each vehicle) of no less than _____ minutes during business hours. Qualifying transit routes must have paired route service (service in opposite directions during all posted service times) during business hours. Only trips in one direction are counted towards the threshold. If a qualifying transit route has multiple stops within the required walking distance, only trips from _____ stop are counted towards the threshold. Transit service must be existing or the Offeror must demonstrate to the Government's reasonable satisfaction that such transit service will exist by the Government's required occupancy date.

D. Transit Accessibility:

A commuter rail station shall be located within the immediate vicinity of the Building, but generally not exceeding a safely accessible, walkable _____ from the principal functional entrance of the Building, as determined by the LCO. The station must provide paired route service (service in opposite directions during all posted service times) during business hours, and provide at least _____ trips per weekday. Only trips in one direction are counted towards the threshold.

Section 1.04 Synopsis: Confirm the offered property can meet the parking and area amenities requirements of this section. While these items may seem like minor requirements, the GLC can and may come back to the property owner after the lease is signed to seek verification that these items have been met per the requirements stated in the lease. If there are any questions regarding requirements the property must meet for this section, then contact the GLC for clarification. Make sure to get a written response from the GLC on any clarifications or exceptions taken by the property owner in this section. See also section 3.06.P.

1.05 LIST OF RLP DOCUMENTS (SEP 2015)

The following documents are attached to and included as part of this RLP package:

DOCUMENT NAME	NO. OF PAGES	EXHIBIT
Lease No. _____(Form L100)		
Agency's Requirements		
Security Requirements for Level _____		
GSA Form 3516, Solicitation Provisions		
GSA Form 3517B, General Clauses		
Proposal to Lease Space (GSA Form 1364)		
GSA Form 1217, Lessor's Annual Cost Statement		
GSA Form 3518-SAM, Addendum to System for Award Management (SAM) Representations and Certifications (Acquisitions of Leasehold Interests in Real Property)		
GSA Form 12000 for Prelease Fire Protection and Life Safety Evaluation for an Office Building (Part A or Part B) (See Section 3 for applicable requirements)		
Security Unit Price List [FOR FSL I AND II ONLY]		
Seismic Offer Forms [FOR SEISMIC AREAS YELLOW AND RED ONLY]		

Section 1.05 Synopsis: Review the documents in this section, if need be, with the GLC to confirm that the RLP document package includes the documents referenced in the RLP document list in this section. Discuss with the GLC what is required for the forms included in the list along with those documents that may not be applicable to the property being offered as part of the RLP. See also L100 section 1.07 in Volume II.

1.06 AMENDMENTS TO THE RLP (JUN 2012)

This RLP may be amended by notice from the LCO. Amendments may modify the terms of this RLP, or the terms, conditions, and requirements of the Lease contemplated by the RLP.

Section 1.06 Synopsis: Keep track of all amendments issued during the RLP transaction process. These amendments should be prominently referenced in the final lease documents if they modify lease terms, requirements and conditions.

1.07 LEASE DESCRIPTION (SEP 2015)

A. Offeror shall examine the Lease form included in the RLP documents to understand the Government's and the Lessor's respective rights and responsibilities under the contemplated Lease.

B. The Lease contemplated by this RLP includes:

1. The term of the Lease, and renewal option, if any.

2. Terms and Conditions of the Lease, including Definitions, Standards, and Formulas applicable to the Lease and this RLP.

3. Building Shell standards and requirements.

4. Information concerning the tenant agency's buildout requirements, to be supplemented after award.

5. Security Requirements.

6. A description of all services to be provided by the Lessor.

C. Should the Offeror be awarded the Lease, the terms of the Lease shall be binding upon the Lessor without regard to any statements contained in this RLP.

D. The Lease contemplated by this RLP is a fully serviced Lease. Rent shall be based upon a proposed rental rate per Rentable Square Foot (RSF), limited by the offered rate and the maximum ABOA SF solicited under this RLP. Although certain Tenant Improvement (TI) requirements information is provided with this RLP and will be incorporated into the Lease, the TIs to be delivered by the Lessor will be based on the final design to be developed after award of the Lease, which reflects the Agency's full requirements. The Lessor shall design and build the TIs and will be compensated for TI costs, together with design and project management fees to be set under the Lease. Although the TI requirements will not be developed fully until after award, Offerors shall provide the allowance stated in the Tenant Improvement Allowance paragraph of the Lease. Offerors are encouraged to consider the use of existing fit-out and other improvements to minimize waste. However, any existing improvements must be deemed equivalent to Lease requirements for new construction, and Offerors are cautioned to consider those requirements before assuming efficiencies in its TI costs resulting from use of existing improvements.

Unless the Government prepares Design Intent Drawings (DIDs), after award the Lessor must prepare DIDs for the leased Space conforming to the lease requirements and other Government-supplied information related to the client agency's interior build-out requirements. The Government will have the opportunity to review the Lessor's DIDs to determine that the Lessor's design meets the requirements of the Lease. Only after the Government approves the DIDs and a final price for TIs is negotiated will the Lessor be released to proceed with buildout. The Lease also provides that the Government may modify the TI requirements, subject to the Lessor's right to receive compensation for such changes.

D. The Lease contemplated by this RLP is a fully serviced, turnkey Lease with rent that covers all Lessor costs, including all shell upgrades, TIs, operating costs, real estate taxes, and security upgrades. Rent shall be based upon a proposed rental rate per Rentable Square Foot (RSF), limited by the offered rate and the maximum ABOA SF solicited under this RLP. The Tenant Improvements to be delivered by the Lessor shall be based upon information provided with this RLP and Lease, including Agency Specific Requirements. The Lessor shall be required to design and build the TIs and will be compensated for the TI costs based upon turnkey pricing established under the Lease. Offerors are encouraged to consider the use of existing fit-out and other improvements to minimize waste. However, any existing improvements must be deemed equivalent to Lease requirements for new construction, and Offerors are cautioned to consider those requirements before assuming efficiencies in its TI costs resulting from use of existing improvements.

After award, the Lessor must prepare Design Intent Drawings (DIDs) for the leased Space conforming to the Agency Specific Requirements. The Government will have the opportunity to review the Lessor's DID's to determine that the Lessor's design meets the requirements of the Lease. Only after the Government approves the DIDs will the Lessor be released to proceed with buildout. The Lease also provides that the Government may modify the TI requirements, subject to the Lessor's right to receive compensation for such changes.

E. The security pricing process is described in a separate paragraph.

F. Upon completion and acceptance of the leased Space, the Space will be measured for establishing the actual annual rent, and the lease term shall commence. During the term of the Lease, rent will be adjusted for changes to the Lessor's operating costs and real estate taxes, pursuant to paragraphs set forth in Section 2 of the Lease.

G. Offerors are advised that doing business with the Government carries special responsibilities with respect to sustainability, fire protection and life safety, and security, as well as other requirements not typically found in private commercial leases. These are set forth both in the lease form and in the GSA Form 3517B, which will be part of the Lease.

Section 1.07 Synopsis: This section details the steps the GLC expects the property owner to take from lease award up to the occupancy period of the lease term. The property owner and the property owner's attorney need to understand this section along with what the lease performance expectations are for both the tenant agency and the property owner.

1.08 RELATIONSHIP OF RLP BUILDING MINIMUM REQUIREMENTS AND LEASE OBLIGATIONS (JUN 2012)

The Lease establishes various requirements relating to the Building shell. Such requirements are not deemed TIs. Certain of these Building requirements are established as minimum requirements in this RLP. If the Lessor's Building does not meet the requirements at the time of award, the Lessor may still be awarded the Lease. However, as a condition of award, the Government will require Lessor to identify those Building improvements that will bring the Building into compliance with RLP requirements. Upon award of the Lease, completion of those Building improvements will become Lease obligations.

Section 1.08 Synopsis: If the offered property has requirement deficiencies that do not meet the minimum requirements as stated in the RLP and the lease, the GLC and the property owner should seek to have these deficiencies agreed to in writing, detailing how these deficiencies will be treated if the property owner is awarded the lease.

1.09 PRICING OF SECURITY REQUIREMENTS (SEP 2012)

A. This proposed Lease contains an attachment with the security requirements and obligations for the Building, which are based on the facility security level (FSL). The Federal Government determines the facility's FSL rating, which ranges from FSL I to FSL IV. The FSL is based on client agency mix, required size of space, number of employees, use of the space, location, configuration of the site and lot, and public access into and around the facility.

B. The security requirements attached to this Lease includes a list of security countermeasures that must be installed in the leased Space. The Offeror shall use the Security Unit Price List to provide the Government with itemized costs of these security countermeasures, and he or she shall amortize the cost of any Building Specific Amortized Capital (BSAC) into the rent.

B. The security requirements attached to this Lease includes a general list of countermeasures that may be installed in the leased Space as part of the Building Specific Amortized Capital (BSAC). The final list of security countermeasures will be determined during the design phase and identified in the design intent drawings and construction documents. After completing the construction documents, the Lessor shall submit a list of the itemized costs. Such costs shall be subject to negotiation.

C. There shall be no charge to the Government for any items that already exist in the offered Building or facility.

Section 1.09 Synopsis: The GLC and the property owner should have a clear understanding of how the tenant agency will pay for the BSAC costs listed in this section. Specifically discuss whether the BSAC costs will be a fixed cost to the property owner before the lease is signed; this scenario will usually obligate the property owner to a fixed cost without the property owner being able to negotiate the BSAC costs with the GLC after the design and general contractor bids on the BSAC costs are completed. These discussions and the decisions regarding how the BSAC costs will be paid by the GLC should be memorialized in writing before the lease is signed; this will allow both parties to readily recall their understanding of these costs when the tenant improvement pricing phase starts. See also section 3.08 in this chapter and L100 section 1.03.B. in Volume II.

1.10 SECURITY LEVEL DETERMINATION FOR FACILITY HOUSING OTHER FEDERAL TENANTS (APR 2011)

If an Offeror is offering Space in a facility currently housing a Federal agency, the security requirements of the facility may be increased and the Offeror may be required to adhere to a higher security standard than other Offerors competing for the same space requirement. If two or more Federal space requirements are being competed at the same time, an Offeror submitting on both or more space requirements may be subject to a higher security standard if the Offeror is determined to be the successful Offeror on more than one space requirement. It is incumbent upon the Offeror to prepare the Offeror's proposal accordingly.

Section 1.10 Synopsis: If the offered property meets the criteria listed in this section, it is best to check with the GLC to determine if the property meets an exemption from this section. Adherence to this section may increase the overall lease costs due to implementing higher security standards. The costs of adhering to this section are usually borne by the property owner so it is important that the property owner have a written understanding of what is expected from the GLC for the items in this section. Ideally any cost increases to comply section will be agreed to by both the GLC and the property owner before the lease is signed.

1.11 INSPECTION–RIGHT OF ENTRY (JUN 2012)

A. At any time and from time to time after receipt of an offer (until the same has been duly withdrawn or rejected), the agents, employees and contractors of the Government may, upon reasonable prior notice to Offeror, enter upon the offered Space or the Premises, and all other areas of the Building access to which is necessary to accomplish the purposes of entry, to determine the potential or actual compliance by the Offeror with the requirements of the RLP and its attachments, which purposes shall include, but not be limited to:

1. Inspecting, sampling, and analyzing of suspected asbestos-containing materials and air monitoring for asbestos fibers.

2. Inspecting the heating, ventilation and air conditioning system, maintenance records, and mechanical rooms for the offered Space or the Premises.

3. Inspecting for any leaks, spills, or other potentially hazardous conditions which may involve tenant exposure to hazardous or toxic substances.

4. Inspecting for any current or past hazardous waste operations, to ensure that appropriate actions were taken to alleviate any environmentally unsound activities in accordance with Federal, state, and local law.

B. Nothing in this paragraph shall be construed to create a Government duty to inspect for toxic materials or to impose a higher standard of care on the Government than on other lessees. The purpose of this paragraph is to promote the ease with which the Government may inspect the Building. Nothing in this paragraph shall act to relieve the Offeror of any duty to inspect or liability which might arise because of Offeror's failure to inspect for or correct a hazardous condition.

Section 1.11 Synopsis: While it is uncommon for a GLC to make multiple visits to a property being offered as part of the RLP submittal, the GLC is still reserving the right to do so in this section. It is a best practice for the property owner and the GLC to determine specifically what it is the GLC is looking to accomplish as part of their visit to the site along with the desired results of the visit by the GLC. Also, discuss with the GLC how to address property items considered to be harmful or hazardous. These items should be prominently disclosed to the GLC in the course of the RLP submittal process.

1.12 AUTHORIZED REPRESENTATIVES (JUN 2012)

With respect to all matters relating to this RLP, only the Government's LCO designated below shall have the authority to amend the RLP and award a Lease. The Government shall have the right to substitute its LCO by notice, without an express delegation by the prior LCO.

Lease LCO:

[Name]

[Mailing Address] [Office Phone] [Cell Phone] [Fax]

[Email Address]

As to all other matters, Offerors may contact the Alternate Government Contact designated below.

Alternate Government Contact:

[Name]

[Mailing Address] [Office Phone] [Cell Phone] [Fax]

[Email Address]

Section 1.12 Synopsis: Most RLP documents will indicate who the government lease contact ("GLC") is for the RLP transaction. Keep in mind that the GLC may also be the same point of contact on the lease after the lease is awarded and the tenant agency takes occupancy of the space. There may be additional points of contact on the RLP transaction if the GLC is utilizing the services of a private-sector real estate broker. If there are any questions on the GLC's role and authority in the lease transaction, it is fair to ask the GLC to provide in writing what their authorization is for conducting the lease transaction on behalf of the tenant agency. The property owner should also seek out the name of the person on the GLC's team who has authority to sign the lease on behalf of the tenant agency. Challenges may occur if the property owner is unaware of who has authority to negotiate on behalf of the tenant agency or if a GLC makes representations and promises on behalf of the tenant agency, but has no authority to do so.

1.13 BROKER COMMISSION AND COMMISSION CREDIT (SEP 2013)

A. For the purposes of this RLP, _____ (the Broker) is the authorized contractor real estate broker representing GSA. Offerors are advised that there is a potential for a dual agency situation to arise under this procurement, whereby the Broker may represent both GSA and another Offeror under this lease action. By submitting an offer, the Offeror acknowledges the potential for a dual agency situation. Should there be an actual dual agency, the Broker will notify all Offerors of the actual dual agency and request written acknowledgement statements from all Offerors. The Government expects the Lessor to pay a commission to the Broker. By submitting an offer, the Offeror agrees that if the Offeror is paying a commission or fee in connection with this Lease to a listing agent, an offering agent, or broker, property manager, developer, or any other agent or representative, then the Offeror will pay a commission to the Broker to which the Broker would ordinarily be entitled consistent with local business practices, as evidenced through a brokerage agreement between the Offeror and the Broker. The commission will be negotiated between the Offeror and the Broker and will be based on a Lease term not to exceed the Firm Term of the Lease contemplated by this RLP. Commissions will not be negotiated or collected on option periods or for Lease terms beyond the Firm Term of the Lease. As part of the offer, the Offeror shall disclose all commissions and/or fees to be paid by the Offeror including both the Offeror's agent(s), broker(s), property manager, developer or any other agent or representative and the Broker. The Offeror shall enter the commission amounts for its representative and the amount to GSA's Broker in blocks 31a and 31b respectively on GSA Form 1217, Lessors Annual Cost Statement. An executed commission agreement reflecting this agreement shall be submitted with the initial offer.

B. For the benefit of the Government, the Broker has agreed to forego a percentage of any commission that it is entitled to receive in connection with the contemplated Lease. This amount shall be specifically set forth at time of lease award. The resulting total dollar value of the foregone commission (the Commission Credit) shall be applied in equal monthly amounts against rental payments due and owing under the Lease. The rental amount payable shall be reduced by the Commission Credit at the commencement of the Lease, over the minimum number of months that will not exceed the monthly shell rental, until the Commission Credit has been fully recaptured. The parties agree to execute a Lease Amendment setting forth the full nature, extent, terms, and conditions of commissions paid to the Broker and the Commission Credit to be applied against the Government's rental payment obligations under the Lease. Commissions and/or credits shall be treated as confidential financial information and Offerors will refrain from public disclosure or using the information for any other purpose than that for which it was furnished without consent of the GSA LCO.

C. For purposes of price evaluation, the Commission Credit shall be treated as a deduction from the rent in accordance with the Method of Award. The amount of any commission paid to the Broker shall not be considered separately as part of this price evaluation since the value of the commission is included in the rental consideration.

Section 1.13 Synopsis: The RLP document should contain, or make available upon request, the GLC's broker's real estate commission agreement with a reference as to what the commission fees are, how the fees will be paid, and how the commission credit will be calculated if one is due to the tenant agency. If a property owner does not want to pay a commission to the GLC's broker, then it is important to discuss with the GLC what, if any, disadvantages there are for not paying a commission to the GLC broker. Also note under paragraph A of this section the potential for the GLC's real estate broker to be working as a dual agent whereby the GLC's real estate broker may be representing both the GLC and other property owners in the RLP transaction. See also L100 section 1.04 in Volume II.

SECTION 2 ELIGIBILITY AND PREFERENCES FOR AWARD

2.01 EFFICIENCY OF LAYOUT (AUG 2011)

A. In order to be acceptable for award, the offered Space must provide for an efficient layout as determined by the LCO.

B. To demonstrate potential for efficient layout, GSA may request the Offeror to provide a test fit layout at the Offeror's expense. The Government will advise the Offeror if the test fit layout demonstrates that the Government's requirement cannot be accommodated within the Space offered. The Offeror will have the option of increasing the ABOA square footage offered, if it does not exceed the maximum ABOA square footage in this RLP offer package. If the Offeror is already providing the maximum ABOA square footage and cannot house the Government's space requirements efficiently, then the Government will advise the Offeror that the offer is unacceptable.

Section 2.01 Synopsis: The property owner should complete a test fit, if possible, regardless of whether it is requested by the GLC. The test fit should occur before the lease is signed. The results of the test fit should be discussed with the GLC to confirm that both the square footage count and space configuration layout will meet the stated requirements of the lease. See also section 1.01 in Volume II.

2.02 FLOOD PLAINS (JUN 2012)

A Lease will not be awarded for any offered Property located within a 100-year floodplain unless the Government has determined that there is no practicable alternative. An Offeror may offer less than its entire site in order to exclude a portion of the site that falls within a floodplain, so long as the portion offered meets all the requirements of this RLP. If an Offeror intends that the offered Property that will become the Premises for purposes of this Lease will be something other than the entire site as recorded in tax or other property records the Offeror shall clearly demarcate the offered Property on its site plan/map submissions and shall propose an adjustment to property taxes on an appropriate pro rata basis. For such an offer, the LCO may, in his or her sole discretion, determine that the offered Property does not adequately avoid development in a 100-year floodplain.

Section 2.02 Synopsis: The property owner should confirm if the property submitted is located in a 100-year flood plain. If the property is located in a 100-year flood plain, it is best to contact the GLC to discuss how to proceed. This section as written does allow the GLC some flexibility to accept properties located in a flood plain.

2.03 SEISMIC SAFETY - MODERATE SEISMICITY (SEP 2012)

The Government intends to award a Lease to an Offeror of a Building that is in compliance with the Seismic Standards. If an offer is received which is in compliance with the Seismic Standards and the other requirements of this RLP, then other offers which do not comply with the Seismic Standards will not be considered. If none of the offers is in compliance with the Seismic Standards, the LCO will make the award to the Offeror whose offer meets the other requirements of this RLP and provides the best value to the Government, taking into account price, seismic safety and any other award factors specified in this RLP.

An offered Building will be considered to be in compliance with the Seismic Standards if it meets one of the following conditions:

1. The offer include a representation that the Building will have less than 10,000 ABOA SF of Space leased to the Federal Government upon commencement of the lease term (Seismic Form D).

2. The offer includes a Seismic Certificate certifying that the Building is a Benchmark Building (Seismic Form A).

3. The offer includes a Seismic Certificate based on a Tier I Evaluation showing that the Building meets the Seismic Standards (Seismic Form B). The submission must include the checklists and backup calculations from the Tier 1 Evaluation.

4. The offer includes a Seismic Certificate based on a Tier 2 or Tier 3 Evaluation showing that the Building complies with the Seismic Standards (Seismic Form B). If the certificate is based on a Tier 2 or Tier 3 Evaluation, the data, working papers, calculations and reports from the evaluation must be made available to the Government.

5. The offer includes a commitment to retrofit the Building to satisfy all of the Basic Safety Objective requirements of ASCE/SEI 41 (Seismic Form C, Part 1). If the Offeror proposes to retrofit the Building, the offer must include a Tier 1 report with all supporting documents, a narrative explaining the process and scope of retrofit, and a schedule for the seismic retrofit. The Offeror shall provide a construction schedule, concept design for the seismic upgrade, and supporting documents for the retrofit, including structural calculations, drawings, specifications, and geotechnical report to the Government for review and approval prior to award. The documentation must demonstrate the seismic retrofit will meet the seismic standards and be completed within the time frame required.

6. The offer includes a pre-award commitment to construct a new Building, using local building codes (Seismic Form C, Part 2).

The LCO may allow an Offeror to submit a Seismic Certificate after the deadline for final proposal revisions. However, the LCO is not obligated to delay award in order to enable an Offeror to submit a Seismic Certificate.

Definitions. For the purpose of this paragraph:

- "ASCE/SEI 31" means the American Society of Civil Engineers standard, Seismic Evaluation of Existing Buildings. You can purchase ASCE/SEI from ASCE at (800) 548-2723 or by visiting http://www.pubs.asce.org.
- "ASCE/SEI 41" means American Society of Civil Engineers standard, Seismic Rehabilitation of Existing Buildings. You can purchase ASCE/SEI from ASCE at (800) 548-2723 or by visiting http://www.pubs.asce.org.
- "Benchmark Building" means a building that was designed and built, or retrofitted, in accordance with the seismic provisions of the applicable codes specified in Section 1.3.1 of RP 8.
- "Engineer" means a professional engineer who is licensed in Civil or Structural Engineering and qualified in the structural design of buildings. They must be licensed in the state where the property is located.
- "RP 8" means "*Standards of Seismic Safety for Existing Federally Owned and Leased Buildings ICSSC Recommended Practice 8 (RP 8)*," issued by the Interagency Committee on Seismic Safety in Construction as ICSSC RP 8 and the National Institute of Standards and Technology as NIST GCR 11-917-12. RP 8 can be obtained from http://www.wbdg.org/ccb/nist/nist_gcr11_917_12.pdf.
- "Seismic Certificate" means a certificate executed and stamped by an Engineer on the appropriate Certificate of Seismic Compliance form included with this RLP together with any required attachments.
- "Seismic Standards" means the requirements of RP 8 Section 2.2 for Life Safety Performance Level in ASCE/SEI 31 or the Basic Safety Objective in ASCE/SEI 41, unless otherwise specified.
- "Tier 1 Evaluation" means an evaluation by an Engineer in accordance with Chapters 2.0 and 3.0 of ASCE/SEI 31. A Tier 1 Evaluation must include the appropriate Structural, Nonstructural and Geologic Site Hazards and Foundation Checklists.
- "Tier 2 Evaluation" means an evaluation by an Engineer in accordance with Chapter 4.0 of ASCE/SEI 31.
- "Tier 3 Evaluation" means an evaluation by an Engineer in accordance with Chapter 5.0 of ASCE/SEI 31.

2.04 SEISMIC SAFETY - HIGH SEISMICITY (SEP 2013)

A. The Government intends to award a Lease to an Offeror of a Building that is in compliance with the Seismic Standards. If an offer is received which is in compliance with the Seismic Standards and the other requirements of this RLP, then other offers which do not comply with the Seismic Standards must not be considered. If none of the offers is in compliance with the Standards, the

LCO will make the award to the Offeror whose offer meets the other requirements of this RLP and provides the best value to the Government, taking into account price, seismic safety and any other award factors specified in this RLP.

B. An offered Building will be considered to be in compliance with the Seismic Standards if it meets one of the following conditions:

1. The offer includes a representation that the Premises will be in a one-story Building of steel light frame or wood construction with less than 3,000 ABOA SF of space in the Building (Seismic Form D).

2. The offer includes a Seismic Certificate certifying that the Building is a Benchmark Building (Seismic Form A).

3. The offer includes a Seismic Certificate based on a Tier I Evaluation showing that the Building meets the Seismic Standards (Seismic Form B). The submission must include the checklists and backup calculations from the Tier 1 Evaluation.

4. The offer includes a Seismic Certificate based on a Tier 2 or Tier 3 Evaluation showing that the Building complies with the Seismic Standards (Seismic Form B). If the certificate is based on a Tier 2 or Tier 3 Evaluation, the data, working papers, calculations and reports from the evaluation must be made available to the Government.

5. The offer includes a commitment to retrofit the Building to satisfy all of the Basic Safety Objective requirements of ASCE/SEI 41 (Seismic Form C, Part 1). If the Offeror proposes to retrofit the Building, the offer must include a Tier 1 report with all supporting documents, a narrative explaining the process and scope of retrofit and a schedule for the seismic retrofit. The Offeror shall provide a construction schedule, concept design for the seismic upgrade and supporting documents for the retrofit, including structural calculations, drawings, specifications, and geotechnical report to the Government for review and approval prior to award. The documentation must demonstrate the seismic retrofit will meet the seismic standards and be completed within the time frame required.

6. The offer includes a pre-award commitment to construct a new Building, using local building codes (Seismic Form C, Part 2).

C. The LCO may allow an Offeror to submit a Seismic Certificate after the deadline for final proposal revisions. However, the LCO is not obligated to delay award in order to enable an Offeror to submit a Seismic Certificate.

Definitions. For the purpose of this paragraph:

- "ASCE/SEI 31" means the American Society of Civil Engineers standard, Seismic Evaluation of Existing Buildings. You can purchase ASCE/SEI from ASCE at (800) 548-2723 or by visiting http://www.pubs.asce.org.
- "ASCE/SEI 41" means American Society of Civil Engineers standard, Seismic Rehabilitation of Existing Buildings. You can purchase ASCE/SEI from ASCE at (800) 548-2723 or by visiting http://www.pubs.asce.org.

- "Benchmark Building" means a building that was designed and built, or retrofitted, in accordance with the seismic provisions of the applicable codes specified in Section 1.3.1 of RP 8.
- "Engineer" means a professional engineer who is licensed in Civil or Structural Engineering and qualified in the structural design of buildings. They must be licensed in the state where the property is located.
- "RP 8" means "*Standards of Seismic Safety for Existing Federally Owned and Leased Buildings ICSSC Recommended Practice 8 (RP 8)*," issued by the Interagency Committee on Seismic Safety in Construction as ICSSC RP 8 and the National Institute of Standards and Technology as NIST GCR 11-917-12. RP 8 can be obtained from http://www.wbdg.org/ccb/nist/nist_gcr11_917_12.pdf.
- "Seismic Certificate" means a certificate executed and stamped by an Engineer on the appropriate Certificate of Seismic Compliance form included with this RLP together with any required attachments.
- "Seismic Standards" means the requirements of RP 8 Section 2.2 for Life Safety Performance Level in ASCE/SEI 31 or the Basic Safety Objective in ASCE/SEI 41, unless otherwise specified.
- "Tier 1 Evaluation" means an evaluation by an Engineer in accordance with Chapters 2.0 and 3.0 of ASCE/SEI 31. A Tier 1 Evaluation must include the appropriate Structural,
- Nonstructural and Geologic Site Hazards and Foundation Checklists.
- "Tier 2 Evaluation" means an evaluation by an Engineer in accordance with Chapter 4.0 of ASCE/SEI 31.
- "Tier 3 Evaluation" means an evaluation by an Engineer in accordance with Chapter 5.0 of ASCE/SEI 31.

Section 2.03 & 2.04 Synopsis: Seismic safety is an important part of a government lease in an area with seismic activity. If the RLP package includes seismic safety forms, it is best to determine if the property needs to have a seismic evaluation or if the property meets any of the qualifications or exemptions for not completing a seismic evaluation. If it is deemed necessary, a property owner should consult with a seismic safety expert to determine what level of seismicity the property is located in, along with determining what seismic certifications the property needs. It is common for property owners to proceed with a seismic evaluation on a property when an exemption or waiver of the seismic certification can be applied for with the GLC. Ideally a property owner will discuss the seismic certification and evaluation options with an experienced GLC who can give the property owner proper direction before a property owner proceeds with a costly seismic study.

2.05 HISTORIC PREFERENCE (SEP 2013)

A. The Government will give preference to offers of Space in Historic Properties and/or Historic Districts following this hierarchy of consideration:

1. Historic Properties within Historic Districts.

2. Non-historic developed sites and non-historic undeveloped sites within Historic Districts.

3. Historic Properties outside of Historic Districts.

B. Definitions:

1. Determination of eligibility means a decision by the Department of the Interior that a district, site, Building, structure or object meets the National Register criteria for evaluation although the Property is not formally listed in the National Register (36 CFR 60.3(c)).

2. Historic District means a geographically definable area, urban or rural, possessing a significant concentration, linkage, or continuity of sites, Buildings, structures, or objects united by past events or aesthetically by plan or physical development. A district may also comprise individual elements separated geographically but linked by association or history (36 CFR 60.3(d)). The Historic District must be included in or be determined eligible for inclusion in the National Register of Historic Places (NRHP).

3. Historic Property means any prehistoric or Historic District, site, building, structure, or object included in or been determined eligible for inclusion in the NRHP maintained by the Secretary of the Interior (36 CFR 800.16(l)).

4. National Register of Historic Places means the National Register of districts, sites, buildings, structures and objects significant in American history, architecture, archeology, engineering and culture that the Secretary of the Interior is authorized to expand and maintain under the National Historic Preservation Act (36 CFR 60.1).

C. The offer of Space must meet the terms and conditions of this RLP package and its attachments. The LCO has discretion to accept alternatives to certain architectural characteristics and safety features defined elsewhere in this RLP package to maintain the historical integrity of an Historic Building, such as high ceilings and wooden floors, or to maintain the integrity of an Historic District, such as setbacks, floor-to-ceiling heights, and location and appearance of parking.

D. When award will be based on the lowest price technically acceptable source selection process, the Government will give a price evaluation preference, based on the total annual ABOA SF present value cost to the Government, to Historic Properties as follows:

1. First to suitable Historic Properties within Historic Districts, a 10 percent price preference.

2. If no suitable Historic Property within an Historic District is offered, or the 10 percent preference does not result in such property being the lowest price technically acceptable offer, the Government will give a 2.5 percent price preference to suitable non-historic developed or undeveloped sites within Historic Districts.

3. If no suitable, non-historic, developed, or undeveloped site within a Historic District is offered, or the 2.5 percent preference does not result in such property being the lowest price technically acceptable offer, the Government will give a 10 percent price preference to suitable Historic Properties outside of Historic Districts.

4. Finally, if no suitable Historic Property outside of Historic Districts is offered, no historic price preference will be given to any property offered.

E. When award will be based on the best value tradeoff source selection process, which permits tradeoffs among price and non- price factors, the Government will give a price evaluation preference, based on the total annual ABOA SF present value cost to the Government, to Historic Properties as follows:

1. First, to suitable Historic Properties within Historic Districts, a 10 percent price preference.

2. If no suitable Historic Property within a Historic District is offered or remains in the competition, the Government will give a 2.5 percent price preference to suitable non-historic developed or undeveloped sites within Historic Districts.

3. If no suitable, non-historic developed or undeveloped site within an Historic District is offered or remains in the competition, the Government will give a 10 percent price preference to suitable Historic Properties outside of Historic Districts.

4. Finally, if no suitable Historic Property outside of Historic Districts is offered, no historic price preference will be given to any property offered.

F. The Government will compute price evaluation preferences by reducing the price(s) of the Offerors qualifying for a price evaluation preference by the applicable percentage provided in this provision. The price evaluation preference will be used for price evaluation purposes only. The Government will award a Lease for the actual prices proposed by the successful Offeror and accepted by the Government.

G. To qualify for a price evaluation preference, Offeror must provide satisfactory documentation in their offer that their property qualifies as one of the following:

1. A Historic Property within a Historic District.

2. A non-historic developed or undeveloped site within a Historic District.

3. A Historic Property outside of a Historic District.

Section 2.05 Synopsis: Property owners should check whether a property is located in a Historic District, is designated as a Historic Property, or meets any of the price preference qualifications of this section. Property owners commonly do not confirm these items as part of the RLP submittal process. If a property meets any of the items in this section it is best to notify the GLC to discuss what submittal items are required for this section. It is very important when applying for a Historic Preference that the paperwork submitted for the preference is correctly submitted to the GLC with the submittal acknowledged in writing by the GLC to the property owner.

2.06 ASBESTOS (JUN 2012)

A. Government requests space with no asbestos-containing materials (ACM), or with ACM in a stable, solid matrix (e.g., asbestos flooring or asbestos cement panels), which is not damaged or subject to damage by routine operations. For purposes of this paragraph, "space" includes the 1) space offered for lease, 2) common building area, 3) ventilation systems and zones serving the space offered, and 4) the area above suspended ceilings and engineering space in the same ventilation zone as the space offered. If no offers are received for such space, the Government may consider space with thermal system insulation ACM (e.g., wrapped pipe or boiler lagging), which is not damaged or subject to damage by routine operations.

B. ACM is defined as any materials with a concentration of greater than 1 percent by dry weight of asbestos.

C. Space with ACM of any type or condition may be upgraded by the Offeror to meet conditions described in sub-paragraph A by abatement (removal, enclosure, encapsulation, or repair) of ACM not meeting those conditions. If any offer involving abatement of ACM is accepted by the Government, the successful Offeror will be required to successfully complete the abatement in accordance with OSHA, EPA, Department of Transportation (DOT), state, and local regulations and guidance prior to occupancy.

D. Management Plan. If space is offered which contains ACM, the Offeror shall submit an asbestos-related management plan for acceptance by the Government prior to lease award. This plan shall conform to EPA guidance.

Section 2.06 Synopsis: Any ACM materials present in the property needs to be prominently disclosed and discussed with the GLC. Any exceptions, remediation, exemptions, or waivers for the items in this section need to be in writing and included as part of both the RLP and lease documents as applicable. See also L100 section 6.13 in Volume II.

2.07 ACCESSIBILITY (SEP 2013)

The Lease contemplated by this RLP contains requirements for Accessibility. In order to be eligible for award, Offeror must either:

A. Verify in the Lease proposal that the Building, offered Space, and areas serving the offered Space meet the Lease accessibility requirements, or

B. Include as a specific obligation in its Lease proposal that improvements to bring the Building, offered Space, and areas serving the offered Space into compliance with Lease accessibility requirements will be completed prior to acceptance of the Space.

Section 2.07 Synopsis: While this section may not reference the Americans with Disabilities Act (ADA) or the Architectural Barriers Act Accessibility Standards (ABAAS) specifically, the GLC may require that both the leased property and the leased space meet the ADA and/or the ABAAS requirements. ABAAS can be stricter than some local building code accessibility requirements. The ABAAS standards, if applicable, should be discussed with the GLC prior to lease award to confirm if there are any costs to the property owner to be ABAAS compliant. In conjunction with the discussions with the GLC, it is best to have both the architect and general contractor review the property and the offered space to determine what accessibility changes need to be made along with the associated costs to make these changes. See also L100 section 3.21 in Volume II.

2.08 FIRE PROTECTION AND LIFE SAFETY (SEP 2013)

The Lease contemplated by this RLP contains Building requirements for Means of Egress, Automatic Fire Sprinkler System, and Fire Alarm System. In order to be eligible for award, Offeror must either:

A. Verify in the Lease proposal that the Building in which Space is offered meets the Means of Egress, Automatic Fire Sprinkler System, and Fire Alarm System requirements of the Lease, or

B. Include as a specific obligation in its Lease proposal that improvements to bring the Building into compliance with Lease requirements will be completed prior to acceptance of the Space.

Section 2.08 Synopsis: Discuss with the GLC what fire life safety improvements are needed for the GLC to accept the space. The property owner needs to determine what fire life safety upgrades or additions need to be added to the tenant improvement design of the space so as to accurately determine what the associated shell costs are for this item. Ideally this will be done before the lease is signed; at a minimum, property owners should set aside a budget for this item. It is common for property owners to incorrectly account for this cost item, which will cause an unanticipated increase in shell construction costs after the lease is signed. See also L100 sections 3.14 and 3.15 in Volume II.

2.09 ENERGY INDEPENDENCE AND SECURITY ACT (MAR 2016)

A. The Energy Independence and Security Act (EISA) establishes requirements for Government leases relating to energy efficiency standards and potential cost effective energy efficiency and conservation improvements.

B. Unless one of the statutory exceptions listed in sub-paragraph C below applies, GSA may award a lease for a Building only if the Building has earned the ENERGY STAR® label conferred by the U.S. Environmental Protection Agency (EPA) within the most recent year prior to the due date for final proposal revisions. The term "most recent year" means that the date of award of the ENERGY STAR® label by EPA must not be more than 1 year prior to the due date of final proposal revisions. For example, an ENERGY STAR® label awarded by EPA on October 1, 2010, is valid for all lease procurements where final proposal revisions are due on or before September 30, 2011. In lieu of the above, all new Buildings being specifically constructed for the Government must achieve an ENERGY STAR® label within 18 months after occupancy by the Government. In addition, Offerors of the following Buildings shall also have up to 18 months after occupancy by the Government, or as soon thereafter as the Building is eligible for Energy Star® consideration, to achieve an Energy

Star® label: 1) All existing Buildings that have had an Energy Star® label but are unable to obtain a label in the most recent year (i.e., within 12 months prior to the due date for final proposal revisions) because of insufficient occupancy, 2) Newly built Buildings that have used Energy® Star's Target Finder tool and either achieved a "Designed to Earn the Energy Star®" certification or received an unofficial score (in strict adherence to Target Finder's usage instructions, including the use of required energy modeling) of 75 or higher prior to the due date for final proposal revisions and who are unable to obtain a label in the most recent year because of insufficient occupancy, 3) An existing Building that is unable to obtain a label because of insufficient occupancy but that can produce an indication, through the use of energy modeling or past utility and occupancy data input into Energy Star's® Portfolio Manager tool or Target Finder, that it can receive an unofficial score of 75 or higher using all other requirements of Target Finder or Portfolio Manager, except for actual data from the most recent year. ENERGY STAR® tools and resources can be found at www.energystar.gov.

C. EISA allows a Federal agency to lease Space in a Building that does not have an ENERGY STAR® Label if:

1. No Space is offered in a Building with an ENERGY STAR® Label that meets RLP requirements, including locational needs,

2. The agency will remain in a Building it currently occupies,

3. The Lease will be in a Building of historical, architectural, or cultural significance listed or eligible to be listed on the National Register of Historic Places, or

4. The Lease is for 10,000 RSF or less.

D. If one or more of the statutory exceptions applies, and the offered Space is not in a Building that has earned the ENERGY STAR® Label within one year prior to the due date for final proposal revisions, Offerors are required to include in their lease proposal an agreement to renovate the Building for all energy efficiency and conservation improvements that it has determined would be cost effective over the Firm Term of the Lease, if any, prior to acceptance of the Space (or not later than one year after the Lease Award Date of a succeeding or superseding lease). Such improvements may consist of, but are not limited to, the following:

1. Heating, Ventilating, and Air Conditioning (HVAC) upgrades, including boilers, chillers, and Building Automation System (BAS)/Monitoring/Control System (EMCS).

2. Lighting Improvements.

3. Building Envelope Modifications.

NOTE: Additional information can be found at http://www.gsa.gov/leasing under "Green Leasing."

E. The term "cost effective" means an improvement that will result in substantial operational cost savings to the landlord by reducing electricity or fossil fuel consumption, water, or other utility costs. The term "operational cost savings" means a reduction in operational costs to the landlord through the application of Building improvements that achieve cost savings over the Firm Term of the Lease sufficient to pay the incremental additional costs of making the Building improvements.

F. Instructions for obtaining an ENERGY STAR® Label are provided at http://www.energystar.gov/buildings/facility-owners-and-managers/existing-buildings/earn-recognition/energy-star-certification (use "Portfolio Manager" to apply). ENERGY STAR® tools and resources can be found at www.energystar.gov. The ENERGY STAR® Building Upgrade Manual (http://www.energystar.gov/buildings/facility-owners-and-managers/existing-buildings/save-energy/comprehensive-approach/energy-star) and Building Upgrade Value Calculator (http://www.energystar.gov/buildings/tools-and-resources/building-upgrade-value-calculator) are tools which can be useful in considering energy efficiency and conservation improvements to Buildings.

G. If one or more of the statutory exceptions applies, and the offered Space is not in a Building that has earned the ENERGY STAR® Label within one year prior to the due date for final proposal revisions, the successful Offeror will be excused from performing any agreed-to energy efficiency and conservation renovations, and benchmarking with public disclosure (as provided in (I) below), if it obtains the ENERGY STAR® Label prior to the Government's acceptance of the Space (or not later than one year after the Lease Award Date for succeeding and superseding leases).

H. If no improvements are proposed, the Offeror must demonstrate to the Government using the ENERGY STAR® Online Tools why no energy efficiency and conservation improvements are cost effective. If such explanation is unreasonable, the offer may be rejected.

I. As described in Section 3 of the Lease, successful Offerors meeting one of the statutory exceptions above must agree to benchmark and publicly disclose the Building's current ENERGY STAR® score, using EPA's Portfolio Manager online software application. See the Lease for additional details.

J. All new Buildings being specifically constructed for the Government must achieve the ENERGY STAR® Label within 18 months after occupancy by the Government.

K. As part of the cost effective upgrades specified under sub-paragraph D above, existing lighting systems must be upgraded to meet or exceed the stated lighting specifications in the Lease unless, with respect to upgrades otherwise in excess of the minimum stated requirements, Offeror can demonstrate, using the Building Upgrade Value Calculator discussed above, that such additional upgrades are not cost effective over the Firm Term of the Lease.

Section 2.09 Synopsis: This section should be read carefully with the understanding that if the offered property does not meet one of the exemptions or exceptions listed in this section, then the GLC will require the property owner to comply with this section at some point after the lease is signed.

If no exemption or exception is taken here, the property owner should ensure that the general contractor and architect is aware that this item needs to be properly designed and accounted for in the project costs before the lease is signed. See also L100 section 3.16 in Volume II.

2.10 ENVIRONMENTAL CONSIDERATIONS (SEP 2013)

A. The Government requests space with no known hazardous conditions or recognized environmental conditions that would pose a health and safety risk or environmental liability to the Government.

B. Upon request by the Government, Offeror must provide all known previous use of the Building.

C. Offeror must indicate in its written offer any known hazardous conditions or environmental releases with/from the offered Space, Building or Property.

Section 2.10 Synopsis: Property owners need to have a discussion with the GLC regarding any property items that would be considered harmful or hazardous. It is a best practice to include documentation in response to the RLP with a plan to address or alleviate any concerns of harmful or hazardous materials on the property. See also section 1.11.

SECTION 3 HOW TO OFFER

3.01 GENERAL INSTRUCTIONS (JUN 2012)

Offeror shall prepare a complete offer, using the forms provided with this RLP, and submit the completed lease proposal package to the Government as indicated below.

3.02 RECEIPT OF LEASE PROPOSALS (SEP 2013)

A. Offeror is authorized to transmit its lease proposal as an attachment to an email. Offeror's email shall include the name, address and telephone number of the Offeror, and identify the name and title of the individual signing on behalf of the Offeror. Offeror's signed lease proposal must be saved in a generally accessible format (such as portable document format (pdf)), which displays a visible image of all original document signatures, and must be transmitted as an attachment to the email. Only emails transmitted to, and received at, the GSA email address identified in the RLP will be accepted. Offeror submitting a lease proposal by email shall retain in its possession, and make available upon GSA's request, its original signed proposal.

Offeror choosing not to submit its proposal via email may still submit its lease proposal by United States mail or other express delivery service of Offeror's choosing.

B. In order to be considered for award, offers conforming to the requirements of the RLP shall be received in one of the following ways:

1. No later than _____

on the following date at the following designated office and address:

Date: Office: Address:

2. No later than _____ address:

Date:

Email:

Address:

C. Offers sent by United States mail or hand delivered (including delivery by commercial carrier) shall be deemed late if delivered to the address of the office designated for receipt of offers after the date and time established for receipt of offers.

D. Offers transmitted through email shall be deemed late if received at the designated email address after the date and time established for receipt of offers unless it was received at the initial point of entry to the Government infrastructure not later than 5:00 p.m. one Working Day prior to the date specified for receipt of proposals.

E. Offers delivered through any means authorized by the RLP may be also deemed timely if there is acceptable evidence to establish that it was received at the Government installation designated for receipt of proposals and was under the Government's control prior to the time set for receipt of proposals, or if it was the only proposal received.

F. There will be no public opening of offers, and all offers will be confidential until the Lease has been awarded. However, the Government may release proposals outside the Government such as to support contractors to assist in the evaluation of offers.

Such Government contractors shall be required to protect the data from unauthorized disclosure.

Section 3.02 Synopsis: Confirm with the GLC the format for submitting the RLP documents and whether the RLP documents are to be submitted via email or hardcopy. If a property owner is submitting an RLP that is not 100% complete as per the directions in the RLP, then the property owner should confirm with the GLC that the RLP offer will be considered acceptable if submitted incomplete. If the property owner anticipates the offer will be submitted late, then the GLC should be informed in a timely manner. The GLC may decide whether the offer will be accepted late by granting a time extension for submission of the RLP offers.

3.03 PRICING TERMS (SEP 2015)

Offeror shall provide the following pricing information with its offer:

A. GSA Form 1217, Lessor's Annual Cost Statement. Complete all sections of the 1217.

B. GSA Form 1364, Proposal to Lease Space. Complete all sections of the 1364, including, but not limited to:

1. A fully serviced Lease rate (gross rate) per ABOA and RSF, clearly itemizing the total Building shell rental, TI rate, Building Specific Amortized Capital (BSAC) rate, operating costs, and parking (itemizing all costs of parking above base local code requirements or otherwise already included in shell rent).

2. Improvements. All improvements in the base Building, lobbies, common areas, and core areas shall be provided by the Lessor, at the Lessor's expense. This Building shell rental rate shall also include, but is not limited to, property financing (exclusive of TIs and BSAC), insurance, taxes, management, profit, etc., for the Building. The Building shell rental rate shall also include all basic Building systems and common area buildout, including base Building lobbies, common areas, core areas, etc., exclusive of the ABOA Space offered as required in this RLP.

3. The annual cost per ABOA and rentable square foot (RSF) for the cost of services and utilities. This equals line 27 of GSA Form 1217, Lessor's Annual Cost Statement, divided by the Building size (shown on the top of both GSA Form 1364, Proposal to Lease Space, and Form 1217) for ABOA and RSF, respectively.

4. The annual rent to amortize the Tenant Improvements. Such amortization shall be expressed as a cost per ABOA and RSF per year. This shall be all alterations for the Space above the Building shell and BSAC build-out. Such alterations shall be described and identified in the drawings used to construct the Space. If the Offeror chooses to amortize the TI for a period exceeding the Firm Term of the Lease, the Offeror shall indicate the extended time in the offer. If the Government terminates the Lease after the Firm Term or does not otherwise renew or extend the term beyond the Firm Term, the Government shall not be liable for any unamortized TI costs resulting from an extended amortization period.

5. The annual rent to amortize the Building Specific Amortized Capital (BSAC) costs, if any. Such amortization shall be expressed as a rate per ABOA and RSF per year. Refer to the security requirements attached to the Lease.

6. A fully serviced Lease rate per ABOA and RSF for that portion of the lease term extending beyond the Firm Term. The rate proposed for this portion of the term shall not reflect any TIs or BSAC as they will have been fully amortized over the Firm Term.

7. An hourly overtime rate for overtime use of heating and cooling, and annual rate for areas requiring 24/7 HVAC. NOTE: Refer to the Lease document for additional guidance.

8. Adjustment for Vacant Leased Premises. NOTE: Refer to the Lease document for additional guidance.

9. Lessor's Fees to complete Tenant Improvements. Provide a listing of proposed (i) Lessor's Project Management fee and (ii) Lessor's A/E design costs to prepare construction documents, to complete the Tenant Improvements. State the basis for determining each component, (e.g. flat fee, cost per ABOA SF, etc.). State any assumptions used to compute the dollar costs for each fee component.

10. Rent concessions being offered. Indicate either on the GSA Form 1364 Proposal to Lease Space or in separate correspondence.

11. Compensation (expressed as either % or $) to Offeror's broker and/or representative arising from an agreement between the Offeror and the Offeror's representative, agent(s), broker(s), property manager, developer, employee, or any other agent or representative in connection with the Lease contemplated herein shall be entered in block 25.b., and if GSA is using a Tenant

Representative Broker, compensation (expressed as either % or $) to GSA's Broker reflecting the agreement between Offeror and GSA's Broker, shall be entered in block 25.a.

C. Security Unit Price List. The Offeror shall use the Security Unit Price list to provide a cost breakdown of the security countermeasures, which were outlined in the security requirements attachment. The Security Unit Price list includes various improvements and services to be provided by the Lessor. Each item is classified as part of the shell, tenant improvements, or BSAC. There shall be no charge to the Government for any items that already exist in the offered Building or facility.

D. Any Brokerage Commission Agreement between GSA's Tenant Representative and the Lessor for commissions identified in the GSA Form 1217.

Section 3.03 Synopsis: The three forms listed here, along with the brokerage commission agreement, need to be thoroughly reviewed by the property owner for both an understanding of what the cost components are and to ensure that the property owner is fully aware of what they are being obligated to pay and what the expected performance is for each item. The forms referenced in this section are discussed in more detail in Volume II.

3.04 BUDGET SCOREKEEPING, OPERATING LEASE TREATMENT (APR 2011)

The Government will award a Lease pursuant to this RLP only if the Lease will score as an operating lease under Office of Management and Budget Circular A-11, Appendix B. Only offers that are compliant with operating lease limitations will be eligible for award. Offerors are obligated to provide supporting documentation at the request of the LCO to facilitate the Government's determination in this regard.

Section 3.04 Synopsis: The US GSA uses the "90 percent" calculation to determine if a lease is a capital lease or operating lease which is discussed further by the US GSA here:

"Among the criteria to determine an operating lease in Circular No. A-11 is that the 'present value of the minimum lease payments over the life of the lease does not exceed 90 percent of the fair market value of the asset at the inception of the lease.' To determine whether the 90 percent threshold has been reached or exceeded, the designated Portfolio Management employee must conduct a "90 percent" scoring calculation, using the Scoring Evaluation Spreadsheet available in eLease or on the Office of Real Property Asset Management InSite Web page. While all lease transactions are required to be evaluated against the above operating lease criteria, in certain scenarios where the likelihood of the lease scoring as a capital lease is remote and the realty contracting officer and designated portfolio management employee provide sufficient facts about the specific lease transaction to reasonably conclude that it will not score as a capital lease, the '90 percent' scoring calculation is not required to make such a determination."[1]

The GLC will typically alert a property owner if the GLC expects the lease will qualify for a scoring test to determine whether the lease is an operating lease or a capital lease. This scoring determination is not necessarily determined by how large the lease rent payments are but based on the rents versus replacement costs of the property, which can be applicable to small leases in buildings with small footprints.

3.05 PROSPECTUS LEASE (SEP 2013)

A. This RLP is subject to an approved Prospectus issued in accordance with 40 USC § 3307. The Government will only award a lease pursuant to this RLP if the offered rental rate does not exceed the Congressionally-imposed rent limitation set forth in the Prospectus. If a copy of the prospectus is not attached to the RLP, a copy may be obtained from the LCO upon request.

A. This RLP is subject to the Prospectus threshold mandated by 40 USC § 3307. The Government will award a Lease pursuant to this RLP only if the offered rental rate does not exceed said Congressionally-imposed rent threshold. The current threshold is available from the LCO or at the GSA Web site, http://www.gsa.gov, using the keyword "prospectus."

Section 3.05 Synopsis: According to the US GSA: "As part of the authorization process for new construction or leasing proposals, GSA is required to submit for approval a prospectus containing project and cost specifications to the Office of Management and Budget (OMB) and to House and Senate committees. Funding for authorized real property projects is normally provided through annual appropriations acts. Relatively small projects, however, do not require prospectus approval. Prospectus approval is required for new construction or leases in FY 2014 only if the proposals are valued at more than $2.85 million;[2] for projects involving the alteration of leased space, the threshold value is $1.425 million. Thresholds change annually to reflect changing construction costs and market circumstances."[3]

3.06 ADDITIONAL SUBMITTALS (MAR 2016)

Offeror shall also submit with its offer the following:

A. GSA Form 3518-SAM, Addendum to System for Award Management (SAM), Representations and Certifications (Acquisitions of Leasehold Interests in Real Property). Note: This information applies to the status of the Ownership entity and not the authorized representative completing the form.

B. Satisfactory evidence of at least a conditional commitment of funds in an amount necessary to prepare the Space. Such commitments shall be signed by an authorized bank officer, or other legally authorized financing official, and at a minimum shall state: amount of loan, term in years, annual percentage rate, and length of loan commitment.

Section 3.06.B. Synopsis: There is some debate as to whether it is a best practice to share the total project costs with the GLC or to share only those project costs related to the tenant improvements. The GLC should be able to address any questions a property owner has regarding what figure the property owner should input into the funds letter.

C. Evidence that the Property is zoned in compliance with local zoning laws, including evidence of variances, if any, approved by the proper local authority, or the Offeror's plan and schedule to obtain all necessary zoning approvals prior to performance if the same have not been received at the time of submission of offers.

Section 3.06.C. Synopsis: Zoning compliance is a major item for government real estate lease projects because government tenants can sometimes require additional improvements to the property that may require different zoning standards then what the property currently has. If there are extensive renovations required by the government tenant that are outside the normal renovations for the property, then the property owner should contact the local zoning body to review the planned renovations and improvements as part of completing the RLP documents with the GLC.

Additional improvements to the property that often need additional review time by the zoning body can be: the government tenant agency's secured parking and fencing requirements, indoor firing ranges, and on-site storage of hazardous materials.

D. Evidence of ownership or control of Building or site. If the Offeror owns the Property being offered or has a long-term leasehold interest, documentation satisfactory to the LCO evidencing the Offeror's stated interest in the Property and any encumbrances on the Property, shall be submitted.

Section 3.06.D. Synopsis: A property deed may work for this submittal requirement.

E. If the Offeror does not yet have a vested interest in the Property, but rather has a written agreement to acquire an interest, then the Offeror shall submit a fully executed copy of the written agreement with its offer, together with a statement from the current owner that the agreement is in full force and effect and that the Offeror has performed all conditions precedent to closing, or other form of documentation satisfactory to the LCO. These submittals must remain current. The Offeror is required to submit updated documents as required.

Section 3.06.E. Synopsis: This section addresses parties who do not have ownership interests in the property being offered for the RLP submittal. The GLC will often request paperwork from RLP offerors that details the contractual relationship between the current property owner and the offering party intending to purchase the property if they are awarded a lease by the GLC.

It is important to remember that on some government real estate lease projects there may be multiple parties offering the same property to the GLC using various purchase options to purchase the property contingent upon a lease award of the government tenant lease. It is a good idea to ask the GLC if there are other parties offering the subject property being submitted for the government tenant lease. There may be parties who do not have a contractual relationship with the property owner who are offering the property to the GLC for lease to the government tenant agency. If this is the case it is best to contact both the GLC and the property owner to determine if the other parties are qualified offerors on the project, and if not, they might be disqualified by the GLC from offering the property for the RLP. This section is specifically relevant for offerors submitting land parcels for leases where new construction is required and for regions of the US where open listings are standard practice.

F. If claiming an historic preference in accordance with the Historic Preference paragraph in RLP Section 2, Eligibility and Preferences for Award, Offeror must submit one of the following as documentation that the Property is historic or the site of the offered Property is within a Historic District: a letter from the National Park Service stating that the Property is listed in the National Register of Historic Places (NRHP) or eligible for listing, with a date of the listing/decision, a letter from the State Historic Preservation Office stating that the Property is listed in the NRHP, or on a statewide register, or eligible for inclusion, with a date of the listing/decision, or, the NRHP Identification Number and date of listing available from the NRHP Database found at www.nps.gov/nr.

Section 3.06.F. Synopsis: Property owners should check to see if the offered property qualifies for the preferences listed in this section. See also section 2.05.

G. If there is a potential for conflict of interest because of a single agent representing multiple owners, present evidence that the agent disclosed the multiple representation to each entity and has authorization from each ownership entity offering in response to this RLP package. Owners and agents in conflicting interest situations are advised to exercise due diligence with regard to ethics, independent pricing, and Government procurement integrity requirements. In such cases, the Government reserves the right to negotiate with the owner directly.

Section 3.06.G. Synopsis: A property owner should ask all real estate agents involved in the government lease project to state whom they are working for and what, if any, conflicts of interest there are related to the RLP transaction. There are instances where a single real estate agent may submit multiple RLP submittals for multiple properties on a government lease project. Alternatively, it is fair for a property owner to ask the GLC's real estate broker if they are submitting a property also as part of the RLP transaction process. See also section 1.13.

H. The Offeror must have an active registration in the System for Award Management (SAM), via the Internet at https://www.acquisition.gov, prior to final proposal revisions. This registration service is free of charge.

I. The Offeror must submit the Fire Protection and Life Safety (FPLS) Information in I.1, unless the Building meets either exemption in I.2 or I.3 below.

1. FPLS Submittal Information

   a. Completed GSA Form 12000, Prelease Fire Protection and Life Safety Evaluation for an Office Building (Part A or Part B, as applicable).

   b. A copy of the previous year's fire alarm system maintenance record showing compliance with the requirements in NFPA 72 (if a system is installed in the Building).

c. A copy of the previous year's automatic fire sprinkler system maintenance record showing compliance with the requirements in NFPA 25 (if a system is installed in the Building).

d. A valid Building Certificate of Occupancy (C of O) issued by the local jurisdiction. If the Building C of O is not available or the local jurisdiction does not issue a Building C of O, a report prepared by a licensed fire protection engineer with their assessment of the offered Space regarding compliance with all applicable local Fire Protection and Life Safety-related codes and ordinances must be provided.

2. If the Space offered is 10,000 RSF or less in area and is located on the 1st floor of the Building, Offeror is not required to submit to GSA the Fire Protection and Life Safety (FPLS) Submittal Information listed in I.1.a through I.1.d above.

3. If the Offeror provides a Building C of O obtained under any edition of the International Building Code (IBC), and the offered Space meets or will meet all the requirements of the Lease with regard to Means of Egress, Automatic Fire Sprinkler System, and Fire Alarm System prior to occupancy, then the Offeror is not required to submit to GSA the FPLS Submittal Information listed in I.1 above.

Section 3.06.I. Synopsis: Completing the FPLS is an opportune time to review the property's fire alarm and fire safety code compliance requirements. Confirm with the GLC that the property's current fire life safety configuration meets the minimum standards, as local codes themselves may not meet the minimum standards stated in the lease. It is common for leasehold improvements made to the leased space to trigger new fire life safety code requirements by the governing enforcement body where the property is located. There are various ways to be compliant with this section as well as exceptions or exemptions that may be available from the GLC. See also section 2.08.

J. The legal description of the Property and tax ID number associated with the Property, copies of prior year tax notices and prior year tax bills, as well as any other information (such as a fact sheet, 5" wide x 3" high or larger color photograph, site plan, location map, and tax parcel map) in case of multiple tax parcels for an offered Building, and any other information that may affect the assessed value, in order for the Government to perform a complete and adequate analysis of the offered Property. The Offeror is to provide a detailed overview and documentation of any Tax Abatements on the Property as outlined in the "Real Estate Tax Adjustment" paragraph of the Lease.

Section 3.06.J. Synopsis: Property information and the tax information should be submitted with the RLP to make certain that the GLC has a clear understanding of what space is offered for lease. It is common for large office parks, office campuses, and retail centers to have multiple property legal descriptions and tax IDs that may not ideally describe the space being offered for lease.

Confirmation of these items is important in order to ensure that the real estate taxes are adjusted correctly throughout the life of the lease and that any transfer of title will be completed in a timely manner.

K. A plan and short narrative as necessary to explain how the Offeror will meet the parking requirements.

Section 3.06.K. Synopsis: The parking plan and any parking narratives submitted by the property owner to the GLC will often be used as an exhibit to the final lease documents. The plan and narrative are important for both the GLC and property owner to come to an agreement on available parking at the property for the tenant agency. Ensure that any documents or correspondence related to the parking requirements by the GLC can be accomplished as part of the lease to the tenant agency. Overstating the parking available to the GLC can cause property management challenges for property owners after the lease is signed. In situations where the property owner overstates the parking plan and parking narratives, the GLC may require the property owner honor these items, which can add additional project costs for the property owner which have not been previously anticipated. See also section 1.02 in Volume II.

L. The architectural plans for modernization, if the offered Building is not a modern office Building.

M. An asbestos management plan, if the offered Building contains asbestos-containing materials.

N. First generation plans scaled at a minimum of 1/8" = 1'-0" (preferred) shall be submitted for review and consideration and meet N.1 through N.5 noted below.

1. All plans submitted for consideration shall include floor plan(s) for which Space is being offered and floor plan(s) of the floor(s) of exit discharge (e.g., street level(s)). Each plan submitted shall include the locations of all exit stairs, elevators, and the Space(s) being offered to the Government. In addition, where Building exit stairs are interrupted or discontinued before the level of exit discharge, additional floor plans for the level(s) where exit stairs are interrupted or discontinued must also be provided.

2. All plans submitted for consideration shall have been generated by a Computer Aided Design (CAD) program which is compatible with the latest release of AutoCAD. The required file extension is .DWG. Clean and purged files shall be submitted on CD-ROM. Plans shall include a proposed corridor pattern for typical floors and/or partial floors. The CAD file showing the offered Space should show the Poly-Line utilized to determine the square footage on a separate and unique layer. All submissions shall be accompanied with a written matrix indicating the layering standard to verify that all information is recoverable. All architectural features of the Space shall be accurately shown.

3. Photostatic copies are not acceptable. All architectural features of the Space shall be accurately shown. If conversion or renovation of the Building is planned, alterations to meet this RLP shall be indicated.

4. Plans shall reflect corridors in place or the proposed corridor pattern for both a typical full (single-tenant) floor and/or partial (multi-tenant) floor. The corridors in place or proposed corridors shall meet local code requirements for issuance of occupancy permits.

5. GSA will review all plans submitted to determine if an acceptable level of safety is provided. In addition, GSA will review the common corridors in place and/or proposed corridor pattern

to determine whether these achieve an acceptable level of safety as well as to verify that the corridors provide public access to all essential Building elements. The Offeror will be advised of any adjustments that are required to the corridors for determining the ABOA Space. The required corridors may or may not be defined by ceiling-high partitions. Actual corridors in the approved layout for the successful Offeror's Space may differ from the corridors used in determining the ABOA square footage for the lease award. Additional egress corridors required by the tenant agency's design intent drawings will not be deducted from the ABOA square footage that the most efficient corridor pattern would have yielded.

Section 3.06.N. Synopsis: Property owners often do not have floor plans available in the format requested in this section. The property owner should discuss with the GLC the minimum submittal items necessary to be compliant with this section without the property owner having to spend a considerable amount of money to generate new plans that may not be readily available.

The GLC may be able to assist the property owner in arriving at a lower cost solution that is acceptable to the GLC under this section. Property owners are cautioned that this section needs to be adhered to, at a minimum, to the extent necessary to arrive at an absolute understanding that the space being offered for lease will meet the minimum square footage measurements and specifications stated in the lease. See also section 2.01.

O. As provided in the "Amount and Type of Space, Lease Term, and Occupancy Date" paragraph in the RLP, advise whether there are existing vending facilities in the offered Building which have exclusive rights in the Building.

P. Provide evidence demonstrating amenities do or will exist by the Government's required occupancy date. Such evidence shall include copies of signed leases, construction contracts, or other documentation as deemed acceptable by the LCO.

Section 3.06.P. Synopsis: This section is often overlooked but should be adhered to specifically if there are amenity requirements in the lease. The property owner should remember that the GLC may request evidence of these amenities after the lease is signed or sometime after occupancy of the space by the tenant agency. See also section 1.04.

Q. No later than the due date for final proposal revisions, the Offeror must submit to the LCO:

1. Evidence of an Energy Star® label obtained within the 12 months prior to the due date of final proposal revisions.

2. Offerors falling under a statutory exception must also indicate by the due date for final proposal revisions what cost effective energy efficiency and conservation improvements they are proposing to make.

3. If no cost-effective improvements can be made, the Offeror must demonstrate to the Government using the ENERGY STAR® Online Tools referenced in the RLP paragraph, entitled "ENERGY INDEPENDENCE AND SECURITY ACT," why no energy efficiency and conservation improvements are cost effective. This explanation will be subject to review by the LCO. If the explanation is considered unreasonable, the offer may be considered technically unacceptable.

4. If the Offeror is claiming eligibility for additional time to obtain the Energy Star® label per sub-paragraph B of the RLP paragraph entitled "ENERGY INDEPENDENCE AND SECURITY ACT," then the Offeror shall provide such indication with its initial offer and also must provide by the due date for final proposal revisions evidence substantiating their claim for additional time to obtain the Energy Star® label and substantiating their capability of earning the Energy Star®.

5. For new construction, the Offeror need not submit anything regarding compliance with EISA by the date of final proposal revisions, but shall be required to produce prior to the issuance of a permit for building construction a Statement of Energy Design Intent (SEDI) using Energy Star's® Target Finder online tool reflecting an Energy Star® benchmark score of 75 or higher and a certification from EPA of being Designed to Earn the Energy Star®.

R. For projects 10,000 RSF and above, a LEED-NC Silver scorecard documenting the proposed Credits to meet Silver level. Along with the proposed scorecard, the Offeror shall submit a brief statement outlining how each of the credits proposed on the scorecard will be achieved.

S. From the entirety of available LEED Credits, the Offeror must achieve the following Credits on the project:

Water Efficiency	Credit 1	Water Efficient Landscaping - 50% Reduction
Energy and Atmosphere	Credit 3	Enhanced Commissioning
Materials and Resources	Credit 5	Regional Materials, 20% Manufactured Regionally
Indoor Environmental Quality	Credit 2	Increased Ventilation
Indoor Environmental Quality	Credit 3.2	Construction IAQ Management Plan, Before Occupancy
Innovation and Design	Credit 2	LEED Accredited Professional

The Offeror must identify the USGBC LEED Accredited Professionals (APs) as team members, including their roles throughout the project.

T. LEED-CI scorecard documenting the proposed credits to meet Certified level. Along with the proposed scorecard, the Offeror shall submit a brief statement outlining how each of the Credits proposed on the scorecard will be achieved.

U. From the entirety of available LEED Credits, the Lessor must achieve the following Credits on the project:

Water Efficiency	Credit 1	Water Use Reduction 30% Minimum Reduction
Energy and Atmosphere	Credit 1.1	Optimize Energy Performance – Lighting Power
Energy and Atmosphere	Credit 1.3	Optimize Energy Performance - HVAC
Energy and Atmosphere	Credit 2	Enhanced Commissioning
Materials and Resources	Credit 5	Regional Materials
Indoor Environmental Quality	Credit 2	Increased Ventilation
Indoor Environmental Quality	Credit 3.2	Construction IAQ Management Plan, Before Occupancy
Innovation and Design	Credit 2	LEED Accredited Professional

The Offeror must identify the USGBC LEED accredited professionals (APs) as team members, including their roles throughout the project.

Section 3.06.U. Synopsis: All LEED RLP items should be agreed to in writing with the GLC. It is a best practice to have a LEED design and project cost estimate developed and signed off by the GLC and the property owner before the lease is signed. If a property owner overlooks the costs associated with the LEED lease requirements, they may find that the LEED costs make the government lease economically unviable after the lease is signed. See also L100 sections 3.50 and 3.51 in Volume II.

V. Evidence of seismic safety compliance as required in Section 2 of this RLP.

W. Information required under paragraph entitled "DUE DILIGENCE AND NATIONAL ENVIRONMENTAL POLICY ACT REQUIREMENTS - RLP."

X. Information required under paragraph entitled "NATIONAL HISTORIC PRESERVATION ACT REQUIREMENTS - RLP."

Y. If the Offeror requests any deviations, all deviations must be documented on Form 1364 in block labeled "Additional Remarks or Conditions with Respect to this Offer." GSA at its sole discretion will make the decision whether or not to accept the deviation. Any deviations must be requested prior to the request for final proposal revisions. If the Offeror requests any deviations, GSA at its sole discretion will make the decision whether to accept the deviation.

Z. If more than 5,000 square feet of land area is to be disturbed in order to meet the Government's requirements, (as more fully described in the lease paragraph named ENERGY INDEPENDENCE AND SECURITY ACT, sub-paragraph (B)(1)(b)), a statement from Offeror that the Offeror is aware of and will comply with the specific lease requirements concerning maintenance and restoration of the real property's hydrology.

3.07 TENANT IMPROVEMENTS INCLUDED IN OFFER (SEP 2015)

TENANT IMPROVEMENT ALLOWANCE PRICING:

The TI Allowance is _____ per ABOA SF (TIs are the finishes and fixtures that typically take Space from the shell condition to a finished, usable condition.) The TI Allowance shall be used for the build-out of the Space in accordance with the Government approved design intent drawings. All TIs required by the Government for occupancy shall be performed by the successful Offeror as part of the rental consideration, and all improvements shall meet the quality standards and requirements of this RLP package and its attachments.

TENANT IMPROVEMENT ALLOWANCE PRICING:

The TI Allowance for the existing leased Space is _____ per ABOA SF. The TI Allowance for other locations offered is __________ per ABOA SF (TIs are the finishes and fixtures that typically take Space from the shell condition to a finished, usable condition.) The TI Allowance shall be used for the build-out of the Space in accordance with the Government approved design intent drawings. All TIs required by the Government for occupancy shall be performed by the successful Offeror as part of the rental consideration, and all improvements shall meet the quality standards and requirements of this RLP package and its attachments.

A. The TIs for this requirement shall consist of the following:

Repainting of the leased Premises in accordance with the "Painting – TI" paragraph in Section 5 of the Lease.

Re-carpeting of the leased Premises in accordance with the "Floor Coverings and Perimeters" paragraph in Section 5 of the Lease.

Other–See attached Scope of Work.

All TIs required by the Government for occupancy shall be performed by the successful Offeror as part of the rental consideration, and all improvements shall meet the quality standards and requirements of this RLP package and its attachments.

TENANT IMPROVEMENT TURNKEY PRICING

A. An Agency Specific Requirements (ASR) package is provided with this RLP to all Offerors upon which to base their TI pricing. (TIs are the finishes and fixtures that typically take Space from the "shell" condition to a finished, usable condition.) All TIs required by the Government for occupancy shall be performed by the successful Offeror as part of the rental consideration and all improvements shall meet the quality standards and requirements of this RLP and its attachments.

B. The Tenant Improvements shall include all the Offeror's administrative costs, general contractor fees, subcontractor's profit and overhead costs, Offeror's Project Management fee, design costs, and other associated project fees necessary to prepare construction documents and to complete the TIs. It is the successful Offeror's responsibility to prepare all documentation (working/ construction drawings, etc.) required to receive construction permits. NO COSTS ASSOCIATED WITH THE BUILDING SHELL SHALL BE INCLUDED IN THE TI PRICING.

Section 3.07 Synopsis: A majority of tenant improvement costs are amortized over the firm term of the lease with additional tenant improvement cost overruns paid by the GLC via a lump sum payment or amortized into the lease term. This section is important for property owners to understand as it correlates with the expanded tenant improvement information in the L100 that should be thoroughly reviewed before a lease is signed. Regardless of a property owner's experience with government real estate leases, the tenant improvement and shell costs should be discussed in detail with the GLC before a lease is signed. See also L100 section 1.08 and section 5 "Tenant Improvement Components," in Volume II.

3.08 SECURITY IMPROVEMENTS INCLUDED IN OFFER (SEP 2012)

A. The Building Specific Amortized Capital (BSAC) amount is _____ per ABOA SF. The BSAC shall be used for the build-out of security-related improvements in the Building in accordance with the Government-approved design intent drawings, if applicable. All security countermeasures required by the Government for occupancy shall be performed by the successful Offeror as part of the rental consideration, and all improvements shall meet the quality standards and requirements of this RLP package and its attachments.

B. The BSAC shall include all the Offeror's administrative costs, general contractor fees, subcontractor's profit and overhead costs, Offeror's profit and overhead, design costs, and other associated project fees necessary to prepare construction documents and to complete the security countermeasures. It is the successful Offeror's responsibility to prepare all documentation (working/ construction drawings, etc.) required to receive construction permits. No costs associated with the building shell or TI shall be included in the BSAC pricing.

Section 3.08 Synopsis: Determine with the GLC how the BSAC costs will be paid for. Specifically discuss if the BSAC costs will be a fixed cost to the property owner before the lease is signed without the property owner being able to negotiate the BSAC costs with the GLC after the design and bids are completed. It is best to get written clarification from the GLC if there any questions on how the BSAC costs are to be paid. See also section 1.09 and L100 section 1.03.B in Volume II.

3.09 LEED FOR COMMERCIAL INTERIORS (JUN 2012)

The project TIs shall incorporate any necessary design parameters for the Space to meet Leadership in Energy and Environmental Design for Commercial Interiors (LEED-CI) requirements into the Working Construction Drawings. The Lessor must coordinate the requirements to meet LEED-CI Certified level for the TIs with the Building shell requirements.

Section 3.09 Synopsis: As referenced in this Chapter's section 3.06 Synopsis, all LEED project items should be agreed to in writing with the GLC and the property owner's project team members before the lease is signed. It is a best practice to have a LEED design and project cost estimate developed and signed off by the GLC and the property owner before the lease is fully executed. See also L100 section 3.51 in Volume II.

3.10 OPERATING COSTS REQUIREMENTS INCLUDED IN OFFER (JUN 2012)

The Government requires a fully serviced Lease as part of the rental consideration. The base for the operating costs adjustment will be established during negotiations based upon rentable SF. The proposed methodology for operating costs adjustment shall include all items specified in the attached Lease document. The minimum requirements for normal hours, utilities, and janitorial services are specified in the attached Lease document. The offer shall clearly state whether the rental is firm throughout the term of the Lease or if it is subject to annual adjustment of operating costs as indicated above. If operating costs will be subject to adjustment, those costs shall be specified in the proposal.

Section 3.10 Synopsis: Property owners need to accurately budget for how the property's operating costs will be adjusted from year to year. As this specific section paragraph states, the government requires a fully serviced lease, which dictates that most if not all the utilities and building services will be paid for by the property owner and included as part of the rent charged to the tenant agency. The sample L100 in Volume II has lease language that discusses how the operating costs adjustments may be made over the life of the lease. The property owner may have some flexibility as to what option to choose regarding operating cost adjustments. See also section 3.11 and L100 section 1.15 in Volume II.

3.11 UTILITIES SEPARATE FROM RENTAL / BUILDING OPERATING PLAN (JUN 2012)

The Offeror shall specify which utilities, if any, are excluded from the rental consideration. If any such utilities are excluded, the Offeror shall obtain a statement from a registered professional engineer stating that all HVAC, plumbing, and other energy intensive Building systems can operate under the control conditions stated in the Lease. The statement shall also identify all Building systems that do not conform to the system performance values, including the "recommended" or "suggested" values of ANSI/ASHRAE Standard 90.1, "Energy Efficient Design of New Buildings Except Low Rise Residential Buildings," or more restrictive state and local codes.

The Offeror shall submit a building operating plan with the offer. Such plan shall include a schedule of startup and shutdown times for operation of each building system, such as lighting, HVAC, and plumbing. Such plan shall be in effect on the Lease Term Commencement Date.

Section 3.11 Synopsis: If the utility costs are separate from the rental rate then the property owner should include this as part of the RLP submittal, with a specific discussion with the GLC as to what utilities will be separate from the rental rates and paid for directly by the tenant agency. The utilities that are separate from the rental rate should be prominently included in the lease documents to avoid any confusion after the lease is signed as to who is responsible for payment of these items.

SECTION 4 METHOD OF AWARD

4.01 NEGOTIATIONS (JUN 2012)

Negotiations may be conducted on behalf of the Government by the GSA LCO or designated representative. When negotiations are conducted, GSA will negotiate the rental price for the initial term, any renewal periods, and any other aspect of the offer as deemed necessary. The Offeror shall not enter into negotiations concerning the Space leased or to be leased with representatives of Federal agencies other than the LCO or their designee. The LCO or their designated representative will conduct oral or written negotiations with all Offerors that are within the competitive range. The competitive range will be established by the LCO based on cost or price and other factors (if any) that are stated in this RLP and will include all of the most highly rated proposals, unless the range is further reduced for purposes of efficiency. Prior to eliminating an Offeror that is a HUBZone small business concern (SBC) and which has not waived its entitlement to a price evaluation preference from the competitive range, the LCO shall adjust the evaluated prices of all non-small business Offerors proposed for inclusion in the competitive range by increasing the prices by ten (10) percent, solely for the purpose of determining whether the HUBZone SBC Offeror should be included or excluded from the competitive range. Offerors who are not included in the competitive range will be notified in writing.

All Offerors within the competitive range will be provided a reasonable opportunity to submit revisions to their initial offer including any cost or price, technical, or other revisions that may result from the negotiations. Negotiations will be closed with submission of final proposal revisions.

Negotiations may be conducted on behalf of the Government by the GSA LCO or designated representative. When negotiations are conducted, GSA will negotiate the rental price for the initial term, any renewal periods, and any other aspect of the offer as deemed necessary. The Offeror shall not enter into negotiations concerning the Space leased or to be leased with representatives of federal agencies other than the LCO or their designee.

Section 4.01 Synopsis: As discussed in Volume II, it is helpful for the property owner and the GLC to establish an understanding of whether the GLC is negotiating an RLP item with the property owner or simply discussing clarification items related to the property owner's offer. Ask the GLC what the GLC can discuss during negotiations and what the property owner can do to present the best offer to lease space to the GLC.

4.02 HUBZONE SMALL BUSINESS CONCERN ADDITIONAL PERFORMANCE REQUIREMENTS (SEP 2015)

A HUBZone small business concern (SBC) Offeror may elect to waive the price evaluation preference provided in the "Award Based On Price" paragraph or the "Other Award Factors" paragraph of the RLP by so indicating on the GSA Form 1364, Proposal to Lease Space. In such a case, no price evaluation preference shall apply to the evaluation of the HUBZone SBC, and the performance of work requirements set forth in Section 1 of the Lease shall not be applicable should the HUBZone SBC be awarded the Lease. A HUBZone SBC Offeror acknowledges that a prospective HUBZone SBC awardee must be a qualified HUBZone SBC at the time of award of this contract in order to be eligible for the price evaluation preference. The HUBZone SBC Offeror shall provide the LCO a copy of the notice required by 13 CFR 126.501 if material changes occur before contract award that could affect its HUBZone eligibility. If it is determined, prior to award, that the apparently successful HUBZone SBC Offeror is not an eligible HUBZone SBC, the LCO will reevaluate proposals without regard to any price preference provided for the previously identified HUBZone SBC Offeror, and make an award consistent with the solicitation and the evaluation factors set forth herein.

If a HUBZone SBC that has not waived the price preference is awarded the Lease, the certification required by the "Additional Financial and Technical Capability" paragraph of the Lease must be provided within 10 days of award. If it is determined within 20 days of award that a HUBZone SBC Offeror that has been awarded the Lease was not an eligible HUBZone SBC at the time of award, and the HUBZone SBC Lessor failed to provide the LCO with information regarding a change to its HUBZone eligibility prior to award, then the Lease shall be subject, at the LCO's discretion, to termination, and the Government will be relieved of all obligations to the Lessor in such an event and not be liable to the Lessor for any costs, claims or damages of any nature whatsoever.

Section 4.02 Synopsis: Discuss with the GLC to determine if the property qualifies for the HUBZone SBC preference under this section's requirements.

4.03 AWARD BASED ON PRICE (JUN 2012)

A. The Lease will be awarded to the responsible Offeror whose offer conforms to the requirements of this RLP and the Lease documents and is the lowest priced technically acceptable offer submitted. Refer to the "Present Value Price Evaluation" paragraph of this RLP.

B. If after completion of the Price Evaluation, award is proposed to a non-small business Offeror, and there exists as part of the procurement another technically acceptable proposal submitted by a responsible Offeror that is a qualified HUBZone small business concern (SBC) which has not waived its entitlement to a price evaluation preference, the evaluated price of the non-small business Offeror's proposal shall be increased by ten (10) percent, solely for the purpose of determining whether award should be made to the HUBZone SBC Offeror. In such a case, the proposals of the apparently successful non-small business Offeror and the HUBZone SBC Offeror shall be considered in light of the applied price preference, and award made to the lower priced offer. The LCO shall document his/her application of the price preference and further consideration of the offers under this subparagraph.

C. If an offer contains terms taking exception to or modifying any Lease provision, the Government will not be under any obligation to award a Lease in response to that offer.

Section 4.03 Synopsis: It is a best practice to discuss this section with the GLC to understand specifically how the RLP offer will be evaluated for lease award. While a majority of government real estate leases are based on the best offered price, it has become more common for government leases to be awarded based on price with other award factors that include how the property owner's rental rates compare to the market, technical factors, etc. See also section 4.04.

4.04 OTHER AWARD FACTORS (JUN 2012)

A. The Lease will be awarded to the responsible Offeror whose offer will be most advantageous to the Government.

B. The combination of factors below is [significantly more important than price] [approximately equal in importance to price] [significantly less important than price].

C. The following award factor(s) will be considered:

1. ______________________________

2. ______________________________

3. ______________________________

D. If after completion of the Price Evaluation, award is proposed to a non-small business Offeror, and there exists as part of the procurement another technically acceptable proposal submitted by a responsible Offeror that is a qualified HUBZone small business concern (SBC) which has not waived its entitlement to a price evaluation preference, the evaluated price of the non-small business Offeror's proposal shall be increased by ten (10) percent, solely for the purpose of determining whether award should be made to the HUBZone SBC Offeror. In such a case, the proposals of the apparently successful non-small business Offeror and the HUBZone SBC Offeror shall be considered in accordance with the evaluation factors and the applied price preference, and award made to the offer determined to be most advantageous to the Government. The LCO shall document his/her application of the price preference and further consideration of the offers under this sub-paragraph.

E. If an offer contains terms taking exception to or modifying any Lease provision, the Government will not be under any obligation to award a Lease in response to that offer.

Section 4.04 Synopsis: This section when compared to section 4.03, "Award Based on Price," can be a challenge when selecting the best approach for a property owner submitting an RLP based on "Other Award Factors." The property owner should have a discussion with the GLC early on in the RLP submittal process to determine what the best approach is for submitting items listed in this section. It is common for GLCs to make clarifications and adjustments to the "Other Award Factor" section items after the RLP is initially sent to the property owner. Typically an RLP will include either section 4.03 or 4.04 but not both.

4.05 PRESENT VALUE PRICE EVALUATION (SEP 2015)

A. If annual CPI adjustments in operating expenses are included, the Offeror shall be required to submit the offer with the total "gross" annual price per RSF and per ABOA SF and a breakout of the "base" price per RSF and ABOA SF for services and utilities (operating expenses) to be provided by the Lessor. The "gross" price shall include the "base" price. The base price per ABOA SF from which adjustments are made will be the base price for the term of the Lease, including any option periods.

B. The Offeror must submit plans and any other information to demonstrate that the Rentable Space yields ABOA space within the required ABOA range. The Government will verify the amount of ABOA SF and will convert the rentable prices offered to ABOA prices, which will subsequently be used in the price evaluation.

C. Evaluation of offered prices will be based on the annual price per ABOA SF, including all required option periods. The Government will perform present value price evaluation by reducing the prices per ABOA SF to a composite annual ABOA SF price, as follows:

1. Parking and ware yard areas will be excluded from the total square footage but not from the price. For different types of space, the gross annual per ABOA SF price will be determined by dividing the total annual rental by the total ABOA square footage excluding these areas.

2. Free rent will be evaluated in the year in which it is offered. The gross annual price is adjusted to reflect free rent.

3. Prior to the discounting procedure below, the total dollar amount of the Commission Credit (if applicable) will be subtracted from the first year's gross annual rent, unless the provision of free rent causes the credit to apply against rent beyond the first year's term, in which case the Commission Credit will be allocated proportionately against the appropriate year's gross rent.

4. Also as stated in the "Broker Commission and Commission Credit" paragraph, the amount of any commission paid to GSA's Broker will not be considered separately as part of this price evaluation since the value of the commission is subsumed in the gross rent rate.

5. If annual adjustments in operating expenses will not be made, the gross annual price, minus the Commission Credit(if applicable), will be discounted annually at 5 percent to yield a gross present value cost (PVC).

6. If annual adjustments in operating expenses will be made, the annual price, minus the Commission Credit (if applicable) and minus the base cost of operating expenses, will be discounted annually at 5 percent to yield net PVC. The operating expenses will be both escalated at 2.5 percent compounded annually and discounted annually at 5 percent, then added to the net PVC to yield the gross PVC.

7. To the gross PVC will be added:

a. The cost of Government-provided services not included in the rental escalated at 2.5 percent compounded annually and discounted annually at 5 percent.

b. The annualized (over the full term) cost of any items, which are to be reimbursed in a lump sum payment. (The cost of these items is present value, therefore, it will not be discounted.)

c. The annual price for parking to accommodate the minimum number of spaces required for government vehicles, if not included in the shell rent and charged separately. The price will be discounted annually at 5 percent.

d. The cost of relocation of furniture, telecommunications, replications costs, and other move-related costs, if applicable.

e. The fees for architectural and engineering design (A/E) services and the Offeror's project management fees associated with Tenant Improvements. The Offeror is required as part of their offer to identify on GSA Form 1364 any and all fees to complete the tenant improvements, broken down into two components: (1) Fees for architectural and engineering design services (A/E fees), which may be offered as a rate per ABOA SF, percentage rate, or flat fee, and (2) Lessor's overhead, administrative costs, profit, and fees associated with Tenant Improvements (Lessor's PM fees), which may be only offered as a percentage rate. These fees will be evaluated in a multi-step process, as follows.

- The A/E fees are assumed to consume a portion of the total tenant improvement allowance (TIA), thus reducing the amount available for actual construction. The percentage is not a percentage of the TIA, but a percentage of the underlying costs, which together with the A/E fee equals the TIA. The following example is used to illustrate the calculations, and assumes the following: An allowance of $30 per square foot for 10,000 ABOA square feet, which is $300,000, and A/E fees of 5%.
- The underlying costs equals the TIA divided by (1 + A/E fee percentage) $300,000/1.05 = $285,714.29
- A/E fees at 5% of the underlying costs are .05 x $285,714.29 = $14,285.71

- Underlying costs of $285,714.29 plus 5% A/E fees of $14,285.71 = TIA of $300,000
- The Lessor's PM fees are presumed to be in addition to the TIA and calculated as a percentage of the full TIA. Using the same example, if Lessor's PM fees are offered at 5%, the fees are calculated as $300,000 x .05 = $15,000.
- The sum of these fees is then computed as a percentage of the total TIA. Following the example, A/E fees of $14,285.71 plus Lessor's PM fees of $15,000 (total fees of $29,285.71) ÷ $300,000 TIA = 9.762%. The amortized rental rate for the tenant improvement allowance is increased by this percentage for purposes of price evaluation.

f. The annual cost of overtime HVAC based on the offered hourly overtime rate and an estimated usage of _____ hours of overtime HVAC per year for the Space. This cost will be discounted annually at 5 percent.

8. The sum of either sub-paragraphs 5 and 7 or sub-paragraphs 6 and 7, divided by the ABOA SF will be the present value cost per ABOA SF of the offer for price evaluation purposes.

Section 4.05 Synopsis: The GLC should be able to discuss with the property owner in specific detail how a property's offer is being analyzed on a present value basis if it is a basis for lease award. It may help for the property owner to ask the GLC how the RLP offer is being analyzed to confirm that the RLP offer is being properly evaluated by the GLC. An additional item to note is that very rarely will the term "net present value" be used to describe the present value calculation as described in this section, as these two terms have different definitions and calculations.

4.06 AWARD (APR 2015)

A. To document the agreement between the parties, the successful Offeror and the GSA LCO will execute a Lease prepared by GSA, which incorporates the agreement of the parties. The Lease shall consist of the following:

1. Lease No. GS _____ and any associated Lease amendments.
2. GSA Form 3517B, General Clauses.
3. GSA Form 3518-SAM, Addendum to System for Award Management (SAM) Representations and Certifications (Acquisitions of Leasehold Interests in Real Property).
4. The pertinent provisions of the offer.
5. Floor plans of the offered Space.

B. The acceptance of the offer and award of the Lease by the Government occurs upon execution of the Lease by the LCO and mailing or otherwise furnishing written notification of the executed Lease to the successful Offeror.

Section 4.06 Synopsis: The property owner should discuss with the GLC how the GLC intends to make the lease award with a specific discussion regarding when the property owner will actually have an actual lease with the GLC. See also section 1.01.

SECTION 5 ADDITIONAL TERMS AND CONDITIONS

Section 5 Synopsis: This section is often used for adding additional tenant requirements and to document any modifications or changes to the RLP. It is common for government leases to have several modifications, changes, and amendments to the RLP before the lease is fully executed.

CHAPTER SUMMARY

This chapter discussed the following items for a review of the US federal government's request for lease proposal (RLP) document:

- The common elements of an RLP proposal.
- A review of the US GSA's real estate request for lease proposal (RLP) document, the R100, which is currently used for most of the US GSA's real estate lease transactions with the private sector.

NOTES

[1] Determination of Operating or Capital Lease Classification for Budget Scorekeeping Purposes, http://www.gsa.gov/graphics/pbs/Att_1_Determination_of_Operating_Lease_and_Lease_Scoring_w101408_508_R2-n71-h_0Z5RDZ-i34K-pR.pdf.

[2] http://www.gsa.gov/portal/content/101522.

[3] http://congressionalresearch.com/RS22287/document.php?-study=General+Services+Administration+Prospectus+Thresh-olds+for+Owned+and+Leas ed+Federal+Facilities.

The Chicago Picasso, Daley Plaza

APPENDIX A

1. **State of Florida Request for Lease Proposal**
2. **State of Florida Standard Form Lease**
3. **State of California Standard Form Lease**
4. **State of Texas Standard Form Lease**

Department Of Management Services

Request for Proposal ("RFP") for Leased Space

Contents

I. Request for Proposal – Introduction and Overview

The State of Florida's Department of ______________________________(hereinafter referred to as the "Agency"), requests your participation in a space search in _______________ County, Florida (more detailed boundaries are attached hereto as **Attachment B**). The Department of ______________________________ is seeking detailed and competitive proposals to provide built-out office facilities and related infrastructure for occupancy by the Agency. As relates to any space that is required to be built-out pursuant to this Request for Proposal, please see **Attachment "A"** which includes the Agency Specifications detailing the build-out requirements.

All responses to this Request for Proposal (hereinafter referred to as a "Reply" or "Replies") must be received by the date required in Article II, Section A, in written/typed form. The Reply must be sent, within the timeframes provided herein, to the Department of ____________________ located at the address specified in Article II of this Request for Proposal.

The "Offeror" shall mean the individual submitting a Bid to this Request for Proposal, such person being the owner of the proposed facility or an individual duly authorized to bind the owner of the facility. The terms "Bid Reply" or "Replies" shall be the Offeror's response to the Request for Proposal. The term "State" shall mean the State of Florida and its Agencies.

II. Request for Proposal - Timetable

The following schedule of events will be strictly adhered to in all actions relevant to this RFP, unless modified by the department by addendum to this RFP (all times are Eastern times):

A. RFP issued:

B. Pre-Proposal Conference: (Attendance is mandatory/optional)

Location: ______________________________

Date: ______________

C. Deadline for proposer's written questions to be submitted to Issuing Officer:

Name: ______________________________

Address: ______________________________

Telephone: ______________

Fax: ______________

D. Answers issued in Addendum to RFP:

E. Proposal Due Date:

Time: ______________

Location: ______________________________

F. Date, Time and Location of Proposal Opening: ______________________________

____

G. Date and Time of Posting: ______________

H. Intended Date of Occupancy as defined in Section ______________

III. Request for Proposal - Instructions and general information

Definitions of terms

Boundary: The precise geographic area defined by lines, streets, or roads denoting the area for the acceptable location of a site/facility. To be considered within the specified given boundaries, the site/facility must be within or abutting the defined lines of demarcation.

Business Day: Working days occurring Monday through Friday, except legal holidays observed by the State of Florida. The terms "working days" and "business days" may be used interchangeably.

Certificate of Occupancy: The certificate issued by the appropriate official from the jurisdiction or jurisdictions where the offered property of facility is located, which signifies that the building or structure has met all construction requirements of such jurisdiction, and that the structure or facility may be occupied by persons.

Certified Minority Business Enterprise (CMBE): A business which has been certified by the Minority Business Advocacy and Assistance Office.

Common Area: Any area of a building whose use is shared by other tenants. Examples include primary lobby, restrooms, primary (entrance) corridors, etc.

Covenants: Clauses in the lease or underlying deed which define or limit the rights and obligations of lessor or lessee.

Date of Occupancy: The date following the issuance of any applicable certificate of occupancy when a building or facility has been inspected and is accepted by the department.

Day: One calendar day.

Department: The division of Florida State Government which is issuing this Request for Proposal (RFP), or its successor in interest. The complete name of the department which issued this RFP is provided on the first page of this RFP. As used in this document, the word "department" refers to the full formal name of the issuer of this RFP.

Energy Performance Analysis: A number describing the energy consumption and cost of a facility per square foot of floor area per year stated in BTU consumption per square foot per year.

Exclusive Parking Spaces: Parking designated and identified by the lessor for the sole and exclusive use of the lessee 24 hours per day, 7 days per week, without interference from or concurrent use by others. By offering parking spaces, the lessor agrees to take whatever steps are necessary to assure that the department enjoys exclusive use of those spaces as described here unless agreed otherwise in writing.

Existing Building/Facility: To be considered existing, the proposed space must be enclosed with a roof system and exterior walls in place.

Foot-candle: The illumination of a surface one foot distance from a source of one candle, equal to one lumen per square foot. For purposes of this RFP, foot-candles will be measured using a General Electric Type 214 Light Meter or its equal to be supplied by the lessor.

Lease: The contract entered into by a department and the successful proposer to this RFP, which shall incorporate, among other provisions, the contents of this RFP and the successful proposer's response to this RFP, except as specifically provided to the contrary in the lease document, and which gives the department a current possessory interest in the building or facility. The terms "lease" and "contract" may be used interchangeably.

Lessee: A person who acquires the right to possession and use of a premises under a lease.

Lessor: A person who transfers the right to possession and use of a premises under a lease.

Lowest and Best Proposal: That proposal selected by the department following an objective and detailed process to evaluate and compare proposals. "Lowest" refers to the lowest present value cost of a proposal based on the rental rate criteria. "Lowest and Best" refers to the evaluation score. Weights for evaluation criteria are described in each RFP.

Proposal: All materials submitted by a prospective proposer in response to this RFP.

Public Entity Crime: As defined in paragraph 287.133(1)(g), Florida Statutes, means a violation of any state or federal law by a person with respect to and directly related to the transaction of business with any public entity or with an agency or political subdivision of any other state or with the United States, including but not limited to, any proposal or contract for goods or services, any lease for real property, or any contract for the construction or repair of a public building or public work, involving antitrust, fraud, theft, bribery, collusion, racketeering, conspiracy, or material misrepresentation.

Prospective Proposer: Any firm or person who submits a proposal to the department in response to this RFP.

Responsive Proposal: A proposal which conforms in all material respects to this RFP.

Request for Proposal (RFP): The RFP consists of the package of documents by which the department seeks to lease real property to meets its needs. This consists of a group of documents provided to each interested party, including:

1. Cover sheet entitled Request for Proposal.
2. Timetable (Section 1).
3. Instructions and Information (Section 2).
4. A standardized RFP form which is submitted by all proposer's as their basic RFP document (Section 3).
5. Attachments to the RFP package.
6. Any written amendments to this RFP, including written responses submitted by the department to questions received at or before the pre-proposal conference.

Standard Lease Agreement: Lease Form Number 4054 on which leases for real property are written.

State: The State of Florida and its departments, boards and commissions, officers and employees.

Subcontractor: Any person other than an employee of the proposer who performs any of the services listed in this RFP for compensation.

UPS: Uninterruptible power supply.

Throughout this RFP, the singular may be read as plural and the plural as singular. Gender is intended to be neutral.

Requirements for Proposers to Submit Proposals

A. **Control of Property**: For a proposal to be responsive, it must be submitted by one of the entities listed below, and the proposal must include supporting documentation proving such status. This requirement applies to both the building or structure and the proposed parking areas, as well as areas of ingress and egress.

a.) The owner of record of the facility and parking areas - Submit a copy of the deed(s) evidencing clear title to the property proposed.

b.) The lessee of space being proposed - Submit a copy of the underlying lease agreement with documentation of authorization to sublease the facility and parking areas through the term of the base lease and all renewal option periods.

c.) The authorized agent, broker or legal representative of the owner(s) - Submit a copy of the Special Power of Attorney authorizing submission of the proposal.

d.) The holder of an option to purchase - Submit documentation of a valid option to purchase the facility and/or parking areas from the owner of record which, if exercised, will result in the proposer's control of the facility prior to the intended date of occupancy.

e.) The holder of an option to lease the property offered - Submit documentation of an option to lease the facility with authorization to, in turn, sublease. Any lease must encompass the entire time period of the basic lease and any renewal option periods as required by this state. A copy of the lease agreement between the owner and the lessee must be provided to the department at the time of submitting the response to this RFP.

B. If the successful proposer is a legal entity (such as trust, partnership or corporation) to be established, the proposer, by responding to this RFP, certifies that such organization and registration as required by law will be met, and documentation of same will be submitted at the time of lease execution. Such documentation must show that the proposed entity will be in place prior to the date of execution of the lease document.

C. All proposers must submit documentation of proper zoning from the local zoning authority for the intended use. If the present use of the property will change, the department reserves the right to request copies of permits and evidence of concurrence.

D. The proposer agrees that its proposal shall remain valid for a minimum of sixty (60) calendar days following the notice of award date. Any offer submitted to the department pursuant to this RFP must be held open and valid in all respects for no less than 60 days, at any time during which the department may accept that offer and the proposer agrees to enter into such lease agreement as is necessary for the department to accept the offer.

E. The prospective lessor must be an equal opportunity employer. Minority participation is strongly encouraged in all proposals.

RFP Document Package

The RFP is composed of the items and attachments listed below. It is the proposer's responsibility to be familiar with all aspects of the RFP, including attachments. If upon examination, it is found that any part or parts of the package are missing, contact the Issuing Officer listed on the cover sheet of this RFP package. See also the section below entitled Familiarity with Laws.

__________ Cover page containing a copy of the RFP Legal Advertisement

__________ Section 1 - Timetable

__________ Section 2 - Instructions and Information on Submitting RFP

__________ Section 3 - RFP Submittal Form

ATTACHMENTS AS NOTED BELOW

____________ Map showing proposal zone boundaries

____________ Standards for Special Facilities for Physically Disabled

____________ Renovation plan requirements for submittal to State Fire Marshal

____________ Standard Lease Agreement

____________ Disclosure of Ownership Statement

____________ Energy performance calculation method

____________ Special Power of Attorney (if applicable)

____________ Employee Eligibility Verification

Except as requested in the RFP submittal form, proposer's are not required to resubmit Section 1 and Section 2 of the RFP or the above-mentioned standard attachment forms. However, proposer's must conform to these requirements.

Familiarity with Laws

The proposer is required to be familiar with all federal, state and local laws, ordinances, rules and regulations that in any way affect this project. Lack of knowledge by the proposer will in no way allow relief from responsibility. All costs associated with compliance shall be borne by the proposer. The department will exercise due care in response to questions concerning matters of law, but if in error, will not be estopped from asserting the correct principles of law.

Legal Requirements

Applicable provisions of all federal, state, county and local laws and administrative procedures, regulations or rules shall govern the development, submittal and evaluation of all proposals received in response hereto. Florida law, including Florida's provisions on conflict of laws, shall govern any and all claims and disputes which may arise between persons submitting a proposal hereto and the department. Lack of knowledge of the law or applicable administrative procedures, regulations or rules by any proposer shall not constitute a cognizable defense against their effect.

Venue

The validity, interpretation and performance of the lease shall be controlled by and construed under the laws of the State of Florida. Any and all litigation arising under the lease shall be instituted in the appropriate court in ______________________ County.

Waiver

The failure of any party to the lease resulting from this RFP to object to or take affirmative action with respect to any conduct or the other which is in violation of the terms of the lease shall not be construed as a waiver of the violation or breach, or of any future violation or breach.

Public Access to Records

All documents, papers, letters or other materials relating to the lease that are made or received by the lessor in conjunction with the lease, are required to be available for public access and copying in the manner specified by Chapter 119, Florida Statutes. Such records shall be maintained for a period of at least three years after the expiration of the lease. The department may unilaterally cancel any lease resulting from this RFP for Lessor's refusal to allow access to public records.

Indemnification

The lessor shall act as an independent contractor and not as an employee of the department in the performance of the tasks and duties which are subject of the lease. Lessor shall be liable, and agrees to be liable for, and shall indemnify, defend and hold the department, the State of Florida, its officers and employees, harmless from all claims, suits, judgments or damages (including litigation costs and reasonable attorney's fees) arising from the Lessor's performance of the tasks and duties which are subject of the lease whether accomplished by subcontractor or not, including:

1. Obtaining consent of any nature whatsoever,

2. Any and all claims arising from contracts between the lessor and other parties made pursuant to the lease,

3. Actions resulting from hidden defects in the property which a reasonable inspection of the premises did not reveal.

Subcontracting

The lessor may enter into written subcontracts for performance of work under the lease but only with prior written approval of the department. The department shall have the continuing right throughout the term of any lease resulting from this RFP to disapprove subcontractors if such disapproval would be in the best interest of the department. The department shall have the right to inspect and acquire copies of any of the documents executed between the lessor and the subcontractor. No subcontract which the lessor enters into with respect to performance under the lease shall in any way relieve the lessor of any responsibility for performance of duties required by law or required in any lease resulting from this RFP.

Unauthorized Aliens

NOTICE TO LESSOR. The department shall consider the employment by any contractor of unauthorized aliens a violation of Section 274A(e) of the Immigration and Nationality Act. Such violation shall be cause for unilateral cancellation of the lease.

Public Entity Crime

A person or affiliate who has been placed on the convicted vendor list following a conviction for public entity crime may not submit a proposal on a contract to provide any goods or services to a public entity, may not submit a proposal on a contract with a public entity for the construction or repair of a public building or public work, may not submit bids/proposals on lease of real property to a public entity, may not be awarded or perform work as a contractor, supplier, subcontractor, or consultant under a contract with any public entity, and may not transact business with any public entity in excess of the threshold amount provided in Section 287.017, Florida Statutes, for category two for a period of thirty-six (36) months from the date of being place on the convicted vendor list.

Taxes and Insurance

A. The department is generally exempt from all federal, state and local taxes and no such taxes shall be included in the price of the proposal. The department shall have no responsibility for the payment of taxes which become payable by lessor or its subcontractors in performance of the lease, including real estate taxes.

B. The lessor is responsible for fire insurance and general liability coverage on the demised premises but is not liable for fire insurance coverage of the person and property of the lessee or any other person or property which may be placed in the demised premises.

C. The lessor shall be solely responsible for any and all damage to the leased premises between the time an offer is made pursuant to this RFP and acceptance of the property (not merely the offer) by the department.

Alternatives

For evaluation purposes, each proposal submitted will be evaluated against the requirements of this RFP. If a proposer desires to propose alternatives to the required specifications, he may do so by attaching a sheet to the RFP submittal document titled "Alternatives." However, these alternatives will not be presented to any evaluator for the department for use in comparison of proposals and can only be considered after an award is made. Selection of a proposal does not imply acceptance of any accompanying alternatives. However, once submitted as part of this proposal, they may be considered and accepted individually with separate notification.

Historical Properties

If the facility being offered is a historical property, proof of such historical property designation shall be provided with the proposal. Failure to provide this proof will not prevent the evaluation of the proposal, but as specified in 267.061, Florida Statutes, no preference in property use will be given.

Pre-proposal Conference

If attendance at the pre-proposal conference scheduled in the RFP or associated advertisement is not mandatory, information and explanations provided at the conference must be complied with by the proposer and non-attendance shall not be an excuse for noncompliance, nor for additional costs to the state subsequent to award. However, if attendance is mandatory, the proposal form must be signed by someone in attendance at the pre-proposal conference.

Note: The purpose of the pre-proposal conference is to provide proposer's an opportunity to ask questions. Remarks and explanations at the conference shall not be binding and shall not change the provisions of the RFP. The department will orally respond, to the best of its ability and knowledge, to questions raised at the conference. However, the department will not be bound to its preliminary answers given at the conference. Changes or amendments to the RFP will be accomplished only in writing and will be sent to all those who express in writing an interest in submitting an offer pursuant to this RFP.

Any person requiring special accommodation because of a disability at any public meetings relating to this RFP should contact ______________ at (xxx-xxx-xxxx) extension __________ (voice), or through the Florida Relay Service at 1-800-955-8771 (TTD) at least 48 hours prior to the scheduled meeting.

Mandatory Requirements

The department has established certain mandatory requirements which must be included as part of any proposal. The use of the terms "shall," "must," or "will," (except to indicate simple futurity) in this RFP indicate a mandatory requirement or condition.

The words "should" or "may" in this RFP indicate desirable attributes or conditions, but are permissive in nature. Deviation from, or omission of, such a desirable feature will not by itself cause rejection of a proposal.

Interpretation of RFP Documents

A. From the date this RFP is issued until a determination to award or reject is made, no contact related to this RFP will be allowed between a proposer and any department staff, with the exception of the Issuing Officer. Contact initiated by the department may be responded to by individuals designated by the Issuing Officer. Any unauthorized contact may disqualify the proposer from further consideration.

B. Questions concerning an interpretation of meaning, ambiguity, conditions and specifications of the RFP, and/or requests for changes to conditions and specifications, must be in writing, addressed to the Issuing Officer. The envelope should be identifiable as questions regarding the RFP. Copies of such questions should be received no less than 15 working days prior to proposal opening so that final answers can be mailed to all prospective proposers who requested a copy of this RFP, in the form of written Addendum. The terms and conditions of this RFP will be incorporated in the resulting lease.

C. Any prospective proposer who disputes the reasonableness or appropriateness of the terms, conditions or specifications of this RFP and wishes to protest same, shall file a formal written protest in accordance with Section 120.57(3), Florida Statutes, Chapter 28-110, Florida Administrative Code within 72 hours (excluding state holidays, Saturdays and Sundays) of the receipt of this RFP package. Any proposer who disputes the department's notice of decision shall file a formal written protest pursuant to Chapter 120, Florida Statutes, within 72 hours (excluding state holidays, Saturdays and Sundays) of the posting of the disputed notice.

D. Any person who files a formal written protest shall, at the time of filing the formal written protest, post a bond as set forth in Section 255.25(3)(c), Florida Statutes. Failure to both file a formal written protest and to post a bond shall constitute a waiver of proceedings under Chapter 120, Florida Statutes.

Preparation and Submission of Proposals

A. Proposals must be submitted on the RFP Submittal Form. **Proposals not submitted on the RFP Submittal Form will be rejected as Non-Responsive.**

B. Proposers shall deliver the original and __________ copies of their proposal no later than the date and time specified in the Timetable in Section 1. The original proposal must contain original documents required to be submitted by proposers.

C. Each proposer must complete the RFP Submittal Form providing acknowledgments as requested.

D. Each proposal submitted shall be signed by the owner(s), corporate officials, or legal representative(s). The corporate, trade, or partnership title must be either stamped or typewritten beside the actual signature(s). If the RFP is signed by a legal representative, agent or broker, written evidence as described in paragraph 2.2 from the owner of record of his/her authority must accompany the proposal. All proposal signatures must be original signatures. **This written notice must be on the Special Power of Attorney Form (Attachment_____).**

E. All RFP Submittal Form sheets and required documents must be properly executed and must be submitted in a sealed and titled envelope or wrapper. The face of the envelope shall be addressed to the Issuing Officer identified on the cover sheet of this proposal package. It shall show proposal opening date, time and lease number as indicated on the first page of this proposal package as follows:

To: ____, Issuing Officer

Proposal Opening Date: _______________________, 20_____.

Time: ____EST.

Lease Number: ____________________________________

F. The address listed on the cover sheet is the Issuing Officer's office address, which may not be the address at which the proposal opening is to be held.

It is the proposer's responsibility to assure that his proposal is delivered at the proper time and place of the proposal opening as stated in the advertisement. Proposals arriving late will not be considered.

Cost of Developing and Submitting Proposal: Ownership

A. Neither the department nor the state is liable for any of the costs incurred by a proposer in preparing and submitting a proposal.

B. All proposals become the property of the department upon receipt and will not be returned to the proposer's once opened. The department shall have the right to use any and all ideas or adaptations of ideas contained in any proposal received in response to this RFP without the payment of any fee or royalty for that use. Selection or rejection of the proposal will not affect this right.

Withdrawal of Proposals

A. A proposal may be withdrawn in person by a proposer or authorized representative who presents proper identification and signs a receipt for the proposal, but only if the withdrawal is made prior to the exact deadline set for receipt of proposals.

B. Errors and omissions on the part of the proposer in preparation of the proposal confers no right to withdrawal of the proposal after it has been opened.

Opening of Proposals

A. Proposals will be opened publicly at the local time and place stated in the Timetable (Section 1). The Issuing Officer, whose duty it is to open them, will decide when the specified time has arrived. No proposal received thereafter will be considered and will be returned unopened. No responsibility will be attached to any officer for the premature opening of a proposal not properly sealed, addressed or identified.

B. At the time fixed for the opening of proposals, only the proposer, location and lease rates will be made public for the information of proposer's and others interested who may be present.

C. Upon written request, proposal tabulations will be furnished in the form of a standard department proposal synopsis.

Inspection or Examination of Proposals

Proposals are not public records subject to the provisions of Section 119.01(1), Florida Statutes, until such time as the department provides notice of a decision pursuant to Section 120.53(5), Florida Statutes, or within 10 days after proposal opening, whichever is earlier. After 10 days or notice of decision, whichever is earlier, proposal files may be examined during normal working hours **by appointment.**

Evaluation of Proposals

A. Terms and Conditions: All proposals submitted to the department are subject to the department's terms and conditions contained in the RFP. Any and all additional terms and conditions submitted by proposers are rejected and shall have no force or effect.

B. The department reserves the right to make an award with or without further negotiations with the highest scoring proposer. Therefore, proposals should be submitted with the most favorable terms the proposer can offer. The department may reject any and all proposals that are conditional, incomplete, or which contain irregularities, as this will be deemed to be a counteroffer. **Issuance of the RFP in no way constitutes a commitment by the department to award a contract or to enter into a lease.**

C. Proposals received are first evaluated to determine technical responsiveness, this includes submittal on Proposal Submittal Form, inclusion of required information, data, attachments, signatures and such other fatal criteria as are set out herein. Non-responsive proposals will be withdrawn from further consideration. Non-responsive proposers will be informed at the time of posting. Any protest must be filed within 72 hours of posting, excluding state holidays, Saturday and Sunday. Protests filed after the 72-hour posting notice will be considered untimely.

D. Responsive proposals will be evaluated against how well they meet the criteria set out in this RFP. This may include a visit to each proposed facility. After an application of the evaluation criteria to each proposal, the results will be presented to the department official having award authority for final evaluation and determination of which, if any, offer will be selected for further negotiation.

E. The department reserves, in its sole discretion, the right to waive any minor irregularities or technicality not limited to the correction of simple mistakes or typographical errors and to seek clarification of proposals received, when such is in the best interest of the state. The department also reserves the right to negotiate a different level of services, e.g., full service to non-full service for a corresponding reduction in rate.

Non-Responsive Proposers

A. Proposals which do not meet all mandatory requirements of this RFP or which fail to provide all required information, documents or materials will be rejected as non-responsive. The department reserves the right to determine which proposals meet the mandatory requirements of the RFP.

B. Proposers which in the department's judgment, after the evaluation of documents required to be submitted in response to this RFP, do not possess the capability to perform the contract requirements or the integrity and reliability to assure good faith performance based on past experience, shall be rejected as non-responsive.

Additional Information

The department reserves the right to request additional information from proposers in order to make a thorough review and fair comparison of all proposals submitted. Failure to request additional information is not to be construed as an error on the part of the department.

Evaluation Criteria (Award Factors)

The successful proposal will be that one determined to be lowest and best and in the best interest of the state. All proposals will be evaluated on the factors below:

A. Associated Fiscal Costs:

1. <u>Rental:</u>

a. Rental rates for basic term of lease. Evaluated using total present value methodology for basic term of lease by application of the present value discount rate of ______________ .

Maximum points: __________ Points Awarded: __________

b. Rental rates for optional renewal terms of lease. Rates proposed are within projected budgetary restraint of the department.

Maximum points: __________ Points Awarded: __________

2. <u>Moving Costs:</u> (optional)

Cost of relocating communication network(s) (voice, video and data), furniture and other equipment as determined by a site survey conducted at each proposed facility by the department's management systems director and/or facility manager.

Maximum points: __________ Points Awarded: __________

B. Location:

The effect of environmental factors (including the physical characteristics of the building and the area surrounding it) on the efficient and economical conduct of department operations planned for the requested space.

1. Proximity of facility to the department's preferred area.

   Maximum points: _________ Points Awarded: _________

   (Optional)

   Facility offered within 1 mile of ______________ ______________ points

   Facility offered within 2 miles of ______________ ______________ points

   Facility offered within 3 miles of ______________ ______________ points

   Facility farther than 3 miles of ______________ ______________ points

2. Frequency and availability of public transportation near the offered space.

   Maximum points: _________ Points Awarded: _________

3. Present condition of physical plant, property the building sits on, adjacent structures and surrounding neighborhood.

   Maximum points: _________ Points Awarded: _________

4. Security issues posed by building, by associated parking and by surrounding neighborhood, as evidenced by police reports, quality of exterior lighting, and obstructed entrances/exits.

   Maximum points: _________ Points Awarded: _________

C. Property:

1. The extent to which the offered space is designed to efficient layout and good utilization of space and energy, for example (house service units in proximity to interdependent units, Sustainable Building Rating or E.A. Energy Analysis).

   Maximum points: _________ Points Awarded: _________

2. The extent to which the building, parking area and property as a whole is conducive to future expansions.

   Maximum points: _________ Points Awarded: _________

3. Providing the aggregate square footage in a single building is preferred. Proposals will be considered, but fewer points given, which offer the aggregate square footage in not more than two buildings connected by overhangs and sidewalks. Buildings which are immediately adjacent or within _________ yards of one another will also be considered but receive fewer points.

   Maximum points: _________ Points Awarded: _________

Aggregate space in a single building ______________ points

Two buildings connected by sidewalks/overhangs ______________ points

Adjacent buildings or within ____________ yards ______________ points

Total Award Factors: _____100

Total Points Awarded: _____

Rejection of Proposals

A. The department reserves the right to reject any and all proposals when such rejection is in the interest of the State of Florida. Such rejection shall not be arbitrary, but be based on strong justification. Notification will be made at the time of posting.

B. If all proposals are rejected, the state reserves the right to change specifications as necessary and reinstate procedures for soliciting competitive proposals.

Proposal Award

A. The department presently intends to enter into a lease agreement based on submission and acceptance of the proposal which is in the best interest of the department and the state.

B. Notification of proposal award or no award will be made by posting at the address shown above in the Timetable and will be made at the **Time of Posting**. Other interested parties also may request to be notified of the award.

C. Notification of proposal award is final when either no protests are submitted or after all protests are resolved by an administrative hearing procedure and approval from the Department of Management Services is obtained for the proposed lease. Subsequent appeals at district court level will not mandate a delay in the proposal award.

D. The lease, which is the subject of this RFP, will not be considered to be entered into until final execution by all parties of the lease document referred to in Attachment __________.

Protest Procedures

A. Any substantially affected person may dispute the specifications of the RFP or an award made pursuant to it through the filing of a protest as provided in Chapter 120, Florida Statutes.

B. Proposal Award: To be considered a protest of an award, a formal protest must be filed in accordance with 120.57(3), Florida Statutes, and Chapter 28-110, Florida Administrative Code.

C. Failure to file a protest bond as required by 287.042(2)(c) and 255.25(3)(d), Florida Statutes, within the deadline prescribed for filing the formal written protest shall result in rejection of the protest with prejudice. Failure to file the protest bond within the deadline for filing the formal written protest shall constitute a waiver of proceedings under Chapter 120.

1. To protest either the specifications or the result of this RFP, a written notice of intent to protest must be filed with the project contact person listed on the cover sheet of this RFP within 72 hours of receipt of the RFP documents or within 72 hours of posting of the results of this RFP (excluding state holidays, Saturday and Sunday). Within 10 calendar days after the notice of intent to protest is filed, and if a protest is still desired, a formal written protest must be filed with the project contact person or the right to protest will be waived.

2. At the time of filing of the formal protest, a bond payable to the department in an amount equal to one percent of the total lease payments over the term of the lease or $5,000, whichever is more, must accompany the formal protest. This bond shall be written by a surety company licensed to do business in Florida and shall be conditioned upon the payment of all costs which may be imposed against the protester in the administrative hearing in which the action is brought and in any subsequent appellate court proceeding. If the department prevails, it should recover all costs and charges which shall be included in the final order or judgment, excluding attorney's fees. Upon payment of such costs and charges by the protester, the remainder of the bond shall be returned. The department shall pay and be responsible for no interest earned on the bond even if interest is earned.

Additional Requirements

A. The proposal submitted will remain valid for a minimum of 60 days following the posting.

B. The successful proposer agrees to enter into a lease agreement on the Department of Management Services' Standard Lease Agreement Form BPM 4054 (included for your information as Attachment ______________).

C. The successful proposer must provide a Disclosure of Ownership using the Department of Management Services' Form FM 4114 (Attachment _____) as soon after the proposal award as practical.

D. If requested, the successful proposer shall provide the legal description (Metes and Bounds, Plat, Government Survey System), of property being offered, as well as the general description, room number, building name, street address, and fire district.

E. If successful, proposer agrees to incorporate as additional covenants and conditions of the lease agreement all of the terms, requirements and conditions (including proposer's response, acknowledgment and rental rate representations) contained in this RFP Form and all attachments which were executed and submitted by lessor as successful proposer for this lease.

F. (Optional Requirement) If successful, the proposer shall furnish as a proposal guarantee, a **Performance Bond or Irrevocable Bank Letter of Credit** to the Department of ________________ ____________ within __________ calendar days from the date the award is final. The Letter of Credit will be in an amount equal to 1/2% of 1% of the proposed lease rental obligation over the base term of the lease.

IV. Request for Proposal - Proposal Submittal Form

Lease Number: ______________ District: ____________________

RFP Opening Date: __________ RFP Opening Time: _________ EST

Location of RFP Opening: ____
____
____

Name of Proposer: ____

Contact Person: ____

Phone No.: _________________

Address: ____

FOR:

Department of ____

County: ____

Issuing Officer: ____

Address: ____

It is the proposer's responsibility to be familiar with all aspects of this RFP. The proposer must write answers where requested. Having thoroughly reviewed the RFP and all attachments, this proposal is submitted in reply:

Net Square Footage Required

_________________ measured in accordance with the Standard Method of Space Measurement (Florida Administrative Code 60H-2.003)

Any and all references to square feet of the Proposed Space contained in a Reply must be "usable square feet" in accordance with the Department of Management Services Standard Method for Measuring Floor Area in Office Buildings, The Agency and Department of Management Services reserve the right to independently verify the space measurement

Note: Restrooms, common tenant lobbies and mechanical rooms are not included in calculating net rentable square footage.

PROPOSER RESPONSE: The net square feet proposed is: _________________________

(Space offered must be within the 3% required.)

Type of Space Required

______________________________, for use as ____________________________________.

Space to Be Located

_____________________ County, Florida, within boundaries shown on the attached map (Attachment ____________).

PROPOSER RESPONSE: ____
(Address of proposed location)

Proposer to mark location of site on map (Attachment ________________), and include with proposal. Note if space is located within preferred area.

Space to be Made Available

Space to be made available ________________ or within ________ days after notification of proposal award, whichever occurs last. Time of availability for the space in this RFP is of the essence. If the successful proposer fails to make the space available when specified in the proposal, the proposer shall be liable to the department for liquidated damages of ____________ per day for each additional day until the space or portion thereof is made available and, where deemed necessary by the department, for the actual cost of re-procurement of the desired space.

If delays are caused by the department, a written extension will be granted to the lessor. Unforeseen circumstances beyond the control of the lessor (such as acts of God or labor strikes), which delay performance may be cause for the lessor to request an extension (in writing) from the project Issuing Officer. Any damage incurred by the department for cost overruns and denied extension requests will be subtracted from the first and, if necessary, succeeding month's rental payments until the balance is zero. A final decision concerning an extension shall be at the sole discretion of the department.

Lessor shall, on notice of award, diligently seek zoning and concurrence, if required, and permits appropriate to the use classification of the local jurisdiction beyond the possibility of appeal so that the proposed property may be used for the purposes specified herein. Permits and/or a concurrence certificate must be obtained within ________ days of bid award. Should zoning, permits and concurrence not be obtained on or before this date, the department may at any time thereafter rescind any award previously made without liability to the lessor, notwithstanding any partial performance which may exist at the time of rescission.

Term of Lease

_____________________ years with an option to renew for ________________ option periods.

Visual Material

As part of the bid submittal, bidders are to provide:

A. Clear photographs (8" x 10") or architect's renderings showing exterior front, sides and rear of the proposed facility (color preferred).

B. A scaled (1/16" or 1/8" or 1/4" = 1'0") floor plan showing present configurations with measurements. The final floor plan will be as described in the specifications.

C. Calculation of the net rentable square footage available using measurements from the floor plan. Refer to Standard Method of Measurement (Attachment _________).

D. A scaled site layout showing the present location of building(s), configuration and number of parking spaces assigned to the department, access and egress routes, and any proposed changes which the prospective lessor will make before the department is to occupy the offered premises.

Final site layout must allow and utilize input from the department so as to best accommodate the needs of the department.

Services

The successful proposer is to furnish all services. Services provided by the lessor shall include all necessary build-out and cleanup and shall provide the department with clean ready to operate space. Services shall also include payment of electric, gas, water, sewage, trash removal, storm water fees, recycling service, interior, common area and exterior maintenance, janitorial services, monthly pest control, and other services as provided for in the RFP package and the Standard Lease Agreement (Attachment _____). (Fire alarm system monitoring and elevator maintenance, phone - optional)

The successful proposer will provide the lease space to the department (lessee) for its exclusive use 24 hours per day, 7 days per week, during the lease term. The space to be leased by the department will be fully occupied during normal working hours from 7:00 a.m. to 6:00 p.m., Monday through Friday, excluding state holidays, Saturdays and Sundays, and may be fully or partially occupied during all other periods of time as necessary or as required at the sole discretion of the department. Services are to be provided during all normal business hours of occupancy at no additional cost to the department (lessee).

Public Transportation

Specify availability of present public transportation to the proposer's proposed facility.

Proposer Response:

_________ Taxi

_________ Bus: Frequency of Service ____________________________

_________ Other: Specify ____________________________________

NOTE: Attach copy of public transportation schedule.

Dining Facilities

Indicate availability of dining facilities within the area of proposed facility, and within appropriate distance from facility.

Proposer Response: (Check one or more)

_________The property contains a cafeteria.

_________The property contains a dining room with food vending machines.

__________ The 3 nearest restaurants are: Distance:

____________________ ____________________

____________________ ____________________

____________________ ____________________

Existing Tenants

If the offered space or any portion thereof (including parking areas) is presently occupied or will be covered by an active lease(s) on the date of occupancy or thereafter, written documentation from the tenant(s) acknowledging the Lessor's proposal and ability to vacate premises by the proposed date or earlier must be presented with your response to allow the proposal to be considered responsive. If existing tenants are on a month-to-month lease, the proposer must provide a letter explaining this.

Proposer Response: (Check one)

__________ Existing tenant acknowledgment(s), included as part of this bid.

__________ Not applicable

NOTE: Include existing tenant acknowledgment with proposal (if applicable).

Parking

A minimum of __________ parking spaces are required, more if required by local zoning provisions. This parking is to be under the control of proposer, off-street, suitably paved and lined, and is to be provided as part of the lease cost to the department.

The lessor will grant to the lessee an (**exclusive, non-exclusive**) right to use ________ or more parking spaces. Lessor shall submit with this proposal a letter certifying that the lessor agrees to the required number of parking spaces on site, states the number of parking spaces per net rentable square feet of space as required by the local zoning jurisdiction, and provides a site plan of the parking lot identifying the number of parking spaces assigned to specific other tenants. The purpose of this submittal is to assure that parking spaces conform to local jurisdiction requirements of number of size, and that the number of parking spaces requested can be achieved without infringing on or combining with the parking requirements of other tenants.

A minimum of __________ of the total required spaces must be full-size parking spaces (as opposed to compact size).

A minimum of __________ of the total required spaces must meet the standards of DCA Accessibility Requirements Manual published by the Department of Community Affairs, latest edition. (Your local building official has a copy.)

Proposer Response:

______________ Exclusive parking spaces available on site

______________ Non-exclusive parking spaces located on site

____________________ Distance from the proposed facility

____________________ Non-exclusive parking spaces located off site

____________________ Distance from the proposed facility

____________________ Spaces required by local zoning jurisdiction

NOTE: Proposer must provide with submittal current evidence of control of all parking spaces being proposed. Permission to park is not control.

Recycling Program

The state is required by law to collect high-grade office paper.

A. The successful proposer will be required:

a.) To coordinate the participation of the janitorial staff in the recycling program,

b.) To supply and maintain standard trash dumpster(s) and recycling dumpster(s),

c.) To provide an external 10' x 15' concrete pad for each dumpster enclosed with fence and/or shrubbery so as not to distract from the aesthetics of the facility. If external recycling dumpsters on the site are impractical, the successful proposer may propose an internal collection room.

B. The janitorial staff will be required:

a.) To remove recyclable material from the office receptacle and/or bulk recyclable loads,

b.) To place recyclable materials and non-recyclable materials in respective dumpsters,

c.) To arrange pickup by recycling contractor.

C. The department will:

Appoint a department recycling monitor who will promote the program and monitor program effectiveness.

D. The recycling contractor will provide and maintain clearly marked:

a.) Individual office sorting containers.

b.) Internal janitorial collection carts.

c.) Exterior storage containers.

BUILDING REQUIREMENTS

Accessibility Standards and Alterations

Lessor agrees that the proposed premises now conform (or that prior to lessee's occupancy, said premises shall, at the Lessor's expense, be brought into conformance) to the requirements of

Section 553.501 – 553.513, Florida Statutes, providing requirements for the physically disabled and with the requirements of Public Law 101-336, July 26, 1990, known as the "Americans with Disabilities Act of 1990" Appendix to Part 1991, prepared by the United States Architectural and Transportation Barriers Compliance Board.

The proposed space must be in an **existing building**. To be considered as existing, the proposed space must be enclosed with a roof system and exterior walls in place. Renovations to bring the facility into compliance with all applicable federal, state and local codes and regulations and/or to meet the desired arrangements are permitted, if carried out in accordance with prescribed procedures:

A. Proposals offering multi-story or multi-level buildings must have all stories/levels serviced by an elevator which meets the requirements of DCA Accessibility Manual (your local building official has a copy).

B. Any renovations required must comply with the Fire Safety Standards of the State Building Code before relocations are commenced as required by Florida Statutes 255.25(5) (NFPA 101). If renovations are required, successful proposer must submit two sets of plans for certification as outlined in (Attachment __________). (Renovations/Construction Plan requirements for Submittal to State Fire Marshal, January 1994). Building codes adopted by local jurisdictions shall be applicable to all lease construction. The property must comply with DCA Accessibility Manual published by the Florida Department of Community Affairs (may be seen at your local building official's office).

C. All construction shall be performed by licensed contractors. The cost of all construction, permits and fees shall be borne by the lessor. Upon plan approval by the department, construction schedules will be provided by the owner to achieve the required occupancy date.

D. Proposals offering multi-story buildings must meet the applicable building code and live load minimum of ______________ pounds per square foot. The successful proposer must obtain certification by a structural engineer registered with the State of Florida.

E. Upon completion of design, proposer shall provide reduced scale reproducible drawings showing layout and room numbers in both hard copy and CAD format.

Proposer Response: (If applicable) ______________ pounds per square foot. (Submit documentation with proposal.)

F. Upon completion of all construction work, the proposer shall provide as-built drawings of the facility, reproducible and in CAD format (AutoCAD preferred), to the Issuing Officer.

Revised Codes

The facility must comply with the latest revision of all applicable codes and standards.

Hazardous Material

<u>**Asbestos:**</u> The successful proposer shall provide to the lessee prior to occupancy an acceptable State of Florida, or AHERA guideline asbestos survey. Additionally, the proposer shall provide copies of all asbestos abatement reports which have taken place in the proposed leased space or building. If asbestos material still exists in the space or building, the lessor shall have or establish an active

Operations and Maintenance (O & M) Plan as recommended by the U.S. Environmental Protection Agency (EPA) and State of Florida. The lessor shall provide a copy of the annual O & M Plan inspection to the lessee no later than 60 days following the yearly anniversary date.

All friable asbestos containing materials, not enclosed, encapsulated, and in poor condition must be removed from any interior area of the building or space prior to occupancy. Materials such as floor tile, gaskets, roofing, ceiling tiles, caulking, etc., that are in good condition and/or meet the requirements of Category I and II non-friable ACM under the NESHAP's requirements (U.S. EPA, 40 CFR Part 61, Subpart M) may remain in the building or space providing that it is not disturbed and does not become friable. In the event renovations or carpet replacement causes the asbestos to become friable, the landlord will be responsible for the cost of removal and/or abatement. The landlord may not capriciously withhold approval of necessary renovations or scheduled carpet replacement.

Should friable asbestos be discovered either during construction remodeling or after occupancy, the owner shall immediately remove the hazardous material and reimburse the department for any and all relocation costs and delays associated with this removal.

Proposer Response:

_____The property contains NO friable asbestos or hazardous asbestos-based fiber materials or PCB transformers.

_____ The property at present does contain hazardous asbestos or hazardous asbestos-based fiber materials. This material will be removed properly before occupancy at Lessor's expense.

_____ PCB transformers shall be disposed of properly

Hazardous Substances

A. The lessor assures that the proposed site does not contain hazardous substances or electromagnetic fields, whether above or below ground level. Further, the lessor agrees to prohibit the generation, storage or disposal of hazardous substances above or below ground level. Should hazardous substances be revealed during the term of this lease, the lessor shall immediately remove material and restore the site in compliance with all applicable regulations, and reimburse the department for any and all relocation costs.

B. Radon Gas: Radon is a naturally occurring radioactive gas. When accumulated in buildings in sufficient quantities, it may present health risks to persons who are exposed to it over time. Levels of radon that exceed federal and state guidelines have been found in buildings in Florida. Additional information regarding radon and radon testing may be obtained from your county's public health unit. Prior to occupancy, certified proof of radon tests must be provided if the space offered is at or below grade level. If radon measurements above 4 CI/L are detected, the lessor shall promptly act to reduce the level to meet the standard. (Radon Hotline: 1-800-543-8279)

The lease number must be identified on each packet of information submitted, including the diskette, if applicable. The engineer must identify the system used and shall stamp and seal the document set.

If documentation has not been returned from DMS at the time of RFP submittal, submit documentation (Priority Mail, Return Receipt or letter of receipt from DMS) that shows it was sent to the department **prior** to RFP opening.

Energy Performance Analysis:

a.) To calculate the Energy Performance Analysis, see Attachment _____.

b) The successful proposer will be required to document the building design as part of the renovation plan submittal process.

A. Energy Star Rating:

The State requires wherever possible that leased space be in an Energy Star Rated Facility.

Does this facility meet the standards of an Energy Star building? Yes _____ or No _____

SPACE REQUIREMENTS

Office and Room Sizes

Number and approximate size of offices and rooms for internal space requirements:

Approximate number & Size		Square Footage	Net Square Footage	Special Requirement
	Offices not to exceed			
	Offices not to exceed			
	Offices not to exceed			
	Offices not to exceed			
	Clerical Areas			
	Central File Room			Fire Rated
	Closed Client File Room			
	Reception			
	Food Stamp Issuance			
	Forms Room (with shelves)			
	Law/Conference			
	Telephone Room			
	Training Center			
	Copy Machine			
	LAN Room			
	Employee Lounge			
	Mail Room			
	Playroom/Storage			

SPACE REQUIREMENTS - Continued

Office and Room Sizes

Number and approximate size of offices and rooms for internal space requirements:

Approximate number & Size		**Square Footage**	**Net Square Footage**	**Special Requirement**
	Interview Room			
	Printer Rooms			
	Storage Rooms			
	Internal Circulation			
Total Square Feet				

Restrooms

In conformity with code requirements, lessor is required to provide a minimum of four (4) restrooms for public use: two (2) men's, two (2) women's, and two (2) restrooms for staff use: one (1) men's, one (1) women's, with a minimum of two (2) per floor. Each is to be equipped as follows:

	MEN'S		WOMEN'S	
	Public	Staff	Public	Staff
Water Closets				
Urinals				
Lavatories with mirrors				

All sinks shall be supplied with cold water.

Note: Must meet requirements of DCA/ADA Accessibility Requirements Manual.

Floor Plans

Final floor plans will be a joint effort of department staff and the successful proposer. The successful proposer is to provide architectural services by a licensed architect to prepare renovation plans. The final floor plan is subject to the department's approval and State Fire Marshal review and approval.

A. Interior Walls shall be extended from floor to ceiling and designed or insulated sufficiently to prevent noise transmission. (Optional)

B. Ceiling Height is to be eight (8) feet minimum. Ceilings may exceed that height if energy efficiency is not adversely affected. Deviation shall be subject to the department's approval.

D. Interior Hall width shall be a minimum of five (5) feet.

E. Design shall maximize the number of exterior window offices and provide natural lighting where possible.

Monthly Construction Meetings

During the course of construction, mandatory monthly progress meetings will be held at the construction site. The facilities services manager will coordinate and chair this meeting. The lessor and/or his contractor agent shall present:

A. Updated progress schedule to achieve the desired completion date,

B. Special problems, remedial actions,

C. Status of fees, permits, building inspection, violations.

Occupancy

The date of lease payment commencement will be determined by the date a Certificate of Occupancy is issued and final acceptance by the State Fire Marshal. In addition, the following criteria has been met:

A. All installations are operational and complete,

B. A letter of acceptance has been signed by the Issuing Officer.

Fire Prevention

Lessor shall conform to all requirements of the State Fire Marshal and shall obtain pre-occupancy inspection and annual inspections by the State Fire Marshal as required by 633.085, Florida Statutes.

Heating, Ventilation and Air Conditioning

Provide sufficient climate control units with adequate ductwork, registers and grills sufficient to uniformly cool and heat the entire leased area. Unit(s) shall be equipped with automatic thermostat(s) fitted with tamper proof covers. Temperatures will be maintained to achieve an average zone temperature of 75 degrees Fahrenheit. Control thermostats will be located in areas to achieve proper zone temperature.

VAV zone boxes shall maintain a minimum air flow (circulation) of a least 25% after the zone temperature reaches its set point (if applicable). Outside fresh air intake vents, dampers, automatic controls, and power driven systems for fresh air (if applicable) shall be fully operational according to design specifications (not closed off). Carbon dioxide monitors (if applicable) shall be calibrated every 3 years at a minimum.

Buildings or spaces older than 20 years, where ductwork has not been retrofitted, with ridged air conveyance ductwork (lined or non-lined on the air side), turning vanes, operational control systems on the air side, air handlers that are to remain in place, shall be thoroughly inspected for excessive buildup of dust and contaminants (i.e., mildew, mold fungi, etc.) by the firm performing the test and balance of the space or building. If excessive buildup of dust, dirt or contaminants is present, the lessor shall contract at his expense with a licensed mechanical firm to have the ductwork, all interior control surfaces, turning vanes, registers, grills and the interior of the air handlers cleaned properly.

The entire air conveyance system shall be inspected, calibrated, tested and balanced by a firm professionally engaged in this type of work, just prior to occupancy, and every 5 years thereafter. The scope of work shall include all the items listed above, and include operating controls, sensors and controls that must be calibrated, inspection of air handlers, pumps, valves, condensate drain lines, condensate pans, coils, ductwork, dampers, VAV boxes, cooling towers, or anything that has a relationship to the air conveyance or operating control system. The test and balance firm shall provide a report in writing to the lessor that the above listed items and specifics have been inspected, and are in proper operating order. A copy of this report shall be provided to the lessee prior to occupancy and after each 5-year re-inspection.

The lessor shall inspect all air handler coils (all layers), condensate drain pans, condensate drain pipes, cooling towers (if applicable), gaskets, or couplings for microbial growth and buildup, due to normal operating conditions, standing water caused by clogs, leaks, etc., on a monthly basis and document any discrepancies. Lessor shall immediately correct any and all problems to current standards or care with due diligence to prevent possible health problems related to the HVAC system and its operation. Fresh air intake vents shall be inspected for any microbial growth, buildup of dirt and thoroughly cleaned, if necessary. Filters (if applicable) on fresh air intake vents shall be cleaned or replaced bi-monthly. A monthly service record shall be maintained by the lessor.

Indoor Air Quality Testing

Lessor shall provide fresh air intake of 20 or more cubic feet per minute per person, as recommended by ASHRAE (the American Society of Heating, Refrigerating and Air Conditioning Engineers). Incoming fresh air to be pre-conditioned (filtered, moisture removed, heated or cooled). Interior humidity shall not exceed 60% relative humidity. The building envelope shall be maintained to a positive pressure to prevent moisture intrusion that may result in micro biological and fungal growth on surfaces, furnishings or interstitial spaces.

In the event a suspected air quality problem arises, the lessee reserves the right to have the indoor air quality tested at its own expense by a CIAQP (Certified Indoor Air Quality Professional), CIEC (Certified Indoor Environmental Consultant), CIH (Certified Industrial Hygienist), or P.E. (Professional Engineer), whose primary business and focus is indoor air quality/environment to determine the cause of the problem. After assessment, if test results indicate conclusively that a problem exists, the lessor shall take immediate corrective action to remedy the situation and reimburse the agency for the costs of conducting such test(s).

Painting and construction shall be conducted under ventilating and occupancy conditions that will not result in indoor air quality complaints.

Security Requirements

A. All outside doors shall be equipped with dead-bolt or dead-latch locks and panic hardware.

B. All interior doors (except restrooms) shall have key lockable locksets, turn-latch of push button on backside, master keyed. (optional)

C. All opening outside windows shall have interior locks.

D. Night illumination is required at all outside doors and all parking areas.

E. Provide keys to all locksets in accordance with a master keying system acceptable to the department. Provide ______ entrance keys.

F. Provide a security alarm system. All perimeter windows and doors shall be connected to a 24-hour central station, police response monitoring system with two (2) programmable keyed terminals, locations to be determined by the department. (Optional)

G. Provide a keycard type access control system for _____ doors. System to be CPU based and integrated with alarm points of the central system. Loss of power shall not cause loss of access. System to track entry/exit to doors of all staff. Permit fee and alarm monitoring to be paid by lessor. (Optional)

Signs

A. Interior identification:

1) Lessor will provide interior main directory showing location of all programs, conference rooms, etc. Provide directory signs on each floor and in entrance suites showing programs and/or room use. Provide directional signs as required.

2) Other ADA compliance, raised letter signs with Braille shall be provided to identify all restrooms (handicap symbol on restrooms for person with disabilities), conference rooms, mechanical equipment, and other special use rooms. All rooms and/or offices are to be numbered consecutively.

B. Exterior identification:

1) For buildings where department occupies 50% or more of the gross lease space, the department shall have the option to require department signage on the building exterior to be provided by the lessor either at the top of the building or at the entrance. Sign lighting encouraged.

2) Lessor is to provide vinyl lettering on all entrance doors to designate program(s).

Note: All signs must meet requirements of DCA/ADA Accessibility Requirements Manual, and are to be maintained by lessor.

Refrigerated Drinking Fountains

A. Provide a minimum of _____ per floor immediately adjacent to restrooms or lobby areas.

Note: Must meet the requirement of ADA/ANSI Standard A117.11980, Specifications for Making Buildings and Facilities Accessible to and Usable by Physically Handicapped People. (Your local building official should have a copy.)

Floor Coverings (optional)

New carpeting will be installed prior to acceptance of the building. All individual office spaces and conference rooms shall have at least _____ oz. weight, 20-26 face weight loop commercial grade anti-soil carpeting to benefit acoustics, comfort and minimum maintenance in cleaning. Lounge areas, reception areas and restrooms will be ceramic tiled or covered with non-slip commercial vinyl sheet flooring. Carpeting shall have UM-44D, ASTM D 3674-81/UM-44D, fire and 3.5 kilovolts electrostatic conductivity rating. All vinyl and carpeting shall be a color and by a manufacturer acceptable to the department, which will choose from an assortment of at least three samples provided by the lessor. Carpeting shall be treated to reduce staining.

Windows (optional requirement)

Window Covering

Exterior windows shall have blinds or shades to facilitate sunlight and energy control. Windows receiving direct sunlight shall be tinted or covered with energy saving film.

Ceiling Fans (optional, at discretion of lessee)

Fans shall be suspended a minimum of eight (8) feet above the finished floor level, where ceiling height permits, in those areas noted.

Lighting

A. All leased space to be provided with fluorescent lights to provide a minimum lighting level of:

10 foot-candles - halls and corridors, etc.

30 foot-candles - other public areas

50 foot-candles - offices, classrooms, conference rooms, etc.

50 foot-candles - computer rooms

(Measured with a General Electric type 214 Light Meter)

B. Interior lighting must include emergency lighting for security and safety. All emergency lights shall have battery packs and be tested monthly.

Electrical Requirements

Lessor shall provide:

A. Two (2) duplex receptacles per office, maximum three (3) offices per circuit,

B. Three (3) dedicated circuits for each break room,

C. Class "B" surge protection on all 120/208 circuit break panels,

D. Dedicated circuits as required for printers, copiers, etc.

E. Ground resistance test to assure less than 5 ohm better,

F. Housekeeping circuits separate from office circuitry,

G. Building must comply with National Electric Code latest edition at the time of occupancy.

Telephone and Computer Requirements (unique agency requirements)

(Area to be completed by Agency)

Janitorial Services

The successful proposer agrees to furnish janitorial and cleaning services as part of this lease agreement. This includes furnishing all cleaning/maintenance equipment and cleaning supplies as required, including but not limited to drinking cups at water fountains, bathroom tissues, paper towels, trash receptacle liners, liquid soap and doormats at entrances. All supplies are to be of good quality suitable for lessee's needs.

Maintenance and Repair

On or about every annual anniversary of the date of occupancy, a maintenance inspection will be conducted by the facilities services manager and the lessor or his representative to review the condition of the building interior, exterior and site. Any discrepancies will be noted and a date of correction completion established. During the term of the lease, if maintenance and repair items appear that are emergencies or recurring problems that have not received attention within three working days, the lessee will have the right to complete the work, by a contractor of Lessor's choice, and send the invoice to the lessor for payment. Non-responsiveness shall be deemed a breach of this lease. Failure by the lessor to correct or repair documented interior problems within 60 days after written notification by the lessee shall result in further legal action to obtain compliance. If the lessee is successful in court, the lessor agrees to pay any and all attorney's fees of the lessee, as well as impact costs due to decreased productivity.

Emergency Repairs

Upon occupancy, the lessor will furnish the names of the contractors who will be available 24 hours daily to service or repair glass, plumbing, HVAC, roofing, hardware (locks), electric, etc.

Interior Painting

All painted surfaces shall be freshly painted before occupancy at the commencement of this lease, and at least once every three years thereafter during the lease term and any renewals thereof. Touch-up painting to be done as needed. The department will be provided samples from which to choose colors and finishes (flat or semi-gloss). High traffic areas shall be repainted annually when requested by the department.

Florida Products and Labor

Florida products and labor shall be used wherever price and quality are equal.

Sales Taxes

The proposer will not be exempted from the state sales tax on materials to be used in the construction.

Miscellaneous Requirements (unique agency requirements)

Certification Regarding Debarment, Suspension, Ineligibility and Voluntary Exclusion Contracts/ Subcontracts

Any person submitting a proposal in response to this RFP must execute the enclosed form (Attachment _____) and submit it with the proposal.

Proposed Rental Rates

The following proposed net square foot per year rental rate includes all necessary remodeling, renovation and/or construction. It also includes payment of electric, water, sewage, trash removal and dumpster, pest control, interior and exterior maintenance, parking facilities and other services as provided in this RFP package and Standard Lease Agreement. The present value discount rate to be used in evaluating proposals received is __________ %.

Basic lease term and proposed rate per square foot per year:

Basic Lease Term	**Rate Per Square Foot**	**Total Annual Rental**
Year 1	$	$
Year 2	$	$
Year 3	$	$
Year 4	$	$
Year 5	$	$
Year 6	$	$
Year 7	$	$
Year 8	$	$
Year 9	$	$
Year 10	$	$
Option Renewal Terms:		
Year 1	$	$
Year 2	$	$
Year 3	$	$
Year 4	$	$
Year 5	$	$

Certification

I hereby certify as owner, officer or authorized agent that I have read the RFP and all its attachments and agree to abide by all requirements and conditions contained therein. I further certify that this Proposal Submittal constitutes my formal proposal in its entirety.

____

Submitting Proposer's Name

If lease is to be written in a name other than proposer's, please insert said name here:

____

FEID or SS number of prospective lessor, whichever is applicable: ________________

______________________	______________________
(Print or type name)	Witness
______________________	______________________
(Print or type title)	Witness

Documentation Required to be Submitted with Proposal for Existing Building

In order for a proposal to be accepted, Items 1 through 10 must be included in the proposal. Items 11 through 16 must be included, if applicable.

Checklist:

______ 1. RFP form properly completed and notarized
______ 2. Map (annotated with location of proposed facility)
______ 3. Photographs
______ 4. Floor plan showing present layout with dimensions
______ 5. Square footage calculations
______ 6. Site layout with all parking spaces and utilization of spaces shown
______ 7. Disclosure of Ownership Statement [Attachment __________]
______ 8. Energy Performance Analysis
______ 9. Evidence of control of parking
______10. Documentation showing proposer as controller of property
______11. Authorization for corporation to conduct business in Florida
______12. Certification letter from an HVAC contractor or engineer
______13. Public transportation schedule
______14. Certification of building live load by a registered engineer
______15. Tenant acknowledgment of lessor proposal
______16. Proof of historical property designation (if applicable)

ATTACHMENT A: AGENCY SPECIFICATIONS

ATTACHMENT B: BOUNDARIES

ATTACHMENT C: LEASE AGREEMENT

Lease Number: ________________

Lease Commencement: __________

Preamble

THIS LEASE AGREEMENT is entered into this _____ Day of _________, 20_____, by and between those Parties listed.

Parties

Lessee: ____

Agency Name

Address: ____
Street City State (Zip Code)

Lessor: ____
Lessor Name

Address: ____
Street City State (Zip Code)

FEID: **OR** **Social Security Number**

1. Description

A. In consideration for the covenants and agreements made here, Lessor agrees to lease to Lessee those premises (hereinafter the "Premises") described as:

Building: ________________
Building Name

County: ________________

Address: ____
Street City State (Zip Code)

consisting of an aggregate area of _________ square feet of net usable space measured in accordance with the Department of Management Services' Standard Method of Space Measurement. This space comprises approximately _____% of the ____________ net square feet in the building.

B. Lessor shall also provide _________ exclusive parking spaces ☐
or_________ nonexclusive ☐ parking spaces as part of this Lease Agreement.

2. Term & Renewals

A. The Lease shall begin on: ____________________ _____, __________
Month Day Year

and end at the close of business on: ____________________ _____, _____
Month Day Year

B. Lessee, however, is hereby granted the option to renew this Lease for an additional ____________ years upon the same terms and conditions or as specified on attached addendum. If Lessee desires to renew this Lease under the provisions of this Article, it shall give Lessor written notice thereof not more than six months nor less than three months prior to the expiration of the term provided in this Article or any applicable renewal period.

3. Notices & Invoices

All Notices to be served upon Lessee shall be sent by receipted mail to:

Lessee: ____
Agency Name

Address: ____
Street City State (Zip Code)

All Notices to be served upon Lessor shall be sent by receipted mail to:

Lessor: ____
Lessor Name

Address: ____
Street City State (Zip Code)

Rental invoice should be submitted monthly to Lessee at:

Lessee: ____
Agency Name

Address: ____
Street City State (Zip Code)

Rental Payments shall be paid to Lessor at:

Lessor: ____
Lessor Name

Address: ____
Street City State (Zip Code)

4. Rent

The rent shall be payable the month following the month of occupancy in accordance with subsection 215.422, Florida Statutes. The rent for any fractional part of the first month shall be prorated.

A. Base Term

Lessee agrees to pay Lessor rent according to the following schedule:

TERM		RATE PER SQUARE FOOT	MONTHLY RENT	ANNUAL RENT
Start (MM/DD/YYYY)	End (MM/DD/YYYY)			

B. Option Term

For the renewal options as specified in Article 3, the rental rate shall be:

TERM		RATE PER SQUARE FOOT	MONTHLY RENT	ANNUAL RENT
Start (MM/DD/YYYY)	End (MM/DD/YYYY)			

5. Utilities

A. The Lessor ☐ or Lessee ☐ will promptly pay all billed utilities including gas, water, sewer, solid waste, storm water, and other power and electric light rates or charges which may become payable during the term of this Lease. If the Lease is for 5,000 square feet or greater, energy use must be separately metered to reflect all energy and fuels consumed by Lessee.

B. Lessor agrees to provide Lessee timely and accurate data on Lessee's monthly consumption or use of electricity, natural gas, LP gas and/or fuel oil, as appropriate, pursuant to Section 255.257, Florida Statutes.

6. Facility Services

A. The Lessor ☐ or Lessee ☐ will furnish daily janitorial services and required janitorial supplies. Janitorial services will include provision of recycling trash disposal for the Premises at the expense of the Lessor ☐ or Lessee ☐.

B. Lessor shall provide for interior and exterior maintenance and repairs in accordance with generally accepted good practices. This includes repainting, replacement of worn or damaged floor covering and repairs or replacement of interior equipment as needed due to normal use. Lessor shall maintain the exterior of the leased facility so to conform to all applicable health and safety laws, ordinances and codes, which are presently in effect or may be enacted during the term of this Lease and any renewal periods.

C. The Lessor ☐ or Lessee ☐ agrees to furnish pest control services for the leased premises during the term of the Lease at the expense of the Lessor ☐ or Lessee ☐.

D. Lessor agrees to install light fixtures for use by Lessee. The Lessor ☐ or Lessee ☐ shall be responsible for replacement of all bulbs, lamps, tubes, and starters used in such fixtures.

E. All services required above shall be provided during Lessee's normal working hours, which are deemed _____ a.m. to _____ p.m., Monday through Friday excluding state holidays, unless otherwise agreed to in writing.

F. Lessee shall, during the term of this Lease, maintain the interior of the Premises in as good a state of repair as it is at the time of the commencement of this Lease. Notwithstanding this obligation, reasonable wear and tear and unavoidable casualties are permissible.

7. Accessibility and Alterations

A. Lessor agrees that the Premises conform, or will be brought into conformance with, the requirements of the Florida Americans With Disabilities Accessibility Implementation Act, Section 553.501 - 553.513, Florida Statutes, and the current Florida Disability Code for Building Construction, providing requirements for persons with disabilities, and with the requirement of Public Law 101-336, enacted July 26, 1990, effective January 26, 1992, Section 28 CFR Part 35 and Appendix to Section 36 CFR Part 1191, known as the "Americans with Disabilities Act of 1990" prior to Lessee's occupancy.

B. Lessor agrees that Lessee shall have the right to make any alterations in and to the Premises during the term of this Lease upon first having obtained written consent of Lessor. Lessor shall not capriciously withhold the consent to any such alterations.

8. Applicable Laws

Due to the size and/or configuration of the space leased, the following laws apply:

A. Section 255.25(3) (e), Florida Statutes relating to tenant improvement costs for which Lessor may be eligible for reimbursement. As applicable, Lessor and Lessee agree that the sum of ______________________________ has been spent by the Lessor for improvements to the Premises and the Lessor does ☐ or does not ☐ intend to seek reimbursement for these improvements.

B. Section 252.385(4) (b), Florida Statutes relating to the use of the Premises as a public hurricane evacuation shelter. As applicable, the facility in which the Premises exist may be required to serve as a public hurricane evacuation shelter at the request of local emergency management agencies. It is hereby agreed and understood that in the event the Premises is selected for use as an emergency shelter Lessor, upon receiving notice from the Emergency Management Center, shall make the building available as a public hurricane evacuation shelter.

9. Heating and Air Conditioning

Lessor agrees to furnish to Lessee heating and air conditioning equipment and maintain same in satisfactory operating condition at all times for the Premises during the term of the Lease at the expense of Lessor. Lessor agrees that thermostats in the Premises will be set to maintain an average zone temperature of 75 degrees Fahrenheit during the heating and cooling seasons.

10. Compliance with Fire Safety Standards

A. Lessor shall provide for fire protection during the term of this Lease in accordance with the fire safety standards of the State Fire Marshal. Lessor shall be responsible for maintenance and repair of all fire protection equipment necessary to conform to the requirements of the State Fire Marshal. Lessor agrees that the Premises shall be available for inspection by the State Fire Marshal, prior to occupancy by Lessee, and at any reasonable time thereafter.

B. To assure Lessee of facility compliance with Florida's Fire Safety Standards, Lessor agrees to provide Lessee with written Fire Safety Inspection prior to the approval of this Lease. Fire Safety Inspection is to be conducted by State Fire Marshal or local fire officials.

C. In the event that the entirety or majority of the Premises is destroyed by fire, lightning, storm or other casualty, Lessor may repair the damage to Premises at its own cost and expense. Rental payments shall cease until the completion of repairs. Lessor will immediately refund the pro rata part of any rentals paid in advance by Lessee prior to the destruction. Should the Premises be only partly destroyed, leaving the major part in usable condition, then the rental shall abate on the damaged portion until the Premises is restored by Lessor. Upon the completion of such repairs, the full rental shall commence and the Lease shall then continue the balance of the term.

D. Lessor certifies that no asbestos was used in the construction of the demised Premises or that if asbestos was used, actions have been completed to correct the hazards caused by the use of asbestos.

E. Lessor certifies that if any radon is present, it is at a measurement level less than 4 PCI/L.

11. Injury or Damage to Property

All property of any kind that may be on the Premises during the term of this Lease shall be at the sole risk of Lessee, and except for any negligence of Lessor, Lessor shall not be liable to Lessee for loss or damage to the property.

12. Expiration of Term

At the expiration of the term, Lessee will peaceably yield the up Premises to Lessor in good and tenantable repair. Lessor and Lessee agree that Lessee shall have the right to remove from the Premises all personal property of Lessee including all fixtures, machinery, equipment, appurtenances and appliances placed or installed on the Premises by Lessee provided that Lessee agrees to restore the Premises to as good a state of repair as found prior to the removal.

13. Right to Inspect

Lessor, at all reasonable times, may enter into and upon the Premises for the purpose of viewing the same and for the purpose of making any such repairs as Lessor is required to make under the terms of this Lease.

14. Taxes and Insurance

Lessor shall pay all real estate taxes and fire insurance premiums on the Premises. Lessor shall not be liable to carry fire insurance on the person or property of Lessee or any other person or property that may occupy the Premises now or later.

15. Subletting and Assignment

Lessee, upon obtaining written consent of Lessor, shall have the right to sublet all or any part of the Premises or to assign all or any part of the Premises. Lessor shall not capriciously withhold written consent.

16. Wavier of Defaults

No waiver by Lessee of any breach of this Lease by Lessor shall be construed as a waiver of any subsequent breach of any duty or covenant imposed by this Lease.

17. Breach of Covenant

A. If Lessee neglects or fails to perform or observe any covenant herein, and such default continues for a period of thirty (30) days after receipt of written notice thereof from Lessor, then Lessor may lawfully, immediately, or at any time thereafter, and without further notice or demand, enter into and upon the Premises, and repossess the same as of their former estate and expel Lessee and remove its effects forcefully, if necessary.

B. This action by Lessor shall not be deemed as any manner of trespass and thereupon any remedy which might otherwise be used by Lessor for arrears of rent or for any breach of Lessee's covenants herein contained shall terminated, without prejudice.

18. Availability of Funds

Pursuant to Section 255.2502, Florida Statutes, Lessor acknowledges that the State of Florida's performance and obligation to pay under this contract is contingent upon an annual appropriation by the Legislature.

19. Acknowledgment of Assignment

Upon the request of Lessor, Lessee shall execute such acknowledgment(s), or any assignment(s), of rentals and profits made by Lessor to any third person, firm, or corporation. Notwithstanding this obligation, Lessor shall not make such request unless required to do so by the mortgagee under a mortgage, or mortgages executed by Lessor.

20. Not Consent to Sue

No provisions, terms, or conditions of this Lease shall be construed as consent of the State of Florida to be sued because of said leasehold.

21. Right to Terminate

Lessee shall have the right to terminate this Lease without penalty in the event a State-owned building becomes available to Lessee for occupancy, and upon the giving six (6) months advance written notice to Lessor by Certified Mail, Return Receipt Requested.

22. Public Entity Crime Statement

Section 287.133, Florida Statutes places the following restrictions on the ability of persons convicted of public entity crimes to transact business with public entities, including the department:

A person, or affiliate, who has been placed on the convicted vendor list, following a conviction for a public entity crime, may not submit a bid on a contract to provide any goods or services to a public entity, may not submit a bid on a contract with a public entity for the construction or repair of a public building or public work, may not submit bids on leases of real property to a public entity, may not perform work as a contractor, supplier, subcontractor, or consultant under a contract with any public entity, and may not transact business with any public entity in excess of the threshold amount provided in Section 287.017, Florida Statutes for CATEGORY TWO for a period of 36 months from the date of being placed on the convicted vendor list.

23. Discrimination

Section 287.134 Florida Statutes places the following restrictions on the ability of persons on the discriminatory vendor list to transact business with public entities, including the department:

An entity who has been placed on the discriminatory vendor list may not submit a bid or proposal to provide goods or services to a public entity, may not submit a bid or proposal with a public entity for the construction or repair of a public building or public work, may not submit bids or proposals on leases of real property to a public entity, may not perform work as a contractor, supplier, subcontractor or consultant under contract with any public entity and may not transact business with any public entity.

24. Use of Premises

Lessee will not make or suffer any unlawful, improper, or offensive use of the Premises or any use or occupancy thereof contrary to the laws of the State of Florida or to such ordinances of the city or county in which the Premises are located, now or hereinafter made, as may be applicable to Lessee.

25. Failure to Comply

A. In the event that Lessor fails to comply with any term or provision of this Lease after written notice, Lessee reserves the option to:

i. setoff and deduct from the rental amount due Lessor under this Lease such sums as Lessee determines are required to remedy the default of Lessor, and/or

ii. fulfill Lessor's obligations under the terms of this Lease, whereby Lessor shall reimburse Lessee on demand for any reasonable expenses which Lessee may incur in thus effecting compliance with Lessor's obligation under this Lease. Should Lessee elect this option, Lessee shall use its best efforts to mitigate damages caused thereby, and/or

iii. terminate this Lease and vacate the Premises, but without prejudice to any remedy which might otherwise be used by Lessee for any breach of Lessor's covenants contained herein, and/or

iv. bring suit for damages against Lessor for any expense (including reasonable attorney's fees) Lessee may incur by Lessor's failure to comply with any term or provision of the Lease. However, Lessee shall not bring suit for damages incurred due to a delay in the Commencement Date of this Lease if any such delay is caused solely by any delay, default or omission of Lessee.

B. Lessee is required to give Lessor written notice setting forth in reasonable detail the nature and extent of such failure and Lessor will be given thirty (30) days to cure such failure. If such failure cannot reasonably be completely cured within that thirty (30) day period, the length of such period shall be extended for the period reasonably required thereof, only if Lessor commences curing such failure within such thirty (30) day period and continues the curing thereof with reasonable diligence and continuity.

C. Reason for setoff of amounts due under this Lease shall include, but are not limited to, remedying heating and air conditioning equipment and roofing deficiencies.

D. Each occasion of setoff of rental amounts due under this Lease shall be contingent upon the prior approval of Lessee's legal counsel.

26. Definition of Terms

A. The terms "Lease," "Lease Agreement," or "Agreement" shall be inclusive of each other and shall also include any renewals, extensions or modifications of this Lease.

B. The terms "Lessor," "Sublessor." "Lessee" and "Sublessee" shall include the successors and assigns for the parties hereto.

C. The singular shall include the plural and the plural shall include the singular whenever the context so requires or permits.

27. Additional Terms

A. No additional covenants or conditions form a part of this Lease

B. All additional covenants or conditions appear on attached Addendum(s):

IN WITNESS WHEREOF, the parties hereto have hereunto executed this instrument for the purpose herein expressed, this

_____ day of __________, **20**______.

ANY MODIFICATION OF A LEASE AGREEMENT SHALL NOT BECOME LEGALLY EFFECTIVE UNTIL APPROVED/ACCEPTED BY THE DEPARTMENT OF MANAGEMENT SERVICES.

ORIGINAL SIGNATURES REQUESTED ON ALL COPIES

As to Lessor - Lessor, or authorized representative and two witnesses must sign, print name and enter date.

X________________ Lessor or Authorized Representative	________________ Printed Name	___/___/____ Date
X________________ Witness #1	________________ Printed Name	___/___/____ Date
X________________ Witness #2	________________ Printed Name	___/___/____ Date

As to Lessee Agency - Agency head, or authorized delegate, and representative of agency general counsel must sign, print name and enter date.

X________________ Agency Head or Authorized Delegate	________________ Printed Name	___/___/____ Date
X________________ Agency Office of General Counsel	________________ Printed Name	___/___/____ Date

As to the Department of Management Services - Chief Real Property Administrator, or authorized delegate, and Secretary, or authorized delegate must sign, print name and enter date.

X________________ Chief Real Property Administrator	________________ Printed Name	___/___/____ Date
X________________ Secretary or Authorized Delegate	________________ Printed Name	___/___/____ Date
X________________ Office of General Counsel	________________ Printed Name	___/___/____ Date

STATE OF FLORIDA
DEPARTMENT OF MANAGEMENT SERVICES

ADDENDUM FOR ASSESSING LIQUIDATED DAMAGES

ADDENDUM NUMBER: ______________

LEASE NUMBER: ______________

As a condition precedent to lessee's obligation to occupy and pay rent, the leased premises shall be renovated and completed in accordance with the Invitation to Negotiate issued for the above referenced lease.

Should lessor fail to complete renovations within the time frame specified in the Invitation to Negotiate, liquidated damages in the amount of $________ per day shall be assessed until specified renovations are completed. This provision for liquidated damages shall in no way affect Lessee's right to terminate the lease for failure to have the renovations completed by the commencement date of the Lease. The Lessee's exercise of the right to terminate the lease shall not release the Lessor from his obligation to pay said liquidated damages in the amount stated above.

_________________________ _________________________

Lessee Signature Lessor Signature

(SEAL)

STATE OF FLORIDA
DEPARTMENT OF MANAGEMENT SERVICES

JANITORIAL SERVICES

ADDENDUM NUMBER: ______________

LEASE NUMBER: ______________

The lessor agrees to furnish janitorial and cleaning services as part of this lease agreement. This includes furnishing all cleaning/maintenance equipment and cleaning supplies as required, including but not limited to, drinking cups at water fountains, bathroom tissues, paper towels, trash receptacle liners, hand soap (preferably liquid) and doormats at entrances to the facility. All supplies are to be of good quality acceptable in the janitorial profession and of satisfactory quality suitable to the needs of personnel.

Cleaning of the facility shall be accomplished in accord with the following schedule:

FLOORS	
DAILY:	Carpeted Areas - Vacuum Non-carpeted Areas - Dust mop Remove gum and other materials. Spot damp mop and to remove stains or spots.
WEEKLY:	Non-Carpeted Areas - Damp mop and spray buff.
SEMI-ANNUALLY:	Machine clean carpets in hallways. Other areas to be cleaned if their condition so dictates. Strip, reseal and wax all normally waxed floors.
ANNUALLY:	Machine clean all carpets throughout the facility.
WALLS, CEILINGS, INTERIOR DOORS, LEDGES, ETC.	
WEEKLY:	Spot clean.
	Clean light switch plates and surrounding wall areas.
	Dust windowsills, ledges, fixtures, etc.
MONTHLY:	Dust or vacuum HVAC registers.
ANNUALLY:	Clean all light fixtures diffuses and dust light bulbs.
WINDOWS AND GLASS	
DAILY:	Spot clean entrances and vicinity glass both in and outside. Spot clean directory and internal glass or windows.
SEMI-ANNUALLY:	Clean inside of external windows.
WATER FOUNTAINS	
DAILY:	Clean and sanitize.
	Replenish supply of disposable cups (if applicable).
FURNISHINGS	
AS NEEDED, BUT AT LEAST WEEKLY:	Dust tables, chairs, desks, credenzas, file cabinets, bookcases, etc. Do not disturb any papers lying on desks or cabinets. Dust and clean all ornamental wall decorations, pictures, charts, chalkboards, etc. Dust draperies, venetian blinds, or curtains.
SEMI-ANNUALLY:	Vacuum all drapes, venetian blinds, or curtains.

TRASH AND REFUSE	
DAILY:	Empty and clean all trash receptacles. Receptacle liners are to be used. Change as necessary. Remove all collected trash to external dumpsters or trash containers. In conference rooms, reception areas, etc., remove accumulated trash, i.e. paper cups, soda cans, etc.
CIGARETTE URNS AND ASHTRAYS	
DAILY:	Empty and clean all cigarette urns. Empty and damp wipe all ashtrays.
ELEVATORS (If Applicable)	
DAILY:	If carpeted, vacuum. If not carpeted, dust mop, remove gum and other materials, spot damp mop to remove stains or spots. Clean hardware and control panels.
WEEKLY:	Vacuum door tracks. Damp mop floors and spray buff if not carpeted.
STAIRWELLS (If Applicable)	
DAILY:	Remove accumulated trash. Spot sweep as required.
WEEKLY:	Sweep. Dust mop to remove stains. Dust handrails, ledges, etc. Spot clean walls and doors.
RESTROOMS	
DAILY:	Maintain in a clean and sanitary condition: floors, walls, doors, stalls, partitions, shelves, sinks, commodes, urinals, bath facilities, soap and towel dispensers. Clean and polish mirrors. Empty and sanitize trash and sanitary napkin receptacles. Replenish supplies of tissue, towels, and soap. Check and replace, as necessary, deodorizer bars/room air freshener units.
MONTHLY:	Clean ceramic tile surfaces with a strong cleaner or bleach so that tile and grout have a uniform color.

LOUNGE AND KITCHEN AREAS (If Applicable)	
DAILY:	Clean and sanitize sinks and counter areas.
EXTERIOR	
DAILY:	Sweep outside area immediately adjacent to building entrances. Keep parking lot and surrounding grass areas free of trash.
WEEKLY:	Sweep all exterior access areas, i.e. sidewalks, porches, verandas, etc.

MAINTENANCE SERVICES

In reference to Articles III and V of the lease agreement:

1. Filters for HVAC shall be changed every 90 days at a minimum and more often as conditions warrant.
2. All painted surfaces in the facility shall be freshly painted at the commencement of this lease, if needed, and at least once every three years thereafter during the lease term and any renewals thereof. Touch up painting to be done as needed.
3. Perform such other services as are necessary to keep the facility clean and in a sanitary condition.

In providing any or all of the before mentioned services:

1. Janitorial staff are to only use necessary lighting in the areas in which they are actually working and turn off unnecessary lighting. Air conditioning equipment is not to be turned on for the exclusive use of the janitorial staff.
2. Only actual employees of the janitorial contractor are to be admitted to the premises.
3. During after hours cleaning, all outside doors are to be locked and janitorial staff are not to provide access into the facility to anyone.
4. Janitorial staff are to check exterior doors and windows to ensure the facility is secure at the time of leaving the facility.

____________________________ Lessee Signature

____________________________ Lessor Signature

(SEAL)

STATE OF FLORIDA
DEPARTMENT OF MANAGEMENT SERVICES

ADDENDUM NUMBER: ______________

LEASE NUMBER: ______________

Employment Eligibility Verification

Pursuant to Executive Order #11-02 (as Superceded by 11-116), Lessor agrees that it will enroll and participate in the Employment Eligibility Verification Program ("E-Verify Program") administered by the U.S. Department of Homeland Security ("DHS"), under the terms provided in the "Memorandum of Understanding" with DHS governing the program, to verify the employment eligibility of all persons it employs under the lease term to perform duties in Florida. Lessor further agrees to provide to the Lessee, as part of the leasing documents, documentation of such enrollment in the form of a copy of the "Edit Company Profile" page in E-Verify, which contains proof of enrollment in the E-Verify Program. (This page can be accessed from the "Edit Company Profile" link on the left navigation menu of the E-Verify employer's homepage.) Information regarding "E-Verify" is available at the following website: http://www.dhs.gov/files/programs/gc_1185221678150.shtm#1.

Lessor further agrees that it will require each subcontractor that performs work under this lease to verify the employment eligibility of its employees hired during the term of this contract by enrolling and participating in the E-Verify Program within ninety days of the effective date of this lease or within ninety days of the effective date of the contract between the Lessor and the subcontractor, whichever is later. The Lessor shall obtain from the subcontractor(s) a copy of the "Edit Company Profile" screen indicating enrollment in the E-Verify Program and make such record(s) available to the Agency and other authorized state officials upon request.

Lessor further agrees to maintain records of its participation and compliance with the provisions of the E-Verify Program, including participation by its subcontractors as provided above, and to make such records available to the Agency and other authorized state officials upon request.

Compliance with the terms of this Employment Eligibility Verification provision (including compliance with the terms of the "Memorandum of Understanding" with DHS) is hereby made an express condition of this lease.

______________________	______________________
Lessee	Lessor
______________________	______________________
Date	Date

ATTACHMENT D: DISCLOSURE OF OWNERSHIP

STATE OF FLORIDA Disclosure Statement

Department of Management Services Form 4114

Lease Number: __________

Purpose

This form is used to collect the information required pursuant to subsections 255.249(4)(h), 255.249(4)(i) and 255.01, Florida Statutes.

1. **Ownership - Indicate the type of ownership of the facility in which this lease exists.**

   a. Publicly Owned Facility

   b. Privately Owned Facility Individually held Entity held (e.g., corporate, LLC, partnership, etc.)

   c. Name of titleholder: ____________________

   Titleholder FEIN or SSN: ____________________

   Name of facility: ____________________

   Facility street address: ____________________

   Facility city, state, zip code: ____________________

2. **Disclosure Requirements**

   a. Does a corporation registered with the Securities and Exchange Commission and/or registered pursuant to chapter 517, Florida Statutes, own the facility listed above? Yes No

   If "Yes," please proceed to section 4.

   b. Does any party have a 4% or greater ownership interest in the facility or the entity holding title to the facility? Yes No

   If "Yes," please proceed to 2.c.

   c. Does any public official, agent, or employee hold any ownership interest in the facility or the entity holding title to the facility? Yes No

   If "Yes," please proceed to 2.d.

   d. Is the facility listed above financed with any type of local government obligations? Yes No

   If "Yes," please stop and immediately contact your state leasing representative.

3. **Ownership Disclosure List - (additional pages may be attached)**

a. Name	Government Agency (if applicable)	Extent of Interest (Percent)
______	______	______
______	______	______
______	______	______
______	______	______
______	______	______
______	______	______
______	______	______

b. The equity of all others holding interest in the above named facility totals: ______________

4. Signatures

By signing this form, the undersigned acknowledges that the information provided is true and complete, to the best of their knowledge.

a. Publicly Owned Facilities

Signature: ______________________________
Name: ______________________________
Government Entity: ______________________________
Date: ______________________________

b. Private Individually-held Facilities

Signature: ______________________________
Name: ______________________________
Government Entity: ______________________________
Date: ______________________________

Signature: ______________________________
Name: ______________________________
Government Entity: ______________________________
Date: ______________________________

c. Entity-held Facilities

This is to certify, that the undersigned is authorized to conduct business as a representative of the entity listed in section 1.c. of this Disclosure Statement.

Signature: ______________________________
Name: ______________________________
Government Entity: ______________________________
Date: ______________________________

ATTACHMENT E: DIVISION OF STATE FIRE MARSHALL PLANS REVIEW FEES, PROCEDURES AND REQUIREMENTS

DIVISION OF STATE FIRE MARSHAL

Plans Review Fees, Procedures and Requirements

The plans for all construction of any new state owned or state lease building and renovation or alteration of any existing state owned or state leased building are subject to review and approval of the Division of State Fire Marshal for compliance with the Uniform Fire Safety Standards prior to commencement of construction or change of occupancy. The Division of State Fire Marshal may inspect state owned and state leased spaces as necessary prior to occupancy or during construction, renovation, or alteration to ascertain compliance with the uniform fire safety standards as per Florida Statutes 633.085 and 69A-52, Florida Administrative Code.

69A-3.009 (12), FAC, defines a state owned building as:

(a) "State-owned building," as used in Chapter 633, F.S., and any rule adopted by the State Fire Marshal, except as provided in paragraph (b) of this subsection, means any structure used or intended for supporting or sheltering any use or occupancy of which the state, any state agency or department, or the Trustees of the Internal Improvement Trust Fund is the record owner of the legal title to such structure.

(b) "State-owned building" does not mean or include a pole barn, a picnic shelter, a lift station, an animal pen, an animal feeder, a pump house, a one-family private residence, a two-family private residence, a forestry fire tower or other fire tower, a radio tower, a building no longer in use, an empty building, or a greenhouse.

DESIGN CRITERIA:

The Life Safety portion of the plans shall be designed in accordance with the National Fire Protection Association (NFPA) 101, Life Safety Code, NFPA 1, Fire Prevention Code, and adopted NFPA Standards. **See Florida Administrative Code 69A-3.012 for the adopted edition of NFPA 101 & 1 and a list of adopted NFPA Standards.**

(https://www.flrules.org/)

PLANS REVIEW FEES:

The fee for plans review is determined by multiplying the estimated construction/ renovation cost of the building, by the constant 0.0025. The minimum fee is $100.00. This does not include the cost of the land, site improvements, civil work or furniture & equipment.

Example:

$1,000.000.00 Construction Cost x .0025 = 2,500.00 Fee

1

METHOD OF PAYMENT

After plans are received an invoice will be prepared and sent at which time payment can be made by personal check, money order or, if a state agency is paying, a Samas - Journal Transfer. Please make check or money order payable to the Department of Financial Services. Fill in the memo portion with "SFM Plans Review fee" and return payment with invoice.

WHAT TO SUBMIT

Plans and specifications are required to be signed and sealed in accordance with Florida Statute. Submit completed application form DFS-K3-1973 and two sets of plans and one set of specifications to:

If Sending By Regular Mail

Division of State Fire Marshal

Plans Review Section

If Sending By Overnight Service

Division of State Fire Marshal

Plans Review Section

PLANS SUBMISSION:

The Division of State Fire Marshal will require the submitter to furnish two sets of plans and one set of specifications for review to the Plans Review Section. The submitter may, however, submit plans at an earlier stage, i.e., design review, in which case only one unsigned set needs to be submitted. **Only one design review will be allowed per project**. When the documents are approved for construction, the plans and specs will be stamped "APPROVED" and returned to the submitter. The stamped set of plans must be kept on the job site for the fire safety inspector's use at the time of inspection. It shall be the responsibility of the submitter to see that the "approved" set of plans is on the construction site before work begins and remains there until final inspection and approval has been issued. Plan approval is good for one year from the date of issue. The construction contract must be let within this period or the approval will expire and the plans must be re-submitted with another review fee.

The editions of the pertinent codes that will apply to your project will be those that are adopted at the date of your first submittal, regardless of phase, i.e. 50% or final, and will not change even if a newer edition is adopted during the review process.

Any change orders or redesign during construction that affect life safety shall be submitted for review with the State Fire Marshal's file number indicated. There is no additional fee required for changes.

The review process allows 30 calendar days for review of all state-owned property and 10 working days for review of state leased property.

If there are any special circumstances or hazards that require further clarification, the reviewer will attempt to contact you, therefore, please include the name and telephone number of a contact person with your plan submission. Please remember that if you are called and asked for additional information or clarification, the reviewer needs this information in writing before he can approve the project. If the statutory time (10 working days on a lease or 30 calendar days on state owned) expires he must disapprove the project and a re-submittal process may add further delay to the project.

PLAN INFORMATION

The following items are areas where we must have your assistance. Please ensure that all submittals address these necessary items where applicable and help us prevent lost time due to disapprovals based on lack of information.

- **Renovation or Alteration** - Any alteration or any installation of new equipment shall be installed under the requirement of new construction. The scope of work shall be identified clearly. Show the number of floors in the building and the location of the project under consideration in comparison to the entire floor and building.
- **Equivalency Concepts** - Any requirement of the code that a designer wishes to modify by alternative arrangements shall in no case afford less safety to life than the code presently requires. Any request to use equivalency concepts will only be considered when technical documentation is submitted.
- **Classification of Occupancy** - Plans shall indicate the type of occupancy based on N.F.P.A. 101, Chapter 6.
- **Change of Occupancy** - The designer shall identify the existing type of occupancy and clearly identify the new occupancy use and areas.
- **Floor Area** - The gross square footage of the building shall be indicated on the plans. All assembly rooms shall indicate the net floor area.
- **High Hazard Area** - Any areas of a building, structure, or parts thereof, containing highly combustible, flammable, explosive products or materials which are likely to burn rapidly shall be identified on the submittal. The designer shall identify amounts and types of hazardous materials used throughout the facility.
- **Means of Egress** - All three components of the means of egress (exit access, exit and exit discharge) shall be clearly identified. Travel distance to exits shall be detailed.
- **Occupant Load** - The occupant load for each floor and calculations showing how the load was obtained shall be shown. All assembly rooms, spaces, or areas shall be identified and calculated with calculations shown on plans.
- **Construction Type** - The type of construction shall be identified as per N.F.P.A. 220.
- **Atrium** - Any building in which the designer has incorporated an atrium shall have the atrium area clearly defined on the contract document. Atrium shall be in accordance with NFPA 101, 8.2.5.6.
- **Penetration of Smoke or Fire Barriers** - Passage of pipes, conduits, bus ducts, cables, wires, air ducts, pneumatic ducts and similar service equipment through smoke and/or fire barriers shall be detailed on the contract documents.

- **Fire Detection, Alarm and Communication Systems** - All existing or new systems shall be clearly identified on the plans. The type of system and the appropriate N.F.P.A. standard that was used for the design and installation shall be indicated on the plans and signed and sealed by the Engineer of Record.
- **Automatic Sprinkler System, Standpipes and Fire Pumps** - All existing or new systems shall be clearly identified on the plans. The type of system and appropriate N.F.P.A. standard, which was used for the design and installation, shall be indicated on the plans and signed and sealed by the Engineer of Record. Hydraulic calculations, also signed and sealed by the Engineer of Record, shall accompany the plans where applicable.
- **Correction Facilities** - The use condition of the area shall be clearly indicated as per NFPA 101, Chapter 22.
- **Lease Spaces** - If the leased space is on a floor located above the level of exit discharge (LED) a plan of the LED is required to be submitted to ensure proper exiting from the building.
- The plan shall have the correct name of the facility: Building Number, Office/Complex Name, Street Address, and City, County, and Zip Code, and any assigned lease number noted on the document.
- Include site plan to scale showing project, distances to nearby buildings, fences, parking, and location of hazardous features such as fuel storage or incinerators, and fire lanes if required by NFPA 1.
- Include floor plan(s) drawn to scale showing walls and partitions, openings, door swings, built-in features, changes in elevation such as steps or ramps, dimensions, and notes to indicate what is shown and the use (room name) of each space.
- Schedules for doors, windows and hardware.
- Drawings of HVAC systems.
- Show the following on plans, if applicable: exit markings, emergency lighting (type and location), fire extinguisher(s) (type and location), nationally tested wall assembly details for rated walls, stair and handrail details, interior finishes and their flame spread ratings.
- Show any special fire extinguishing systems such as dry chemical hood systems.

CONSTRUCTION INSPECTIONS

The review fee will cover plans review and up to three (3) construction site inspections. (1) an underground fire main inspection (if applicable), (2) an intermediate inspection at approximately 65% completion (before covering walls and ceilings), (3) and a final inspection prior to occupancy. The intermediate (65%) inspection is optional at our discretion, and depends upon the size and complexity of the construction project. The purpose of construction site inspections is to ensure that the project is in fact constructed in accordance with the approved construction documents.

Any re-inspection required as a result of deficiencies found during the final occupancy inspection shall result in additional fees billed to the Contractor for re-inspection at a rate of $65.00 per hour, per Inspector, portal to portal, plus expenses. With this in mind, the contractor should have completed his own systems testing and inspection punch list and made the corrections necessary in order to eliminate re-inspections as much as possible.

HOW TO REQUEST AN INSPECTION

The following inspections must be considered:

1. Underground: **REQUIRED** if an underground fire main is installed. This inspection must be performed before cover-up.
2. Intermediate: **REQUIRED** if so indicated on the approval letter, or required by the SFM inspector during the initial on-site meeting.
3. Final: **REQUIRED.**

The construction documents must be approved prior to commencing construction of the project. Any request for the use of an alternative system, or change made to the approved plans must be approved by the Plans Review Section prior to its installation. Throughout the various construction phases, ALL requests for inspection shall be made at least five (5) working days in advance using the enclosed DFS Form DI4-1528.

The request may be forwarded by mail or facsimile to the Plans Review Section (see form for fax # and address).

The Plans Review Section will route the request to the appropriate field office where the local field inspector will then contact the requestor to make final arrangements for the inspection.

This request form has to be completed in its entirety, otherwise, the request for inspection will not be granted. Additionally, if the plans are found to be disapproved or rejected by this office, the inspection will not be performed and a stop work order may be issued until the plans are submitted, approved, and the plans review fee is paid in full. Should you have any questions, please notify the Plans Review Section (850) 413-3733 prior to mailing this request form.

Should the project not pass inspection due to various deficiencies, a re-inspection within 30 days should be scheduled with the Inspector at that time. If the corrections cannot be made within that required time frame, it is the responsibility of the agency or requesting party to complete the attached inspection request form (DI4-1528) and submit it to Plans Review Section in Tallahassee, noting the date in which the project will be ready for re-inspection in order for him to reschedule the site for a re-inspection.

The following checklists have been provided for your use in preparing plans that contain sprinkler and fire alarm systems.

FIRE ALARM CHECKLIST

1. The fire alarm contractor shall be licensed for the scope of work submitted.
2. Provide contractor's name, address, phone and license number.
3. Provide job site address, occupancy type, design criteria (NFPA standard)

4. General description of how the system will operate. What will activate the system, will it go into general alarm or ring by zone, will it annunciate, will it be monitored by a central station, will the air handling system be shut down, elevator recall, etc.

5. Itemized list of equipment to be used showing quantity, manufacturer, model number, type of device, and CFM number.

6. Calculations to be complete. Indicate all electric current required in supervision and alarm conditions. Provide calculations on battery manufacturer's standard form.

7. Denote capacity of battery, and confirm adequate size when operating under the full-calculated load.

8. Voltage drop calculations showing that voltage drop does not exceed 5% drop.

9. Cut sheets for each type of device being installed.

10. Drawing showing location of devices, wire runs, number of conductors, zones, end-of-line resistors, and typical wiring method used on the devices.

11. If fire alarm work is resultant from an inspection (State Fire Marshal, fire department, etc.) provide copy of report.

12. Submittal must be complete. Examples: Candela ratings of strobes shall be identified. Ceiling heights shall be indicated when ceiling mounted strobes are used. Reflected ceilings are to be clearly denoted. Include light fixture types/locations, HVAC opening types/locations, and all architectural features (joist, beams, coffers, furrs, etc.) extending more than 4 inches from the ceiling plane. Rooms, spaces and areas shall be identified.

13. Differentiate between all existing and proposed components. If system or portion is existing, indicate date of existing system installation, or date of prior substantial system renovation.

SPRINKLER SYSTEM CHECKLIST

1. Occupancy class of each area or room identified.

2. All sprinklers identified by make, type, orifice size, temperature rating, thermal sensitivity, including all existing heads affecting the scope of work.

3. For large storage areas, provide storage height, method of storage, description of commodities, etc. If project is specialized storage design (NFPA 231, 231C, etc.) provide complete design statement denoting methodology for arriving at project area/densities.

4. All piping identified by size, type, inside diameter, and schedule, including all existing piping affecting the scope of work.

5. All ceiling information: heights, types, architectural profiles (vaults, coffers, furrs, etc.), construction assembly (combustible ceiling or framing, significant combustibles in ceiling cavity, etc.)

6. Sprinkler obstructions denoted (suspended light fixtures, duct work, architectural items, etc.)

7. H.V.A.C. openings shown

8. Method of maintaining sprinkler system at or above 40 degrees F identified. Describe all unheated areas and explain methodology of all types, sizes, locations, etc. of freeze protection devices.

9. Graphically highlight each hydraulic area, title each area on the plans, with matching title on each calculation set.

10. Location and rating of firewalls, unprotected vertical openings, and other assemblies affecting sprinkler design.

11. Size of city main at street, denoting dead end or circulating (or denote private supply)

12. Total area protected by each system on each floor.

13. Location, type, and listing of hangers.

14. Underground pipe size, length, location, type, point of connection to city main, bury depth, thrust blocks, and all appurtenances (valve types, water meters, valve pits, backflow preventers, etc.)

15. All hydraulic name plate information.

16. Setting for pressure reducing valve denoted.

HYDRAULIC CALCULATIONS FOR SPRINKLER SYSTEMS

1. Verify the water supply, test location, date (must be 12 months current) peak demand time (or calculated adjustment), and account for test elevation at calculations.

2. Verify hazard classification (light, ordinary, special occupancy, etc.).

3. Verify the design criteria (density/sq. ft. over the hydraulic design area).

4. Verify the location of the area calculated (most hydraulically demanding is not always the most physically remote)

5. Verify the dimensions of the area calculated (design area shall not extend beyond designated area served by each sprinkler). Sufficient length parallel to the branch lines or cross-mains, as required.

6. Verify the densities (sprinklers flowing at or above minimum required flow rate).

7. Verify the pipe sizes, lengths, equivalent lengths of fittings, and flow paths (account for all pressure losses).

8. Verify the hose demand.

9. Confirm that the system demand is at or less than the available water supply (include demand vs. supply graph).

MATERIAL CUT SHEETS FOR SPRINKLER SYSTEMS

1. Sprinklers, pipes, valves, pressure-reducing devices, flow switches, backflow preventers, water meters (all system devices effecting hydraulic design, whether existing or proposed).
2. Fire pump type, size, and design curves (provide current pump test for existing pump).

DEPARTMENT OF FINANCIAL SERVICES
Division of State Fire Marshal- Bureau of Fire Prevention

APPLICATION FOR PLAN REVIEW

By submitting this form you are requesting that the State Fire Marshal's Office complete a plan review in accordance with F.S. 633. This form must be completed in its entirety. Partial or incomplete submittals may result in delay of processing this request.

1. CONTACT INFORMATION		
a. Applicant's Name:	Email:	Phone:
b. State Agency Contact:	Email:	Phone:
c. Architect of Record:	Email:	Phone:
d. Engineer of Record for Fire Alarm System:	Email:	Phone:
e. Engineer of Record for Fire Sprinkler System:	Email:	Phone:

2. PROJECT NAME OR DESCRIPTION	
3. TYPE OF SUBMITTAL	a. ☐ Design Review (<100% Construction Documents) b. ☐ 100% Construction Documents c. ☐ Revision for SFM # : (Complete items 1a and 7 only) d. ☐ Shop Drawings for SFM # : (Complete items 1a and 7 only) e. ☐ Other:

4. BUILDING INFORMATION		
	a. ☐ State Owned*	b. ☐ State-Leased,** lease #:
	c. Design or State Agency Project #:	
	d. Project Square Footage:	e. State Agency or University:
	f. Building Name:	g. Building #:
	h. Building Street Address:	
	i. City/State/Zip:	j. County:
	k. NFPA Occupancy Type: (check all that apply) Ambulatory Health Care ☐ Detention and Correctional ☐ One and Two Family ☐ Hotels and Dormitories ☐ Lodging or Rooming Houses ☐ Residential Board and Care ☐ Storage ☐	Apartments ☐ Day-Care ☐ Mercantile ☐ Health Care ☐ Business ☐ Industrial ☐ Assembly ☐
	l. Is this a change in occupancy? ☐ Yes ☐No	m. FBC Construction Type:
	n. Building Height:	o. Number of Stories:
	p. Life Safety Systems: (check all that apply) ☐ Fire Alarm System ☐Fire Sprinkler ☐Standpipe ☐Other:	
	q. Estimated Construction Cost (not including the cost of land, site improvement, civil work or furniture and equipment):	

DFS-K3-1973 REV 04/09
Adopted in Rule 69A-52.003 F.A.C.

ATTACHMENT F: ENERGY PERFORMANCE INDEX

STATE OF FLORIDA
DEPARTMENT OF MANAGEMENT SERVICES

ENERGY PERFORMANCE ANALYSIS (EPA)

ADDENDUM NUMBER: ______________

Overview

Pursuant to Section 255.254, Florida Statutes, no state agency shall lease a facility without having secured from the Department of Management Services (DMS) an evaluation of life-cycle costs based on sustainable building ratings. DMS implements Section 255.254, Florida Statutes, through Rule Chapter 60D-4 of the Florida Administrative Code (FAC). Pursuant to Rule 60D-4.007, FAC, an Energy Performance Analysis (EPA) is required before an agency considers leasing the following facilities:

- buildings larger than 5,000 gross square feet
- spaces larger than 5,000 square feet of rentable area within an existing building

The EPA requirements include the following procedures:

- the Energy Star rating of the proposed lease -or- the energy performance index for facilities not eligible for an Energy Star rating (see EPA Procedures below)
- the energy cost projection (see EPA Procedures below)
- the computer-based simulation when required in the EPA Procedures (also see Computer-Based Simulation Requirements below for additional information)
- the EPA Submission (see EPA Submission Requirements below)

EPA Procedures

1. **Energy Star Rating:**
   a. An Energy Star rating shall be developed for the proposed lease space with one of the following free software tools:
      1. the Energy Star Portfolio Manager software, which is available at: http://www.energystar.gov/index.cfm?c=evaluate_performance.bus_portfoliomanager
   b. the Energy Star Target Finder software, which is available at: http://www.energystar.gov/index.cfm?c=new_bldg_design.bus_target_finder
   c. The minimum acceptable Energy Star rating is 50.
   d. The Energy Star rating shall be developed with the annual energy consumption for only the lease space being proposed. Use the following two scenarios as a guide:

1. Whole-Building Scenario: When the proposed lease space is an entire building or section of a given building that is separately metered by the utility provider, the Energy Star rating may be developed with actual utility bill data for the previous 12-month period. If actual utility bill data does not exist or the space has been unoccupied for more than 30 days, then the Energy Star rating must be developed with the annual energy consumption results of a computer-based simulation (see Computer-Based Simulation Requirements below for additional information).

2. Partial-Building Scenario: When the proposed lease space does not account for all rentable space within a given building or is not separately metered by the utility provider, a computer-based simulation shall be performed that computes the expected annual energy consumption for the proposed lease space. The results of the computer-based simulation shall be used to generate the Energy Star rating. *Note: An Energy Star rating for the entire building in this scenario will not be accepted.*

a. Exception: When the proposed lease does not meet the eligibility criteria for an Energy Star rating regarding the type or allocation of space, an energy performance index (kBTU per gross square foot per year) shall be developed manually in lieu of the Energy Star rating using one of the following sources:

- actual utility bill data for the previous 12 months
- the expected annual energy consumption developed with a computer-based simulation

b. Low Energy Star Ratings: For circumstances where the Energy Star rating of a proposed lease space is less than 50, a computer-based simulation may be performed that simulates energy conservation measures that are sufficient to raise the Energy Star rating to 50 or higher.

c. Renovations: When renovations that alter HVAC and/or lighting systems are either planned, necessary, or have been performed to make the proposed lease space suitable for the new tenant agency, a computer-based simulation shall be performed to provide the expected annual energy consumption required to develop one of the following:

1) an Energy Star rating for the proposed lease

2) the energy performance index (kBTU per gross square foot per year) for proposed lease spaces that are not eligible for an Energy Star rating

3. Energy Cost Projection:

a. Annual energy cost: The total expected annual energy cost for the proposed lease space shall be derived from one of the following sources:

1) the average annual energy costs based on actual utility bills for the previous three years

2) current utility rates and a computer-based simulation when a computer-based simulation is required to develop the Energy Star rating.

b. A cost utilization index (total energy cost per gross square foot per year) shall be developed with the annual energy cost data described above.

c. The cost utilization index (total energy cost per gross square foot per year) shall be projected forward for each contract year of the proposed lease based on one of the following:

1) the average annual energy escalation rate derived from actual utility bill data for the previous three years

2) an escalation rate approved by the agency when actual utility bill data for the previous three years is not available.

Computer-Based Simulation Requirements

When a computer-based simulation is required to develop the EPA (see EPA Procedures above), the computer-based simulation shall be consistent with the following requirements:

1. The computer-based simulation shall be performed by an engineer licensed in Florida.
2. The computer-based simulation program shall be one of the following commercially-available software programs:
    a. DOE-2
    b. BLAST
    c. eQuest
    d. EnergyPlus
    e. Carrier HAP
    f. Trane TRACE
    g. Other programs determined by DMS to be consistent with Rule 60D-4.005, FAC.
3. The computer-based simulation shall model total energy consumption for the proposed lease space.
4. The computer-based energy simulation shall model all of the following loads that exist or shall exist as a result of renovations in the proposed lease space:
    a. lighting
    b. internal equipment loads
    c. service water heating
    d. space heating
    e. space cooling
    f. fans
    g. pumps

EPA Submission Requirements

The EPA submission shall contain all of the following information:

1. A description of the proposed lease space that includes:
    a. gross square footage
    b. rentable square footage
    c. type of space
    d. current number of occupants
    e. proposed number of occupants (this is the tenant agency's requirement)
    f. weekly operating schedule
    g. address of the facility
2. Copies of the utility bill statements for the previous one year (provide when such data is used to develop the Energy Star rating). Historical consumption and cost data supplied by the utility provider will be considered acceptable in lieu of utility bill copies.
3. Copies of the actual utility bill statements for the previous three years (provide when such data is used to develop the energy cost projection). Historical consumption and cost data supplied by the utility provider will be considered acceptable in lieu of utility bill copies.
4. Input and output sheets from the computer-based simulation program (provide when a computer-based simulation is required).
5. The name, address, firm name, and license number of the engineer who performed the computer-based simulation (provide when a computer-based simulation is required).
6. Energy Star software forms:
7. "Statement of Energy Performance" (provide when Energy Star Portfolio Manager is used)
8. "Target Energy Performance Results" (provide when Energy Star Target Finder is used)
9. Energy performance index and calculations (provide when the proposed lease is not eligible for an Energy Star rating).
10. The cost utilization index, projection, and calculations. A brief description of the type and size of the existing HVAC and lighting systems.
11. A detailed description of all renovations planned, necessary, or performed to make the proposed lease space suitable for the tenant agency.
12. A detailed description of all energy conservation measures proposed to raise the Energy Star rating to the minimum accepted level (provide when energy conservation measures are proposed and also include the revised Energy Star reports).

13. Delivery: The energy performance analysis shall be mailed or delivered to the department pursuant to Section 255.254(1), Florida Statutes at the address listed here:

DMS EPA Review

STATE OF FLORIDA

Standard Lease Agreement

Department of Management Services Form 4054

Lease Number: ______________________

Lease Commencement: _______________

Preamble

THIS LEASE AGREEMENT is entered into this _____ day of _____, 20_____ by and between those Parties listed below.

Parties

Lessee: ____
Agency Name

Address: ____
Street City State Zip Code

Lessor: ____
Lessor Name

Address: ____
Street City State Zip Code

FEID: _________________OR Social Security Number: ________________________

1. Description

A. In consideration for the covenants and agreements made here, Lessor agrees to lease to Lessee those Premises (hereinafter the "Premises") described as:

Description:

Building: ____
Building Name

County: ____

Address: ____
Street City State Zip Code

consisting of an aggregate area of ____ square feet of net rentable space measured in accordance with the Department of Management Services' Standard Method of Space Measurement. This space comprises approximately _____ of the _____ net square feet in the building.

B. Lessor shall also provide _______ exclusive parking spaces and _________ nonexclusive parking spaces as part of this Lease Agreement.

2. Term & Renewals

A. The Lease shall begin on: __________________ _____, _________

Month Day Year

and end at the close of business on: __________________ _____, _________

Month Day Year

for a term of _____ months.

B. Lessee, however, is hereby granted the option to renew this Lease for an additional ____ upon the same terms and conditions as specified in Article 5. B. of this Lease. If Lessee desires to renew this Lease under the provisions of this Article, it shall give Lessor written notice thereof not more than six months nor less than three months prior to the expiration of the term provided in this Article or any applicable renewal period.

3. Notices, Rental Invoices & Rental Payments

A. All Notices to be served upon Lessee shall be sent by receipted mail to:

Lessee: ____

Agency Name

Address: ____

Street City State Zip Code

B. All Notices to be served upon Lessor shall be sent by receipted mail to:

Lessor: ____

Lessor Name

Address: ____

Street City State Zip Code

C. Rental invoices shall be submitted monthly to Lessee at:

Lessee: ____

Agency Name

Address: ____

Street City State Zip Code

D. Rental Payments shall be paid to Lessor at:

Lessor: ____

Lessor Name

Address: ____

Street City State Zip Code

4. Rent

The rent shall be payable the month following the month of occupancy in accordance with subsection 215.422, Florida Statutes. The rent for any fractional part of the first month shall be prorated.

A. Base Term

Lessee agrees to pay Lessor rent according to the following schedule:

TERM				
Start (MM/DD/YYYY)	End (MM/DD/YYYY)	RATE PER SQUARE FOOT	MONTHLY RENT	ANNUAL RENT
			$0.00	$0.00
			$0.00	$0.00
			$0.00	$0.00
			$0.00	$0.00
			$0.00	$0.00
			$0.00	$0.00
			$0.00	$0.00
			$0.00	$0.00
			$0.00	$0.00
			$0.00	$0.00

B. Option Term

For the renewal options as specified in article 2, the rental rate shall be:

TERM				
Start (MM/DD/YYYY)	End (MM/DD/YYYY)	RATE PER SQUARE FOOT	MONTHLY RENT	ANNUAL RENT
			$0.00	$0.00
			$0.00	$0.00
			$0.00	$0.00
			$0.00	$0.00
			$0.00	$0.00
			$0.00	$0.00
			$0.00	$0.00
			$0.00	$0.00
			$0.00	$0.00
			$0.00	$0.00

5. Utilities

A. The Lessor ☐, Lessee ☐, see Addendum __________ ☐ will promptly pay all billed utilities including gas, water, sewer, solid waste, storm water, and other power and electric light rates or charges which may become payable during the term of this Lease.

B. Lessor agrees to provide Lessee timely and accurate data on Lessee's monthly consumption or use of electricity, natural gas, LP gas and/or fuel oil, as appropriate, pursuant to Section 255.257, Florida Statutes.

6. Facility Services

A. The Lessor ☐ or Lessee ☐ will furnish daily janitorial services and required janitorial supplies. Janitorial services will include provision of recycling trash disposal for the Premises at the expense of the Lessor ☐ or Lessee ☐.

B. Lessor shall provide for interior and exterior maintenance and repairs in accordance with generally accepted good practices. This includes repainting, replacement of worn or damaged floor covering and repairs or replacement of interior equipment as needed due to normal use. Lessor shall maintain the exterior of the leased facility so to conform to all applicable health and safety laws, ordinances and codes, which are presently in effect or may be enacted during the term of this Lease and any renewal periods.

C. The Lessor ☐ or Lessee ☐ agrees to furnish pest control services for the leased Premises during the term of the Lease at the expense of the Lessor ☐ or Lessee ☐.

D. Lessor agrees to install light fixtures for use by Lessee. The Lessor ☐ or Lessee ☐ shall be responsible for replacement of all bulbs, lamps, tubes, and starters used in such fixtures.

E. All services required above shall be provided during Lessee's normal working hours, which are deemed 7:30 a.m. to 5:30 p.m., Monday through Friday excluding state holidays, unless otherwise stipulated below:

Day	From	To
____________	____________	____________
____________	____________	____________
____________	____________	____________
____________	____________	____________
____________	____________	____________
____________	____________	____________
____________	____________	____________
____________	____________	____________
____________	____________	____________

F. During the term of this Lease, Lessee shall maintain the interior of the Premises in as good a state of repair as it is at the time of the commencement of this Lease. Notwithstanding this obligation, reasonable wear and tear and unavoidable casualties are permissible.

7. Accessibility and Alterations

A. Lessor agrees that the Premises conform, or will be brought into conformance with, the requirements of the Florida Americans With Disabilities Accessibility Implementation Act, Section 553.501 - 553.513, Florida Statutes, and the current Florida Disability Code for Building Construction, providing requirements for persons with disabilities, and with the requirement of Public Law 101-336, enacted July 26, 1990, effective January 26, 1992, Section 28 CFR Part 35 and Appendix to Section 36 CFR Part 1191, known as the "Americans with Disabilities Act of 1990" prior to Lessee's occupancy.

B. Lessor agrees that Lessee shall have the right to make any alterations in and to the Premises during the term of this Lease upon first having obtained written consent of Lessor. Lessor shall not capriciously withhold the consent to any such alterations.

8. Applicable Laws

Due to the size and/or configuration of the space leased, the following laws apply:

A. ☐ Section 255.25(3)(e), Florida Statutes relating to tenant improvement costs for which Lessor may be eligible for reimbursement. As applicable, Lessor and Lessee agree that the sum of _______ has been spent by the Lessor for improvements to the Premises and the Lessor does ☐ or does not ☐ intend to seek reimbursement for these improvements.

B. ☐ Section 252.385(4)(b), Florida Statutes relating to the use of the Premises as a public hurricane evacuation shelter. As applicable, the facility in which the Premises exist may be required to serve as a public hurricane evacuation shelter at the request of local emergency management agencies. It is hereby agreed and understood that in the event the Premises is selected for use as an emergency shelter Lessor, upon receiving notice from the Emergency Management Center, shall make the building available as a public hurricane evacuation shelter.

9. Heating and Air Conditioning

Lessor agrees to furnish to Lessee heating and air conditioning equipment and maintain same in satisfactory operating condition at all times for the Premises during the term of the Lease at the expense of Lessor. Lessor agrees that thermostats in the Premises will be set to maintain an average zone temperature of 75 degrees Fahrenheit during the heating and cooling seasons.

10. Compliance with Fire Safety Standards

A. Lessor shall provide for fire protection during the term of this Lease in accordance with the fire safety standards of the State Fire Marshal. Lessor shall be responsible for maintenance and repair of all fire protection equipment necessary to conform to the requirements of the State Fire Marshal. Lessor agrees that the Premises shall be available for inspection by the State Fire Marshal, prior to occupancy by Lessee, and at any reasonable time thereafter.

B. To assure Lessee of facility compliance with Florida's Fire Safety Standards, Lessor agrees to provide Lessee with written Fire Safety Inspection prior to the approval of this Lease. Fire Safety Inspection is to be conducted by State Fire Marshal or local fire officials.

C. In the event that the entirety or majority of the Premises is destroyed by fire, lightning, storm or other casualty, Lessor may repair the damage to Premises at its own cost and expense. Rental payments shall cease until the completion of repairs. Lessor will immediately refund the pro rata part of any rentals paid in advance by Lessee prior to the destruction. Should the Premises be only partly destroyed, leaving the major part in usable condition, then the rental shall abate on the damaged portion until the Premises is restored by Lessor. Upon the completion of such repairs, the full rental shall commence and the Lease shall then continue the balance of the term.

D. Lessor certifies that no asbestos was used in the construction of the demised Premises or that if asbestos was used, actions have been completed to correct the hazards caused by the use of asbestos.

E. Radon is a naturally occurring radioactive gas that, when it has accumulated in a building in sufficient quantities, may present health risks to persons who are exposed to it over a period of time. Levels of radon that exceed federal and state guidelines have been found in buildings in Florida. Additional information regarding radon and radon testing may be obtained from your county health department. (Chapter 404.056(8), Florida Statutes. Lessor certifies that if any radon is present, it is at a measurement level less than 4 PCI/L.

11. Injury or Damage to Property

All property of any kind that may be on the Premises during the term of this Lease shall be at the sole risk of Lessee, and except for any negligence of Lessor, Lessor shall not be liable to Lessee for loss or damage to the property.

12. Expiration of Term

At the expiration of the term, Lessee will peaceably yield up to Lessor the Premises in good and tenantable repair. Lessor and Lessee agree that Lessee shall have the right to remove from the Premises all personal property of Lessee including all fixtures, machinery, equipment, appurtenances and appliances placed or installed on the Premises by Lessee provided that Lessee agrees to restore the Premises to as good a state of repair as found prior to the removal.

13. Right to Inspect

Lessor, at all reasonable times, may enter into and upon the Premises for the purpose of viewing the same and for the purpose of making any such repairs as Lessor is required to make under the terms of this Lease .

14. Taxes and Insurance

Lessor shall pay all real estate taxes and fire insurance premiums on the Premises. Lessor shall not be liable to carry fire insurance on the person or property of Lessee or any other person or property that may occupy the Premises now or later.

15. Subletting and Assignment

Lessee, upon obtaining written consent of Lessor, shall have the right to sublet all or any part of the Premises or to assign all or any part of the Premises. Lessor shall not capriciously withhold written consent.

16. Wavier of Defaults

No waiver by Lessee of any breach of this Lease by Lessor shall be construed as a waiver of any subsequent breach of any duty or covenant imposed by this Lease.

17. Rental Commencement

Notwithstanding the provisions of Article 2 "Term" and Article 4 "Rent" of this Lease, term shall not commence until date of completion of the renovations of the demised premises to Lessee's satisfaction and thereby made ready for occupancy by lessee. At the time of occupancy, the rent for any fractional part of the first month of occupancy shall be prorated.

18. Availability of Funds

Pursuant to Section 255.2502, Florida Statutes, Lessor acknowledges that the State of Florida's performance and obligation to pay under this contract is contingent upon an annual appropriation by the Legislature.

19. Breach of Covenant

A. If Lessee neglects or fails to perform or observe any covenant herein, and such default continues for a period of thirty (30) days after receipt of written notice thereof from Lessor, then Lessor may lawfully, immediately, or at any time thereafter, and without further notice or demand, enter into and upon the Premises, and repossess the same as of their former estate and expel Lessee and remove its effects forcefully, if necessary.

B. This action by Lessor shall not be deemed as any manner of trespass and thereupon any remedy which might otherwise be used by Lessor for arrears of rent or for any breach of Lessee's covenants herein contained shall terminated, without prejudice.

20. Not Consent to Sue

No provisions, terms, or conditions of this Lease shall be construed as consent of the State of Florida to be sued because of said leasehold.

21. Right to Terminate

Lessee shall have the right to terminate this Lease without penalty in the event a State-owned building becomes available to Lessee for occupancy, and upon the giving six (6) months advance written notice to Lessor by Certified Mail, Return Receipt Requested.

22. Public Entity Crime Statement

Section 287.133, Florida Statutes places the following restrictions on the ability of persons convicted of public entity crimes to transact business with public entities, including the department:

A person, or affiliate, who has been placed on the convicted vendor list, following a conviction for a public entity crime, may not submit a bid on a contract to provide any goods or services to a public entity, may not submit a bid on a contract with a public entity for the construction or repair of a public building or public work, may not submit bids on leases of real property to a public entity, may not perform work as a contractor, supplier, subcontractor, or consultant under a contract with any public entity, and may not transact business with any public entity in excess of the threshold amount provided in Section 287.017, Florida Statutes for CATEGORY TWO for a period of 36 months from the date of being placed on the convicted vendor list.

23. Discrimination

Section 287.134 Florida Statutes places the following restrictions on the ability of persons on the discriminatory vendor list to transact business with public entities, including the department:

An entity who has been placed on the discriminatory vendor list may not submit a bid or proposal to provide goods or services to a public entity, may not submit a bid or proposal with a public entity for the construction or repair of a public building or public work, may not submit bids or proposals on leases of real property to a public entity, may not perform work as a contractor, supplier subcontractor or consultant under contract with any public entity and may not transact business with any public entity.

24. Use of Premises

Lessee will not make or suffer any unlawful, improper, or offensive use of the Premises or any use or occupancy thereof contrary to the laws of the State of Florida or to such ordinances of the city or county in which the Premises are located, now or hereinafter made, as may be applicable to Lessee.

25. Failure to Comply

A. In the event that Lessor fails to comply with any term or provision of this Lease after written notice, Lessee reserves the option to:

   i. setoff and deduct from the rental amount due Lessor under this Lease such sums as Lessee determines are required to remedy the default of Lessor, and/or

   ii. fulfill Lessor's obligations under the terms of this Lease, whereby Lessor shall reimburse Lessee on demand for any reasonable expenses which Lessee may incur in thus effecting compliance with Lessor's obligation under this Lease. Should Lessee elect this option, Lessee shall use its best efforts to mitigate damages caused thereby, and/or

   iii. terminate this Lease and vacate the Premises, but without prejudice to any remedy which might otherwise be used by Lessee for any breach of Lessor's covenants contained herein, and/or

   iv. bring suit for damages against Lessor for any expense (including reasonable attorney's fees) Lessee may incur by Lessor's failure to comply with any term or provision of the Lease. However, Lessee shall not bring suit for damages incurred due to a delay in the Commencement Date of this Lease if any such delay is caused solely by any delay, default or omission of Lessee.

B. Lessee is required to give Lessor written notice setting forth in reasonable detail the nature and extent of such failure and Lessor will be given thirty (30) days to cure such failure. If such failure cannot reasonably be completely cured within that thirty (30) day period, the length of such period shall be extended for the period reasonably required thereof, only if Lessor commences curing such failure within such thirty (30) day period and continues the curing thereof with reasonable diligence and continuity.

C. Reason for setoff of amounts due under this Lease shall include, but are not limited to, remedying heating and air conditioning equipment and roofing deficiencies.

D. Each occasion of setoff of rental amounts due under this Lease shall be contingent upon the prior approval of Lessee's legal counsel.

26. Definition of Terms

A. The terms "Lease," "Lease Agreement," or "Agreement" shall be inclusive of each other and shall also include any renewals, extensions or modifications of this Lease.

B. The terms "Lessor" and "Lessee" shall include the successors and assigns for the parties hereto.

C. The singular shall include the plural and the plural shall include the singular whenever the context so requires or permits.

27. Additional Terms

A. No additional covenants or conditions form a part of this Lease.

B. All additional covenants or conditions appear on attached Addendum(s):

IN WITNESS WHEREOF, the Parties hereto have hereunto executed this instrument for the purpose herein expressed,

this ____ day of ______________, 20_____.

ANY MODIFICATION OF A LEASE AGREEMENT SHALL NOT BECOME LEGALLY EFFECTIVE UNTIL APPROVED/ACCEPTED BY THE DEPARTMENT OF MANAGEMENT SERVICES.

ORIGINAL SIGNATURES REQUESTED ON ALL COPIES

As to Lessor - Lessor, or authorized representative and two witnesses must sign, print name and enter date.

X______________________ Lessor or Authorized Representative	______________________ Printed Name	___/___/____ Date
X______________________ Witness #1	______________________ Printed Name	___/___/____ Date
X______________________ Witness #2	______________________ Printed Name	___/___/____ Date

As to Lessee Agency - Agency head, or authorized delegate, and representative of Agency's Office of General Counsel, must sign, print name and enter date.

X______________________ Agency Head or Authorized Delegate	______________________ Printed Name	___/___/____ Date
X______________________ Agency Office of General Counsel	______________________ Printed Name	___/___/____ Date

As to the Department of Management Services - Chief Real Property Administrator (or authorized designee) and Secretary (or authorized delegate) must sign, print name and enter date. When applicable, DMS Office of General Counsel, shall sign, print name and enter date..

X______________________ Chief Real Property Administrator	______________________ Printed Name	___/___/____ Date
X______________________ Secretary or Authorized Delegate	______________________ Printed Name	___/___/____ Date
X______________________ Office of General Counsel	______________________ Printed Name	___/___/____ Date

STATE OF CALIFORNIA
DEPARTMENT OF GENERAL SERVICES REAL ESTATE SERVICES DIVISION

STANDARD LEASE FORM

LEASE COVERING PREMISES LOCATED AT
LESSOR'S FED. TAX. I.D., NO. OR SOCIAL SECURITY NO.
TENANT AGENCY

Lease File No.: ________________

Project No.: __________________

Preamble

THIS LEASE, made and entered into this _____ day of __________ by ______________ and between ______________

hereinafter called the Lessor, without distinction as to number or gender, and the State of California, acting by and through the Director of the Department of General Services, hereinafter called the State,

WITNESSETH

Description

1. The Lessor hereby leases unto the State and the State hereby hires from the Lessor those certain premises with appurtenances situated in the City of , County of , State of California, and more particularly described as follows:

Approximately net usable square feet of office space on the floor of the building located at as outlined in red on the attached Exhibit "A" plan, together with specifications marked Exhibit "B" and administrative requirements marked Exhibit "C", said Exhibits "A" and "B" and "C", Project No. dated , hereby being incorporated into this lease, and including nonexclusive unobstructed parking spaces contiguous to the subject building, and unlimited use of the building's common facilities. The State shall have access to and use of the leased premises 24 hours per day, seven (7) days per week with no exceptions.

Term

2. The term of this lease shall commence on ________, and shall end on ________, with such rights of termination as may be hereinafter expressly set forth.

Early Termination

3. The State may terminate this lease at any time effective on or after ___________, by giving written notice to the Lessor at least thirty (30) days prior to the date when such termination shall become effective. If the State fails to complete its move out within the notice period and remains in the premises, additional rent shall be paid and prorated on a thirty (30) day month, based on the actual number of days the State occupies the premises following the effective date of termination.

Rent

4. Rental payments shall be paid by the State, from legally available funds and subject to the California Constitution, in arrears on the last day of each month during said term as follows:

Rental payable hereunder for any period of time less than one month shall be determined by prorating the monthly rental herein specified based on the actual number of days in the month. Rental shall be paid to Lessor at the address specified in Paragraph 5 or to such other address as the Lessor may designate by a notice in writing. If the premises are not complete pursuant to Paragraph 6 by the date shown in Paragraph 2, it is understood and agreed by and between the parties that, at the State's sole option, the dates shown in Paragraphs 2 and 3 and the dates and dollar amounts shown in Paragraph 4 may be adjusted to the first of the month following the State's acceptance of the completed premises, such acceptance shall not unreasonably be withheld. If the State exercises this option, it is agreed the State will complete unilaterally an amendment to the lease to revise the herein above stated dates. Any accrued rents for the period of time prior to the unilaterally adjusted commencement date will be paid in accordance with Paragraph 8. Additionally, it is understood and agreed between the parties that, at the State's option, the dates shown in the "CPI Escalator Operating Expenses" paragraph, if incorporated herein, shall be adjusted to reflect the time delay between lease commencement and the first of the month following the actual acceptance date. In the event this lease agreement contains a provision granting the State an Option to Purchase the premises, it is further agreed herein by the parties that, notwithstanding the provision of the Option to Purchase paragraph herein, the effective dates and corresponding purchase option prices of said Option to Purchase shall be adjusted consistent with any adjustment to the lease commencement date. Said "adjusted" purchase option dates shall be established consistent herewith and incorporated into said lease with a unilateral amendment by the State.

Notices

5. All notices and correspondence herein provided to be given, or which may be given by either party to the other, shall be deemed to have been fully given when made in writing and either: 1) deposited in the United States Mail, certified and postage prepaid, or 2) sent via an alternate commercial overnight delivery service (i.e. FedEx or similar) with receiver's signature required, and addressed as follows:

To the Lessor: ____
____
____
____

Phone No. ( )____________

Fax No. ( )____________

Email ____________

To the State: **DEPARTMENT OF GENERAL SERVICES,** **Phone No.**
REAL ESTATE SERVICES DIVISION **FAX No.**
LEASE MANAGEMENT

ALL NOTICES AND CORRESPONDENCE MUST REFERENCE TENANT AGENCY AND PREMISES ADDRESS

Rental warrants shall be made payable to: ____________________________

and mailed to: ____
____
____

Nothing herein contained shall preclude the giving of any such written notice by personal service. The address to which notices and correspondence shall be mailed to either party may be changed by giving written notice to the other party.

Completion and Compliance with Plans and Specifications

6. Lessor agrees that, prior to ________, and at Lessor's sole cost and expense, all required construction, improvements and/or alterations, if any, shall be completed and the leased premises made ready for State's occupancy in full compliance with Exhibit "A", consisting of # of pages sheets titled, "Office Quarters, Project No." dated , and in accordance with Exhibit "B", consisting of ________ pages, titled, "Outline Specifications, Project No." dated ________, and Exhibit "C" consisting of sixteen (16) pages titled, "Administrative Requirements Project No." dated ________, which Exhibits "A" and "B" and "C" are by this reference incorporated herein.

Notice of Completion and Access to Premises during Construction

7. Lessor shall notify the State in writing by certified mail of the date the leased premises will be completed and ready for occupancy at least thirty (30) days prior thereto. Such notice shall be a condition precedent to the accrual of rental hereunder, except however, that if the State occupies the premises prior to the receipt of such notice or prior to the expiration of the notice period of such notice, rental shall commence to accrue as of the date of occupancy.

Following execution of this lease, and not more than sixty days (60) prior to completion of construction and occupancy under this lease, State or its contractors or other representatives shall have the right to enter the premises for the purpose of installing certain equipment such as, but not limited to, modular system furniture, and electrical and telecommunications cabling and equipment.

State agrees to indemnify and hold Lessor harmless from and against any claims, damages, or other injury suffered by Lessor as a result of the work to be performed pursuant to this right to enter the premises prior to State's acceptance and occupancy of the premises. Lessor agrees to indemnify and hold State and its agents, contractors or other representatives harmless from and against any claims, damages, injury or other harm suffered by reason of the negligence or other wrongful act of Lessor or any of Lessor's agents, contractors, or other representatives.

In no event shall the exercise of this right of entry be construed so as to cause an acceleration of the occupancy date of this lease or the obligation of the State to pay rent.

Lessor and State shall each make all reasonable efforts to ensure that the respective construction and installation work is scheduled in such a manner so as to not interfere with or delay the other.

In the event that one or the other party causes a delay in the other party's work, such injured party shall be compensated in the following manner:

Delays caused by the Lessor:

Credit the State a compensating day of delay in the occupancy date and corresponding day of delay in payment of rent.

Delays caused by the State:

Credit the Lessor a compensating day of payment of rent from the actual date of occupancy. Compensation will be in one day increments.

The parties agree that this shall be the sole remedy for delay, in that the calculation of damages in any other manner is too uncertain and not susceptible of accurate determination.

Early Occupancy

8. Lessor agrees that if the leased premises are ready for occupancy prior to the completion date specified above in Paragraph 6, State may elect to occupy the premises on the earliest date practical after its receipt of the herein required completion notice. The rent payable for any such early occupancy by the State shall be at the rate of $______ per month, and shall be prorated on a daily basis for any partial month.

Time limit and Prior Tenancy

9. No rental shall accrue under this lease, nor shall the State have any obligation to perform the covenants or observe the conditions herein contained until the leased premises have been made ready for occupancy in accordance with the provisions hereof. It is specifically agreed that in the event the leased premises are not completed and ready for occupancy by the State on or before ________________, then and in that event the State may, at its option and in addition to any other remedies it may have, terminate this lease and be relieved of any further obligations hereunder, providing that a fair and reasonable allowance for the following delays shall be added to said time for completion:

A. Acts of the State, its agents or employees, or those claiming under agreement with or grant from the State,

or by

B. The acts of God which Lessor could not reasonably have foreseen or guarded against, or by

C. Any strikes, boycotts or like obstructive actions by employees or labor organizations and which are beyond control of Lessor, and which cannot be reasonably overcome, or by

D. Restrictive regulations by the Federal Government which are enforced in connection with a National Emergency.

In the event that the State elects to occupy premises before the work on the premises specified in Exhibit A, B, and C is fully completed, the State will provide the Lessor with a punch list of work remaining to be completed (referenced as the State's "Punch List"). Lessor agrees that Lessor shall complete the remaining work no later than 14 calendar days from the date of receipt of said Punch List. If said Punch List is not completed within the specified 14-day period, Lessor agrees that, beginning on the first day after said 14-day period following occupancy of premises by the State, rent may at the State's sole option be reduced to $___ which is seventy percent (70%) of the base rent specified in paragraph 4 herein (excluding any amortization payments) until such time that the Punch List work is completed in full and that such completion of work is inspected and accepted by the State. The portion of the rent specified for amortization of tenant improvements, if any shall continue to be paid in full without interruption.

It is understood and agreed that the rent reduction specified above does not relieve Lessor of its obligation to complete said work and the State shall maintain all other remedies specified in the Lease.

It is understood by all parties hereto that it shall be the Lessor's responsibility to remove any prior tenant.

Conformity to Exhibits

10. Occupancy of the leased premises by the State shall not relieve Lessor in any respect from full compliance at all times with aforesaid Exhibits "A" and "B" and "C". It is further understood and agreed that any installation not in conformity with said Exhibits "A" and "B" and "C" shall be immediately corrected by the Lessor at Lessor's sole cost and expense. In the event Lessor shall, after notice in writing from the State requiring the Lessor to comply with the requirements of this paragraph in regard to a specified condition, fail, refuse or neglect to remedy such condition, State may terminate this lease without further obligation, or as to such specified condition, at its option and in addition to any other remedy the State may have, withhold rent due and bring the leased premises into conformity with said Exhibits at its own cost including State's Administrative costs, if any, and deduct the amount thereof from the rent that may then be or thereafter become due hereunder.

Asbestos

11. Lessor hereby warrants and guarantees that the space leased to the State will be operated and maintained free of hazard from Asbestos Containing Materials (ACM) and agrees to the conditions for survey, testing, and abatement of ACM described in Exhibit "B" as applicable. Lessor specifically agrees that, in the event the State elects to exercise its rights under the provisions of Paragraph 16 of this lease, any costs related to abatement or hazard from asbestos shall be the Lessor's responsibility as described in the aforementioned Exhibit "B."

Parking

12. Lessor, at Lessor's sole cost and expense, shall clearly mark the parking spaces described hereinabove as assigned to the State of California. Said parking spaces will be arranged and maintained so as to provide unobstructed access to each parking space at any time. In addition to any assigned parking spaces, State and its invitees shall have equal access to common spaces provided to all tenants on a first-come, first-served basis.

Services, Utilities, and Supplies

13. Lessor, at Lessor's sole cost and expense, during the term of this lease shall furnish the following services, utilities, and supplies to the area leased by the State, and also to the "common" building areas (if any) such as lobbies, elevators, stairways, corridors, etc., which State shares with other tenants, if any:

A. Sewer, trash disposal, and water service, including both hot and cold water to the lavatories except lavatories in Employment Development Department public toilet rooms in lobby areas which need only cold water.

B. Elevator (if any) service.

C. Electricity and/or gas as necessary to provide power for heating, ventilating, and air conditioning, and electrical or gas service as needed for State's operations.

D. Janitorial services sufficient to maintain the interior in a clean well-maintained condition, that is, to eliminate all visible dust, dirt, litter, grime, stains, smears, finger marks, etc., to the greatest practical degree possible, by performing at least the following:

Daily:

(1) Empty and clean all trash containers, and dispose of all trash and rubbish.

(2) Clean and maintain in a sanitary and odor-free condition all floors, wash mirrors, basins, toilet bowls, and urinals.

(3) Furnish and replenish all toilet room supplies (including soap, towels, seat covers, toilet tissue, and sanitary napkins). Furnish and replenish paper towel supply in all areas of the leased space.

(4) Sweep or dust mop all hard surface floors, and carpet sweep all carpeted areas, including stairways and halls. Offices with hard surface floors in the public lobby area shall be damp-mopped daily.

(5) Remove finger marks and smudges from all glass entrance doors.

(6) Specifically check, and if action is needed, then:

a. Dust the tops of all furniture, counters, cabinets, and window sills (which are free of interfering objects).

b. Remove spots and/or spills from the carpets, floors, and stairways.

As needed, but not less frequently than:

Twice Weekly: Vacuum all carpets.

Weekly:

(1) Damp mop all hard surface floors.

(2) Dust all window blinds.

(3) Treat stainless steel fountains and sinks to eliminate stains and mineral deposits.

(4) Spot clean the walls.

Quarterly:

(1) Strip all hard surface floors and apply a new coat of floor finish, buff as necessary to produce a uniformly shining appearance.

(2) Treat carpets for static electricity control (if not integrated in the fabric).

Semi-annually:

Wash all windows, window blinds, light fixtures, walls, and painted surfaces.

Annually:

(1) Steam clean carpets to remove all stains and spots.

(2) Clean window coverings.

In the event of failure by the Lessor to furnish any of the above services or supplies in a satisfactory manner, the State may furnish the same at its own cost, and, in addition to any other remedy the State may have, may deduct the amount thereof, including State's administrative costs, from the rent that may then be, or thereafter become due hereunder.

Repair and Maintenance

14. A. During the lease term, the Lessor shall maintain the leased premises in good repair and tenantable condition, so as to minimize breakdowns and loss of the State's use of the premises caused by deferred or inadequate maintenance, including, but not limited to:

(1) Generally maintaining the leased premises in good, vermin-free, operating condition and appearance.

(2) Furnishing prompt, good quality repair of the building, equipment, and appurtenances.

(3) Furnishing preventative maintenance, including, but not limited to, manufacturer's recommended servicing of equipment such as elevator (if any), heating, ventilating and air conditioning equipment, and fixtures.

(4) Furnishing ongoing maintenance and prompt repair of any and all special equipment and systems referenced in Exhibits A and B including but not limited to, security and access control systems, fire suppression systems, special HVAC systems for computer rooms, and UPS systems.

(5) Furnishing and promptly replacing any inoperative light bulbs, fluorescent tubes, ballast, starters, and filters for the heating, ventilating and air conditioning equipment as required.

(6) Furnishing remedial painting as necessary to maintain the premises in a neat, clean and orderly condition.

(7) Annual testing and maintenance of all fire extinguishers in or adjacent to the leased premises.

(8) Repairing and replacing as necessary intrabuilding network cable and inside wire cable used for voice and data transmission.

(9) Repairing and replacing parking lot bumpers and paving as necessary. Repaint directional arrows, striping, etc., as necessary.

(10) On a weekly basis, sweeping parking areas and sidewalks, maintaining landscaped areas, including sprinklers, drainage, etc., in a growing, litter-free, weed free, and neatly mowed and/or trimmed condition.

(11) Repairing and replacing floor covering as necessary. Lessor, at Lessor's sole cost, shall arrange for moving of furniture and equipment prior and subsequent to the repairing or replacement of floor covering.

(12) Keeping all walkways, parking lots, entrances, and auxiliary areas free of snow, water, oil spills, debris, or other materials which may be hazardous to users of the building.

B. Lessor shall provide prompt repair or correction for any damage except damage arising from a willful or negligent act of the State's agents, employees or invitees.

C. Except in emergency situations, the Lessor shall give not less than 48 hour prior notice to State tenants, when any pest control, remodeling, renovation, or repair work affecting the State occupied space may result in employee health concerns in the work environment.

D. In case Lessor, after notice in writing from the State requiring the Lessor to comply with the requirements of this paragraph in regard to a specified condition, shall fail, refuse or neglect to comply with such notice, or in the event of an emergency constituting a hazard to the health or safety of the State's employees, property, or invitees, the State may terminate this lease without further obligation or at its option, perform such maintenance or make such repair at its own cost and, in addition to any other remedy the State may have, may withhold rent due and deduct the amount thereof, including necessary costs incurred by the State required for the administration of such maintenance and repairs, from the rent that may then be or thereafter become due hereunder.

Painting

15. In addition to any painting completed prior to the commencement of this lease, and touch-up painting required after initial occupancy upon receipt of written request from the State, Lessor agrees at Lessor's sole cost and expense to repaint all painted surfaces (☐ interior and ☐ exterior) of the leased premises in accordance with the attached Exhibits "A" and "B". In no event shall Lessor be required to repaint more than once during the first sixty (60) month period of this lease after the painting completed prior to the commencement date, and once during any succeeding sixty (60) month period.

Lessor shall, within forty-five (45) days from the giving of any such notice, arrange for and complete the painting. All painting of interior premises shall be performed after business hours or as otherwise agreed upon by the State. Colors are to be approved by the State. Lessor, at Lessor's sole cost, shall arrange for moving of furniture and equipment prior and subsequent to the repainting, and provide drop cloths, and covers as necessary.

Change Orders and Alterations

16. The State shall have the right during the existence of this lease to make change orders and alterations, attach fixtures, and erect additions, structures, or signs in or upon the leased premises. Such fixtures, additions, structures, or signs so placed in or upon or attached to the premises under this lease or any extension hereof shall be and remain the property of the State and may be removed therefrom by the State prior to the termination or expiration of this lease or any renewal or extension hereof, or within a reasonable time thereafter.

In the event alterations, fixtures, additions, structures, or signs in or upon the leased premises are desired by State and State elects not to perform the work, any such work, when authorized in writing by the State shall be performed by the Lessor in accordance with plans and specifications provided by State. Lessor agrees to obtain competitive bids from at least three licensed contractors and to contract with the lowest bidder. Lessor further agrees that the overhead and profit for the work shall not exceed fifteen percent (15%) total for Lessor and any general contractor combined. Within forty-five (45) days after receiving Lessor's notice of completion of the requested work and an invoice requesting payment therefor, together with a complete detailed accounting of all costs for each trade, State agrees to reimburse Lessor by a single total payment for the cost of such work.

Assignment and Subletting

17. The State shall not assign this lease without prior written consent of the Lessor, which shall not be unreasonably withheld, but shall in any event have the right to sublet the leased premises.

Quiet Possession

18. The Lessor agrees that the State, while keeping and performing the covenants herein contained, shall at all times during the existence of this lease, peaceably and quietly have, hold, and enjoy the leased premises without suit, trouble, or hindrance from the Lessor or any person claiming under Lessor.

Inspection

19. The Lessor reserves the right to enter and inspect the leased premises at reasonable times, and to render services and make any necessary repairs to the premises.

Destruction

20. If the leased premises are totally destroyed by fire or other casualty, this lease shall terminate. If such casualty shall render ten percent (10%) or less of the floor space of the leased premises unusable for the purpose intended, Lessor shall effect restoration of the premises as quickly as is reasonably possible, but in any event within thirty (30) days.

In the event such casualty shall render more than ten percent (10%) of such floor space unusable but not constitute total destruction, Lessor shall forthwith give notice to State of the specific number of days required to repair the same. If Lessor under such circumstances shall not give such notice within fifteen (15) calendar days after such destruction, or if such notice shall specify that such repairs will require more than ninety (90) days to complete from date such notice is given, State, in either such event, at its option may terminate this lease or, upon notice to Lessor, may maintain occupancy and elect to undertake the repairs itself, deducting the cost thereof from the rental due or to become due under this lease and any other lease between Lessor and State.

In the event of any such destruction other than total, where the State has not terminated the lease as herein provided, or pursuant to the terms hereof has not elected to make the repairs itself, Lessor shall diligently prosecute the repair of said premises and, in any event, if said repairs are not completed within the period of thirty (30) days for destruction aggregating ten percent (10%) or less of the floor space, or within the period specified in Lessor's notice in connection with partial destruction aggregating more than ten percent (10%), the State shall have the option to terminate this lease or complete the repairs itself, deducting the cost thereof from the rental due or to become due under this lease and any other lease between Lessor and State.

In the event the State remains in possession of said premises though partially damaged, the rental as herein provided shall be reduced by the same ratio as the net square feet the State is thus precluded from occupying bears to the total net square feet in the leased premises.

"Net square feet" shall mean actual inside dimensions and shall not include public corridors, stairwells, elevators, and restrooms.

It is understood and agreed that the State or its agent has the right to enter its destroyed or partially destroyed leased facilities no matter what the condition. At the State's request, the Lessor shall immediately identify an appropriate route through the building to access the State leased space. If the Lessor cannot identify an appropriate access route, it is agreed that the State may use any and all means of access at its discretion in order to enter its leased space.

Subrogation Waived

21. To the extent authorized by any fire and extended coverage insurance policy issued to Lessor on the herein leased premises, Lessor hereby waives the subrogation rights of the insurer, and releases the State from liability for any loss or damage covered by said insurance.

Prevailing Wage Provision

22. For those projects defined as "public works" pursuant to Labor Code §1720.2, the following shall apply:

A. Lessor/contractor shall comply with prevailing wage requirements and be subject to restrictions and penalties in accordance with §1770 et seq. of the Labor Code which requires prevailing wages be paid to appropriate work classifications in all bid specifications and subcontracts.

B. The Lessor/contractor shall furnish all subcontractors/employees a copy of the Department of Industrial Relations prevailing wage rates which Lessor will post at the job site. All prevailing wage rates shall be obtained by the Lessor/contractor from:

Department of Industrial Relations

Division of Labor Statistics and Research

For further information on prevailing wage:
http://www.dir.ca.gov/dlsr/statistics_research.html

C. Lessor/contractor shall comply with the payroll record keeping and availability requirement of §1776 of the Labor Code.

D. Lessor/contractor shall make travel and subsistence payments to workers needed for performance of work in accordance with the Labor Code.

E. Prior to commencement of work, Lessor/contractor shall contact the Division of Apprenticeship Standards and comply with §1777.5, §1777.6, and §1777.7 of the Labor Code and Applicable Regulations

Fair Employment Practices

23. During the performance of this lease, the Lessor shall not deny benefits to any person on the basis of religion, color, ethnic group identification, sex, age, physical or mental disability, nor shall they discriminate unlawfully against any employee or applicant for employment because of race, religion, color, national origin, ancestry, physical handicap, mental disability, medical condition, marital status, age, or sex. Lessor shall insure that the evaluation and treatment of employees and applicants for employment are free of such discrimination.

Lessor shall comply with the provisions of the Fair Employment and Housing Act (Government Code, Section 12900 et seq.), the regulations promulgated thereunder (California Administrative Code, Title 2, Section 7285.0 et seq.), the provisions of Article 9.5, Chapter 1, Part 1, Division 3, Title 2 of the Government Code (Government Code, Sections 11135-11139.5), and the regulations or standards adopted by the awarding State agency to implement such article.

DVBE Participation

24. The State of California supports the use of Disabled Veteran Business Enterprise (DVBE) and we encourage the Lessor to utilize DVBEs when contracting for tenant improvements and services. Lessor shall complete the DVBE Program Certification Sheet (Form F) attached in Exhibit "C" herein prior to acceptance and occupancy of this lease. Lessor may refer to the following internet link for DVBE guidelines and instructions. http://www.documents.dgs.ca.gov/RESD/RELPS/leaserequirements/DVBEGuidelines.pdf

Service Companies

25. Within fifteen (15) days after occupancy of the leased premises by the State, Lessor shall provide the State with the name, address, and telephone number of an agency or person convenient to the State as a local source of service regarding the Lessor's responsibilities under this lease as to repairs, maintenance, and servicing of the premises and any or all related equipment, fixtures, and appurtenances.

Service Credit

26. Lessor agrees that the rental provided under the terms of Paragraph 4 hereof is based in part upon the costs of the services, utilities, and supplies to be furnished by Lessor in accordance with Paragraph 13 hereof. In the event the State vacates the premises prior to the end of the term of this lease, or, if after notice in writing from the State, all or any part of such services, utilities, or supplies for any reason are not used by the State, then, in such event, the monthly rental as to each month or portion thereof as to which such services, utilities, or supplies are not used by the State shall be reduced by an amount equal to the average monthly costs of such unused services, utilities, or supplies during the six-month period immediately preceding the first month in which such services, utilities, or supplies are not used.

Holding Over

27. In the event the State remains in possession of the premises after the expiration of the lease term, or any extension or renewal thereof, this lease shall be automatically extended on a month to month basis, subject to thirty (30) days termination by either party, and otherwise on the terms and conditions herein specified, so far as applicable. If the last rental amount shown in Paragraph 4 included the amortization of a capital sum expended by Lessor for certain alterations and improvements, as described in a separate paragraph herein, and the capital sum has been fully amortized, the holdover rent shall be reduced by the amount of the monthly amortization. If the State fails to vacate the premises within the notice period and remains for an extended period, additional rent shall be paid and prorated on a thirty (30) day month, based on the actual number of days the State occupies the premises following the effective date of termination.

Surrender of Possession

28. Upon termination or expiration of this lease, the State will peacefully surrender to the Lessor the leased premises in as good order and condition as when received, except for reasonable use and wear thereof and damage by earthquake, fire, public calamity, the elements, acts of God, or circumstances over which State has no control or for which Lessor is responsible pursuant to this lease. The State shall have no duty to remove any improvements or fixtures placed by it on the premises or to restore any portion of the premises altered by it, save and except in the event State elects to remove any such improvements or fixtures and such removal causes damages or injury to the leased premises, and then only to the extent of any such damage or injury.

Time of Essence, Binding upon Successors

29. Time is of the essence of this lease, and the terms and provisions of this lease shall extend to and be binding upon and inure to the benefit of the heirs, executors, administrators, successors, and assigns to the respective parties hereto. All of the parties hereto shall be jointly and severally liable hereunder.

No Oral Agreements

30. It is mutually understood and agreed that no alterations or variations of the terms of this lease shall be valid unless made in writing and signed by the parties hereto, and that no oral understanding or agreement not incorporated herein, shall be binding on any of the parties hereto.

Service Contracts Wages and Benefits

31. All janitorial and housekeeping services, custodians, food services workers, laundry workers, window cleaners and security guards provided by Lessor pursuant to the provisions of this lease, shall be in full compliance with the requirements of Government Code (GC) 19134 if applicable, including but not limited to the following:

a) Lessor agrees that service contract agreements for such services will provide employee wages and benefits that are valued at eighty-five (85%) of the State Employer cost of providing comparable wages and benefits to state employees performing similar duties. For these purposes, benefits include health, dental, vision, retirement, holiday pay, sick pay and vacation pay.

b) Lessor shall ensure that each contractor and subcontractor providing such services is provided a copy of the applicable regulations for GC 19134.

c) Lessor agrees to certify on a quarterly basis that all contracts executed by Lessor are in compliance with GC 19134.

d) Lessor agrees to include in the service contract agreements the applicable reporting, audit and termination for breach provisions as described in the applicable regulations for GC 19134.

Construction-Related Accessibility Standard Compliancy Act

32. Pursuant to California Civil Code §1938, the Lessor states that the leased premises:

☐ have not undergone an inspection by a Certified Access Specialist (CASp).

☐ have undergone an inspection by a Certified Access Specialist (CASp) and it was determined that the leased premises met all applicable construction-related accessibility standards pursuant to California Civil Code §55.51 et seq.

☐ have undergone an inspection by a Certified Access Specialist (CASp) and it was determined that the leased premises did not meet all applicable construction-related accessibility standards pursuant to California Civil Code §55.51 et seq.

IN WITNESS WHEREOF, this lease has been executed by the parties hereto as of the dates written below.

STATE OF CALIFORNIA Approval Recommended	LESSOR
DEPARTMENT OF GENERAL SERVICES REAL ESTATE SERVICES DIVISION	
By ______________________ Date ______________	By ______________________ Date ______________
Approved DIRECTOR OF THE DEPARTMENT OF GENERAL SERVICES	By ______________________ Date ______________
By ______________________ Leasing Manager, Real Estate Leasing and Planning Section Date ______________	By ______________________ Date ______________

EXHIBIT 'B' OUTLINE SPECIFICATIONS

STATE OF CALIFORNIA

PROJECT: PROJECT NO.:

AGENCY: LEASE NO.:

LOCATION: DATE:

TITLE **PAGE**

PROJECT CONTACT: PHONE:
FAX:
EMAIL:

Confirmation Statement

I/we have read this Exhibit 'B' Outline Specifications and understand it is incorporated into, and is part of, this lease. I/we have acknowledged each and every page by placing my/our initials on this cover sheet.

Initials ____________

DIVISION 1 - GENERAL REQUIREMENTS

1.1 SUMMARY

A. The Outline Specifications describe minimum standards of quality and performance for premises occupied by the State. Construction methods or materials other than those stated herein may be acceptable if, in the opinion of the State, they provide equal quality and performance.

1.2 RELATED DOCUMENTS

A. Lease

B. Exhibit "A" - Plans or Facility Design Program (written narrative)

C. Exhibit "B" - Division 3 Special Provisions:

1. Refer to Division 3 of this specification for Special Provisions, which may amend and or supersede Division 1 and 2 requirements.

D. Exhibit "B" - Division 4 Technical Requirements:

1. Refer to Division 4 of this specification for Technical Requirements, which may amend and or supersede Division 1 and 2 requirements.

E. Exhibit "C" - Administrative Requirements

1. Refer to Exhibit "C" for specific requirements related to the following:

a. State Fire Marshal Procedures

b. Access Compliance Procedures (CBC/ADA)

c. Green Building Practices

1.3 GENERAL PROVISIONS

A. Wherever reference is made to "State," "Agency," "Department," or other State of California administrative department, this shall be construed to mean Department of General Services, Real Estate Services Division, Real Estate Leasing & Planning Section, here and after referred to as DGS.

B. The State's intent is to achieve adequate standards of quality while avoiding unnecessary alterations, so that in all cases where an existing feature is acceptable to DGS, the Lessor's obligation is only to maintain that feature as it exists.

C. The Lessor shall immediately address conflicts, omissions, or errors if discovered within the Exhibits, or any questions regarding interpretation or clarification, by submitting in writing to the State, a Request for Information (RFI). Responses from the State will not change any requirement of the lease Exhibits unless so noted by the State in the response to the RFI. In case of conflicts between Exhibit "A" and the Exhibit "B", the Exhibit "A" supersedes these specifications.

D. Lessor shall patch, repair, and refinish to match, all existing surfaces disturbed by the new construction. Upon completion of the project, there shall be no visual difference between the new work and the existing conditions. No changes, modifications, or substitutions shall be made to the premises as shown, except with the prior written approval of DGS.

E. <u>LEED Certification</u>: In the event the lease contract provides for a LEED certified facility, see Division 3 Special Provisions.

F. <u>Prevailing Wage</u>: For those projects defined as "public works" pursuant to Labor Code §1720.2, Lessor/contractor shall comply with prevailing wage requirements and be subject to restrictions and penalties in accordance with §1770 et seq. of the Labor Code which requires prevailing wages be paid to appropriate work classifications inall bid specifications and subcontracts.

G. <u>Project Schedule:</u> Upon execution of the lease, Lessor shall issue to DGS, a complete and detailed Critical Path Method (CPM) schedule for the project, which may be adjusted by mutual agreement as the project proceeds. The schedule shall include allowances for periods of time necessary for the installation of State-owned equipment and modular systems furniture.

H. <u>Construction Cost:</u> Prior to construction, Lessor shall provide to the State competitive bids from at least three licensed contractors/subcontractors and shall contract with the lowest acceptable bidder. The bids shall include all charges such as, but not limited to labor, materials, tools, equipment, fees, taxes, shipping, handling, permits, inspections, and fabrication for the work defined in the lease exhibits. The bids shall also include any architectural and engineering fees. The bids shall be itemized unit cost construction estimates developed by using the Construction Specification Institute (CSI) format, titles, and numbering system. Lump sum cost estimates are not acceptable.

I. New Shell Condition: The following items shall be provided by the Lessor and shall not be construed as tenant improvements:

a. Exterior Window Coverings

b. Capital improvements to the building's core and shell

c. Building's perimeter walls and core walls with drywall finish ready for paint

d. Fire sprinkler main loop including drops and heads

e. Electrical service at a minimum of 5 watts per square foot f. HVAC equipment and ducting to the premises

g. Code required toilet room facilities

h. Americans with Disability Act (ADA) and California Building Code (CBC) compliance work to correct all deficiencies to comply with current code

J. Previously Constructed and Occupied Space (Second Generation Condition): In addition to items in Paragraph I above, Lessor shall provide the following at no cost to the State:

a. Code compliant ceiling

b. Code compliant lighting systems

c. Any code required exit door and frame assemblies

K. Usable Area Calculation: For the purpose of determining the net useable square feet, State leased space shall be calculated as follows:

1. Net usable office area includes all areas assigned to the State such as: offices, conference rooms, reception rooms, special use and supply rooms, hallways within the space, laboratories, private toilet rooms/showers, break rooms, auditoriums, cafeterias, and spaces exclusively used by State. Net usable office area does not include stairwells, stacks/shafts, janitor closets, mechanical rooms, electrical rooms, code required toilet rooms, code required common area corridors, and common area lobbies. Net usable office area is measured from the finished surface of the office side of the corridor and other permanent walls, the dominant surface (wall or glazing) of the exterior walls, and from the centerline of demising walls separating other building tenants.

L. Record Documents: Lessor, at Lessor's sole cost and expense, shall provide the State accurate architectural drawings of the "as-is" condition of the space to be leased, including building common areas, site/parking plan, and path of travel. The drawings shall be in an electronic format to be determined by DGS. Any required re-design work caused by discrepancies with the "as-is" drawings shall be the responsibility of the Lessor.

M. Green Building Practices: The Lessor Shall operate and maintain the leased premises in accordance with best practices to achieve energy efficiency, sustainability, improved air quality, reduce water usage and enable maximum recycling efforts throughout the term of the lease.

1. New and renegotiated state building leases shall reduce energy and resource use to the extent possible and economically feasible.

2. New (state) building leases shall, where economically feasible, include sub-meters and provide energy use data into Energy Star's Portfolio Manager.

3. Renegotiated state (building) leases for buildings where the State is a sole tenant shall provide energy use data into Energy Star's Portfolio Manager.

4. New and renegotiated state building leases shall encourage landlords to participate in utility sponsored energy conservation measures, using alternative financing.

5. Lessors are encouraged to implement measures of the California Green Building Standards Code, (CalGreen), related to indoor environmental quality, where economically feasible, for all new or renegotiated leases.

6. The State will identify and pursue opportunities to provide electric vehicle charging stations, and accommodate future charging infrastructure demand, at employee parking facilities in new and existing buildings.

7. All equipment and appliances provided by Lessor shall be Energy Star labeled if Energy Star is applicable to the equipment or appliance.

8. Wherever restroom fixtures are replaced during construction the California Green Building Standards voluntary measures are to be met to achieve a further reduction in water usage for state leased space (Tier 1, 30% reduction minimum).

9. Lessor to implement annual irrigation system audits, including leak detection and perform immediate repairs to minimize any water loss.

N. Submittals: Lessor shall submit shop drawings, product data, and samples to the State for review prior to construction or fabrication.

O. Material Safety Data Sheet (MSDS): Prior to construction and upon request by State, Lessor shall provide MSDS of all products or materials used in the maintenance, repair, or renovation of the premises.

1.4 CONSTRUCTION AND CODE CRITERIA

A. Construction Documents: The Exhibit "A" Plan or the Exhibit "A" Facility Design Program (written narrative) are design development guidelines only. Lessor shall provide all required construction documents and calculations necessary to obtain a building permit from the local Building Department and to construct the improvements as indicated. The use of Exhibit "A" Plan in lieu of construction documents is not acceptable to the State.

1. Prior to submitting construction documents to the local building department for plan check and or permitting, Lessor shall submit said construction documents to DGS for review. Any DGS comments to the construction documents shall be construed as advisory only and shall not relieve the Lessor in any respect from full compliance with Exhibits "A", "B", and "C" or any other exhibits.

2. Lessor's architect, engineers, consultants, and contractors shall have current and valid license/certifications as issued by the State of California.

3. During construction of building's core, shell, and or tenant improvements, Lessor shall maintain at the project site, a complete set of lease Exhibits consisting of Exhibit "A", "B", "C" and any other exhibits for DGS use.

B. State Fire Marshal: Concurrent with submission to the building department for permitting, Lessor shall submit a complete set of construction documents, including fire sprinkler plans and fire alarm plans, to the State Fire Marshal for review and approval and shall arrange for periodic inspections of the work (refer to Exhibit "C" for procedures). No construction should commence without approved plans.

C. Access Compliance: Lessor shall ensure that all new work and existing conditions comply with the requirements of CCR Title 24, California Building Code (CBC), and Americans with Disabilities Act (ADA). State agencies are public entities and shall comply with Title II of the ADA. Exceptions to the code for existing buildings are not permitted. Where CBC requirements conflict or differ with ADA requirements, the most stringent requirement shall take precedence. Access compliance shall apply to exterior areas such as, but not limited to, path of travel to and from public transportation and public right-of-way, parking, passenger drop-off and loading zones, walks and sidewalks, curb ramps, ramps, and all stairs. Access compliance shall also apply to interior areas such as, but not limited to, entrances and exits, lobbies, building common areas, elevators, access lifts, doors and gates, access to and through all rooms and spaces, restrooms, signs and identification, counters, waiting, and seating areas, assistive listening systems, telephones, drinking fountains, alarms, and horizontal/vertical access. See Exhibit "C" for procedures.

D. Codes and Ordinances: All new work and existing conditions shall comply with all current regulations, laws, and ordinances of the governmental authorities having jurisdiction and the applicable editions of the following codes including, but not limited to:

1. Title 8 CCR, Industrial Relations
2. Title 17 CCR, Public Health
3. Title 19 CCR, Public Safety, State Fire Marshal Regulations
4. Title 24 CCR, Part 1 - Building Standard Administrative Code
5. Title 24 CCR, Part 2 - California Building Code (CBC), Vols. 1 & 2
6. Title 24 CCR, Part 3 - California Electrical Code (CEC)
7. Title 24 CCR, Part 4 - California Mechanical Code (CMC)
8. Title 24 CCR, Part 5 - California Plumbing Code (CPC)

9. Title 24 CCR, Part 6 - California Energy Code
10. Title 24 CCR, Part 9 - California Fire Code (CFC)
11. Title 24 CCR, Part 11 - California Green Building Standards Code
12. Title 24 CCR, Part 12 - California Reference Standards Code

If fire-life safety, health hazards, and/or non-compliant code conditions are discovered either before or after occupancy, then Lessor, at Lessor's sole cost and expense, shall correct the condition.

E. Building Permit: Lessor shall obtain a building permit for the required construction from the local building department if required. In the event there is no local building department, Lessor, at Lessor's sole cost and expense, shall provide a third party, independent Inspector of Record (IOR). The IOR shall perform periodic inspections of the work for conformance with all regulations, laws, and ordinances.

F. Safety Evacuation Plans: Lessor shall provide safety evacuation plans of the leased premises. The safety evacuation plans shall clearly delineate evacuation routes, exits, fire extinguishers, and fire alarm pull station locations. The plans shall be a minimum of 8" x 10" in size, framed and under glass or clear plastic. The plans shall be installed in all assembly occupancies including conference rooms, break rooms, reception areas, and where requested by SFM.

G. Fire Extinguishers: Lessor shall provide and install fire extinguishers. Fire extinguishers shall be housed in semi-recessed cabinets and shall be located as required by CA Title 19 CCR, Public Safety. Above each fire extinguisher, at approximately 90" A.F.F., Lessor shall furnish and install a red triangular shaped 3-D sign with printed text "Fire Extinguisher" with an arrow pointing down. Lessor shall provide annual servicing of the fire extinguishers throughout the term of the lease.

H. Seismic Performance: The State will consider only those facilities that can demonstrate the ability to meet a seismic performance level as set forth in:

1. 1998 Edition or subsequent editions of the California Building Code or,

2. 1976 Edition or subsequent editions of the Uniform Building Code and the building does not have any one of the enumerated characteristics or conditions listed below:

a) Unreinforced masonry elements, whether load-bearing or not, not including brick veneer

b) Precast, pre-stressed or post-tensioned structural or architectural elements, except piles.

c) Flexible diaphragm (e.g., plywood) shear wall (masonry or concrete) structural system constructed pursuant to editions of the Uniform Building Code prior to the 1997 edition.

d) Apparent additions, alterations, or repairs to the structural system made without a building permit.

e) Constructed on a site with a slope with one or more stories partially below grade (taken as 50% or less) for a portion of their exterior.

f) Soft or weak story, including wood frame structures with cripple walls or if construction is over first-story parking.

g) Seismic retrofit of the building, whether voluntary or mandated, whether partial or complete.

h) Repairs following an earthquake.

i) Welded steel moment frames (WSMF) that constitute the primary seismic force-resisting system for the building, and the structure was designed to code requirements preceding those of the 1997 edition of the Uniform Building Code, and the building site has experienced an earthquake of sufficient magnitude and site peak ground motions that inspection is required when any of the conditions of Section 3.2 of FEMA 352 indicate an investigation of beam-column connections is warranted.

j) Visible signs of distress or deterioration of structural or non-structural systems, e.g., excessively cracked and/or spalling concrete walls or foundations, wood dry rot, etc.

3. Certification of the above requirements must be provided by an independent licensed structural engineer at the Lessor's expense.

4. Lessor shall provide and install all hardware required to brace and anchor all storage cabinets, lockers, bookcases, shelving units and similar furnishings 5'-0" or more in height whether provided by State or Lessor, in accordance with seismic design requirements of the Code.

1.5 SUBSTANTIAL COMPLETION AND PROJECT COMPLETION

A. Premises shall fully conform to all lease Exhibits and shall be constructed in accordance with industry standards and best practices. Lessor guarantees that all mechanical, electrical, plumbing systems and other features (including architectural finishes, paint, hardware, doors, floor covering, etc.) are of quality capable of giving satisfactory service in accordance with these specifications for the term of this lease.

B. Substantial completion is achieved when the, building core, shell, and tenant improvements as defined in the lease exhibits, including the installation of any modular systems furniture (MSF) are sufficiently completed to allow the State to lawfully and physically occupy the premises for its intended purpose. Any work required to complete any outstanding punch list items shall not interfere with, or interrupt the State's daily operations. DGS planner will make the final determination of when substantial completion is achieved.

C. Lessor shall operate the HVAC system to provide continuous air for a minimum of 24 hours per day for 7 days prior to occupancy.

D. State employees, agents, and invitees shall have ready access to the building and premises through the main building entry and lobby. Elevators, stairs and restrooms shall be operational.

E. The premises shall be free of all construction debris and thoroughly cleaned. Lessor shall touch up and restore damaged or defaced painted surfaces throughout the premises subsequent to installation of State's furnishing and equipment. All painting shall be coordinated with DGS planner.

F. Upon project completion, Lessor shall obtain final approvals from the authorities having jurisdiction and all punch-list items shall have been completed, and re-inspected by the State. Lessor shall submit to the State the following completed documents, if applicable, with all appropriate signatures:

1. Building Permit

2. Building Inspection Card

3. Certificate of Occupancy

4. Fire Department approvals

5. State Fire Marshal Final Construction Approval - Exhibit "C" Form D

6. CBC/ADA Access Compliance Fee Calculation - Exhibit "C" Form E

7. CBC/ADA Access Compliance Verified Report - Exhibit "C" Form G

8. LEED Certification - when applicable

9. Air Balance Report

10. Operation manuals and training for equipment such as, but not limited to intrusion alarm system, video conferencing equipment, and appliances.

1.6 HAZARDOUS MATERIALS

A. Lessor warrants and guarantees that the premises leased to the State will be operated and maintained free of hazard from asbestos, lead, mold, and PCB's.

1. The areas include:

a. Premises leased to the State and air plenums in the same HVAC zone.

b. Common public areas which state employees or its invitees would normally and/or reasonably use.

c. Building maintenance areas, utility spaces, and elevator shafts within or servicing areas described in items a. and b. above.

2. Lessor shall be responsible for all costs associated with the abatement of hazardous materials including but not limited to the following, clean up of contaminated State Leased space, State-owned equipment, furnishings and materials and all required monitoring reports. Copies of all air monitoring reports shall be furnished to the State.

3. The State Leased space shall be maintained at or below the permissible exposure levels for all substances regulated under Title 8 California Code of Regulations Section 5155. If it is determined by the State that the tenant must be relocated to prevent exposure above

the permissible level, the Lessor shall provide comparable accommodating space at no cost to the State. In addition, the Lessor shall pay for all costs associated with this move including but not limited to, administrative, furniture, communications contracts and equipment costs.

4. In the event that after written notice is provided by the State, the Lessor fails, refuses, or neglects to diligently pursue abatement of any hazardous material, the State may effect such abatement. The State may deduct all reasonable costs of such abatement of Hazardous materials from the rent.

5. The Lessor shall indemnify, defend, and hold the State of California, its officers, and employees harmless from and against any and all losses, damages, judgments, expenses (including court costs and reasonable attorney fees), or claims whatsoever, arising out of, or in any way connected with or related to, directly or indirectly, the presence of hazardous materials within the State-leased space or the building in which the leased premises are located.

B. Asbestos

1. For buildings constructed prior to January 1, 1979, the Lessor shall provide the State with a current written asbestos survey of the areas listed in Section 1.6.A.1. An independent California Division of Occupational Safety and Health (DOSH) Certified Asbestos Consultant shall complete the survey.

2. For buildings constructed after December 31,1978, and prior to any tenant improvements or major repairs, the Lessor and his construction contractor are responsible for sampling any suspected asbestos containing material (ACM) to be disturbed during the project. Where ACM is suspected to be present, the Lessor shall provide the State with a written asbestos survey covering all materials to be disturbed during the project. An independent California Division of Occupational Safety and Health (DOSH) Certified Asbestos Consultant shall complete the survey.

3. Where asbestos containing material (ACM) or suspect ACM have been identified by survey, the Lessor shall provide the State with a copy of a written Operations and Maintenance (O&M) plan. This O&M Plan must be effective in minimizing damage or disturbance of any ACM or suspect ACM and provide for quick repairs of the same.

4. If damaged ACM or suspect ACM is found, or the physical condition of ACM indicates possible fiber release, a response action in accordance with the approved O&M Plan shall be conducted. The approved O&M plan shall include provisions for air sampling by an independent Certified Industrial Hygienist during and at the completion of all response actions, analysis of air samples shall be conducted utilizing Transmission Electron Microscopy (TEM). The standard for re-occupancy of an affected area shall be concentrations at or below 70 asbestos structures per millimeter squared (structures/mm2).

5. Lessor shall perform asbestos notification as required by Chapter 10.4 of the Health and Safety Code. Any abatement work shall be performed by a licensed contractor with

asbestos certification (ASB). The State reserves the right to establish consultant oversight of any asbestos related work program at its expense.

6. In addition to any other remedies it may have, in the event the Lessor fails to diligently pursue abatement of hazard from ACM, as required under the provisions of this lease, the State may, by notice in writing, terminate this lease. Lessor shall be liable to the State for all expenses, losses, and damages reasonably incurred by the State as a result of such termination, including but not limited to, additional rental necessary to pay for an available, similar replacement facility. This rental shall extend over the period of what would have been the remaining balance of the lease term plus any option periods, costs or any necessary alterations to the replacement facility, administrative costs, and costs of moving furniture, data processing, and telephone equipment.

C. Lead Material:

1. Any material suspected of containing lead within the areas listed in Paragraph "A" shall be tested and identified through sampling by an independent California Department of Public Health Certified (CDPH) Lead-Related Construction Inspector/Assessor.

2. In the event lead removal is required, Lessor shall provide an independent CDPH Certified Lead-Related Construction Inspector/Assessor to inspect the quality of work for compliance with applicable regulations, perform air monitoring, final clearance visual inspection, wet wipe sampling/lab analysis, and ensure proper handling and/or disposal of hazardous waste.

D. Mold:

1. The Lessor shall operate and maintain the leased premises to be free of hazard from mold.

2. If mold is detected within the State Leased Space, an immediate response action in accordance with industry standard practices shall be undertaken by the Lessor. The Lessor shall contract for the services of an independent California Division of Occupational Safety and Health (DOSH) Certified Industrial Hygienist to determine the appropriate response action.

3. Lessor shall be responsible for all costs associated with any hazard response action.

E. Underground storage tanks (UST):

Lessor shall comply with the requirements of the California Health and Safety Code, Section 25280-25299.8 (Underground Storage Tanks).

END OF DIVISION 1

For items that are shown with strikethrough (~~strikethrough~~) please refer to Division 3, Special Provisions for amendments to the requirements.

DIVISION 2 - DESIGN REQUIREMENTS

2.1 FLOOR CONSTRUCTION AND FINISHES

A. Concrete Floor:

1. Concrete floor construction is the standard for comparison. Floors of other material may be acceptable provided its use does not produce or transmit sound or vibration to a greater degree than a 4" reinforced concrete slab.

   a. Lessor shall provide certification that the concrete slab is level and does not exceed a variance of ¼ inch in 10 feet from a true flat plane.

   b. Where slab is out of compliance, leveling shall be achieved using a high-strength concrete topping compound i.e.: Mapei, Ardex, Inc., K-500, Hacker Ind., Firm Fill 4010, Maxxon, Level-Right, or approved equal.

2. Concrete floors in janitor closets, mechanical, and/or electrical utility rooms shall be cleaned and treated with epoxy coating. Office areas throughout shall have carpet or other floor covering with 4" high cove base, unless noted otherwise. Floors in toilet rooms shall be of nonabsorbent material impervious to moisture such as ceramic tile, or approved equal, with minimum 4" high cove base. Floor covering shall extend under counters and cabinets. Colors and patterns shall be as selected or approved by State.

3. Prior to the installation of any finish floor material, Lessor shall perform a quantitative moisture test to the concrete slab. The test shall be administered in accordance with the flooring material manufacturer's written guidelines or recommendations. In the event the moisture content exceeds the flooring material manufacturer's recommendation, the Lessor, at Lessor's sole cost and expense, shall provide and install a waterproofing sealer as recommended by the flooring material manufacturer.

4. Exposed concrete floors are not acceptable in toilet rooms, locker rooms, or shower rooms.

B. Carpet Flooring - General:

1. Lessor shall provide and install carpet and cove base where shown in Exhibit "A". All carpet shall comply with ANSI/NSF 140-2007 Platinum level.

2. Where requested by DGS, Lessor shall submit carpet samples to DGS for selection. The samples shall be from a minimum of three different manufacturers and consist of a variety of patterns, textures, colors, and styles.

3. Carpet shall have random graphic pattern loop non-generic branded, 6 or 6.6 nylon face yarn with inherent static control.

4. Broadloom loop pile carpet shall have inherent static control capability to assure a maximum 3.5 KV rating at 20% relative humidity and 70F degrees as measured by AATCC-Test Method 134.

5. Carpet with anti-microbial properties shall be used for healthcare, senior care or childcare, and 'clean' areas.

6. Carpet shall be installed according to manufacturer's guidelines. The carpet shall be securely attached, have a firm cushion, pad or backing, be of level loop, textured loop, level-cut pile, or level-cut/uncut pile texture. The maximum pile height shall be ½ inch.

7. The carpet backing shall have a minimum 10-year guarantee against tuft pull and zippering, and surface wear shall not be more than 10% within 10 years.

8. Carpet adhesives shall be non-toxic, low odor, solvent free, and shall not produce toxic vapors or contain carcinogenic materials.

9. Carpet shall meet Federal, State, and Local flammability standards.

10. Carpet shall be installed in accordance with the Carpet and Rug Institute CRI Carpet Installation Standard. The installation shall be guaranteed against bubbling, wrinkling, stretching/shrinking, opening seams, or other evidence of poor materials and workmanship for a period of two years following installation. This guarantee shall cover normal wear and tear and note deficiencies occurring as a result of damage, negligence and/or alterations. The materials shall be guaranteed against wear, delamination, tuft bind and be lightfast for a period of 10 years. The material shall remain colorfast as a result of atmospheric contaminants for a period of 5 years after installation.

11. Lessor shall maintain the carpet according to manufacturer's guidelines.

C. Broadloom Carpet Requirements:

1. Density: 6000 minimum, heavy commercial use.

2. Density: 36x finished pile weight divided by pile height.

3. Tuft bind for broadloom shall be minimum 6 lbs., ASTM D 1335 - 98, Standard Test Method for Tuft Bind (edge ravel) of Pile Yarn Floor Coverings, tested wet or dry. Warranty edge ravel for 10 years.

4. Face yarn weight: Minimum 22 oz./sq. yd.

5. Minimum of 10 lbs backing delamination test, ASTM D3936 - 05 Standard Test Method for Resistance to Delamination of the Secondary Backing of Pile Yarn Floor Covering.

6. Minimum rating of 7 anti-stain tests, AATCC Test Method 175-2008 Stain Resistance Pile Floor Coverings.

7. Lessor shall provide 2% of product overage including accent carpet up to a maximum of 100 sq. yards from the same dye-lot for future repairs.

D. Carpet Tile Requirements:

1. Density: 5000 minimum, heavy commercial use.

2. Tuft bind strength shall be minimum 5 lbs., ASTM D 1335-98: Standard Test Method for Tuft Bind (edge ravel) of Pile Yarn Floor Coverings, tested wet or dry. Warranty edge ravel for 10 years.

a. Face yarn weight: Minimum 16 oz./sq. yd

b. Minimum of 10 lbs. backing delamination test, per ASTM D3936-05 Standard Test Method for Resistance to Delamination of the Secondary Backing of Pile Yarn Floor Covering.

c. Minimum rating of 7 anti-stain tests, per AATCC Test Method 175-2008 Stain Resistance Pile Floor Coverings.

d. Lessor shall provide 2% of product overage including accent carpet up to a maximum of 100 sq. yards from the same dye-lot for future repairs.

E. Ceramic Tile Flooring Requirements:

Ceramic Tile Flooring shall have a coefficient of friction of at least 0.6 per ASTM C1028 (0.8% on sloped surfaces steeper than 6%). Unless otherwise noted by DGS, provide slip resistant floor tile with matching ceramic base, include all inner and outer corner and trim pieces. All adhesives, mastics, and grouts shall be non- toxic and low in VOC emissions and shall be as recommended by the ceramic tile manufacturer. All grout shall be sealed and maintained according to manufacturer's guidelines.

F. Resilient Flooring Requirements:

1. Resilient Flooring shall meet ASTM F 1066, FS SS-T-312B, Type IV, Composition 1, Class 2, 12" x 12" having uniform thickness of 1/8" with square true edges of manufacturer's standard color and pattern as selected. Product shall comply with all regulations controlling the use of volatile organic compounds (VOC's). Provide one carton (40 pieces) of additional matching floor tile.

2. Resilient Flooring shall have a coefficient of friction of at least 0.6 per ASTM D2047. It shall be installed in strict accordance with manufacturer's approved installation instructions using the appropriate recommended 100% solvent free adhesive.

G. Rubber Base Requirements:

1. Lessor shall provide and install cove wall base at all carpet and resilient floor finish areas. Wall base shall be extruded rubber cove, 1/8" thick x 4" high complying with ASTM F-1861. The color shall be selected by DGS.

2.2 EXTERIOR WALLS

A. Exterior walls, including door and window assemblies, shall be weatherproof. All cracks that allow outside air to penetrate the building's envelope shall be sealed.

B. Exterior walls shall be insulated to comply with CCR Title 24.

2.3 INTERIOR WALLS AND PARTITIONS

A. Walls and partitions shall be ceiling height unless otherwise noted in Exhibit "A" or Division 3 'Special Provisions'. Subject to code limitations, those indicated as new partitions may be wood or metal stud with plaster or gypsum wallboard or other construction of equal sound transmission coefficient (STC). Provide a minimum STC 32. Demising walls separating State premises and other building tenants shall extend to the under-side of structure above and shall be constructed to achieve a sound transmission coefficient of 50.

B. Walls of equipment rooms, toilet rooms, conference rooms, hearing rooms, quiet rooms, training rooms, interview rooms, employee break rooms, and where indicated in Exhibit "A", shall be insulated to prevent transmission of sound or vibration. Wall construction shall achieve a minimum rating of 50 STC as set forth in ASTM E90.Furnish and install insulation batts above the finished ceiling on each side of the wall for the entire length of the wall.

C. Moisture resistant wainscot of ceramic wall tile or other DGS approved material shall be installed to all plumbing fixture walls and adjacent walls in the toilet rooms. Wall tile shall be a minimum of 4" x 4" glazed ceramic tile. Wainscot shall extend a minimum of 4'-0" A.F.F. unless noted otherwise.

D. Glazed openings in office partitions shall be set in metal frame assemblies and comply with Consumer Product Safety Commission impact-safety standards.

2.4 ROOF AND INSULATION

A. Roof shall be weather tight and provided with suitable drainage system that will effectively dispose of roof water without interfering with use of premises.

B. Roof shall be insulated such that the heat transfer values from roof to occupied areas comply with CCR Title 24.

2.5 ACOUSTICAL CEILINGS

A. Ceilings of office areas including reception, private offices, open office areas, corridors, and office storage areas shall have suspended "T" bar systems with acoustical lay-in tiles or other approved material with equivalent acoustical qualities. Ceiling heights shall be a minimum of 9'-0" and a maximum of 12'-0" unless otherwise approved by DGS.

B. Where existing "T" bar system with acoustical lay-in tiles are reused, Lessor shall modify ceiling system as necessary to comply with all seismic safety regulations. "T" bar system and ceiling tiles shall be free of all dirt, dust, stains, and damage. Where replacement tiles are installed, all tiles shall be arranged as necessary to provide a uniform appearance in each enclosed space.

2.6 DOORS

A. All interior doors shall be solid-core flush wood doors with wood veneer suitable for stain or paint finish. Doors shall be a minimum dimension of 3'-0" x 6'-8" x 1-3/4".

B. Doors shall be manufactured per Window & Door Manufacturers Association (WDMA) and Architectural Woodwork Standards (AWS).

C. The formaldehyde emission level of all new doors shall not exceed 20 ppm.

D. Glass vision panels in interior doors and sidelights shall be minimum 3/8" clear tempered glass set in metal frame assemblies. Fire protective glass assemblies shall be provided where required by code.

E. Fire rated door and frame assemblies shall be installed where noted in Exhibit "A" or as required by code. Doors and frames shall bear Underwriters Laboratory (UL) label for required fire resistive rating.

F. Doors separating conditioned and non-conditioned space shall have weather stripping to effectively limit air infiltration. Adhesive foam-type or felt weather stripping is not acceptable.

G. Where indicated on plans, or required by code, a roll-down steel fire shutter bearing a UL 3/4 hour, "C" label shall be provided. Emergency operation shall be by smoke detectors with adjustable time delay, initially set at 45 seconds.

H. Where existing door and frame assemblies are reused, Lessor shall patch, repair, adjust, and refinish the assemblies to provide a new looking appearance.

2.7 DOOR HARDWARE

A. Lessor shall provide and install door hardware and related items including keying of locksets necessary for a complete installation and operation of doors.

B. All hardware shall be CBC/ADA access compliant, heavy-duty commercial quality equal to Schlage, Von Duprin, or Falcon.

C. Door hardware shall include, but is not limited to, cylindrical lock and latch sets, door butt hinges, doorstops, push plates, door pulls, closers, and exit devices.

D. Hinges for exterior outswing doors shall have non-removable pins.

E. Doorstops shall be provided and installed wherever an opened door or any item of hardware thereon would strike a wall, column, equipment, or other parts of building construction. Doorstops shall be floor mounted.

F. Lessor shall key all keyed locksets as directed by tenant agency and shall provide a minimum of 3 keys for each lock.

G. Metal thresholds and weatherstrips shall be provided to all exterior doors. Thresholds shall have non-slip abrasive finish.

H. Adjustable door closers shall be provided on entrance doors, toilet room doors, vestibule doors, doors with access-control hardware, and where shown on plans, and required by code.

I. 10" high metal kick plates shall be provided and installed on the push side of all doors equipped with door closers.

2.8 MILLWORK

A. Lessor shall provide and install new millwork as shown and where indicated in Exhibit "A".

B. All millwork shall be manufactured and installed in accordance with the Architectural Woodwork Standards (AWS) latest edition, for custom grades. Prior to fabrication, Lessor shall submit to the DGS, shop drawings of all new millwork.

C. Cabinets shall be of sizes and type as indicated in the Exhibit "A". Base cabinets shall have one row of drawers and one adjustable shelf below with concealed hinged doors, unless noted otherwise. Lessor shall provide a 4" toe space at base cabinets. Upper cabinets shall have two rows of adjustable shelves and hinged doors, unless noted otherwise.

D. Counter tops shall be finished with plastic laminate or solid surface material. Counter tops shall be self-edged unless otherwise noted. Counter tops with sinks shall be fully formed and have a no-drip edge, and coved splash joint. All counter tops shall have a back and side splash unless otherwise noted. Sinks shall have a sanitary metal rim or be a self-rim stainless steel sink. Other materials may be submitted to the State for approval.

E. Shelving units shall be a minimum of 3/4" thick white melamine, per AWS. Cover exposed edges with plastic laminate or hardwood edgebound.

F. Face of millwork shall be high-pressure decorative plastic laminate. NEMA LD-3 grades as required by AWS.

G. Lessor shall provide cabinet hardware such as, but not limited to concealed hinges, pulls, catches, shelf rests, standards and brackets, and drawer slides. All hardware shall comply with ANSI A156.9-01 and Builders Hardware Manufacturers Association.

H. All millwork shall be installed in accordance with all seismic safety requirements of the Code.

I. Base Cabinets containing sinks shall be CBC/ADA/access compliant. Unless otherwise noted, Lessor shall provide cabinet doors with attached toe kicks with rubber base to conceal clear space below.

2.9 GYPSUM BOARD FINISH/PAINTING/WALLCOVERING/SEALANTS

A. Gypsum board finish shall be a smooth, blemish-free, monolithic surface and free of tool marks and ridges. *Heavy textured wall surfaces are not acceptable*.

B. Water-based paints shall not be formulated with aromatic hydrocarbons, formaldehyde, halogenated solvents, mercury or mercury compounds, or tinted with pigments of lead, cadmium, chromium VI, antimony and their oxides. All architectural paints and coatings shall comply with VOC limits of the California Green Standards Code unless more stringent local limits apply.

C. All wall texture and paint colors shall be selected and or approved by DGS.

D. New Surfaces:

1. New partitions without factory finish shall be painted with one coat of primer/sealer and two finish coats of premium quality latex, eggshell paint. *Flat paint is not acceptable*.

2. Breakrooms, toiletrooms, and janitorial closets shall be painted with semi-gloss enamel paint.

3. Paint-grade doors and trim shall be latex semi-gloss enamel paint.

4. Stained or natural finish wood shall be finished with sealer and two coats lacquer. They shall be finished using non-toxic, water-based urethanes or similar environmentally sensitive products.

E. Existing Surfaces:

1. Interior walls and plaster or gypsum board ceilings shall be finished in latex eggshell paint.

2. Heavy textured walls shall be sanded smooth and prepared for a new paint finish.

3. Existing wall coverings shall be removed unless otherwise noted, wall surface shall be prepared, and receive a new paint finish.

4. Doors and frames shall be refinished to provide a new looking appearance.

5. HVAC registers and grilles shall be in a newly painted condition.

6. Stained or natural finished wood shall be refinished with sealer and lacquer.

7. Metal toilet stall partitions shall be repainted using electrostatic paint process.

F. Where alteration work occurs, new painted surfaces shall extend to the natural break.

G. Where wall covering is specified, the product shall be 'breathable' to prevent mold and bacteria development. All adhesives used shall be non-toxic, low in VOC emissions, and shall be as recommended by the wall-covering manufacturer.

H. Interior sealants shall not contain mercury, butyl rubber, neoprene, SBR (styrene butadiene rubber), nitride, aromatic solvents (organic solvent with a benzene ring in its molecular structure), fibrous talc or asbestos, formaldehyde, halogenated solvents, lead, cadmium, hexavalent chromium, or their components.

2.10 BUILDING SPECIALTIES

A. Toilet Room Partitions and Accessories: In addition to any Code required toilet room accessories, Lessor shall furnish, install, maintain, and replenish where appropriate, the following accessories:

1. Coin-operated sanitary napkin dispenser (one per women's toilet room)

2. Folding utility shelf and coat hook (one per toilet stall)

3. Mirror with metal frame assembly (one per lavatory, two or more lavatories may have one continuous mirror)

4. Paper towel dispensers (one per every two lavatories)

5. Sanitary napkin waste receptacle (one per women's toilet stall)

6. Soap dispensers (one per lavatory)

7. Toilet paper dispenser, continuous toilet-paper flow, capable of holding two rolls (one per toilet stall)

8. Toilet seat-cover dispenser (one per toilet stall)

9. Trash receptacles (one per toilet room)

B. All accessories shall be constructed of stainless steel and exposed surfaces shall have satin finish.

C. Toilet Room Partitions - New toilet stall partitions shall match building standard.

1. Lessor shall furnish and install privacy screen at all urinal locations – screens shall match toilet partitions.

D. Paper Towel and Soap Dispensers:

1. Where sinks and lavatories are provided for State's exclusive use, Lessor shall provide, install, and replenish paper towel and soap dispensers. Dispensers shall be constructed of stainless steel and exposed surfaces shall have satin finish.

E. Window Treatment:

1. Lessor shall provide and install horizontal or vertical window blinds or other DGS approved device for privacy to all windows and interior glazed openings, including interior door side-lites.

2. At sun-exposed areas, Lessor shall provide and install solar screens, reflective glass coatings, reflective glass panes, or other State and Lessor approved device for sun control.

F. Knox Box:

1. Where State occupies an entire building, Lessor shall furnish and install a Knox Box near building entrance as directed by Fire Department.

G. Signage:

1. Lessor shall provide and install room identification signage for all rooms.

2. Lessor shall verify signage content, room number designation, and submit mock-ups of signage types to DGS for review and approval prior to fabrication.

3. All signage located within the State's premises shall be tactile identification signage with raised letters and raised numbers between 5/8″ and 2″ high with a width-to-height ratio of between 3:5 and 1:1 and a stroke width to height ratio between 1:5 and 1:10. Letters shall be raised 1/32″ above the background, Sans Serif uppercase characters. Signage shall be installed 60″ A.F.F. to centerline of sign. Signage for all private offices shall have a clear 3″ - 4″ high x 6″ wide x 1/16″ thick non-glare lens slide-out.

a. Characters and background of signage shall be eggshell, matt, or other non-glare finish. Characters shall contrast with their background.

4. Grade 2 California Braille dots shall be raised 1/40" above the background. Braille shall be 1/10th inch on center within each cell and 2/10th inch between cells. Braille dots shall be domed or rounded.

5. In addition to room identification signage, Lessor shall provide and install tactile exit signs and tactile exit route signs.

6. Where signs are mounted on glass, such as sidelights, furnish and install a blank of equal material, width, height, and background color to the opposite side of said glass.

7. State of California Identification:

a. On or near the suite entrance door, install the words "STATE OF CALIFORNIA", the name of State tenant/Department/Agency and suite numbers and shall include Braille and tactile text and numbering. Signage shall be building standard and subject to approval by the State. Painted or pressure sensitive vinyl letters are not acceptable. Provide agency identification in the building directory, where available.

8. Lessor shall provide "Maximum Occupancy" signage(s) on the wall above or near the entry door for all conference, meeting, lunch, auditorium, and assembly rooms.

9. Exterior signs: (applicable only if building is totally occupied by the State) Lessor shall provide and install exterior signs. Letters shall be of cast aluminum alloy, bronze, black anodized finish, dimensional plastic. Submit samples to DGS for approval. The words "STATE OF CALIFORNIA" and the name of the occupying department, and street address shall be in scale with the building elevation.

a. Lessor shall be solely responsible for any additional permits and fees.

H. Assistive Listening Devices:

1. Lessor shall provide an assistive listening device system for all meeting, conference, quiet, assembly, and gathering rooms. The system shall comply with all accessibility requirements.

2. Occupant Load less than 50:

a. One portable system per floor can be shared between rooms with occupant loads less than 50. The system shall be designed to accommodate the largest room size that is being shared. The portable, wireless FM based system shall include high output acoustic headset(s) such as the Centrum Motiva PFM 360 (or current model) with disposable ear plugs, neck-loop(s), conference microphones and a lockable charger/accessory carry case large enough to hold all equipment. The system shall be hearing aid compatible. Lessor shall provide signage at reception area indicating that the device is available.

3. Occupant Load of 50 or more:

a. Rooms with more than 50 person occupant load and fixed seating must have a fixed assistive listing device system for 4% of the total number of seats in these rooms, but not less than two. Lessor shall provide signage inside each room and in the common hallway and or corridor indicating that the device is available.

I. Modular Systems Furniture (MSF):

1. The State may elect to furnish and install MSF in lieu of traditional office furniture. MSF may be comprised of any combination of freestanding partition panels, panel supported work surfaces, files, components, and access raceways.

2. Where State elects to install MSF as described above, Lessor, at Lessor's sole cost and expense, shall provide the following:

a. Obtain any required permits from the local jurisdiction.

b. Electrical engineering and installation of all wiring systems and components as necessary or required from the building's electrical system to the MSF for a complete and fully operational system.

c. Provide a minimum of four 20A circuits to each base feed and/or power pole feed. Each 20A circuit shall serve a maximum of four workstations. Coordinate electrical junction box locations with State furnished MSF plans. See Division 3 Special Provisions for MSF wiring diagram.

d. Installation of voice and data communication cabling from the data communication closet to the final point of termination at the MSF panel.

e. Cut and assemble the supplied power pole to the appropriate length, insert pole into top trim of panel, align the pole true and plumb, seismically brace pole, cutting the correct size hole in the ceiling tile, routing the electrical conduit through the pole, and installing the ceiling escutcheon plate to complete the pole installation.

f. Coordinate the installation of new wall mounted equipment to prevent interference with the MSF such as electrical panels, lighting control switching, thermostats, and fire extinguisher cabinets.

g. Relocate any existing wall-mounted equipment as required to accommodate MSF.

h. State or its representative shall provide MSF layout drawing(s) to Lessor for use in the preparation of construction documents.

i. State shall complete all procurement procedures for purchase of MSF.

j. In the event that the Lessor fails to complete the required construction, improvements, and/or alterations prior to the scheduled MSF delivery date, Lessor, at Lessor's sole cost and expense shall be responsible for all additional shipping, handling, and storage fees, including any "overtime" labor costs.

k. Where the State utilizes MSF, and the existing floor coverings are to be replaced as defined in the lease exhibits, Lessor, at Lessor sole cost and expense shall lift the existing MSF and disconnect as necessary, all power, voice, and data cabling. The MSF shall be lifted using a MSF lift system as recommended by the MSF manufacturer. Upon completion of the installation of floor coverings, Lessor shall reconnect all power, voice, and data cabling and lower the MSF into place. Lessor shall realign and adjust the MSF to its original location and condition. Prior to lifting or moving the MSF, Lessor shall perform an inspection with State representatives and contractor to observe and document the condition of the MSF. In the event the MSF is damaged during the performance of any tenant improvement work, Lessor, at Lessor's sole cost and expense shall repair and/or replace the MSF with approved equal product. MSF manufacturer's authorized installers shall perform all repair work.

J. Flagpoles:

1. Where State is the sole or major tenant of the building, (occupying more than 50% of the available space), the United States flag and California State flag shall be prominently displayed upon or in front of the building or grounds in conformance with all flag displaying protocols and etiquettes.

a. Lessor shall furnish and install the flagpole and flags.

b. Freestanding flagpole shall extend 30' above grade.

c. Flagpoles mounted to building shall extend 14' above building parapet.

d. Flagpoles shall be equipped with lockable halyard box.

e. Flagpole and halyard shall be CBC/ADA access compliant.

f. Flags shall be in scale with building and flagpole.

g. Lessor shall provide automatic lighting for nighttime illumination.

2.11 PLUMBING

A. Lessor shall furnish and install plumbing fixtures in quantity and type as shown in Exhibit "A" and as required by Code. Where State occupies multiple floors, Lessor shall provide accessible toilet rooms on each floor. Lessor shall provide one or more drinking fountains within close proximity to office quarters or as indicated on plan. Drinking fountains shall be CBC/ADA access compliant.

B. Lessor shall provide hot and cold water at each lavatory and sink. Domestic water heaters shall be located not more than 25 feet from furthest point of use unless a hot water recirculation or other temperature maintenance system is provided. Water heaters shall initially delivery water at 110° F.

C. Where new toilet rooms, locker rooms with showers, shower rooms are provided and where shown on plans, Lessor shall provide floor drains.

D. Domestic water supply systems shall be constructed with copper piping and tubing. Soldered connections on water supply lines shall use ASTM B32, Tin Antimony solder. Lead solder is not permitted.

2.12 HEATING, VENTILATING, AND AIR CONDITIONING

A. Lessor shall provide a climate control system consisting of a fully automatic heating, ventilating, and air conditioning system capable of providing conditioned air continuously during occupied hours to the premises.

The HVAC system shall be designed and capable of maintaining the following temperatures in all occupied areas:

Design Criteria	Operating Criteria
Winter: 76° F	Winter: 68° F
Summer: 72° F	Summer: 78° F

B. Lessor shall provide and install thermostats with automatic change over from heating to cooling. Thermostats shall have dead-band with adjustable range where no heating or cooling is activated. The temperature range of the thermostats shall be minimum 55°F to 85°F. Thermostats shall be cleaned, calibrated, and initially adjusted to 68°F maximum for heating and 78°F minimum for cooling. Thermostats shall be located within each zone. In multi-tenant buildings, thermostats shall not be shared with other building tenants.

C. Lessor shall furnish and install lockable, tamperproof covers to all thermostats within the leased premises.

D. Lessor shall furnish and install a dedicated air conditioning system with separate thermostat for the computer room, telecommunication room, server room, and other similar spaces. The system shall be capable of providing conditioned air 24 hours per day, 7 days a week. The operating temperature shall comply with the telecommunication equipment manufacturers.

E. Lessor shall submit detailed heating and cooling calculations, Title 24 compliance information, equipment selection data, and "as-built" mechanical drawings to DGS upon request.

F. The cooling load for conference rooms, quiet rooms, hearing rooms, public lobbies, waiting rooms, and employee break rooms shall be based on occupancy of 15 square feet per person. Cooling load for all other areas shall be based on occupancy of 100 square feet per person.

G. Systems shall be zoned for each building exposure and for interior zones where appropriate. Each zone shall be of a size and shape to ensure even air distribution and temperature control throughout the leased premises. Each conference room, quiet room, hearing room, public lobby, waiting room, and employee break room shall be zoned separately.

H. In multi-tenant buildings, HVAC zones shall not be shared with other building tenants.

I. All fan systems supplying 2,000 cfm and above shall be equipped with an economizer system that will use outdoor air up to 100% of fan capacity for cooling of the premises. Operation of the economizer cycle shall be controlled by outside dry bulb air temperature.

J. All lunchrooms and break rooms with microwave oven or other food-heating appliances shall include a general exhaust fan.

K. Toilet rooms shall be provided with a mechanical exhaust system providing a minimum of 15 air changes per hour. Replacement air shall be supplied directly or indirectly from the building system. Individual supply ducts or sound-lined transfer ducts are acceptable. Each exhaust fan shall be interlocked with the associated HVAC unit supply fan serving the room. Exhaust air shall be ducted to the building exterior.

L. Ductwork construction and installation shall conform to the appropriate Sheet Metal and Air Conditioning Contractors National Association, Inc. (SMACNA) low velocity or high velocity duct construction standards. Ductwork shall be concealed or aesthetically compatible with the architectural design of the interior space. Individual supply and return air outlets and ductwork shall be provided in each enclosed area. Undercutting of doors, door grilles, or jumper ducts is not acceptable. Return air shall be conducted through registers connected to ductwork or plenum above ceilings, except as otherwise approved by the State.

M. Air distribution system shall be equipped with air volume controls and shall be capable of draftless operation at an acceptable noise level while handling the design flow of air. The acceptable noise level shall comply with ASHRAE Handbook - HVAC Applications.

N. The complete HVAC system shall be checked, adjusted, and balanced. The air balance report shall be submitted to the State upon project completion.

O. Lessor shall provide vibration isolation supports for all mechanical equipment, piping, and ductwork to prevent transmission of vibration to building structure.

P. Where the heating design of outdoor temperature is below 35° F, Lessor shall provide one winter night setback thermostat for each HVAC system. The thermostat shall cycle the heating system to maintain 55° F.

Q. Lessor shall provide automatic-control time clocks (7-day-programmable) or energy management systems (microprocessors) to allow the shutoff and startup of the HVAC equipment according to the State's occupancy schedule. State shall determine maximum daily hours of operation. Lessor shall provide one-hour by-pass timers for each HVAC system for after-hours operation.

R. Indirect evaporative cooling, desiccant dehumidification, and passive solar design measures are acceptable when approved by DGS.

2.13 ELECTRICAL

A. General Electrical Requirements:

1. Lessor shall provide electrical engineering and installation of all transformers, main switchboard, subpanels, branch circuits, wiring devices, electrical switching, energy management systems, lighting, receptacles, and control equipment for HVAC systems.

2. Service and metering equipment shall be in accordance with utility company requirements. An Electrical Arc-Flash Hazard Analysis and Short-Circuit and Protective Device Coordination Study shall be performed based on the available fault current from the utility system and contribution from the facilities motors. Electrical equipment warning labels shall be provided based upon the available arc hazard energy at each piece of Electrical Equipment. Labels shall comply with the requirements of the California Electrical Code and NFPA 70E.

3. Where electrical service panels are installed to provide service to State premises, Lessor shall provide and install panels with a minimum of 20 percent more circuit capacity than the Lessor's calculated load total.

4. The electrical panels serving the State's premises shall be accessible from the building core or from within the State's quarters. The location of the panels shall be coordinated and approved by the DGS prior to installation.

5. All appliances and all energy-consuming devices shall be Energy Star® certified by the Environmental Protection Agency (EPA).

B. Power Requirements:

1. Duplex convenience outlets shall be 20A, 125V, 3 wire grounding type provided in quantities indicated on the Exhibit "A". Lessor shall provide a minimum of two convenience outlets in each private office.

2. Electrical/data/telephone outlet heights:

a. Existing receptacles may remain at 12" A.F.F. New receptacles shall be installed at 15" A.F.F. or as noted on plans.

3. Lessor shall furnish and install all special use outlets, dedicated circuits, and isolated ground convenience outlets for copy machines, electronic communications equipment, and where noted on plan.

a. Dedicated circuits shall have individual ungrounded circuit conductors from each device to panel board circuit breaker and individual grounded circuit conductors from each device to the neutral bus located in the panel board. Equipment grounding conductors shall be connected to the grounding electrode system through a ground bus located in the panel board.

C. General Lighting Requirements:

1. Lighting Design Guidelines:

a. Lighting shall comply with the design guidelines of the current edition of IESNA Lighting Handbook.

2. Where existing light fixtures are reused, Lessor shall modify fixtures as necessary to comply with all seismic guidelines. Lessor shall thoroughly clean fixture housings, lamps, and fixture lenses. All lenses shall be free of damage and discolor. There shall be no visual discrepancy between existing lamp color temperature and new lamp color temperature in each enclosed space. Lessor shall replace incandescent lamp fixtures with new high efficiency lamp fixtures where applicable.

3. Premises shall have sufficient light fixtures properly spaced and be capable of providing the recommended levels of illumination indicated in the following table.

a. Minimum Lighting Levels:

AREA:	FOOTCANDLES:
Work Surfaces (includes task lighting)	50
Work Area Ambient Lighting	30
Telecommunications rooms and closets	50
Special Purpose Area(s)	75
Repair Garage	50
Hallways, Aisles, Corridors	25

Conference / Meeting Rooms	70
Incandescent Lighting	10 - 30
Drafting Areas	50
High Density Filing Areas	50
Document Processing Area/Room	30
Circulation Space around work areas	30
Building Entries	25
Restrooms	40
Waiting and Lounge Areas	15
Coffee Counters	20
Lunch Rooms/ Break Rooms	30
Warehouse	2

4. Minimum requirements for new or replacement linear fluorescent lighting systems:

   a. Minimum Color Rendering Index (CRI) of 70

   b. Option of common Color Temperature lamps (CCT) (3000° K through 4100° K)

   c. Minimum power factor of 90%

   d. Minimum system efficacy of 90 lumens per watt

   e. High frequency electronic ballast

   f. Maximum Total Harmonic Distortion (THD) of 20%

   g. Minimum lamp life of 20,000 hours

5. Minimum requirements for compact fluorescent lighting systems:

   a. Minimum Color Rendering Index (CRI) of 75%

   b. Option of common Color Temperature lamps (CCT) (2700° K through 4100° K)

   c. Minimum power factor of 90%

   d. Minimum system efficacy of 60 lumens per watt

   e. Electronic ballast

   f. Maximum Total Harmonic Distortion (THD) of 20%

   g. Minimum lamp life of 10,000 hours

6. Minimum requirements for LED lighting systems:

   a. Minimum Color Rendering Index (CRI) of 80

   b. Option of common Color Temperature lamps (CCT) (3000° K through 4100° K)

   c. Minimum power factor of 90%

   d. Minimum system efficacy of 90 lumens per watt

   e. Internal LED Driver

   f. Lamps capable of being dimmed from 100% to 0% of maximum lighting output

g. Minimum lamp life of 50,000 hours

7. Pairs of one-lamp or three-lamp recessed fluorescent luminaries and continuous mounted fluorescents that are (1) on the same switch control, (2) in the same area, (3) within 10 feet of each other in accessible ceiling spaces, and (4) do not use electronic ballasts, shall be tandem wired and shall not use single lamp ballasts.

8. Where required, lighting panel switches including exterior lighting shall have a two schedule, programmable, 7-day with holiday setting, battery- backup time clock. Time clock operation shall have manual override with a two-hour bypass. Override shall be accessible to the tenant.

9. Where exterior illumination is required, lessor shall provide and install exterior solid-state luminaires that are designed for and exclusively use LED lamp technology. Luminaires shall include integrated controls and the required Backlight, Uplight, and Glare (BUG) ratings based on the Lighting Zone the luminaires are in for accent light and outdoor building security lighting. All building entrances shall be illuminated.

D. Communication Equipment Requirements:

1. Lessor shall provide and install all conduits and telephone service cabling from the building's main point of entry (MPOE) to the tenant agency's Telecommunication closet.

2. Lessor shall furnish and install telephone terminal backboard. Backboard shall be 4' x 8' x ¾" thick, fire retardant plywood, and painted to match adjacent surfaces.

3. Lessor shall furnish and install termination blocks, cable management hardware, and terminate and label all cables at both ends.

4. Lessor shall provide and install all components as required by the telephone service provider's requirements.

5. Unless otherwise noted, Lessor shall furnish and install a complete structured cabling system from the tenant agency's telecommunication closet to the final point of termination. Lessor shall provide all components such as, but not limited to, cabling, cable labels, cable trays, cable management hardware, patch panels, cross connects, patch cords, faceplate, jacks, and wall outlets, MSF workstation outlets, as necessary or required for a complete and operational system.

6. Lessor shall provide and install all conduit and outlet boxes with pull-wire.

7. The system shall be tested pursuant to and meet ANSI/TIA/EIA standards.

8. BICSI Certified cabling installers shall perform all work, and shall comply with all ANSI/TIA/EIA cabling standards.

9. The system shall comply with the requirements of the tenant agency's specifications.

10. The State shall not be required to remove any communication equipment and or cabling described herein either during the lease term or upon termination of this lease.

2.14 PARKING AND PAVING

A. Parking areas and access from the public way shall be paved. Each parking stall shall have individual unobstructed access. All stalls shall be marked with 4" wide painted stripes using white traffic grade paint. Traffic areas shall have appropriate painted directional arrows and any other graphics noted on Exhibit "A". Lessor shall furnish and install appropriate signage as required by local jurisdiction.

B. Pavement at existing parking areas shall be free of holes, patches, divots or badly weathered surface conditions. If new material is used, the existing asphalt shall be ground and used for fill in the parking area.

END OF DIVISION 2

DIVISION 3 - SPECIAL PROVISIONS

The following Special Provisions supplement the requirements specified in Divisions 1 and 2. Where Division 3 requirements conflict with Divisions 1 & 2, Division 3 supersedes those requirements.

There are NO SPECIAL PROVISIONS for this Project.

END OF DIVISION 3

DIVISION 4 - TECHNICAL REQUIREMENTS

The following Technical Requirements supplement the requirements specified in Divisions 1 and 2. Where Division 4 requirements conflict with Divisions 1 & 2, Division 4 supersedes those requirements.

There are NO TECHNICAL REQUIREMENTS for this Project.

END OF DIVISION 4

EXHIBIT 'C' – ADMINISTRATIVE REQUIREMENTS

STATE OF CALIFORNIA

PROJECT: PROJECT NO.:

AGENCY: LEASE NO.:

LOCATION: DATE:

TITLE **PAGE**

PROJECT CONTACT: PHONE:
FAX:
EMAIL:

Confirmation Statement

I/we have read this Exhibit 'C' Administrative Requirements and understand it is incorporated into, and is part of, this lease. I/we have acknowledged each and every page by placing my/our initials on this cover sheet.

Initials ____________

1.00 GENERAL

A. The State of California and its governing agencies have mandated that the Department of General Services (DGS), Real Estate Services Division (RESD) adhere to all regulations, policies and state statutes for all state agencies leasing private sector building space.

B. This Exhibit 'C' document is a binding part of the lease document and shall function with Exhibits 'A' and 'B'.

C. The forms contained in Division 4 are for the Lessor's reference. A separate Lessor's forms packet will be provided by RESD for the Lessor's use. The forms contained in the "Lessor's Packet" are to be used by the Lessor to accomplish the processes required by this document.

D. Federal Americans with Disabilities Act (ADA) and California Building Code (Title 24) accessibility requirements are combined and noted hereafter as **CBC/ADA**.

E. Abbreviations: State Fire Marshal (SFM), Division of the State Architect (DSA), Real Estate Services Division (RESD).

1.01 STATE FIRE MARSHAL AUTHORITY

A. Section 13108 of the California State Health and Safety Code gives the State Fire Marshal (SFM) authority for enforcement of fire protection regulations for State owned and State occupied leased buildings or premises. This authority encompasses both plan review and construction inspections of all leased facilities.

B. If at any time during the Design, Construction Document Review, or Construction Inspection processes, a conflict arises between the State and local authorities, the Lessor/architect will compile all pertinent information and present the situation through the RESD Space Planner to the SFM. The SFM has final authority in the determination of compliance and will take the lead in the resolution of problems or suitable interpretation of code.

1.02 ACCESS COMPLIANCE AUTHORITY

A. California law incorporates the Americans with Disabilities Act requirements. California Government Code provides that buildings shall be made accessible to, and usable by, persons with disabilities, whether they are leased, rented, contracted, sublet, or hired by any municipal, county, or State divisions of government, or special district. California Building Standards Code defines that all State facilities shall meet the federal Architectural Barriers Acts.

B. These statutes, in addition to the California Building Code, Title 24, generate the need for a standard process to ensure access compliance with respect to State leased facilities.

C. The **Division of the State Architect (DSA)** is charged with the responsibility of ensuring compliance with the above standards.

D. If at any time during the Design, Construction Document Review, or Construction Inspection processes, a conflict arises between the State and local authorities, the Lessor/architect will compile all pertinent information and present the situation to the RESD Space Planner.

E. The DSA has delegated a component of the access compliance responsibility to RESD for leased facilities. Conforming to DSA delegation, RESD is requiring the Lessor to ensure compliance by utilizing one of the two procedures defined in this document. Refer to Division 3 (below) for specific requirements and procedures.

F. Public right-of-way access is required for all State leased facilities. If the existing conditions do not meet the required codes and regulations, the design professional (Lessor's architect) must demonstrate and document a diligent effort to request that the authority having control over the public right-of-way, makes the necessary modifications to secure right-of-way access. All correspondence shall be documented and provided to the RESD Space Planner for the project file.

End of Authority and Policy Requirements

2.00 RESD LEASE EXHIBIT 'A'

A. Prior to the lease execution, the RESD Space Planner is responsible for the development and submittal of the lease Exhibit 'A' space plan(s) to the SFM for a general code compliance review and approval. The approved Exhibit 'A' plan(s) will reflect the design concept for the proposed lease within the configuration of the existing building shell. If RESD elects to use a narrative Facilities Design Program (FDP) in place of the Space Plan, the SFM review and approval will follow lease execution and development of preliminary architectural drawings by the Lessor.

2.01 CONSTRUCTION DRAWINGS

A. The Exhibit 'A' Plan or the Exhibit 'A' FDP are design development guidelines only. Lessor, at Lessor's sole cost and expense, shall provide all required construction documents and calculations necessary to obtain a building permit from the local Building Department and to construct the improvements as indicated. The use of Exhibit 'A' Plan in lieu of construction documents is not acceptable to the State.

2.02 PLAN REVIEW AND APPROVAL

A. The Lessor's architect is required to submit the construction drawings to the SFM for plan review and approval prior to construction. **All** specific technical elements of the construction such as fire alarm and smoke detection systems, fire sprinklers, construction details of fire assemblies, etc. shall be included with the construction drawings. For projects with no alterations that would require a building permit the Lessor is not required to submit construction drawings to the SFM.

B. The Lessor's architect shall submit the SFM **Plan Review Application** Form A (attached) and the construction drawings to the State Fire Marshal in Sacramento. There is no fee associated with the SFM review process.

C. The **Plan Review Application form** and all submittals shall be sent to: Office of State Fire Marshal, Code Enforcement
1131 S Street
Sacramento, California, 95814

This form must be filled out completely, including the address to which the approved documents shall be returned. Plan review time is generally consistent with local building authority permitting process, however the architect shall verify the estimated review time for this project review at submittal. The architect shall make the necessary adjustments to the overall project schedule accordingly.

D. The approved drawings or revisions requests will be returned to the address shown on the Plan Review Application and will be accompanied by either a SFM **Plan Review Approval** Form B or a SFM **Plan Review Transmittal** Form C (attached). The Lessor/architect shall provide a copy of the approved form to the RESD Space Planner.

2.03 CONSTRUCTION INSPECTION

A. The regional SFM office will inspect and approve the construction in the State leased building. There are two regions, Code Enforcement North and Code Enforcement South. Call (916) 445-8550 to determine the local contact information. The Lessor, architect, or contractor shall be responsible for contacting the regional Deputy State Fire Marshal for coordination of the inspections based on the proposed construction schedule.

B. After completion of each successive SFM construction inspection, any deficiencies shall be recorded on the SFM **Fire Safety Correction Notice** Form D (attached). This form is to be signed by a Lessor's representative on site. When final approval by the Deputy SFM is recorded on this document the Lessor shall send a copy to the RESD Space Planner.

End of SFM Process

3.00 GENERAL

A. To comply with the accessibility requirements and ensure that the facility has complied with all accessibility codes and regulations, the Lessor is required to complete one of the two processes defined below. In each case the RESD Space Planner will remain the primary contact. The facilities are categorized according to size as either Group I or Group II projects. Each category has specific requirements as defined. Group I projects are submitted to RESD and Group II facilities are submitted to DSA for plan review and approval. The Lessor is required to follow the procedure of the applicable process and is responsible for the associated costs.

3.01 FEE REQUIREMENT

A. The Lessor is required to submit the project fee to RESD for Group I or directly to the DSA regional office for Group II facilities. The RESD Space Planner will calculate the required fee using the **CBC/ADA Access Compliance Fee Calculation *Form E*** (attached) and include this in the Exhibit C lease document.

3.02 DETERMINATION OF FACILITY GROUP

A. The group is determined by the category and the size of the State's net usable leased area. The respective administrative process is defined in the following Sections 3.03 (Group I) and 3.04 (Group II). The Group Types are defined below:

GROUP I:

Building Type:	**Net Usable Square Footage:**
Existing Office Buildings	Less than 100,000 square feet
Existing Warehouse Buildings	Less than 500,000 square feet
Any Building to be Constructed	Less than 30,000 square feet

GROUP II:

Building Type:	**Net Usable Square Footage:**
Existing Office Buildings with Alterations	100,000 sq. ft. or greater
Existing Warehouse Buildings with Alterations	500,000 sq. ft. or greater
Any Building to be Constructed	30,000 sq. ft. or greater

Note: Certain Group I projects, at the discretion of the State, may be determined compatible with Group II process regardless of the building size. The RESD Space Planner shall inform the Lessor which process applies to this particular project during lease negotiations.

3.03 GROUP I FACILITY PROCEDURE

For Group I facilities the Lessor's architect is required to complete the requirements outlined in paragraphs A through D below:

A. Accessibility Survey: The Lessor must have an accessibility survey completed prior to the finalization and approval of the construction documents. The survey must be completed using the DGS' Accessibility Checklist for State-Leased Buildings and Facilities. The following consultants are acceptable:

1. DSA certified accessibility consultants trained for Leased facilities http://www.dgs.ca.gov/resd/Programs/LeasingandPlanning/NewLease/LeaseRequirements.aspx

2. Certified Access Specialist (CASp) http://www.dgs.ca.gov/dsa/Programs/programCert/casp.aspx#t1

3. ICC Accessibility Inspector/Plans Examiner https://av.iccsafe.org/EWEB/DynamicPage.aspx?Site=icc&WebKey=b7afd990-2e14-4013-a186-aeb405641a95&FromSearchControl=Yes

4. Architect licensed in the State of California

A.1.1 The consultant will survey the facility and site per CCR Title 24, California Building Code (CBC), and Americans with Disabilities Act (ADA). State agencies are public entities and shall comply with Title II of the ADA. Exceptions to the code for existing buildings are not permitted. Access compliance shall apply to exterior areas such as but not limited to path of travel to and from public transportation and public right-of-way, parking, passenger drop-off and loading zones, walks and sidewalks, curb ramps, ramps, and all stairs. Access compliance shall also apply to interior areas such as but not limited to entrances and exits, lobbies, building common areas, elevators, access lifts, doors and gates, access to and through all rooms and spaces, restrooms, signs and identification, counters, waiting, seating areas, assistive listening systems, telephones, drinking fountains, alarms, and horizontal/vertical access. Consultants will observe and record all deficiencies, as well as provide solutions needed to bring facility into compliance with sufficient detail to allow Lessor or his/her agent to develop a cost estimate for proposed barrier removal. Should all areas mentioned above not be fully constructed, consultants shall review the construction documents in addition to the physical evaluation.

B. Fee Payment: The Lessor shall prepare a check payable to the Dept. of General Services, Real Estate Services Division. Lessor shall enclose a copy of the **CBC/ADA Access Compliance Fee Calculation** Form E (attached) as prepared by the RESD Space Planner, along with payment and mail to DGS, RESD (Include the project number on the check to RESD).

C. Construction Documents: The Lessor's Architect will incorporate all items defined in the accessibility survey into the construction documents. The Lessor shall submit the completed drawings to RESD for review.

D. Verified Report: Following the completion of construction, the Lessor's architect is responsible for verifying that the items outlined in the accessibility survey and incorporated into the construction documents have been completed. The **Verified Report** Form G (attached) shall be signed by the Lessor's architect. The architect shall forward the signed Verified Report to RESD Space Planner prior to the final inspection that will be performed by RESD. The project will not be accepted for occupancy prior to receipt of this document.

End of Group I Procedure

3.04 GROUP II FACILITY PROCEDURE

The Lessor is required to submit plans and specifications to the **Division of the State Architect (DSA)** for access compliance review and approval. Although the formal process for access compliance plan review and approval is processed through DSA, the DGS RESD Space Planner will continue as the project manager. The Lessor's architect shall inform RESD of the status of plan review/approval from DSA.

For Group II facilities the Lessor's architect is required to complete the requirements outlined in paragraphs A through F below:

A. Accessibility Survey: The Lessor must have an accessibility survey completed prior to the finalization and approval of the construction documents. The survey must be completed using the DGS Accessibility Checklist for State-Leased Buildings and Facilities. The following consultants are acceptable:

  1. DSA certified accessibility consultants trained for Leased facilities http://www.resd.dgs.ca.gov/Branches/PSB/LeaseRequirements.htm

  2. Certified Access Specialist (CASp) http://www.dgs.ca.gov/dsa/Programs/programCert/casp.aspx#t1

  3. ICC Accessibility Inspector/Plans Examiner https://av.iccsafe.org/EWEB/DynamicPage.aspx?Site=icc&WebKey=b7afd990-2e14-4013-a186-aeb405641a95&FromSearchControl=Yes

  4. Architect licensed in the State of California

  Note: See Section 3.03, paragraph A.1.1 (Group I Facility Procedure) for parameters of survey.

B. Construction Drawings and Specifications: The Lessor is required to retain an architect licensed in the State of California to design and develop plans and specifications in accordance with the lease exhibits and applicable codes and regulations. The Lessor's architect will incorporate all items defined in the accessibility survey into the construction documents. The architect is required to stamp and sign the construction documents.

C. Fee Payment: In accordance with the calculation of fees per the **CBC/ADA Access Compliance Fee Calculation** Form E (attached), the Lessor shall prepare a check payable to the Division of the State Architect. This check along with a copy of the CBC/ADA Access Compliance Fee Calculation Form E shall be forwarded directly to the appropriate regional DSA office in the submittal package.

D. Submittal Package: The submittals shall be sent to the appropriate DSA regional office. The state is divided into four regions, San Francisco Bay Area, Sacramento, Los Angeles and San Diego. The DSA regional office that will review this project can be confirmed by calling DSA at (916) 445-8100. The submittal package must be complete before the DSA accepts the project for review. Proceed to the DSA website using the link below for instructions on this process: http://www.dgs.ca.gov/dsa/Programs/progProject/overview/projsubmitintro.aspx

  Upon receipt of the submittal package, a DSA application number is assigned to the project for tracking purposes. A preliminary review of your submittal is performed within a few days.

Plan review is scheduled after DSA verifies that a complete submittal package has been received. The Lessor's architect shall verify the estimated time for this project review with DSA at submittal. The architect shall make the necessary adjustments to the overall project schedule accordingly.

E. DSA Plan Approval: Once approval has been granted by DSA, the Lessor is required to construct the project in compliance with the plans, specifications and lease exhibits. The Lessor shall provide a copy of DSA's letter of approval to the RESD Space Planner. Construction shall not commence until this process has been completed.

F. Verified Report: Following completion of construction, the Lessor's architect shall visit the site to verify that the building and site are in compliance with the DSA approved plans and specifications. The **Verified Report** Form G (attached) shall be completed and signed by the Lessor's architect. The architect shall forward the Verified Report to RESD Space Planner prior to the final construction inspection by RESD. The project will not be accepted for occupancy prior to receipt of this document.

End of Group II Procedure

4.00 SFM PLAN REVIEW APPLICATION, FORM A

STATE OF CALIFORNIA - THE RESOURCES AGENCY Edmund G. Brown Jr., Governor

DEPARTMENT OF FORESTRY AND FIRE PROTECTION OFFICE OF THE STATE FIRE MARSHAL
Fire and Life Safety Division
Web Site: www.fire.ca.gov

PLAN REVIEW APPLICATION

Please Print or Type - Must be Submitted with all Plans, Specifications and Deferred Approvals

Application Date: ______

State Department Project: ______________________

Building Name: ______________________

DGS Project # (DGS Only): ______________________

Please check one of these boxes/do not leave blank **Bill To: SRF ☐ ARF ☐ Agency ☐**

Project Address: ______________________

City: ____________ Zip Code: ________ County: ________

Scope of Project: ______________________

Estimated Contract Cost: ______________________

Bid Date: ____________ Contract Start Date: ____________

Submitting Firm/Agency: ______________________

Address: ______________________

City: ____________ Zip Code: ________ County: ________

Contact Person: ______________________

Telephone Number: ( ) - Email Address: ____________

SFM USE ONLY – BELOW THIS LINE

Date Received: ____________ Database ID #: ____________

Received By: ____________

SFM FILE #: ____________

4.01 SFM PLAN REVIEW APPROVAL, FORM B

(This is for Reference Only - The Lessor will receive this Plan Review Approval form or the Plan Review Transmittal form (next page) with the plans that were submitted for review and approval to the SFM)

STATE OF CALIFORNIA - THE RESOURCES AGENCY Edmund G. Brown Jr., Governor

OFFICE OF THE STATE FIRE MARSHAL Code Enforcement - North
DEPARTMENT OF FORESTRY AND FIRE PROTECTION

1131 "S" Street (95811)
P.O. Box 944246 (94244-2460) Sacramento, CA
Web Site: http://osfm.fire.ca.gov

PLAN REVIEW APPROVAL

TO: ______________________ DATE: ______________________
______________________ CSFM: ______________________
____
____

FACILITY NAME: ______________________

FACILITY ADDRESS: ______________________

PROJECT DESCRIPTION: ______________________
____
____

Reproducible plans and specifications for the project described and included in the plan review transmittal dated _________ are approved by this office and were stamped_________.

Nothing in our review shall be construed as encompassing structural integrity. Approval of this plan does not authorize or approve any omission or deviation from applicable regulations. Final approval is subject to field inspection. One set of approved plans shall be available on the project site at all times.

If you have any questions, please contact me at __________________.

____
Deputy State Fire Marshal

cc: ☐ Code Enforcement - North
☐ Code Enforcement - South
☐ Field File

RECORD #: ______________
RECEIVED DATE: __________

4.02 SFM PLAN REVIEW TRANSMITTAL, FORM C

STATE OF CALIFORNIA - THE RESOURCES AGENCY Edmund G. Brown Jr., Governor

OFFICE OF THE STATE FIRE MARSHAL Code Enforcement - North
DEPARTMENT OF FORESTRY AND FIRE PROTECTION

1131 "S" Street (95811)
P.O. Box 944246 (94244-2460) Sacramento, CA
Web Site: http://osfm.fire.ca.gov

PLAN REVIEW TRANSMITTAL

FACILITY NAME: ______________________________

FACILITY ADDRESS: ______________________________

PROJECT DESCRIPTION: ______________________________

____

____

As requested, we have reviewed ☐ Plans ☐ Specifications ☐ Change Order ☐ Addendum ☐ Instructional Bulletin ☐ Request for Information ☐ Equipment Submittal for the project listed above to determine conformance with the fire and life safety standards of Titles 19 and 24, California Code of Regulations. By copy of this transmittal we are:

☐ advising you that the items listed above were found to be in accordance with the applicable provisions of Title 19 and 24.

☐ returning the items listed above to you for review. Consideration must be given to all comments noted in red pencil on the documents.

☐ requesting that you contact our office at the telephone number listed below for an appointment for our stamp of approval or back check. Submit the plans with our official comments at the time of the back check.

Nothing in our review shall be construed as encompassing structural integrity. Approval of this plan does not authorize or approve any omission or deviation from applicable regulations. Final approval of this project is subject to field inspection.

If you have any questions, please contact me at ______________.

____
Deputy State Fire Marshal

cc: ☐ Code Enforcement - North
☐ Code Enforcement - South
☐ Field File

RECORD #: ______________
RECEIVED DATE: ______________

4.03 SFM FIRE SAFETY CORRECTION NOTICE

and/or

FINAL CONSTRUCTION APPROVAL - FORM D

STATE OF CALIFORNIA - THE RESOURCES AGENCY

Edmund G. Brown Jr., Governor

OFFICE OF THE STATE FIRE MARSHAL Code Enforcement - North
DEPARTMENT OF FORESTRY AND FIRE PROTECTION

1131 "S" Street (95811)
P.O. Box 944246 (94244-2460) Sacramento, CA
Web Site: http://osfm.fire.ca.gov

Fire Safety Correction Notice

File Number: ________________

Name: ____

Address: ____

____

The California Health and Safety Code and the State Fire Marshal's regulations require the following fire safety deficiencies be corrected.

The above deficiencies are to be corrected within __________days. **When ALL deficiencies have been corrected, sign and return the certification on the opposite side of this form**. If you have any questions, contact the Office of the State Fire Marshal at (   ) _____ - _____

ISSUED BY (Deputy State Fire Marshal) RECEIVED BY DATE

4.04 CBC/ADA ACCESS COMPLIANCE FEE CALCULATION FORM E

RELPS Planner: ____________________

Date: __________

Agency: ____________________

Address: ____________________

____

Project Number: __________

Project Name: ____________________

For GROUP I Facilities

Send to:
Dept. of General Services
Real Estate Services Division
Professional Services Branch

707 3rd Street, Suite 5-305
West Sacramento, CA 95605

For GROUP 2 Facilities

Send to:
DSA Regional Office
See DSA Website for offices in your area at www.dsa.dgs.ca.gov/contact/default.htm

	Project Type	Project Size (net usable s.f.)		Project Value (PV)
☐	Existing Warehouse Buildings		$20/sf	$ -
☐	Existing Office Buildings		$50/sf	$ -
☐	New Construction Build-to-Suit		$150/sf	$ -

GROUP I (Under $5,000,000)	Project Value	Multiplier	Fee
PV X 0.2% of 1st $500,000 =	$ -	0.002	
Remainder of PV x 0.1% =	$ -	0.001	
Remainder between 2M and 5M x .01%	$ -	0.0001	
Calculated total =	$ -		
x 10% (QA or $200 Minimum) = Total Fee			$ 200

GROUP II (Over $5,000,000)	Project Value		Fee
PV x 0.5% of 1st $500,000	$ -	0.005	$ -
PV between 500,000 and 2M x .25%	$ -	0.0025	$ -
PV over 2M x .1%	$ -	0.001	$ -
Total Fee			$ -

Total Lessor Fee Obligation:	**$ 200**

4.05 DVBE PROGRAM CERTIFICATION SHEET, FORM F

CALIFORNIA DISABLED VETERAN BUSINESS ENTERPRISE PROGRAM CERTIFICATION SHEET

Lessor must complete and sign to certify if DVBE Participation was or was not obtained

LEASE AMOUNT/DVBE CERTIFICATION Lease Project No.: ______________

I hereby certify that the Lease Contract Amount, as defined below, is in the amount of $______of which $______was awarded to a certified DVBE firm resulting in ____________% DVBE participation. I understand that the Lease Contract Amount is the total dollar figure against which the DVBE participation will be evaluated.

______________________________	______________________
Lessor Name	Date
______________________________	______________________
Lessor's Signature	Printed Name

DEFINITION: Lease contract amount is the total amount of lease costs expended by the Lessor over the firm term of the lease which are attributable to expenditures by the lessor to make the leased property sufficient for state occupancy. This typically includes, but is not necessarily limited to, tenant improvements, extraordinary maintenance, and janitorial services specified in the lease. In the case of a build-to-suit facility, the total of the construction and off-site development costs, as well as architectural and engineering costs, would be included.

4.06 VERIFIED REPORT, FORM G

State Leased Buildings and Facilities
Verified Report - Form G

The Architect having general responsible charge of the work of construction on the plans and specifications, is responsible for the submission of this report to the Department of General Services/Real Estate Services Division, Planner (DGS/RESD) prior to the state tenant taking occupancy.

RESD Project Info:	Agency:		RESD Project #
	Project Type (Scope of Work):		Date:
	RESD Planner:	Phone:	Fax:

Facility Info:	Building Name	Hours of Operation:	
	Address:		Suite
	City:		Zip:
	Lessor Contact	Phone	Fax

Contractor:	Company Name	License #	Phone

This report includes all construction work through the date of: ________ month _____ day _____ year

Exterior Work	% Compliant	Interior Work	% Compliant
		Accessible Main Entrance	
Parking & Accessible Stalls		Doors & Gates	
Walks & Sidewalks		Information/Reception Counter	
Curb Ramps		Elevators/Ramps/Lifts	
Stairways		Sanitary Facilities/Sinks/Drinking Fountains	
Ramps & Landings		Stairwells/Exits	
Accessible Main Entrance		Conference/Meeting /Assembly Rooms	
Wayfinding & Signage		Wayfinding & Signage	
		Fire Alarms	
		Total Project Percentage of Completion	

*All items required to be 100% complete unless Hardship approved by DSA or Mitigation Plan outlined in lease.

List work and % to be completed (attach additional pages as necessary):

I declare under penalty of perjury that I have read the above report and know the contents thereof, that all of the above statements are true and that I know of my own personal knowledge that the work during the period covered by the report has been performed and materials used and installed, and in every material respect are in compliance with the duly approved plans and specifications therefore.

Architect:	Signature	Date
	Name	Architect #
	Company/Firm	Phone
	Address	Fax

Submit completed forms to location indicated below:
DGS/RESD Real Estate Services Division Attn: Planner 707 Third Street, Suite 5-305 West Sacramento, CA 95605

TEXAS STATE LEASE

____

THE STATE OF TEXAS §

COUNTY OF TRAVIS §

1. PARTIES

This Agreement is made and entered into on this _____day of _______________, <20____, by and between LESSOR, ____________________, and LESSEE, STATE OF TEXAS, acting by and through the Texas Facilities Commission (TFC).

2. PROPERTY LEASED

______________________________________ Total Square Feet, occupied by the

______________________________________ (Occupying State Agency/ies) located in the

______________________________________ (Building/Property Name) at

______________________________________ (Street Address) in

______________________________________ (City, Zip Code) in

______________________________________ County, Texas

Lessor promises, in return for the consideration described herein to be paid by the Lessee and the covenants set out herein to be kept by Lessee, to hereby lease, unto the Lessee, the Property and Premises described herein.

Lessor also promises to furnish any and all requirements related to such Property and Premises as set out in this lease, **and the Request for Proposal (RFP)**, all of which are incorporated herein by reference and made a part hereof for all purposes.

3. TERMS OF LEASE

This lease shall be for a period of ________ months commencing on the ___ day of ________, **20**___ (the Commencement Date), and ending on the ___ day of ________, **20**___ (the Termination Date), unless sooner terminated as hereinafter provided. **This lease is contingent upon the majority approval by a quorum of the Commission members of the Texas Facilities Commission. If the Commission does not approve the Lease, it may be terminated by the State of Texas without liability upon 30 days notice to the Lessor.**

4. MONTHLY RENTAL

The Lessee agrees to pay Lessor a base Monthly Rent during the term of this lease in accordance with the Rent Schedule as detailed in Exhibit A. The rental payments provided for herein shall be due and payable by Lessee in advance on the first day of the month for which said rentals are due.

This lease contract is made and entered into in accordance with and subject to the provisions of the Texas Constitution and the Texas Government Code, Title 10, Subtitle D, and is made contingent upon the continuation of the availability of money appropriated by the legislature to pay for the lease. In the event the Legislature or the Executive Branch of the State of Texas cease to fund the lease, or the agency ceases to exist as a result of the Legislative sunset review process, then the Texas Facilities Commission, hereinafter referred to as Commission, may assign another state agency to the space, or a part thereof, covered by this lease. Should the Commission be unable to find another State agency or agencies to fill, or partially fill the space, the Commission, upon written notice to the Lessor, either may terminate this lease, or sublet in whole or in part to a private third party.

5. RENEWAL OPTION

By mutual agreement between Lessee and Lessor, this lease may be renewed up to ___ times for a period up to ___ months each, under the same terms and conditions. Lessee shall give Lessor written notice of intention to exercise this option at least 180 days prior to expiration of this lease.

6. CPI ESCALATION CLAUSE

A. On each anniversary date of the lease commencement, the total monthly rent of the lease may be adjusted by changes in the Consumer Price Index (CPI) reflecting percentage increases.

B. To receive the CPI adjustment, the Lessor must submit a request in writing **by certified mail, return receipt requested,** and received by the Texas Facilities Commission (TFC) no later than thirty (30) days after the anniversary date for that year. In determining whether to grant Lessor's request for a CPI increase, in whole or in part, TFC may review and consider Lessor's performance under this lease and whether any issues with the leased premises remain unresolved, as provided in Section 7(k) below.

C. The percent escalation allowable will be based on the percent change in the CPI for Urban Wage Earners and Clerical Workers, Current Series (CPI-W, U.S. City Average, All Items) published by the United States Department of Labor, Bureau of Labor Statistics. The index may be obtained from the U.S. Bureau of Labor Statistics web site at www.bls.gov. The index month three (3) months prior the anniversary month for the current year and the previous year shall be used to determine the percent increase.

D. A Base Factor of 50%, 40%, 35% or 25% of the monthly rent will be used in the calculation for the escalation, depending on the apportionment of the Lessor's and Tenant's obligation for payment of utilities and janitorial service, in accordance with the following schedule:

BASE FACTOR PERCENT	PAYING UTILITIES	PAYING JANITORIAL
50%	Lessor	Lessor
40%	Lessor	Tenant
35%	Tenant	Lessor
25%	Tenant	Tenant

E. EXAMPLE (Calculation formula with a 50% Base Factor):

Part 1. CPI Current Year	CPI Previous Year		Difference		Divided by Previous Year		% Change
(Mar 04) 182.9	- (Mar 03) 180.3	=	2.6	/	180.3	=	1.4

Part 2. Current Monthly Rent		% Base Factor			% Change		Rent Increase
$2,500.00	x	50%	= $1,250.00	x	1.4	=	$17.50

Part 3. Current Monthly Rent		CPI Increase		New Monthly Rent
$2,500.00	+	$17.50	=	$2,517.50

F. The first eligible CPI rent adjustment for this lease will be ________________, 20___, based upon the percent change in the CPI from ________________, 20___ and ________________, 20___ using a Base Factor of 50%, 40%, 35%, or 25%. Each succeeding year, the same procedure as outlined above will be used.

7. GENERAL TERMS AND CONDITIONS

A. Lessor covenants and agrees to pay all taxes of whatever nature, levied and assessed and to be levied or assessed, on or against the leased Property and improvements during the term of the lease, and to keep the leased Premises, Property and buildings in good repair and condition during the continuance of the term of this lease, said maintenance is to include, but is not limited to, the following services: repair and patch wall, ceiling and floor surfaces, painting as needed, replacement of broken window glass, repair of window shades, blinds and/or drapes, fasteners and sash cord or chains, roof and ceiling leaks, building exterior, interior, plumbing, heating, air conditioning and ventilating equipment and filters, fire protection equipment, miscellaneous valves, woodwork, locks, floor surfaces and coverings, lighting fixtures, and the replacement of all defective or burned-out light bulbs, fluorescent tubes, ballasts and starters. If the occupying agency, or its agents, cause damage to said Property that goes beyond "normal wear and tear," the occupying agency is responsible to pay for those repairs.

B. Lessor hereby covenants and agrees that hereafter and during the term of this lease, it will not rent, lease or otherwise furnish space in this or any adjacent buildings under its control to any enterprise which, in the usual exercise of its business, could be expected to create noise or odors injurious or disruptive to the occupying agency's normal governmental activity. Lessor covenants and agrees it will not lease space that would locate or collocate any regulated parties which have an interest in the occupying agency/ies or whose occupation of these Premises would cause the occupying agency to be in violation of State statute.

C. Lessor warrants that the demised Premises is not in violation of any city, state or local ordinance or statute or any restriction imposed against the demised Premises and that said Lessor will indemnify said Lessee for any direct or indirect loss sustained by Lessee as a result of the existence of such restriction, ordinance or statute.

D. Lessor hereby covenants and agrees that the Lessee may bring on the leased Premises any and all furniture, fixtures and equipment reasonably necessary for the efficient exercise of

Lessee's governmental responsibilities and the parties agree that all such Property shall remain the Property of the Lessee.

E. Any signs necessary to indicate Lessee's name, location and governmental purpose shall be prepared and installed consistent with signage for other lessees in the Property and in keeping with building decor. Any special requirements of Lessee contrary to the above must be stated in writing and made a part of this lease. Any cost of compliance with this paragraph in excess of the amount that would be required for Lessor's standard signage shall be borne by Lessee.

F. On termination of this lease, by lapse of time or otherwise, Lessee may, within a reasonable time thereafter, at its option and expense, remove from said Premises any and all improvements, equipment, appliances or other Property placed or owned by it thereon. Lessee shall deliver the Premises and Property to Lessor in good order and condition, provided however, the reasonable use and ordinary wear and tear are expected.

G. If during the term of this lease, said Premises, or any portion thereof, shall be condemned for any public purpose, Lessee hereto shall have the option of terminating and canceling this lease upon thirty (30) days notice to the Lessor of its election to do so.

H. It is mutually agreed between the Lessor and the Lessee that if said building and Premises shall, during the term of this lease, be damaged by flood, fire or any other cause or causes, the same shall be promptly repaired by the Lessor. During the time of such repair, if the space cannot be fully utilized by Lessee, lease payments due hereunder shall be either reduced or withheld in accord with the degree of non-use. But, if said building and Premises be so damaged as to render said Premises unfit for occupancy, then, and from the date of such damage, this lease shall cease and be void, and rent and other obligations hereunder shall be due and payable only to the date of such damage. The determination as to whether the building and Premises are damaged so as to render them unfit for occupancy shall be made by Lessee. If the Lessor has available under his control space which will meet Lessee's needs and offers same to Lessee, the Lessee may at its option, occupy that space under the same terms and conditions as this lease. Lessor will be responsible for any relocation costs that may be incurred, included but not limited to, cost of the space, moving, communications equipment and computer expenses.

I. Lessee is not obligated to pay rent and other sums under this lease until the premises are available to Lessee for full occupancy and are suitable for use as office space for a state agency. If Lessor is unable to give Lessee full possession of the premises on Commencement Date for any reason, Lessor shall give Lessee immediate written notice of the cause for the delay and the date the premises will be ready for occupancy, Lessee may terminate this lease without liability to the State of Texas and seek other leased space.

Except as provided in Paragraphs 3 and 4, Lessee may not terminate the lease if the delay of occupancy is caused by Lessee, or by conditions beyond Lessor's control, such as strikes, fire, unavoidable casualties or other unusual circumstances that constitutes a justifiable delay.

If the Lessee so elects, the Lessee may continue to treat this lease as if in full force and effect for a period of no more than 120 days after the lease commencement date. During this time, or for as long as possession does not commence, the rent shall not be paid. In the event Lessee either terminates the lease under this paragraph or is unable to occupy the premises on Commencement Date due to reasons other than a justifiable delay as determined by Lessee using reasonable discretion, Lessor will be liable in damages for any rents Lessee pays for other leased space substantially equal to the premises or for any holdover charges associated with a delay in occupying the premises and for any other related losses sustained by Lessee. Payment hereunder shall not begin until possession of the premises is given or the premises are available for full occupancy by the Lessee. Based upon the possession date of the premises, the lease shall be amended to reflect the new lease term.

J. Lessee reserves the right to assign any agency of State government to occupy all or any part of the space described herein or to assign or sublet all or any part of the leased Premises to any private entities (persons or corporations).

K. In the event Lessor shall breach or be in default in the strict performance of any of the covenants or obligations imposed upon Lessor by this lease, and shall remain in default for a period of thirty (30) days after written notice of such default, Lessee shall have the right and privilege of terminating this lease and declaring the same at an end, and shall have the remedies now or hereafter provided by law for recovery of damages occasioned by such default. In lieu of a formal declaration of default and resulting termination as provided above, Lessee may withhold payment of rent from Lessor, until such time as the violations have been corrected or the Lessee may correct all or any part of the violations and deduct the cost from rentals due the Lessor.

L. If Lessee fails to pay rentals or other charges hereunder or otherwise fails to perform its obligations hereunder and this failure is not cured within 30 days after written notice from Lessor to Lessee of such failure, then Lessee is in default, and Lessor may terminate this Lease and may enter and take possession of premises, and will have the remedies now or hereafter provided by law for recovery of rent, repossession of premises and damages occasioned by Lessee's default. No provision, covenant or agreement contained in this Lease shall be deemed a waiver of sovereign immunity of the State of Texas from tort or other liability.

M. The failure of the Lessee or Lessor to insist in any one or more instances on a strict performance of any of the covenants of this lease shall not be construed as a waiver or relinquishment of such covenants in future instances, but the same shall continue and remain in full force and effect.

N. This agreement and each and all of its covenants, obligations and conditions hereof shall inure to the benefit of and be binding upon the heirs, personal representatives, successors and assigns of Lessor, and the successor in office of Lessee.

O. This agreement shall be governed by Texas law.

P. Lessor understands that acceptance of funds under this contract acts as acceptance of the authority of the State Auditor's Office, or any successor agency, to conduct an audit or investigation in connection with those funds. Lessor further agrees to cooperate fully with the State Auditor's Office or its successor in the conduct of the audit or investigation, including providing all records requested. Lessor will ensure that this clause concerning the authority to audit funds received indirectly by subcontractors through Lessor and the requirement to cooperate is included in any subcontract it awards.

Q. Lessor warrants and represents that any use, storage, treatment, or transportation of Hazardous Substances that has occurred in or on the Premises prior to Commencement Date of this Lease has been in compliance with all applicable federal, state, and local laws, regulations, and ordinances. Lessor additionally warrants and represents that no release, leak, discharge, spill, disposal, or emission of Hazardous Substances has occurred in, on, or under the Premises, and that the Premises are free of Hazardous Substances as of Commencement Date.

Lessor shall indemnify Lessee from any and all claims, damages, fines, judgments, penalties, costs, liabilities, or losses (including, without limitation, any and all sums paid for settlement of claims and for fees of attorneys, consultants, and experts) arising during or after the lease term from or in connection with the presence or suspected presence of Hazardous Substances in or on the Premises, unless the Hazardous Substances are present solely as a result of negligence, willful misconduct, or other acts of Lessee or Lessee's agents, employees, contractors, or invitees. Without limitation of the foregoing, this indemnification of the site or any cleanup, removal, or restoration mandated by a federal, state, or local agency or political subdivision, unless the Hazardous Substances are present solely as a result of negligence, willful misconduct, or other acts of Lessee, Lessee's agents, employees, contractors, or invitees. This indemnification shall specifically include any and all costs due to Hazardous Substances that flow, diffuse, migrate, or percolate into, onto, or under the Premises after the lease term commences.

As used herein, "Hazardous Substance" means any substance that is toxic, ignitable, reactive, or corrosive and that is regulated by any local government, the State of Texas, or the United States Government. "Hazardous Substance" includes any and all material or substances that are defined as "hazardous waste," "extremely hazardous waste," or a "hazardous substance" pursuant to state, federal, or local governmental law. "Hazardous Substance" includes but is not restricted to asbestos, polychlorobiphenyls ("PCBs"), solvents, pesticides, and petroleum.

R. At all times during the lease term, Lessor must maintain a policy of all-risk property insurance, issued by and bonded upon an insurance company licensed in the State of Texas, covering the Leased Premises and leasehold improvements (exclusive of contents), in an amount equal to not less than 80% percent of the replacement cost thereof. Lessee shall have no interest in the policy or policy proceeds and Lessor shall not be obligated to insure any furnishings, equipment, trade fixtures, or other personal property that Lessee may place or cause to be placed upon the Leased Premises. Lessor must also maintain a policy or policies of comprehensive general liability insurance insuring Lessor against loss of life, bodily injury and/or property damage with respect to Common Areas, operation of the Building, parking lots and other improvements associated with the land upon which the Leased Premises are located, and any other losses caused by or related to the duties and obligations of Lessor under this Lease.

Lessor acknowledges that, because Lessee is an agency of the State of Texas, liability for the tortious conduct of the agents and employees of Lessee (other than medical liability of medical staff physicians) or for injuries caused by conditions of tangible state property is provided for solely by the provisions of the Texas Tort Claims Act *(Texas Civil Practice and Remedies Code,* Chapters 1010 and 104), and that Workers' Compensation Insurance coverage for employees of Lessee is provided by Lessee as mandated by the provisions of *Texas Labor Code,* Chapter 503. Lessor further acknowledges that, as an agency of the State of Texas, Lessee has only such authority as is granted to Lessee by state law or as may be reasonably implied from such law, and that Lessee shall have the right, at its option, to (a) obtain liability insurance protecting Lessee and its employees and property insurance protecting Lessee's buildings and the contents, to the extent authorized by Section 51.966 of the *Texas Education Code* or other law, or (b) self-insure against any risk that may be incurred by Lessee as a result of its operations under this lease. Any obligation by Lessee under this Lease to obtain insurance is expressly made subject to the Lessee's authority under state law to obtain such insurance. No insurance carrier of either party shall have a right of subrogation against the other party to this lease.

8. LEASE REQUIREMENTS

Lessor and Lessee shall comply with all provisions of Exhibit B entitled Lease Requirements which is incorporated herein for all purposes.

9. OTHER TERMS AND CONDITIONS

A. This lease shall be effective as of the date that all parties execute this lease contract. All proposals, negotiations, notices, and representations with reference to matters covered by this lease are merged in this instrument and no amendment or modification thereof shall be valid unless evidenced in writing and signed by all parties as identified below.

B. Any statement or representation of Lessee in any Estoppel Certificate delivered pursuant to this lease which would modify the rights, privileges or duties of Lessor or Lessee hereunder shall be of no force and effect and may not be relied on by any person.

C. Should Lessor require Lessee to provide an Estoppel Certificate at any time during the term of this lease, Lessor will give Lessee thirty (30) days prior written notice whereupon TFC will deliver to Lessor a completed signed original of same utilizing its standard Estoppel Certificate form.

10. SPECIAL PROVISIONS:

N/A

OR (Reserved for special or unusual conditions or requirements of the lease)

Language for lease consolidation leases:

The Lessee shall have the right to cancel the lease contract should a state-approved lease consolidation facility or a state-owned facility become available, by giving the Lessor written notice of cancellation <180/365> days prior to the desired cancellation date. Lease may not be cancelled prior to <date/consolidation plan date>. **Note: You may want to set a critical date ahead.**

****

LESSOR:

Lessor Name
Address
City, State, Zip
Tel.:
Fax:
Email:

By: ________________________________
Signature

____
Printed Name

LESSEE:

STATE OF TEXAS,
Acting by and through the
TEXAS FACILITIES COMMISSION

Tel.:
Fax:
Email:

By: ________________________________
Director of Planning and Real Estate, Management Division

cc: Agency(ies)

EXHIBIT A RENT SCHEDULE
EXHIBIT B LEASE REQUIREMENTS
EXHIBIT B1 AGENCY SPECIFIC REQUIREMENTS / ROOM SCHEDULE / FLOORPLAN
EXHIBIT C GENERAL CONSTRUCTION NOTES
EXHIBIT C1 NEW CONSTRUCTION NOTES

EXHIBIT A

RENT SCHEDULE

Occupying Agency	Usable Sq. Ft.	Annual Base Rate/SF	Annual Base Rent	Monthly Base Rent

EXHIBIT B

LEASE REQUIREMENTS

A. In signing this lease contract, the Lessor certifies that the leased Premises to be occupied shall comply with all applicable federal, state and local laws, statutes, ordinances, codes, rules and regulations, which include compliance with all applicable handicapped accessibility requirements. Acceptance of the space does not exonerate the Lessor from meeting all the requirements. No requirement may be waived by the Lessee or the occupying agency.

B. Lessor specifically covenants and warrants that the space will at all times comply with the Texas Accessibility Standards (TAS) requirements for persons with disabilities administered by the Texas Department of Licensing and Regulations.

C. Lessor attests that it has sufficient and appropriate title to said Premises and attests that it has the financial capability to fully execute obligations in this lease contract. Lessor further covenants that it has the power and authority to execute this lease and to place Lessee in possession of the Premises in full satisfaction of and compliance with the terms and conditions herein.

D. Lessor also agrees that it will not attempt to impose upon Lessee any requirements of other legal instruments related to these Premises not referred to herein or made a part hereof. Lessor warrants to Lessee the leasehold interest created hereunder and agrees to defend Lessee against the claims of all persons to the leasehold interests of the Lessee. Any person or entity executing this lease as agent for the Lessor shall attach to this lease sufficient evidence of authority to act in the capacity shown.

E. SITE PLAN & CONCEPT FLOOR PLAN DRAWINGS shall be provided by Lessor to Lessee _____ days from execution of the lease, Lessor shall provide lessee dimensioned Auto Cad drawing files of the floor plans of the leased premises. Site plan shall show the building footprint and parking lot(s).

F. COMPLETED CONSTRUCTION PLANS shall be provided by Lessor to Lessee _____ days from execution of the lease or earlier, for Lessee approval prior to commencement of construction. Lessor shall also provide Lessee a construction schedule showing all critical dates of construction or substantial renovation **<15/30/45/90 (this choice should be the same above - *use 90 days for OAG*) >** days from execution of the lease and prior to the commencement of construction of the Premises covered by this lease.

G. ALL CONSTRUCTION, REPAIRS AND ALTERATIONS shall be completed by Lessor _____ days prior to occupancy. Lessee shall have full access to the premises during that period, at no charge to Lessee, in order to prepare the Premises for occupancy on the Commencement Date. All non-economic terms and conditions of the Lease shall be in force. Lessee may do whatever is necessary during said period to ensure it is able to commence normal business operations on the Commencement Date. **CERTIFICATE OF OCCUPANCY (CO)**, issued by the appropriate local authority, shall be provided by Lessor to Lessee _____ prior to occupancy.

H. Lessee reserves the right of inspection and may reject space based on adverse building conditions, including but not limited to general cleanliness, appearance of carpet or tile, grounds, finished interiors or exteriors, odors, pests, insects, or other problems relating to improper extermination or any other condition that would create unsanitary, unattractive or unsafe conditions.

I. As a condition of occupancy, Lessor certifies that the leased space contains the minimum usable square footage specified in the lease contract.

J. Lessee shall have the right to survey and inspect Property during the construction process to ensure the leased space complies with all requirements as set forth in this lease agreement.

K. Prior to occupancy, Lessor shall thoroughly clean the leased Premises. Cleaning operations shall include, but not be limited to, the following:

1. Removal of non-permanent protection and labels.
2. Polish glass of all windows and doors.
3. Clean exposed finishes.
4. Clean all mirrors.
5. Remove all waste and debris.
6. Clean light fixtures and replace dimmed or burned out light bulbs.
7. Sweep and wash paved areas as needed.
8. Clean yards and grounds.
9. Vacuum all carpeted areas.
10. Wax and polish all hard surface flooring.
11. Clean blinds.

L. The Lessee may, upon written notice to the Lessor at least 30 days prior to termination of this lease or any extension, remain in possession of the leased Premises for a period specified in the notice, not to exceed 180 days. The Lessee shall pay the Lessor for each month or part of a month, a pro-rata sum equal to the Monthly Rent in effect at the termination of this lease for the space occupied by the agency during this period.

M. Lessor shall provide, at Lessor's expense, access to all utilities services, meters, and connections necessary for the proper and intended use of the space. These utilities include telecommunications facilities, continuous hot and cold water, wastewater, electricity and natural gas, if required for heating and or cooling.

N. UTILITIES shall be paid by **LESSOR.**
Utility bills for telephone, data transmission, and telecommunications will be paid by the Occupying Agencies. The Occupying Agencies' normal weekly hours of operation shall be 7:00 a.m. to 7:00 p.m., Monday through Friday, and 7:00 a.m. to 12:00 noon on Saturday.

At Lessee's reasonable request, Lessor shall also make available all utilities at other times necessary at an hourly reimbursement rate based on Building Owners and Managers Association International (BOMA) standards, to be provided by the Lessor to the Occupying Agencies prior to award of the Lease.

In the event that Lessee desires to assume payment of any utility, Lessee will provide thirty (30) days notice to Lessor. Upon receipt of such notice, Lessor shall immediately provide to Lessee copies of all past utility bills in order to facilitate Lessee's utility management. The monthly rental amount shall be reduced in an amount equivalent to the average monthly cost of the service assumed by the Lessee, based upon the preceding year's billing records. Lessor shall allow Lessee to separately meter the Premises, at Lessee's sole cost and discretion, at any time during the term of the lease.

UTILITIES shall be paid by **LESSEE.**
Electricity for the leased space shall be separately metered, or, if the Premises are located in a building where electrical service is shared with other tenants, Lessor may calculate Lessee's pro rata share of electricity costs, excluding any taxes, using Lessee's usable square footage as the numerator and the usable square footage of the total shared area as the denominator. Copies of all electric bills received by the Lessor will be provided to the Lessee upon receipt of same by Lessor in order to verify the requested pro rata bill contribution by Lessee.

O. JANITORIAL SERVICES AND SUPPLIES shall be paid by **LESSOR / LESSEE.**

If LESSOR shall provide JANITORIAL SERVICES AND SUPPLIES, services shall include:

a. On a Daily Basis (Monday through Friday, no earlier than 5:00 p.m. and must be completed by 7:00 a.m. the next work day):

   1. Vacuum, sweep and/or dust mop all floors and vestibules.
   2. Detergent mop, rinse, and dry all non-carpeted floors, vacuum carpets and floor rugs, and spot clean carpet and floor rugs as necessary.
   3. Spot clean around light switches and door levers.
   4. Clean and disinfect all restrooms, urinals, toilets, wash basins and drinking fountains.
   5. Empty and clean all restroom receptacles.
   6. Clean and refill all restroom dispensers.
   7. Empty and clean waste baskets and place refuse in proper container. Replace trash can and waste basket liners.
   8. Thoroughly clean break room(s), with cleaning to include, but not limited to, wiping table(s), counter(s), and sink(s).
   9. Remove all refuse from building and place in proper container(s).

10. Set security alarm and lock the building after last janitorial employee is out of building, if applicable.

b. On a Weekly Basis:

1. Clean all baseboards and door frames.
2. Clean and wash all entrance doors.
3. Perform dusting on desks, files, etc.

c. On a Monthly Basis:

1. Perform dusting on all partitions, doors and window ledges.
2. Brush down all walls, ceiling vents and light fixtures.
3. Clean and wax all desks, if requested by the occupying agency/ies.

d. On a Semi-Annual Basis:

1. Steam clean all carpet and floor rugs.
2. Non-carpeted floors to be waxed or buffed.
3. Clean fluorescent light lenses and diffusers when needed and/or as requested by Lessee.
4. Wash all windows, blinds, glass doors, glass partitions, etc.

e. Should the Lessee exercise its right to assume janitorial services, the Lessor will continue to provide and pay for the following services:

1. Exterior of windows washed twice yearly.
2. Daily sanitization of restrooms with germicidal detergent, and restocking of soap and paper products for restrooms that are not within the occupying agency/ies space and for their exclusive use.

P. Lessor shall provide and install labels for all individual electrical circuits in all electrical breaker/fuse boxes.

Q. Lessor shall be responsible for furnishing appropriate outside trash and refuse receptacles and for the removal of trash and refuse from the Premises.

R. Lessor shall maintain the exterior of the building and adjacent grounds in an appropriate manner. Lessor agrees to make diligent efforts to landscape with Texas flora. All grass, trees, shrubbery and other landscaping must be maintained on a regular basis. Water used by Lessor for landscaping and/or decorative purposes shall be paid for by Lessor.

S. The Lessor shall provide monthly interior and quarterly exterior pest extermination services. Any extermination service must be performed after normal business hours.

T. Lessor shall have building maintenance personnel available to respond to routine calls within twenty-four (24) hours and emergency calls within four (4) hours. "Emergency" repair or maintenance shall include, but not be limited to, situations involving the air conditioning, electrical, plumbing, roof leaks, disruption of water-delivery to or drainage from any portion of the plumbing system, access into and out of the leased space, and environmental control. Lessor shall, at a minimum, acknowledge emergency calls within two (2) hours.

U. Space to be occupied under this lease shall be designated a "non-smoking area".

V. Lessor shall provide off-street parking for _____ vehicles. Parking must be under the direct control of the Lessor and must be located within a reasonable distance of the entry to the lease space. <See agency specific requirements for parking.>

W. Lessor shall furnish and maintain exterior lighting for the building, connecting walkways and parking area(s) as necessary for appropriate security. The light fixtures shall be equipped with a light level-sensing device that will operate the units automatically. Lessor shall provide a minimum level of illumination to comply with normal business standards. Lessor shall pay all utility costs associated with exterior lighting.

X. Cost of furnishing and installing light fixtures at inception of lease and replacement light bulbs shall be at Lessor's expense.

Y. Exit lights, shall be provided to the outside of the building in accordance with applicable codes. Electric and/or luminous directional arrows shall be strategically placed to identify the way leading to the outside.

Z. Lessor shall provide an emergency lighting system for one and one-half (1-1/2) hours of illumination in the event of failure of normal lighting.

AA. Each room and area shall have a light switch.

BB. All lighting and electrical accessories shall comply with all Municipal, County, State and Federal ordinances, rules and regulations for any new construction. All electrical work shall conform to the standards and requirements of the latest editions and applicable sections of the National Electrical Code (NEC) Handbook. All lighting fixtures shall have light diffusing panels or elements. Fluorescent lighting fixtures shall have energy efficient ballasts.

CC. Lessor shall provide all life safety equipment, including but not limited to fire extinguishers and smoke alarms, in accordance with the requirements of all applicable municipal building codes. In the absence of a local municipal code, Lessor agrees to comply with minimum requirements as set forth by the International Building Code and the Life Safety Code, as published by the National Fire Protection Administration.

DD. Lessor shall provide access to telecommunication and automation service providers under contract to the occupying agencies at appropriate times during construction.

EE. Lessor shall not unreasonably withhold the right of the Lessee to install a security system in the lease space, as requested by the Lessee. The security system shall remain the Property of the Lessee or occupying agency/ies and may be removed at the end of the lease term.

FF. All exterior doors shall be keyed with non-duplicating keys. Lessor shall furnish keys, individually numbered, as requested by Lessee. All exterior exit doors shall be solid core doors (where applicable) and equipped, unless otherwise required by code, with deadbolt locks with a minimum one-inch throw bolt. All door hardware and automatic door closers shall be of sufficiently sturdy construction to ensure security.

GG. All offices and work areas shall have finished ceiling surfaces, unless otherwise approved by Lessee. Broken or stained acoustical tiles shall be replaced by Lessor in a timely manner. Ceiling tiles must be of sufficient quality and weight to not become dislodged due to the opening and closing of doors.

HH. All demising walls between Lessee space and other tenant space shall be extended from wall to the deck above the finished ceiling at Lessor's expense. The location of the HVAC unit(s) shall not unduly inconvenience the occupying agency, either due to maintenance requirements or noise levels. Lessor shall furnish a cost efficient central heat and cooling system. The heating and cooling temperatures shall be maintained in accordance to meet the goals of the Energy Management Plan Guide as set forth by the State Energy Conservation Office or TFC. The building must have a mechanical system that provides an indoor environment that is healthful, comfortable and free of objectionable odors. The heating, air conditioning and ventilation system shall comply with the requirements of the latest American Society of Heating, Refrigeration, and Air Conditioning (ASHRAE) Standards for Ventilation for Acceptable Indoor Air Quality (currently ASHRAE 62-1989) and the latest ASHRAE Standards for Thermal Environmental Conditions for Human Occupancy (currently ASHRAE 55-1992). Forced air cooling and heating shall be ducted and vented throughout the space to provide the most efficient manner of operation and occupant comfort. Conditioned air shall be vented into each room and area with the exception of closets. Thermostats shall be provided as necessary to control conditions throughout the leased space. Numbers and locations of thermostats and associated zones or equipment shall accommodate all internal and external loads to provide uniform temperatures throughout the space. HVAC controls/ thermostats shall have locking covers and one master key or tool shall be provided to the Occupying Agency. Lessor is responsible for balancing the HVAC system.

EXHIBIT B1

AGENCY SPECIFIC REQUIREMENTS & ROOM SCHEDULE / FLOORPLAN

ROOM SCHEDULE					
	Full Time Employees	**13**		**Date**	
Item	Space Use/Room Name	Number	SF Per	SF Ext.	Adjacency/Comments
	Family Health Services (FHS)				
1	FHS - Nurse Manager	1	120	120	Office
2	FHS - IMM Nurse	1	120	120	Office
3	FHS - TBE Nurse	1	120	120	Office
4	SW - Human Serv Specialist	1	120	120	Office
5	FHS - Human Serv Tech (reception area)	1	64	64	System Furn, with transaction counter
6	FHS - Clerk (Itinerant staff)	1	48	48	System Furn
	Women Infants and Children Program (WIC)				
7	WIC - Nutritionist	1	80	80	System Furn, adj. to conference/ training rm
8	WIC - Contractor	1	0	0	
9	WIC - Clerks (reception area)	4	48	192	System Furn, with transaction counter
	Support Area				
10	Office Machine Area	1	45	45	adj. to Clerks & Human Srv Tech.
21	TBE Waiting Area	1	100	100	near waiting area and adj. to TBE Nurse
22	Supply/Mail Room	1	90	90	Central to all staff
23	Tele/Data Room	1	60	60	Central to all staff
24	Break Room	1	160	160	Central to all staff
25	Client Restrooms	1	60	60	1 unisex restroom, adj. to waiting area
26	Employees Restroom		0	0	per building code, not included in usable SF
			Sub-total	2,857	
		Open Plan Circulation	60%	323	
		Built-out Circulation	30%	695	
			Total Circulation	1,019	
			Total SF	**3,876**	

Rest rooms to be provided by lessor in accordance with local building code and are not included in the usable square footage of this lease.

USABLE SQUARE FEET DEFINITION:

Parking requirements: ____________________

Standard Parking Spaces: ________

ADA/TAS____________________

Exhibit C

GENERAL CONSTRUCTION NOTES

Lessor shall design, in consultation with Lessee, and construct the Premises based upon all of the specifications outlined in this Lease and Exhibits as well as the following criteria at no additional cost to Lessee. Lessor understands that Lessee has no provision for payment of additional construction costs. Any unforeseen costs associated with compliance herein shall be at Lessor's sole cost.

Lessee, not the Occupying Agency of the lease space, has sole authority for the initiation of any changes or modifications (Change Order) to the scope of work contained in this lease.

Should any Occupying Agency cause or request changes by the Lessor to exceed the scope of work described below, Lessor shall first obtain written and signed authorization from the Texas Facilities Commission prior to being obligated to proceed with the work.

1. The space to be occupied must comply with all applicable federal, state, and local laws, statutes, ordinances, codes, rules and regulations. In lieu of applicable local building codes, the International Building Code will apply. Acceptance of the space does not exonerate the Lessor from meeting all the requirements. No requirement may be waived by the Commission or the Occupying Agency.

2. The Leased space shall meet all zoning and building code requirements of the Local Government(s) in which the space is located. Lessor shall comply with all Local Government(s) rules and regulations regarding land development including, but not limited to, subdivision requirements, zoning ordinances, site reviews, plan reviews, development and building permits, inspections, and certificates of occupancy. If Lessor seeks or acquires an exemption from such rules and regulations regarding land development without TFC approval, such action shall be grounds for termination of the lease by the Texas Facilities Commission in accordance with paragraph 7(k) of the State Lease contract.

3. The Texas Accessibility Standards (TAS) requirements for persons with disabilities are administered by the Texas Department of Licensing and Regulation (TDLR), Architectural Barriers Division, P. O. Box 12157, Austin, TX 78711, Telephone: 512-463-3211, website http://www.license.state.tx.us.

4. Lessee reserves the right to survey or inspect construction/renovation to ensure space complies with all requirements at any time.

5. Any new construction for the Premises shall be constructed by Lessor to conform to New Construction Notes in Exhibit C1 and Lease Requirements outlined in Exhibit B and B1.

Exhibit C1

New Construction Notes

Initial New Construction: If requested by Lessee, Lessor agrees to construct, in accordance with the New Construction specifications outlined in this Exhibit.

1. WALLS

A. All new interior walls to be taped, bedded, textured and painted. Existing walls to be repainted or cleaned to a like new condition. Color to be selected by tenant.

B. Provide ceramic tiles in Restrooms and Shower Room if applicable.

C. New demising walls shall be full height to structural deck with insulation and fire caulking at all penetrations.

2. FLOORS

A. Provide new anti-static VCT, locations to be determined by Lessee.

B. Provide new building standard commercial grade carpet throughout, subject to Lessee approval unless noted otherwise, color to be approved by Lessee.

C. Provide new 4" rubber cover base throughout, color to be selected by Lessee.

3. CEILING

A. Ceiling grid to be minimum 9'-0" Above Finished Floor (A.F.F.) with new matching 2' x 4' or 2' x 2' ceiling tiles.

4. DOORS & HARDWARE

A. Use building standard doors, frames, and lever hardware throughout.

B. Re-paint or re-finish exterior doors and touch-up to like new condition.

C. All entrance, exit and interior doors to meet ADA/TAS required code.

5. ELECTRICAL

A. Lessor shall provide 120 volt electrical duplex wall outlets as follows: Walls in excess of twenty feet in length will require one every ten feet. A minimum of one in each hallway, hallways in excess of 50 feet in length will require one every 25 feet.

B. Lessor shall provide ring and string for telecommunication and automation station wiring in walls, ceiling or power poles, as applicable. The Lessee anticipates the need for cable drops at every workstation, office and other areas per the room schedule as will be identified during the Construction Documentation preparation phase.

C. Lessee will connect the furniture to the power and data drops.

D. Lessee shall provide cable. Lessor shall provide all necessary raceway, conduit or pathways per code and pull strings as necessary, to accommodate all work stations, offices etc. per Room Schedule.

E. Lessor shall provide conduit from access point on building exterior to the data/telecom IDF closet for telephone lines and data circuits.

F. All branch circuit ground wires must be tied to a common ground at the distribution panel, to a service ground, or suitable building ground. The conduit must not be the sole means of grounding. The system neutral must be electrically isolated from the ground conductor except at the building ground station. All branch circuits shall be on the same primary transformer. All dedicated circuits shall be identifiable by use of orange colored plates on the outlets.

G. Provide adequate electrical for an 8-wire cube for all work stations. Provide j-boxes in the ceiling to feed into power-poles when furniture is not adjacent to a wall or column.

H. Lessor to provide 120-volt electrical duplex outlets: (these are approx. numbers for preliminary bidding)

1. (3) in each Office

2. (4) in each Storage/Break Room

3. (1) in each hallway every 25"

4. (2) in Wait Room

5. (4) in Reception area

6. (1) at each ceiling mounted j-boxes at each exterior door for tenant provided security system.

I. Provide sufficient dedicated quad. outlets @ LAN room to meet Lessee's requirements.

J. Relocate to provide normal office lighting coverage.

K. All electrical panels are to be labeled with circuits identified to all J boxes to be used for power to furniture, equipment, etc.

L. To the extent not covered above Lessor shall provide required electrical service to the furniture and equipment identified by the Lessee during the Construction Documentation phase.

M. Wiring covered by molding carried across open floor will not be permitted.

N. Building to have standard lighting throughout. (2x4 florescent acrylic lenses or Parabolic desired).

6. MECHANICAL

A. All units will be cleaned to eliminate any debris in all ducts.

B. Thermostats to be added or relocated shall be approved as to location by Lessee.

C. Landlord Mechanical Contractor to balance HVAC system if new or redesign, reconfigure and re-balance the existing HVAC system as required and will provide a final report to Lessee.

7. PLUMBING

A. Provide hot and cold water in Break Room(s).

B. Provide grab bars as per ADA/TAS requirements, paper towel dispensers, soap dispensers, trash receptacles, sanitary napkin receptacles and toilet paper dispensers in all restrooms.

8. WINDOW TREATMENT

A. Provide new building standard window treatment if not existing. Provide blinds if there are no building standard window treatments.

B. If existing, clean and or replace damaged blinds and window coverings to like new condition.

9. MILLWORK

A. Provide upper and lower plastic laminate clad cabinets in break rooms.

B. Uppers to have (2) adjustable shelves and lowers to have (1) adjustable shelf.

10. ADA/TAS

A. Provide opening below sinks to meet ADA/TAS.

B. Building must meet all ADA/TAS standards and regulations.

C. See required specs, if applicable, indicated on lease.

11. SECURITY

Lessor shall provide conduit/wire pull to boxes located by Lessee for Lessee security system.

NOTE: Above items are subject to change if noted otherwise on TFC approved Construction Documents.

APPENDIX B

GLOSSARY OF TERMS

Alteration

Remodeling, improving, enlarging, reducing, or making other changes to a facility, exclusive of maintenance repairs. Alteration includes planning, engineering, architectural work, and other similar actions. (US 2011)

ANSI/BOMA Office Area (ABOA)

Standard for measuring space recognized by the government and documented in the American National Standards Institute/Building Owners and Managers Association (ANSI/BOMA) international standard (265.1-1996) definition for office area, also known as ABOA. It is the area where a tenant normally houses personnel and/or furniture, for which a measurement is to be computed. ABOA is computed by measuring the area enclosed by the finished surface of the room side of corridors (corridors in place as well as those required by local codes and ordinances to provide an acceptable level of safety and/or to provide access to essential building elements) and other permanent walls, the inside face of the dominant portion of building exterior walls, and the center of tenant separating partitions. Where alcoves, recessed entrances, or similar deviations from the corridor are present, ABOA square footage is computed as if the deviation were not present. (US 2011)

Appurtenant Areas

Appurtenant areas are defined as those areas and facilities on the property that are not located within the premises, but for which rights are expressly granted under the lease, or for which rights to use are reasonably necessary or reasonably anticipated with respect to the government's enjoyment of the premises and express appurtenant rights. (US 2013)

Architectural Barriers Act Accessibility Standards (ABAAS)

Public buildings service (PBS) accessibility standards under the Architectural Barriers Act (ABA) of 1968. The ABA requires that buildings and facilities designed, built, altered, or leased with federal funds be accessible to persons with disabilities. The United States Access Board develops and maintains accessibility guidelines under the ABA that serve as the basis for the standards used to enforce the ABA. GSA is one of four Federal agencies responsible for the standards. ABAAS comprises ABA chapters 1 and 2 and chapters 3 through 10 of the Americans with Disabilities Act and Architectural Barriers Act Accessibility Guidelines published by the US Access Board on July 23, 2004. (US 2011)

Assignable Purchase Options

A purchase option gives GSA the right to buy a property at some future date. An assignable purchase option allows GSA to transfer this right to a third party (such as a potential lessor). This right allows GSA to select the preferred site in advance, obtain an assignable purchase option on the site, and have all developers bid to construct on the same site. Unless specifically authorized, assignable purchase options must be at "no cost" or nominal consideration. (US 2011)

Automatic Fire Sprinkler System

An electronically supervised, integrated system of underground and overhead piping, designed in accordance with NFPA 13, Standard for the Installation of Sprinkler Systems. The system is usually activated by heat from a fire and discharges water over the fire area. The system includes an adequate water supply. (US 2011)

Base Year
This is the starting year the operating costs and real estate taxes are fixed with any operating or real estate tax increases after this year passed through to the tenant based on this base year. (Scruggs 2016)

Best Value Tradeoff
A source selection method where award is based on the evaluation of price and other nonprice factors to determine the best value to the Government. The tradeoff concept provides the opportunity for a cost/technical trade-off and does not require that an award be made to the offeror submitting the lowest price or to the highest technically rated offer, although the ultimate decision may be to select the lowest priced offer or the highest technically rated offer. The Source Selection Authority (SSA) has the authority to make the cost/technical tradeoffs in a manner consistent with the award methodology stated in an SFO. (US 2011)

Broker
An individual who acts on behalf of another person as an agent to negotiate for the lease, purchase, or sale of office space, buildings, land, or any other real estate. Sellers and lessors will often be represented by a broker, and the government has retained brokers to represent it in some lease procurements. (US 2011)

Building
The building(s) situated on the property in which the premises are located shall be referred to as the building(s). (US 2013)

Building Common Area
The areas of a building that provide services to building tenants but are not included in the occupied area of any specific tenant. These areas typically include (but are not limited to) main and auxiliary lobbies, atrium spaces at the level of the finished floor, concierge stations and security desks, building lounges and vending areas, health and fitness centers, community locker and shower facilities, mail rooms, fire control rooms, fully enclosed courtyards outside the exterior walls, and building core and service areas such as fully enclosed mechanical and equipment rooms. Specifically excluded from building common area are floor common areas, parking space, portions of loading docks outside the building line, and major vertical penetrations. (US 2011)

Building Rentable Area
Equal to the total of all of the Floor Rentable Areas within a building. (US 2011)

Building-Specific Amortized Costs
Generic term generally applied to a government tenant's security improvement costs that are outside the standard tenant improvement costs paid for by the property owner. (Scruggs 2016)

Buildout
The construction of new or relet space in accordance with a tenant's specifications, including configuring (space planning and design), and finishing (construction). (US 2011)

Build-to-Suit Lease
This lease involves construction of a building "to suit" requirement of the tenant agency and may include an option to purchase the building at some point in the lease term. The tenant leases space, usually as a sole tenant, at a rental rate based upon market competition. The tenant participates in limited development decisions for the building shell and common areas. The lease rate includes the owner's construction costs, developer profit, tax obligation, and interest. (CA 2009)

Central Business Area (CBA)
The centralized community business area and adjacent areas of similar character, including other specific areas that may be recommended by local officials in accordance with Executive Order 12072. CBAs are designated by local government and not by federal agencies. Also sometimes referred to as the central business district (CBD) or central enterprise area (CEA). (US 2011)

Certificate of Occupancy (C of O)
A certificate issued by a local government stating that a building and/or a tenant suite is in a condition suitable for occupancy, sometimes called an Occupancy Permit. A certificate of occupancy is essential and required for PBS acceptance of space, but it is not in itself sufficient for that purpose. The certificate of oc-

cupancy verifies that the space meets local legal and code requirements, but it does not verify compliance with the lease. If the local jurisdiction does not issue a Certificate of Occupancy, then the lessor must obtain the services of a licensed fire protection engineer to verify that the offered space meets all applicable local codes and ordinances to ensure that an acceptable level of safety is provided. (US 2011)

Co-Locate
This term refers to locating two or more independent office groups together in the same building. The office groups would typically have one or more similar office characteristics, such as benefiting a similar clientele, servicing a similar geographic area, or having compatible functions that may lead to sharing service areas, employee areas, or meeting rooms. (CA 2009)

Commission Credit
If GSA awarded this Lease using a broker, and the broker agreed to forgo a percentage of its commission to which it is entitled in connection with the award of the lease, the amount of this credit is referred to as the commission credit. (US 2013)

Common Area Factor (CAF)
The common area factor (CAF) is a conversion factor determined by the building owner and applied by the owner to the ABOA SF to determine the RSF for the leased space. The CAF is expressed as a percentage of the difference between the amount of rentable SF and ABOA SF, divided by the ABOA SF. For example 11,500 RSF and 10,000 ABOA SF will have a CAF of 15% [(11,500 RSF-10,000 ABOA SF)/10,000 ABOA SF]. For the purposes of the lease, the CAF shall be determined in accordance with the applicable ANSI/BOMA standard for the type of space to which the CAF shall apply. (US 2013)

Comparables
Examples of executed leases demonstrating characteristic lease terms available in the market. Comparables are used for analyzing the relative value of a proposed lease by comparing its characteristics to those of executed leases for similar competing space. (US 2011)

Competition in Contracting Act (CICA)
A federal statute (41 USC. § 251 et seq.) enacted to encourage competition in the award of all types of government contracts. Its purpose is to increase the number of competitors and to increase savings through lower, more competitive pricing. It requires contracting officers to provide for full and open competition by using one or more competitive procedures identified in the act. Deviations from full and open competition must be documented in writing and authorized by the appropriate government official. (US 2011)

Competitive Range
Once the general evaluations of a lease offer are completed the GLC will typically proceed to preparing an abstract of all the lease offers received for a given lease transaction to give the GLC an idea of the range of rental rates and responses to the RLP technical factors submitted by the property owners for the lease proposal process. The competitive range can also include market rental rates that are included in the analysis for properties that are not being submitted as part of the lease proposal process. (Scruggs 2016)

Competitive Solicitation
An invitation to bid (ITB), invitation to negotiate (ITN), or request for proposal (RFP) must be used to procure a private lease over 5,000 square feet. DMS requires each agency to justify which type of solicitation is used to best meet the needs of the department. (FL 2009)

Consolidatable
State agency offices that may be located with other agency offices in a joint-use office facility where the agencies have no unique program or client requirement or facility needs. (CA 2009)

Consolidation Lease
"Consolidation lease" refers to a consolidation of space requirements from different locations (i.e., federal and/or leased locations) into a single lease space requirement. (US 2011)

Consumer Price Index (CPI)
The measurement of change in the prices paid for a basket of consumer goods and services over a period of time. (Scruggs 2016)

Contract
Contract and contractor mean lease and lessor, respectively. (US 2013)

Contracting Officer's Representative (COR)
A qualified individual appointed by the lease contracting officer to assist in the technical monitoring or administration of a contract. A COR must be a government employee and possess the necessary qualifications (training) and experience commensurate with the responsibilities delegated to him or her. A COR can be a GSA employee or someone selected and nominated by the client agency and then formally appointed to the contract by the lease contracting officer. Also known as a contracting officer's technical representative (COTR). Designations of CORs must be in writing and enumerate the specific authorities being delegated. (US 2011)

Core Factor
Synonym for common area factor. (US 2011)

Cost-Benefit Analysis
A comparative analysis of the anticipated cost differential of remaining in place compared to moving to another space. The cost-benefit analysis includes anticipated market rates, moving costs, as well as costs to reproduce or build out the space and infrastructure to meet the tenant agency's mission. This analysis, which demonstrates whether the overall cost to the government is greater or lesser than the cost of remaining at the current location, provides the foundation for an OFOC used to justify a succeeding lease. (US 2011)

Covenant of Quiet Enjoyment
Landlord covenants and agrees that tenant, upon paying the rent and upon observing and keeping the covenants, agreements, and conditions of the lease on its part to be kept, observed, and performed, shall lawfully and quietly hold, occupy and enjoy the premises (subject to the provisions of the Lease) during the term without hindrance or molestation by landlord or by any person or persons claiming to be under the landlord. (CH 2015)

Critical Path Method
A project management method where there are several activities needed to complete a project schedule, with some activities needing to be completed before other activities can start. (Scruggs 2016)

Customer Workplace Standards
Customer agency guidelines, regulations, and policies that address the allocation or construction of the customer's physical work environment. It often includes space allocation standards, utilization rate guidelines, support space recommendations, and special build-out requirements that would be followed during construction. In some cases, it also includes performance standards that the workspace must meet. (US 2011)

Davis-Bacon Act of 1931
A federal statute governing wages paid under federal contracts. Under the provisions of the act, contractors or their subcontractors must pay on-site workers no less than the locally prevailing wages and fringe benefits paid on projects of a similar character. Lease contracting officers are to include the *Labor Standards* paragraph in lease solicitations when the delivery schedules are long enough to permit satisfaction of the requirements through construction of a building. If an offeror proposes to satisfy the requirements through new construction or the complete rehabilitation or reconstruction of an existing building, and where the government is the sole or predominant tenant of the facility, various FAR clauses implementing the Davis-Bacon Act will apply to the base build out and tenant improvement work. Davis-Bacon provisions are incorporated into all leases involving new construction. (US 2011)

Days
All references to "day" or "days" in the lease shall mean calendar days, unless specified otherwise. (US 2013)

Delineated Area
The specific boundaries within which space will be obtained to satisfy an agency space requirement. The delineated area for each lease procurement is defined by specific geographic boundaries. (US 2011)

Design Intent Drawings (DIDs)
Fully dimensioned drawings of leased space that consist of enough information to prepare construction

drawings for the space including: (1) furniture, wall, door, and built-in millwork locations; telephone, electrical, and data outlet types and locations; and repositioned sprinklers, ceilings, and lighting, where affected; (2) specifications necessary for calculation of electrical and HVAC loads; and (3) all finish and signage selections. DIDs do not contain mechanical, electrical, or plumbing specifications or drawings. They do not carry furniture or computer and telecommunication specifications, nor do they contain signage, artwork, keying, or hardware schedules. (US 2011)

Distributive Negotiations
Also known as "*The fixed pie*" or "*Win-Lose*" negotiations. In this type of negotiation there's typically a fixed amount of resources available to both parties, which creates an environment where there is a lot of haggling with one side usually having the advantage over the other. (Scruggs 2016)

Dual Agency
Offerors are advised that there is a potential for a dual agency situation to arise under this procurement, whereby the Broker may represent both GSA and another Offeror under this lease action. By submitting an offer, the offeror acknowledges the potential for a dual agency situation. Should there be an actual dual agency, the broker will notify all offerors of the actual dual agency and request written acknowledgement statements from all offerors. (US 2013)

Effective Date (Lease)
The effective date of the lease is the date when the terms and conditions of the lease contract become binding on the lessor and the government. For some purposes, different GSA practices over the years have also interpreted it to mean the day the government begins paying rent or the start date for tenant agency occupancy. Leasing specialists must be cognizant and careful of the different applications of the term. (US 2011)

Emergency Acquired Lease
If an existing state-owned or -leased facility is destroyed or rendered uninhabitable by an act of God, fire, malicious destruction, or structural failure or by legal action, Section 255.25 (10), F.S. enables agencies to request DMS approval to obtain leased space noncompetitively. In addition, under the *Emergency Management Powers of the Governor,* Section 252.36 (5)(a), F.S. allows for the governor to waive any statutory or rule requirement normally applicable to the leasing program. (FL 2009)

Energy Performance Index (EPI)
A number describing the energy requirements at the building boundary of a facility, per square foot of floor space or per cubic foot of occupied volume, as appropriate under defined internal and external ambient conditions over an entire seasonal cycle. The EPI serves as a measure of building performance with respect to energy consumption. (FL 2009)

Energy Star
A joint program of the US Environmental Protection Agency and the US Department of Energy introduced in 1992 to promote energy efficiency. It administers a voluntary labeling program designed to identify and promote energy-efficient products to reduce greenhouse gas emissions. The Energy Star label appears on more than 60 product categories, including major appliances, office equipment, lighting, home electronics, new homes, and commercial and industrial buildings. (US 2011)

Equivalent Level of Safety
An alternative design or system (which may include automatic fire sprinkler systems), based upon fire protection engineering analysis, that achieves a level of safety equal to or greater than that provided by automatic fire sprinkler systems. (US 2011)

Escalation
An increase in rent during the lease term specified in the lease contract. The escalation may be a periodic fixed increase, tied to a government cost of living index or calculated as an adjustment based on changes in expenses paid by the landlord (tax increases, increased maintenance costs, etc.). (US 2011)

Executive Orders
Official documents, numbered consecutively, through which the President of the United States manages the operations of the executive branch of the government. (US 2011)

Extension (Lease)
Extension of the expiration date of a lease to provide for continued occupancy on a short-term basis, with substantially the same terms and conditions. An extension is generally executed when there are evolving agency requirements, delays in delivery of a New or Replacing lease, or delays in a move to other federally controlled space. (US 2011)

FAR/GSAR
All references to the FAR shall be understood to mean the Federal Acquisition Regulation, codified at 48 CFR Chapter 1. All references to the GSAR shall be understood to mean the GSA supplement to the FAR, codified at 48 CFR Chapter 5. (US 2013)

FedBizOpps or Federal Business Opportunities (FBO)
Web-based portal that allows vendors to review Federal procurement opportunities over $25,000. It is designed as a single point of entry for federal buyers to publish and for vendors to find posted federal business opportunities across departments and agencies. Operation and maintenance of the FBO system and website is managed by the GSA Office of Acquisition Systems (OAS). As outlined under GSAM 505.101(c), FBO is used to publicize potential leasehold procurements in lieu of, or in conjunction with, newspaper advertisements. (US 2011)

Federal Acquisition Regulation (FAR)
Codification of uniform policies for acquisition of supplies and services by executive agencies. The official FAR appears in the Code of Federal Regulations at 48 CFR Chapter 1. It is issued and maintained jointly under the statutory authorities granted to the Secretary of Defense, Administrator of General Services, and the Administrator of the National Aeronautics and Space Administration. Statutory authorities to issue and revise the FAR have been delegated to the procurement executives in DOD, GSA, and NASA. The GSA FAR Secretariat publishes the FAR on behalf of all three FAR issuing agencies. (US 2011)

Federal Government
The government of the United States of America. (US 2011)

Federal Management Regulation (FMR)
Subchapter C (parts 102-71 to 102-84) contains the scope and philosophy of GSA's real property policies as they apply to Federal agencies (including PBS) operating under, or subject to, the authorities of the Administrator of General Services. These policies cover the acquisition, management, utilization, and disposal of real property by federal agencies that initiate and have decision-making authority over actions for real property services. This Desk Guide is the procedural guide for operating within the structures of the FMR. (US 2011)

Final Proposal Revisions (FPRs)
Last opportunity for offerors to revise their proposals before award. Previously known as "best and final offer." At the conclusion of discussions, each offeror still in the competitive range is given an opportunity to submit a final proposal revision. The lease contracting officer is required to establish a common cut-off date only for receipt of final proposal revisions, not necessarily for each round of negotiations.

Requests for final proposal revisions should advise offerors that the final proposal revisions must be in writing and that the government intends to make award without obtaining further revisions. After an offeror submits its final proposal revision, no further negotiations are allowed—only clarifications to achieve an accurate understanding are permitted. (US 2011)

Firm Term/Non-Firm Term
The firm term is that part of the lease term that is not subject to termination rights. The non–firm term is that part of the lease term following the end of the firm term. (US 2013)

Fiscal Year
For the federal government, the fiscal year begins on October 1 of each calendar year and ends 12 months later on the following September 30, e.g., Fiscal Year 2011 began October 1, 2010, and ended September 30, 2011. (US 2011)

Floor Common Area
Refers to the area on a floor such as washrooms, janitorial closets, electrical rooms, telephone rooms,

mechanical rooms, elevator lobbies, and public corridors that are available primarily for the use of tenants on that floor. (US 2011)

Floor Common Area Factor
Refers to the conversion factor, that when applied to ANSI/BOMA office (or store) area or building common area, gives the basic rentable area of the office, storage, or building common area. (US 2011)

Floor Rentable Area
Refers to the result of subtracting from the gross measured area of a floor the major vertical penetrations on that same floor. It is usually permanently fixed and rarely changes as a result of changes in corridor size or configuration. (US 2011)

Full Service Lease
The landlord pays for the tenant's share of the cost of operating expenses, including direct and common area utilities, taxes, insurance, maintenance, landscaping, and repairs to the leased premises. These operating expenses are paid for by the tenant and included in the rental payment as part of "full service" rent in the first year of the lease term (the base year). In subsequent years, the tenant's share of operating expense exceeding the tenant's share of operating expense in the base year may be passed through to the tenants. (CA 2009)

GC
General contractor. (Scruggs 2016)

Generation Space
Generic term to identify the age of improvements in a space from when the property was constructed or last renovated. First generation space indicates that no major renovations have occurred since the property was constructed or underwent its last major renovation. (Scruggs 2016)

GLC
Government lease contact. (Scruggs 2016)

Gross Absorption
Total leasing and user sale activity in the marketplace in a given period. (CA 2009)

Gross Building Area
Refers to the total constructed area of a building and is generally not used for leasing purposes. (US 2011)

Gross Lease
A lease that includes all the tenant improvement and operating costs be paid for by the property owner. (Scruggs 2016)

Gross Square Feet (GSF)
The total amount of floor space within the exterior building shell of a building. GSF is calculated by combining the tenant's usable square feet with all other use of space including the outside perimeter wall of the building. This includes stairwells, restrooms, public corridors, elevators, lobbies, duct shafts, equipment rooms, and wall thicknesses. (CA 2009)

Hazardous Areas
Those areas in a building referred to as hazardous areas in NFPA 101, Life Safety Code, or any successor standard. Examples include areas used for the storage of combustibles or flammables; toxic, noxious, or corrosive materials; and heat-producing appliances. (US 2011)

High-Rise Building
A building greater than 75 feet in height, where the building height is measured from the lowest level of fire department vehicle access to the floor of the highest occupied floor (IBC 2009 or NFPA 101 2009). A building that is six stories or more in height is typically considered a high-rise building. (US 2011)

Historic District
A geographically definable area, urban or rural, possessing a significant concentration, linkage, or continuity of sites, buildings, structures, or objects united by past events or aesthetically by plan or physical development. A district may also comprise individual elements separated geographically but linked by association or history (36 CFR 60.3(d)). The historic district must be included in or be determined eligible for inclusion in the National Register of Historic Places. (US 2011)

Historic Property
Any prehistoric or historic district, site, building, structure, or object included in or determined eligible for inclusion in the National Register of Historic Places maintained by the Secretary of the Interior (36 CFR 800.16(1)). (US 2011)

Holdover
Retaining possession of leased space after the lease expiration or termination date. (US 2011)

Hoteling
The temporary leasing of a small block or blocks of space in a shared office arrangement, typically for use by an agency as swing space or for emergencies or special projects. A hoteling lease contains all the basic, generic features of a typical fully serviced office lease with standard operational services and it typically includes expanded services and amenities such as the use of office furniture, phone instruments, phone service, computers, Internet access, conference rooms, break rooms, and security. (US 2011)

Independent Government Estimate (IGE)
An internal PBS document estimating an appraisal and pricing of a lease or other contract for goods or services. It is typically used as a reference point for comparison when examining tenant build-out costs. (US 2011)

Independent Market Analysis
An analysis to determine current market rates for a particular location. (FL 2009)

Integrative Negotiations
Also known as *"Win-Win"* negotiations, involves both parties seeking to integrate the goals and aims of both parties into the negotiation process. (Scruggs 2016)

Justification for Other than Full and Open Competition (Justification or OTFO)
Document that justifies proceeding with a lease action without providing full and open competition, such as a sole-source contract, or a contract resulting from an unsolicited proposal. (US 2011)

Leadership in Energy and Environmental Design (LEED)
A green building certification system, developed by the private sector, nonprofit entity known as the US Green Building Council, to provide third-party verification that a building or community uses strategies to improve performance across metrics such as energy savings, water efficiency, CO_2 emissions reduction, improved indoor environmental quality, and stewardship of resources. LEED helps building owners and operators identify solutions for green building design, construction, operations, and maintenance. The system can be applied to both commercial and residential buildings and throughout the building life cycle (design and construction, operations and maintenance, tenant build-out, and retrofit alterations). (US 2011)

Lease Actions
This term refers to any of the following: a new lease whether it is competitively solicited or not; a modification to an existing lease, such as changing the description, increasing or decreasing square footage, changing the effective date or term or extending the term on a month-to-month basis; a renewal of an existing lease; a reassignment of a lease; an emergency acquired lease; or a lease cancellation. (FL 2009)

Lease Acquisition
The acquisition by lease of an interest in real property for use by the government, whether the space already exists or must be constructed. (US 2011)

Lease Award Date
The Lease award date is the date of execution of the lease by the LCO and the mailing or otherwise furnishing written notification of the executed lease to the successful offeror (and on which the parties' obligations under the lease begin). (US 2013)

Lease Buyouts
A lease buyout occurs when the property owner and the GLC terminate a real estate lease based on some form of payment or compensation made to the property owner by the GLC. The lease buyout by the GLC may include incentives beyond monetary payment to the property owner. (Scruggs 2016)

Lease Construction
Government-planned/government-required new construction of a building resulting from a lease solicitation. Lease construction occurs when the government requires a new construction solution to satisfy an agency's space requirements. Lease construction can also occur as a result of a solicitation for leased space that does not specify construction. (US 2011)

Lease Contracting Officer (LCO)
An individual holding a valid government-issued warrant providing authority to enter into and administer leases on the government's behalf. The lease contracting officer's job classification is GS-1170, Realty Specialist. (US 2011)

Lease Coordinator
In the Central Office, the designated individual in the Support Services Office responsible for processing lease actions. The district secretary is responsible for designating the lease coordinator in the district. (FL 2009)

Lease Cost Relative to Market (LCRM)
A measure that compares the PBS cost of leased space with comparable private commercial asking rates to determine whether PBS negotiates competitive rates for its leases. (US 2011)

Leasehold Improvements
Generally defined as improvements made to the leased space paid for by the tenant. (Scruggs 2016)

Lease in Dispersed Lease Space
The state leases space at the current market rental rates in buildings not owned by the state, with no prospects of ownership. The state participates only in the design of the leased premises (net square feet occupied by the state agency). (CA 2009)

Lease Term Commencement Date
The Lease Term Commencement Date means the date on which the lease term commences. (US 2013)

Leasing Specialist (LS)
PBS personnel (classified GS-1170, Realty Specialist) who assist lease contracting officers and may perform all duties that do not legally obligate the government. (US 2011)

Lessee
The entity that enters into a contract with the lessor. In all PBS leases, the United States acting by and through the US General Services Administration (GSA) is the lessee. The tenant is the occupant agency or other entity so designated by the lessee. (US 2011)

Lessor
Any individual, firm, partnership, limited liability company, trust, association, state or local government, or legal entity that is the rightful owner of the property leased to the federal government. Synonym for landlord. (US 2011)

Local Serving Agencies
Agencies providing service to a specific city or neighborhood. (CA 2009)

Lowest and Best Responsive Quote
A response that is responsive, cost-effective, and best meets the requirements of the department. (FL 2009)

Lowest Price Technically Acceptable (LPTA)
Source selection approach in which award is made to the offeror presenting the lowest priced offer that is technically acceptable (meets the government's minimum requirements). (US 2011)

Low-Rise Building
A building equal to or less than 75 feet in height where the building height is measured from the lowest level of fire department vehicle access to the highest occupied floor (IBC 2009 or NFPA 101 2009). A building that is five stories or less in height is typically considered a low-rise building. (US 2011)

Major Vertical Penetrations
Refers to stairs, elevator shafts, flues, pipe shafts, vertical ducts, and similar building penetrations and their enclosing walls. Atria, light wells, and similar penetrations above the finished floor are included. Excluded are vertical penetrations for the private use of a tenant occupying office areas on more than one floor, as well as structural columns, openings for vertical electric cable or telephone distribution, and openings for plumbing lines. Vertical penetrations are not considered part of a building's rentable area. (US 2011)

Market Research
Any methodical effort to gather information about the market or customers in order to gain insight or improve business decisions. It may involve consulting commercial databases, real estate brokers, and other sources of expertise. It may or may not involve directly contacting commercial lessors. Market research generates useful information for setting negotiation objectives by helping to identify ranges of fair and reasonable costs for the type of space desired. (US 2011)

Market Survey
A mechanism for gathering information about and visiting specific properties in the market to determine whether suitable property is competitively available and how to satisfy a lease requirement in the most competitive manner. Market surveys must not be used to target a single specific property to lease. The characteristics of each building inspected for a market survey must be documented. (US 2011)

Memorandum of Agreement (MOA)
A document that records an understanding of parties to cooperatively work together on an agreed-upon project or meet an agreed objective. It outlines the terms of the parties to work in partnership and lists their agreed responsibilities. It is not intended to be a legally enforceable contract. (US 2011)

Memorandum of Understanding (MOU)
A document confirming agreed-upon terms, indicating an intended common line of action, and setting forth the basic principles and guidelines under which the parties will work together to accomplish their goals. It is not intended to be a legally enforceable contract. (US 2011)

Minimum Loss Strategy
A strategy to negotiate a lease where the property owner loses the least amount on the lease rents and project costs. (Scruggs 2016)

Mold (Actionable)
Actionable mold is mold of types and concentrations in excess of that found in the local outdoor air. (US 2013)

National Register of Historic Places
A formally authorized list of districts, sites, buildings, structures, and objects that are judged significant in American history, architecture, archeology, engineering, and culture. The Secretary of the Interior is authorized to expand and maintain the National Register of Historic Places under the National Historic Preservation Act (36 CFR 60.1). (US 2011)

Negotiation Bias
A positive, neutral, or negative response or action from one or both parties to a negotiation. (Scruggs 2016)

Negotiation Goals
These are the long-term results that the parties to negotiations are looking to achieve. (Scruggs 2016)

Negotiation Objectives

These are typically short-term steps taken to reach the various goals of the negotiations. (Scruggs 2016)

Negotiation Strategy
These are the processes or steps taken by parties to a negotiation to reach the negotiation goals. (Scruggs 2016)

Negotiation Tactics
These are the typically steps taken to implement a negotiation strategy during negotiations. (Scruggs 2016)

Negotiation Vacuum
The process by which one party to the negotiation does not share information with the other party or parties to a negotiation. (Scruggs 2016)

Net Absorption
The change in occupied square feet from one period to the next. (CA 2009)

Net Annual Rent
Net annual rent is calculated by excluding only lessor-supplied services and utilities from the gross rent paid to the lessor. (US 2011)

Net Square Feet (NSF)
The modified Building Owner Managers Association calculation of the actual square feet required for each agency, including interior circulation. (CA 2009)

New or Replacing Lease
A lease with new terms and conditions and a new lease contract number, applicable for either a new requirement or for the replacement of an existing expiring lease. (US 2011)

Non-Consolidatable
Space that cannot be housed in a multitenant facility in an urban setting. Non-consolidatable state functions typically have special needs for security, freeway access, public access, or facility design. Spaces typically considered non-consolidatable include field offices of the CHP, DMV, and EDD, as well as parole offices of the Department of Corrections. For example, Unemployment Insurance and Job Services Offices of EDD are typically considered non-consolidatable because they generate excessive pedestrian and vehicular traffic and serve clients in specific geographic areas. It should be noted that some offices categorized as non-consolidatable might be appropriate tenants of a service center in a suburban location where extensive public parking can be more easily provided. (CA 2009)

Non-Priced Evaluation Factor
An evaluation factor other than price used by the government to select awardees, normally in best value trade-off procurements, where award is based on the best value to the government after considering price and technical (non-priced) evaluation factors. Also referred to as an award factor. (US 2011)

North American Industry Classification System (NAICS)
NAICS is the standard used by federal statistical agencies in classifying business establishments for the purpose of collecting, analyzing, and publishing statistical data related to the US business economy. The NAICS code for GSA leasing is 531190. (US 2011)

Notice to Proceed (NTP)
Notification to a contractor by the lease contracting officer that the contractor can begin work subject to the conditions of the contract. The notice is given in writing and binds the government contractually. The performance time of the contract starts from the NTP date. The notice to proceed for tenant improvements can be granted if competition for the construction contract award is deemed adequate; the lessor's cost proposal is accepted (it is based on the lowest bid by a qualified contractor); final DIDs are approved, and all COs are completed; and funds are available via a signed occupancy agreement, adequate BA 53 fund certification, and/or Reimbursable Work Authorization. (US 2011)

Offer Cost Review
The GLC evaluates the lease offer on the basis of how the individual costs elements make up the total lease costs. (Scruggs 2016)

Offeror
A party providing a response to a request for proposal (RLP) document. (Scruggs 2016)

Office Area
For the purposes of the lease, Space is measured in accordance with the standard (Z65.1-1996) provided by American National Standards Institute/Building Owners and Managers Association (ANSI/BOMA) for office area, which means "the area where a tenant normally houses personnel and/or furniture, for which a measurement is to be computed." References to ABOA mean ANSI/BOMA office area. (US 2013)

Open Listing
An open listing is usually a listing agreement with one or more real estate brokers on a nonexclusive basis. Agents who are successful in leasing a property under this type of listing are generally entitled to a commission. Open listings are more common in some regions of the US, while other regions may not allow it or its practice is not commonly used or is discouraged. (Scruggs 2016)

Operating Costs
The portion of leasehold rent associated with the services, maintenance, utilities, and other operating expenses being provided by the lessor. This figure, also referred to in the SFO as the base rate, is used as the basis for calculating future CPI escalations. (US 2011)

Operational Services
Services that support use of a leased property, such as heating, ventilation, air conditioning, utilities, cus-

todial services, landscaping, pest control, and snow removal. (US 2011)

Optimal Pricing Strategy (OPS)
This strategy requires the property owner to identify an optimal price lease rental rate and not go below it, if possible as part of their lease negotiations with the GLC. (Scruggs 2016)

Optimal Rental Rate
The rental rate set by a property owner after determining and accounting for all the fixed and variable lease costs. (Scruggs 2016)

PBS
Refers to the Public Buildings Service, a branch of GSA (see GSA) that acquires, disposes of, and manages the federal government's real estate (buildings, land, real property interests including leases). (US 2011)

Premises
The premises are defined as the total office area or other type of space, together with all associated common areas. Parking and other areas to which the government has rights under the lease are not included in the premises. (US 2013)

Present Value Analysis (PVA)
Analytical method for comparing rent streams among offers to determine the lowest offer. The present value amount provides a single cost representation of various rent streams, variations in operating costs, lump sum payments, and amortizations that allows the government to understand the true price of all offers in today's (present value) dollars. The PVA is calculated on a per square foot basis, using the ANSI/BOMA office area. The leasing specialist and broker contractor should always use the eLease PVA calculator to create a permanent record within eLease of the offers received in response to a solicitation. (US 2011)

Price Analysis
The GLC compares the property owner's lease rental rates to something external to the lease offer. This is usually done via the competitive range of rental rates in the local real estate market or the range of lease rental rates from the multiple offers received from the market. (Scruggs 2016)

Price Negotiation Memorandum (PNM)
A document describing the principal cost elements of a negotiated lease agreement, including documentation of fair and reasonable pricing. The lease contracting officer must include the PNM in the contract file. (US 2011)

Price Negotiation Objectives
Objectives that establish the government's initial and subsequent negotiation position. They assist in the lease contracting officer's determination of fair and reasonable price. (US 2011)

Private-Sector Building
Any building not owned by a governmental agency. (FL 2009)

Pro Forma
A financial estimate of the gross and net income and expenses expected in a new or renovated office building (or any real estate investment venture). (US 2011)

Property
The property is defined as the land and buildings in which the premises are located, including all appurtenant areas (e.g., parking areas) to which the government is granted rights. (US 2013)

Punch List
An itemized list of work to be completed or corrected by the lessor after substantial completion of the build-out/alterations to the space. (US 2011)

Radon
Radon is a colorless, odorless radioactive gas that seeps up from the earth. When inhaled, it gives off radioactive particles that can damage the cells that line the lung. (Scruggs 2016)

Regional Serving Agency
For the purposes of this study, a regional serving agency is one that administers a state program for a service area that includes all five counties in the Bay Area Region. (CA 2009)

Renewal Option
The right, but not the obligation of the government to continue a lease upon specified terms and conditions, including lease term and rent. (US 2011)

Rent and Related Services
The consideration paid for the use of leased property, plus the costs of operational services furnished by the lessor, the government, or both. (US 2011)

Rentable Area
Rentable area is the area for which a tenant is charged rent. It is determined by the building owner and may vary by city or by building within the same city. The rentable space may include a share of building support/common areas such as elevator lobbies, building corridors, and floor service areas. Floor service areas typically include restrooms, janitor rooms, telephone closets, electrical closets, and mechanical rooms. The rentable space does not include vertical building penetrations and their enclosing walls, such as stairs, elevator shafts, and vertical ducts. (US 2011)

Rentable Space or Rentable Square Feet (RSF)
Rentable space is the area for which a tenant is charged rent. It is determined by the building owner and may vary by city or by building within the same city. The rentable space may include a share of building support/common areas such as elevator lobbies, building corridors, and floor service areas. Floor service areas typically include restrooms, janitor rooms, telephone closets, electrical closets, and mechanical rooms. The rentable space does not include vertical building penetrations and their enclosing walls, such as stairs, elevator shafts, and vertical ducts. Rentable square feet is calculated using the following formula for each type of space (e.g., office, warehouse, etc.) included in the premises: ABOA SF of Space x (1 + CAF) = RSF. (US 2013)

Repairs for Emergencies
In the event of an emergency where further delay would lead to material loss or significant damage to the premises or the property occupied by other tenants of landlord and where such emergency is caused by the negligence, vandalism, or misuse of the premises or equipment therein by tenant's employees, invitees, agents, or contractors, landlord may make such emergency repairs subject to full reimbursement to landlord by tenant of costs associated with such emergency repairs excluding any overhead and/or profit. (CH 2015)

Requesting Office
The office submitting a request for a lease action. (FL 2009)

Responsive
Any response that meets all specific criteria established by the requesting office. (FL 2009)

Rural Areas
As defined in 7 USC 1991(a)(13)(A), "any area other than: (a) A city or town that has a population of greater than 50,000 inhabitants; and (b) The urbanized area contiguous and adjacent to such a city or town." (US 2011)

Scoring
Federal government method for distinguishing between capital expenditures and operating expenditures for budget purposes. Capital expenditures are expenditures that are equivalent to the purchase of a capital asset, or fixed asset (such as a building). Operating expenditures represent costs that keep the government operating (such as leases that do not result in the government assuming the risks of ownership or that do not result in the Government ownership of the leased asset). Budgeting for capital leases and operating leases is accounted for differently; therefore, proper classification of leases is important to the government's budgetary process (OMB Circular A-11 applies). The circular is available at the Office of Management and Budget (OMB) website, www.whitehouse.gov. Each lease acquisition is reviewed by the government during the lease acquisition process to verify that the lease is an operating lease and not scored as a capital lease. Depending upon project parameters, scoring may be performed at project initiation, and/or as part of evaluation of final offers. (US 2011)

Shell (Building Shell)
The complete enveloping structure, the base-building systems, and the finished common areas (building common and floor common) of a building that

bound the tenant areas. The completed building shell is the beginning point for tenant improvements. The lease solicitation for offers (SFO) contains a complete shell definition in its entirety. (US 2011)

Sole-Source Lease Acquisition
A lease that is entered into or proposed to be entered into after receiving authorization of a justification for other than full and open competition (OTFO) with only one source. An OTFO is not required if the requirement is made known to the public through a full and open ad, solicitations for offers are available to all interested sources, and all responsible sources are permitted to compete. (US 2011)

Solicitation for Offers (SFO)
A document used to solicit offers for a lease acquisition. The SFO describes government requirements and performance criteria against which a lessor is expected to perform and the evaluation criteria that the government will use to evaluate offers. (US 2011)

Source Selection
The processes and techniques for selecting a source or sources outlined in GSAM part 570. These include both the lowest-priced technically acceptable (LPTA) process and the best value tradeoff process. The objective of source selection is to select the proposal that represents the best value to the government. (US 2011)

Space
The space refers to that part of the premises to which the government has exclusive use, such as Office Area, or other type of space. Parking areas to which the government has rights under the Lease are not included in the space. (US 2013)

Special Requirements
Requirements of the tenant agency that exceed improvements required for standard office space. Examples include security enhancements, LAN wiring specifications, increased HVAC requirements, and other similar requirements. (US 2011)

State-Owned Facility
Any building to which title is vested in the state or a state agency. (FL 2009)

Suboptimal Pricing Strategy
This strategy is used by property owners when they price the rental rates and project costs without having a full understanding of what these costs and rates entail. (Scruggs 2016)

Suboptimal Rental Rate
The rental rate that is not fully developed or understood by the property owner who is proposing the rental rate as part of their offer to lease space to the GLC. (Scruggs 2016)

Substantially Complete
The condition of space in which all work necessary for the government's access, occupancy, use, and enjoyment has been completed, except for minor matters that don't interfere with access, occupancy, use, or enjoyment. If the space cannot be used for its intended purpose and cannot deliver its intended benefits, then it is not substantially complete and PBS may not accept the space. (US 2011)

Succeeding Lease
A noncompetitive (sole source) lease acquisition secured to cover continued occupancy of the current premises at the end of a lease term without a break in tenancy. It establishes new terms and conditions and has a new lease contract number. A succeeding lease is generally used where acceptable new locations are not identified, or else are identified but a cost-benefit analysis indicates that an award to an offeror other than the current lessor will result in substantial relocation costs or duplication of costs to the government, and the government cannot expect to recover such costs through competition. (US 2011)

Superseding Lease
A new lease that replaces an existing lease prior to expiration. It is procured following noncompetitive sole-source procedures. It establishes new terms and conditions and has a new lease contract number. The government considers executing a superseding lease to replace an existing lease when the government needs numerous or detailed modifications to a space that would cause complications or substantially change the existing lease. A superseding lease should be considered where market rates have changed substantially. (US 2011)

Supplemental Lease Agreement (SLA)
Document used to change or modify an existing lease, such as for acquisition of additional space, partial release of space, revision in terms or rental payments, change in ownership or payee, or any other action that changes the lease. The SLA is documented on GSA form 276, Supplemental Lease Agreement. (US 2011)

Sustainable Building Rating
A rating established by the United States Green Building Council (USGBC) Leadership in Energy and Environmental Design (LEED) rating system, the Green Building Initiative's Green Globes rating system, the Florida Green Building Coalition standards, Energy Star, or a nationally recognized, high-performance green building rating system as approved by the department. (FL 2009)

Swing Space
Temporary space for personnel who must be moved out of their leased space during renovation or alterations. (US 2011)

Technical Analysis
The GLC compares the property owner's lease offer to the specifications and requirements in the lease in addition to the non-price-related award factors in the lease. (Scruggs 2016)

Tenant Agency
The tenant agency is the government tenant leasing the space from the private-sector property owner. There may be instances where the tenant agency is a subtenant to the primary holder of the lease with the property owner; this arrangement is common for leases with the US GSA whereby the US GSA holds the master lease with the property owner with the US GSA in turn subleasing the leased space to another US government agency such as the US Social Security Administration under a separate agreement. (Scruggs 2016)

Tenant Broker
A DMS state term contract representative contracted to negotiate leases. (FL 2009)

Tenant Improvements (TIs)
The finishes and fixtures that transform space from its shell condition to a finished, usable condition. A tenant improvement allowance provided by the building owner is the funding source that enables the space to be fitted out for occupancy to meet a customer agency's specific requirements. (US 2011)

Tenant Services Substitution
In the event that the landlord does not provide timely services as required under the lease, the tenant may elect to provide such services at tenant's cost. In such event the tenant shall deduct tenant's costs of such services from the rent due. (CH 2015)

Test Fit
A dimensioned drawing or floor plan created by a property owner or architect to determine if a government tenant's lease requirements can fit into the proposed leased space. (Scruggs 2016)

TICS
Tenant Improvement Cost Summary. (Scruggs 2016)

Unauthorized Improvements
Any improvements to the premises effectuated by the landlord on the tenant's behalf shall only be performed upon written approval and concurrent Notice to Proceed from the Commissioner of the Department of Fleet and Facility Management. Approval from any other city department(s), or anyone acting, or claiming to act, on the tenant's behalf shall be deemed invalid and of no force or effect. (CH 2015)

Unique Requirement
Requirement listed in the Unique Requirements paragraph of the solicitation for offers (SFO), describing features that a building or location must have to adequately accommodate the agency's requirements. Examples would be prescribing a certain floor location (e.g., above the first floor) or proximity to public transportation stops (e.g., within two blocks of XYZ metro line). (US 2011)

Variable Lease Costs
Variable lease costs are the costs in a lease where the property owner states that they "just don't know what

the real cost is for that item," which means that the cost for that item is variable and can create a suboptimal pricing situation for the property owner if not correctly addressed. (Scruggs 2016)

Walk-Through
Inspection of building space by the tenant and the landlord (or their representatives) together to evaluate the quality and completeness of remodeling or construction and to determine whether the space is substantially complete and ready for occupancy by the tenant. During the walk-through a punch list is generated. (US 2011)

Working Days
Working days mean weekdays, excluding Saturdays and Sundays and Federal holidays. (US 2013)

GLOSSARY OF TERMS SOURCES

The glossary of terms is taken from the following sources with names and date of authorship:

(CA 2009): State of California Glossary of Terms 2009.

(FL 2009): State of Florida 2009 (State of FL *PROCESSING LEASES FOR REAL PROPERTY* 2009).

(CH 2015): City of Chicago Lease dated 2015.

(Scruggs 2016): Jamie Scruggs 2016.

(US 2011): US GSA PBS Leasing Desk Guide 2011.

(US 2013): US GSA Form L100 sections dated 2013.

About the Author

Jamie Scruggs

Summary:

Jamie has worked in government real estate leasing since 1998. He started Government Lease Advisors, Inc., in 2001 to assist government agencies and property owners in their government real estate lease transactions, property sales, new construction projects, and lease administration. Jamie has been involved in thousands of government leases in almost every major US market and has experience with government real estate lease assignments with small property owners and national real estate investment trusts.

Company: Government Lease Advisors, Inc.

Title: Executive Director

Year started in industry: 1998

Agency Lease Experience: Federal, state, and local

Service Areas: National

Services Provided:

- Represents both property owners and government agencies on government lease preparation and negotiation of federal, state, and local leases.
- Project management of the design and construction of tenant and shell improvements.
- Consulting on lease administration items.
- Expert witness services.
- Training, coaching, and consulting services.

Education: BS, University of Illinois, Finance

Contact Information:

Jamie Scruggs
Government Lease Advisors, Inc.
Chicago, Illinois
Phone: 630-200-6333
Email: jamie@govleaseadvisors.com
Website: govleaseadvisors.com

Introduction

Dennis Eisen, PhD

Summary:

Dennis has worked in government real estate leasing since 1973. In 1995 he published *Decision Making in Federal Real Estate: How the Government Decides Whether and with Whom to Lease, Build or Buy.* In 2005 he founded the *Journal of Government Real Estate,* and in 2009 founded and has since served as the executive director of the National Federal Development Association (NFDA). Dennis works with property owners of government-leased properties on lease portfolio and acquisition analysis and provides expert witness testimony for litigation support.

Company: National Federal Development Association (NFDA)

Title: Executive Director

Year started in industry: 1973

Agency Lease Experience: Federal, state, and local

Service Areas: National

Services Provided:

- Lease renewal portfolio support.
- Property acquisition support.
- Consulting on lease administration items.
- Expert witness services.
- Training, coaching, and consulting services.

Education: BS, New York University, Engineering; MS, Brown University, Mathematics; PhD, Adelphi University, Mathematics and Computer Science

Contact Information:

Dr. Dennis Eisen
National Federal Development Association (NFDA)
Washington, DC
Phone: 301-762-1441
Email: deisen@nfda.us
Website: nfda.us

Foreword
Diana Parks Curran

Summary:

Diana has worked in government real estate leasing and construction law since 1993, when she went to work for the US GSA as Assistant Regional Counsel in Atlanta. Diana started Curran Legal Services Group in 2006 to provide legal services to private-sector clients involved in leasing and construction. Diana counsels developer and property-owner clients engaged in government contracting from the bidding stage through contract administration and claims issues and has appeared before the US Civilian Board of Contract Appeals, Armed Services Board of Contract Appeals, the US Court of Federal Claims and the Government Accountability Office (GAO)

Company: Curran Legal Services Group, Inc.

Title: President and Managing Partner

Agency Lease Experience: Federal

Services Provided:

- Represents private-sector firms providing leasehold interests and/or construction services on federal projects.
- Transactional specialization in complex financing of real estate and government-leased and -owned construction matters.
- Consulting on federal-sector lease administration matters including sales of assets, real estate tax reimbursement, operating cost impacts, government-driven changes to requirements, or end of lease term matters including holdover, lease renewal, and rental disputes.
- Procurement protests and challenges at the Government Accountability Office (GAO) and the US Court of Federal Claims.

Education: BA, University of Georgia, Political Science; Juris Doctor, University of Georgia

Contact Information:

Diana Parks Curran
Curran Legal Services Group, Inc.
Johns Creek, Georgia 30097
Phone: 404-556-7341
Email: diana@curranlegal.com
Website: www.curranlegal.com

Industry Reviewer

Brian Adelstein

Summary:

Brian's past responsibilities have included client relationships with the US General Services Administration (GSA) and other government agency clients. Brian has managed up to 60 brokers, 10 cobrokers and 30 subcontractors in the fulfillment of services to the US GSA. Brian's US GSA experience includes more than 1,400 transactions, 8 stand-alone consulting projects, and 40 other tasks. During Brian's tenure, his firm has provided service to over 60 federal government client agencies. He has interacted with US GSA executives, regional leaders, brokers, support staff, and federal government tenant agency representatives.

Company: Cushman & Wakefield

Title: Senior Vice President

Year started in industry: 1999

Agency Lease Experience: Federal, state, and local

Service Areas: National

Services Provided:

- Represents government agencies on the procurement of leases.
- Project management of the design and construction of tenant and shell improvements.
- Management of large scale special projects with 100+ simultaneous leasing actions on a national basis.
- Team leadership, management, training, and mentorship.

Education: BS, University of Michigan, Architecture; MBA, Indiana University, Finance and Marketing

Contact Information:

Brian Adelstein
Cushman & Wakefield
Chicago, Illinois
Phone: 312-424-8167
Email: brian.adelstein@cushwake.com
Website: cushmanwakefield.com

INDEX

IMAGE CREDITS

Marin County Civic Center: Connie Zhou / OTTO

Alexander Calder's *Flamingo* by James Droste is licensed under CC BY ND 2.0, https://creativecommons.org/licenses/by-nd/2.0/. No changes were made.

Chicago Picasso: J. Crocker via Wikimedia Commons

www.ingramcontent.com/pod-product-compliance
Lightning Source LLC
LaVergne TN
LVHW080029210926
848481LV00011B/3138
9780998307503